Travel Discoun...

KU-759-702

This coupon entitles you to special discounts
when you book your trip through the

TRAVEL NETWORK®
RESERVATION SERVICE

Hotels ♦ Airlines ♦ Car Rentals ♦ Cruises
All Your Travel Needs

Here's what you get: *

♦ A discount of $50 USD on a booking of $1,000** or
more for two or more people!

♦ A discount of $25 USD on a booking of $500** or more
for one person!

♦ Free membership for three years, and 1,000 free miles
on enrollment in the unique Miles-to-Go™ frequent-
traveler program. Earn one mile for every dollar spent
through the program. Earn free hotel stays starting at
5,000 miles. Earn free roundtrip airline tickets starting
at 25,000 miles.

♦ Personal help in planning your own, customized trip.

♦ Fast, confirmed reservations at any property
recommended in this guide, subject to availability.***

♦ Special discounts on bookings in the U.S. and around
the world.

♦ Low-cost visa and passport service.

♦ Reduced-rate cruise packages.

Visit our website at http://www.travnet.com/Frommer or
call us globally at 201-567-8500, ext. 55. In the U.S., call
toll-free at 1-888-940-5000, or fax 201-567-1838. In
Canada, call toll-free at 1-800-883-9959, or fax 416-922-
6053. In Asia, call 60-3-7191044, or fax 60-3-7185415.

---

* To qualify for these travel discounts, at least a portion of your trip must
include destinations covered in this guide. No more than one coupon discount
may be used in any 12-month period, for destinations covered in this guide.
Cannot be combined with any other discount or program.

**These are U.S. dollars spent on commissionable bookings.

***A $10 USD fee, plus fax and/or phone charges, will be added to the cost of
bookings at each hotel not linked to the reservation service. Customers
must approve these fees in advance.

Valid until December 31, 1997. Terms and conditions of the Miles-to-
Go™ program are available on request by calling 201-567-8500, ext 55.

BOS123

3 FREE Minutes

of weather information and save up to 60% on long distance calls!

Let The Weather Channel® help you pack! Get all the information you need before you leave.

- Current conditions & forecasts for over 900 cities worldwide
- Severe weather information including winter and tropical storm updates
- Wake-up call complete with your local forecast
- Special interest forecasts featuring ski resort, boating and other outdoor conditions

Remove card and see instructions on back.

Plus:

After selecting any additional payment option, you will receive 5 FREE MINUTES of long distance service!

Easy. Convenient. Fast.

It's The Only Phone Card You Will Ever Need!

During your free call, an automated operator will offer you an option to add $10, $20 or $30 to your phone card using any major credit card.

Use your card to:

- Save 20% on comprehensive weather information!
- Save up to 60% on long distance calls to **anywhere** in the U.S., **anytime!**
- Save 20% on other helpful information including lottery, sports, and more!

Domestic long distance service costs $0.25 per minute and all other options cost $0.75 per minute when using your TWC phone card.

Take the worry out of wondering! Carry the power to access all of these essential services with you in your wallet, wherever **Frommer's** may take you!

THE WEATHER CHANNEL ®

No place on Earth has better weather.™

Frommer's® 97

Boston

by Marie Morris

Macmillan • USA

ABOUT THE AUTHORS

Marie Morris is a native New Yorker and graduated from Harvard College where she studied history. She has worked for the *New York Times, Boston* magazine, and the *Boston Herald,* and has covered Boston for *Frommer's New England* as well. She lives in Boston, not far from Paul Revere.

MACMILLAN TRAVEL

A Simon & Schuster Macmillan Company
1633 Broadway
New York, NY 10019

Find us online at **http://www.mgr.com/travel** or
on America Online at Keyword: **Frommer's.**

ISBN: 0-2861135-7
ISSN: 0899-322X

Editor: Philippe Wamba
Production Editor: Lori Cates
Map Editor: Douglas Stallings
Design by Michele Laseau
Digital Cartography by Ortelius Design, Peter Bogaty, and John Decamillis
Maps copyright © Simon & Schuster, Inc.

SPECIAL SALES

Bulk purchases (10+ copies) of Frommer's and selected Macmillan travel guides are available to corporations, organizations, mail-order catalogs, institutions, and charities at special discounts, and can be customized to suit individual needs. For more information write to: Special Sales, Macmillan General Reference, 1633 Broadway, New York, NY 10019.

Manufactured in the United States of America

Contents

List of Maps

An Invitation to the Reader

In researching this book, I have come across many fine establishments, the best of which I have included here. I am sure that many of you will also come across appealing hotels, inns, restaurants, guesthouses, shops, and attractions. Please don't keep them to yourself. Share your experiences, especially if you want to comment on places included in this edition that have changed for the worse. You can address your letters to:

Marie Morris
Frommer's Boston '97
Macmillan Travel
1633 Broadway
New York, NY 10019

An Additional Note

Please be advised that travel information is subject to change at any time—and this is especially true of prices. We therefore suggest that you write or call ahead for confirmation when making your travel plans. The authors, editors, and publisher cannot be held responsible for the experiences of readers while traveling. Your safety is important to us, however, so we encourage you to stay alert and be aware of your surroundings. Keep a close eye on cameras, purses, and wallets, all favorite targets of thieves and pickpockets.

What the Symbols Mean

✪ **Frommer's Favorites**

Hotels, restaurants, attractions, and entertainment you should not miss.

Ⓢ **Super-Special Values**

Hotels and restaurants that offer great value for your money.

The following abbreviations are used for credit cards:

AE	American Express	EU	Eurocard
CB	Carte Blanche	JCB	Japan Credit Bank
DC	Diners Club	MC	MasterCard
DISC	Discover	V	Visa
ER	enRoute		

Welcome to Boston

The Athens of America. The hub of the solar system. The capital of New England. The biggest college town in the world. America's Walking City. As these immodest nicknames suggest, Bostonians are sitting on a good thing, and they know it. In a glorious waterfront setting that has attracted travelers for hundreds of years, Boston offers cosmopolitan sophistication on a comfortable scale. From the narrow, crowded streets near the harbor to the spacious boulevards along the Charles River, a sense of history permeates the city, where 18th-century landmarks sit alongside space-age office towers, and the leaders of tomorrow rush to lectures in red-brick buildings.

Boston manages to strike a careful balance between romantic celebration of the past and forward-looking pursuit of the future. Skyscrapers bear plaques describing the deeds and misdeeds of centuries past. The city's museums showcase the treasures of antiquity and cutting-edge technology. And the waterfront has been reclaimed from squalor and disrepair and restored to a condition that outshines its former glory.

It's not perfect, of course. Even a brief visit will confirm that the city's drivers have earned their terrible reputation, and the local accents are as ear-splitting as any in Brooklyn or Chicago. Wander into the wrong part of town and you may be ordered to "pahk yuh cah" (park your car) somewhere else—pronto. And college town or not, there isn't much of a late-night scene outside of convenience stores and photocopy shops, although the "blue laws" restricting the sale of alcohol on Sundays have been considerably relaxed.

Take a few days (or weeks) to get to know Boston, or use it as a gateway to the rest of New England. The Pilgrim heritage of Plymouth, the beaches of Cape Cod, the mountains of western Massachusetts, Vermont, and New Hampshire, the historical and literary legacy of Lexington and Concord, and the rugged coast and maritime tradition of the North Shore are all within easy driving distance and well worth exploring.

Here's hoping your experience is memorable and delightful.

1 Frommer's Favorite Boston Experiences

- **A Bird's-Eye View:** On a clear day, you can see for at least 30 miles from the John Hancock Observatory or the Prudential Center Skywalk—not exactly forever, but an impressive view nonetheless. On a clear night, especially in winter, the cityscape looks like black velvet studded with twinkling gems.

Boston Orientation

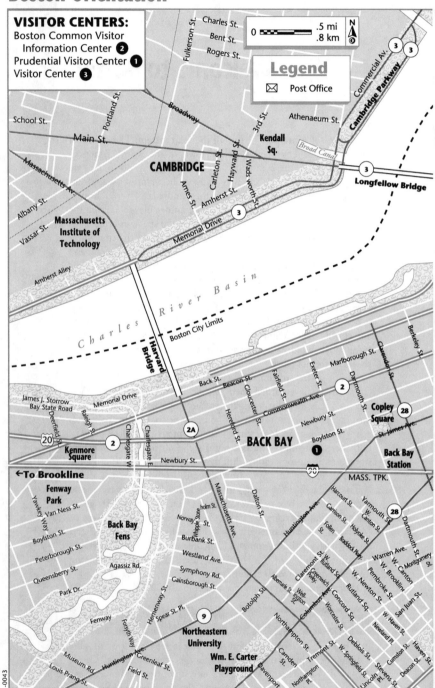

VISITOR CENTERS:
Boston Common Visitor
Information Center **2**
Prudential Visitor Center **1**
Visitor Center **3**

0   .5 mi   .8 km

N

Legend
✉ Post Office

Charles St.
Bent St.
Rogers St.
Fulkerson St.
Commercial Av.
Cambridge Parkway
Athenaeum St.
3rd St.
Broad Canal
School St.
Broadway
Portland St.
Main St.
Massachusetts Av.
Kendall Sq.
Hayward St.
Carleton St.
Wadsworth St.
CAMBRIDGE
Ames St.
Amherst St.
Albany St.
Vassar St.
Longfellow Bridge
3
Massachusetts Institute of Technology
Memorial Drive
Amherst Alley

Charles   *River Basin*
Boston City Limits
Harvard Bridge

James J. Storrow
Bay State Road
Memorial Drive
Back St.
Beacon St.
Gloucester St.
Fairfield St.
Exeter St.
Marlborough St.
Dartmouth St.
Clarendon St.
Berkeley St.
Deerfield St.
Raleigh St.
20
Kenmore Square
2
Charlesgate W.
Charlesgate E.
2A
Commonwealth Av.
Hereford St.
Newbury St.
BACK BAY
Boylston St.
Copley Square
28
St. James Av.
Back Bay Station
Newbury St.
1
MASS. TPK.
←**To Brookline**
Fenway Park
Yawkey Way
Van Ness St.
Boylston St.
Peterborough St.
Queensberry St.
Park Dr.
Back Bay Fens
Agassiz Rd.
Maple Store holm St.
Norway St.
Burbank St.
St.
Westland Ave.
Symphony Rd.
Gainsborough St.
Massachusetts Ave.
Dalton St.
Harcourt St.
Cumston St.
Garrison St.
Yarmouth St.
W. Canton St.
Holyoke St.
Follen
St.
Baddock Pky.
Huntington Ave.
Warren Ave.
W. Canton St.
W. Brookline
Pembroke St.
W. Newton St.
Dartmouth St.
Montgomery St.
Claremont St.
Rutland Sq.
Greenwich
Pky.
W. Rutland Sq.
Concord Sq.
W. Concord St.
San Juan St.
W. Haven St.
Newland Pl.
Hemenway St.
Spear St. Pl.
Fenway
Forsyth Way
Museum Rd.
Huntington Ave.
Greenleaf St.
Field St.
Louis Prang St.
Albemarle St.
Welt.
Ington
St.
9
Northeastern University
Wm. E. Carter Playground
Botolph St.
Northampton St.
Columbus Ave.
Worcester St.
Camden St.
Davenport
Northampton
Pl.
Tremont St.
W. Springfield St.
Deblois St.
Lincoln Pl.
Stevens St.
Cumston St.
Haven St.
Deacon St.

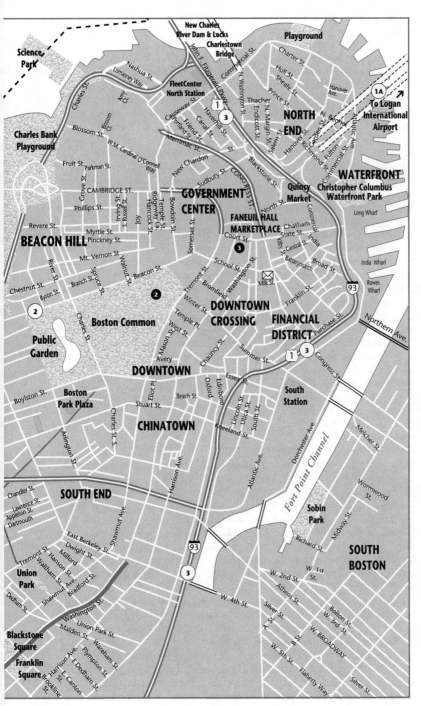

- **A Lunch Break on the Waterfront:** Head for the harbor or the river, settle in at a restaurant or (preferably) on a park bench or a patch of grass, take off your watch, relax, and enjoy the spectacular view of the sailboats, yachts, kayaks, ducks, college crew teams and dancing speckles of sunlight on the water.

- **An Afternoon Red Sox Game:** Since 1912, baseball fans have worshiped at the shrine known as Fenway Park, the "lyric little bandbox of a ball park" (in John Updike's words) off Kenmore Square. The seats are uncomfortable and too close together and the Red Sox haven't won the World Series since 1918, but you won't care a whit as you soak up the atmosphere and bask in the sun.

- **A Few Hours (At Least) at the Museum of Fine Arts:** Whether you're into Egyptian art or contemporary photography, furniture and decorative arts or the Impressionists, you're sure to find something at the MFA that tickles your interest.

- **A Free Friday Flick:** Families, film buffs, and impoverished entertainment-seekers flock to the lawn in front of the Hatch Shell on the Esplanade for free movies (*The Wizard of Oz* or *Raiders of the Lost Ark*, for example) shown on Friday nights in the summer. Bring something to sit on, and maybe a sweater.

- **A Quest for the Ultimate Bargain:** For some people, this is the quintessential Boston experience. Arrive at the legendary Filene's Basement in Downtown Crossing early, before the lunchtime crowds, and set off on a treasure hunt. Prices for the already-discounted merchandise shrink after it's been on the selling floor for two weeks.

- **A Concert Al Fresco:** Boston summer nights swing to the beat of outdoor music, performed by amateurs and professionals. A great spot for free jazz is Christopher Columbus Park, on the waterfront, where performances take place on Fridays at 6pm.

- **A Weekend Afternoon in Harvard Square:** It's not the bohemian hangout of days gone by, but "the Square" is packed with book and record stores, clothing and souvenir shops, restaurants, musicians, students of all ages, and so many people that it's a wonder there are any left at Faneuil Hall Marketplace.

- **A Visit to Faneuil Hall Marketplace:** Specialty shops, an enormous food court, street performers, bars, restaurants, and crowds from all over the world make Faneuil Hall Marketplace (you'll also hear it called Quincy Market) Boston's most popular destination.

- **A Meal at Durgin-Park:** Dinner at this Boston institution might start with oysters, and it might start with a waitress slinging a handful of napkins over your shoulder, dropping a handful of cutlery in front of you, and saying, "Here, give these out." The surly service routine usually seems to be an act, but it's so much a part of the legend that some people are disappointed when the waitresses are nice (as they often are). In any case, the gimmick (or is it?) has worked since 1827.

- **A Walk to the Atlantic Ocean:** Boston Harbor owes its reputation as one of the world's finest ports to its sheltered location and distance from the open sea, which batters the coastline north of the city. To get the full effect of the majestic Atlantic, get out of town. The view from Rockport, at the tip of Cape Ann, or Marblehead, a bit farther south, is worth the trip.

- **A Ride on a Duck:** A Duck Tour, that is. Board one of these reconditioned amphibious Second World War landing crafts (on Huntington Avenue behind the Prudential Center) for a sightseeing ride that includes a dip in the river—for the Duck, not you.

- **A "Ride" at the Museum of Science:** The Mugar Omni Theater, a four-story wraparound auditorium (or torture chamber if you're prone to motion sickness), inundates you with sights and sounds and doesn't let go; whether the film is on volcanoes or sharks, the larger-than-life images will have you believing that you, too, are in the movie. The museum proper (separate admission) is also a great place to explore, especially if you're traveling with children.

- **A Spring Fling in the Public Garden:** Eight square blocks of paradise await you, filled with flowers, ornamental greenery, and flowering trees and shrubs. Pass through for a quick pick-me-up, take to the lagoon for a swan boat ride (or an ice skating session if it's a late spring), or just enjoy the ducklings. They're on view in the flesh, seasonally, and are also immortalized in bronze for year-round viewing.
- **A Walk Around the North End:** Boston's Little Italy (but don't call it that) has an Old World flavor you won't want to miss. Explore the shops on Salem Street, wander the side streets, and whether or not you have a meal, be sure to stop for coffee and a pastry at a Hanover Street caffè.
- **A Pilgrimage to Newbury Street:** From the genteel Arlington Street end to the cutting-edge Massachusetts Avenue end, Boston's legendary shopping destination is eight blocks of pure temptation in the form of galleries, boutiques, jewelry and gift shops, bookstores and more.
- **A Taste of the Countryside:** Actually, at a number of locations in Boston, the country comes to you. From July through November, farmers' markets grace Copley Square (Tuesdays and Fridays) and City Hall Plaza (Mondays and Wednesdays) with everything from fresh herbs and tomatoes to apples and pumpkins.
- **A Vicarious Thrill:** Without so much as lacing up a sneaker, participate in the world-famous Boston Marathon. Stretch a little first, so that you don't cramp up. Drink plenty of fluids. Stake out a slice of sidewalk on Commonwealth Avenue under a tree (the sun can be very draining). Cheer enthusiastically as the runners thunder past. Then relax and put your feet up—you've earned it.

2   The City Today

Boston embodies contrasts and contradictions—it's blue-blood and blue-collar, Yankee and Irish, home to Brahmin bankers and budget-conscious graduate students. It's a proud seaport whose harbor is being reclaimed from crippling pollution, the home of the country's first public school and of an educational system perpetually on the verge of crisis. It's a one-time hotbed of abolitionism with an intractable reputation for racism. It's a magnet for college students from all over the world and others engaged in intellectual pursuits, yet the traditional, parochial obsessions are "sports, politics and revenge." It's a living landmark that you can sometimes mistake for an 18th century New World colony, but where it is theoretically possible (this is an observation, not a suggestion) to spend days without going near anything built before 1960 or even going outdoors.

Whether their association with the city lasts four years or four generations, most Bostonians take pride in their cultural institutions—as do residents of every municipality that boasts more than just a mall and a movie theater. What makes Boston different? Stop 10 Bostonians on the street, ask their three favorite local leisure activities, and you might hear 30 different answers. Here's someone who spends every Fourth of July waiting for the annual outdoor Pops concert but has yet to set foot in Symphony Hall; her friend never skips an exhibit at the Museum of Fine Arts or a chance to sample the clam chowder at a new restaurant; here's a guy who wouldn't miss the Harvard-Yale football game but wouldn't be caught dead at Mount Auburn Cemetery (maybe that's a bad example). Like any city, Boston is what you make of it. And it just happens to have a lot of excellent potential ingredients.

Today you'll find a city of 574,300 at the heart of the Greater Boston area, which encompasses 83 cities and towns and some 4 million people. The hospitals and medical centers are among the best in the world, and the ongoing health-care revolution is a hot topic. The effects of the recession of the late '80s are fading, and the banking and financial services, computer technology, and insurance industries are thriving. The restaurant scene sizzles, with new spots opening and old favorites changing with the times or continuing to do what they've done well for generations. And as they have for more than a century, immigrants flock to the area, where the Irish, eastern European Jews, Italians, Portuguese, African-Americans, Hispanics, West Indians and now Asians as well make their homes and their mark. One pastime that unites many of them is rooting for the city's professional sports teams, which lately is an uphill battle. Boston is still considered a great sports town, but the glory days of the mid-80s exist only as the wistfully recalled stories of old timers to many current fans. (That's good news for visitors, who may find that the once highly coveted Celtics or Bruins tickets are no longer quite so hard to come by.)

The most prominent feature of downtown Boston, today and for the foreseeable future, is not an architectural masterpiece or a natural wonder, but an enormous construction site. The Central Artery (I-93) is being "depressed"—as are many of the people who travel into and through the city every day—in a massive project priced at almost $11 billion. The ultimate goals are to hide the interstate underground, turn the land it currently occupies into green space and smaller surface roads, and link the Massachusetts Turnpike (I-90) directly to Logan Airport through the Ted Williams Tunnel (the tunnel is finished, but the link is not). The target completion date is 2004, and though the site is currently an urban eyesore, other parts of the city are pretty enough to help make up for this temporary blemish on the Boston landscape.

When that's done, Boston will, in a sense, have come full circle. The worst of the traffic will be hidden away, the pedestrians who originally owned the city will once again have easy access to the harbor, and the center of commerce will open onto the waterfront as it did three centuries ago.

3 History 101

Dateline

- 1614 Capt. John Smith maps the New England coast, names the Charles River after King Charles I of England, and calls the area "a paradise."
- 1621 A party of 11 led by Myles Standish explores Boston Harbor, visits with the Massachuset Indians, and returns to Plymouth.
- 1624 William Blackstone settles on the Shawmut peninsula (on Beacon Hill) with 200 books and a Brahma bull.
- 1630 John Winthrop leads settlers to present-day Charlestown in June. The need for a better water supply soon leads them to Shawmut, which they call Trimountain. On September 7, they name it Boston in honor of

continues

Permanently settled in 1630 by representatives of the Massachusetts Bay Company, Boston was named for the hometown of some of the Puritans who left England to seek religious freedom in the New World. Their arrival was greeted with little of the usual strife with the natives, members of the small, Algonquian-speaking Massachuset tribe that roamed the area. They may have used the peninsula they called "Shawmut" (possibly derived from "Mushauwomuk," or "unclaimed land") as a burial place, and they grew corn on some harbor islands, but they made their permanent homes farther inland.

In 1632 the little peninsula became the capital of the Massachusetts Bay Colony, and over the next decade the population increased rapidly during the great Puritan migration. Thanks to its excellent location on the deep, sheltered harbor, Boston quickly became a center of shipbuilding, fishing, and trading. The only thing more important than commerce was religion, and the Puritans exerted such a strongly pious influence that their legacy survives to this day. A concrete reminder is Harvard College's original 1636 mission: preparing young men to be ministers. An early example of puritanical stuffiness was recorded in 1673, when one Captain Kemble was seen kissing his wife on their front steps after returning from a voyage on a Sunday and was sentenced to confinement in the stocks for two hours. He had been away for three years.

In 1684 the colony's charter was revoked, and the inhabitants came under tighter British control. Laws increasing taxes and restricting the colonies' trading activities gradually led to trouble. The situation came to a head after the French and Indian War (also known as the Seven Years' War) ended in 1763. Having helped fight for the British, the notoriously independent-minded colonists were outraged when the Crown expected them to help pay off the war debt. The Sugar Act of 1764 imposed tariffs on sugar, wine and coffee, mostly affecting those engaged in trade; the 1765 Stamp Act taxed everything printed, from legal documents to playing cards, affecting virtually everyone. Boycotts, demonstrations, and riots ensued. The repeal of the Stamp Act in 1766 was too little, too late—the revolutionary slogan "No taxation without representation" had already taken hold.

The Townshend Acts of 1767 imposed taxes on paper, glass and tea, sparking more unrest. The following year, British troops occupied Boston. Perhaps inevitably, tension led to violence. In the Boston Massacre of 1770, five colonists were killed in a scuffle with the redcoats. The first to die was a former slave named Crispus Attucks; another was 17-year-old Samuel Maverick.

Parliament repealed the Townshend Acts but kept the tea tax, and in 1773 granted the nearly bankrupt East India Company the monopoly on the tea trade with the colonies. The idea was to undercut the price of smuggled tea, but the colonists weren't having it. In December, three British ships sat at anchor in Boston Harbor, waiting for their cargo of tea to be unloaded. Before that could happen, the rabble-rousing Sons of Liberty, some disguised as Indians, boarded the ships and dumped 342 chests of tea into

the English hometown of many Puritans. On October 19, 108 voters attend the first town meeting.

- **1632** Boston becomes the capital of Massachusetts.
- **1635** Boston Latin School, America's first public school, opens.
- **1636** Harvard College founded to educate young men for the ministry.
- **1638** America's first printing press established in Cambridge.
- **1639** America's first post office established in home of Richard Fairbank.
- **1682** A free school, ordered to provide for teaching children to write and "cipher," becomes the basis for the public school system.
- **1704** America's first regularly published newspaper, the *Boston News Letter*, is founded.
- **1721** First smallpox inoculations administered at the urging of Dr. Zabdiel Boylston and Cotton Mather, over the violent objections of the populace.
- **1764** "Taxation without representation" is denounced in reaction to the Sugar Act.
- **1770** On March 5, five colonists are killed outside the Old State House, an incident soon known as the Boston Massacre.
- **1773** On December 16, during the Boston Tea Party, 342 chests of tea are dumped into the harbor from three British ships by colonists poorly disguised as Indians.
- **1774** The "Intolerable Acts," which include the closure of the port of Boston and the quartering of British troops in colonists' homes, go into effect.
- **1775** On April 18, Paul Revere and William Dawes spread the word that the British are marching toward Lexington and

continues

Concord. On the 19th, "the shot heard round the world" is fired. On June 17, the British win the Battle of Bunker Hill but suffer heavy casualties.

■ **1776** On March 17, the British evacuate Boston by ship. On July 18, the Declaration of Independence is read from the balcony of the Old State House.

■ **1790s** The China trade helps bring great prosperity to Boston.

■ **1825** The first city census lists 58,277 people.

■ **1831** William Lloyd Garrison publishes the first issue of the *Liberator,* a newspaper dedicated to emancipation.

■ **1839** Boston University founded.

■ **1861** Massachusetts Institute of Technology founded.

■ **1863** Boston College founded. The 54th Massachusetts Colored Regiment of the Union Army suffers heavy casualties in an unsuccessful attempt to capture Fort Wagner in the harbor of Charleston, S.C.

■ **1870** The Museum of Fine Arts is founded.

■ **1872** The Great Fire burns 65 acres and 800 buildings.

■ **1878** Girls Latin School opens.

■ **1881** The Boston Symphony Orchestra is founded.

■ **1895** The Boston Public Library opens.

■ **1897** The first Boston Marathon is run.

■ **1897** The first subway in America opens—a 1.7-mile stretch from Boylston Street to Park Street.

■ **1910** John F. "Honey Fitz" Fitzgerald elected mayor.

■ **1913** James Michael Curley elected mayor for the first time.

■ **1918** The Red Sox celebrate their World Series victory; a championship drought (of 79 years, and counting) begins.

■ **1919** A storage tank at the

continues

the harbor. The Boston Tea Party became a rallying point for both sides.

The British responded by closing the port until the tea was paid for and forcing Bostonians to house the soldiers who began to flood the town. They soon numbered 4,000 (in a town of 16,000). Mutual distrust ran high—Paul Revere wrote of helping form "a committee for the purpose of watching the movements of the British troops"—and when the British commander in Boston, General Gage, learned that the patriots were accumulating arms and ammunition, he dispatched men to destroy the stockpiles.

Troops marched from Boston toward Lexington and Concord late on April 18, 1775. William Dawes and Revere, who alerted the colonists of the British advance on his famous "midnight ride," sounded the warning to the local militia companies, the Minutemen, who mobilized for the impending confrontation. The next day, some 700 British soldiers under Major John Pitcairn emerged victorious from a skirmish in Lexington and then were routed at Concord before reaching the arms depot.

It took the redcoats almost an entire day to make the trip (along the route now marked "Battle Road"), which you can do in a car in about half an hour. Thanks in no small part to Henry Wadsworth Longfellow's poem "Paul Revere's Ride" (*Listen my children and you shall hear / Of the midnight ride of Paul Revere*), Lexington and Concord are closely associated with the beginning of the war. In the early stages there was activity that left its mark all over eastern Massachusetts, particularly in Cambridge. Royalist sympathizers, or "Tories," were concentrated so heavily along one stretch of Brattle St. that it was called "Tory Row." When the tide began to turn, George Washington made his home on the same street (in a house later occupied by Longfellow that's open for tours). On nearby Cambridge Common is the site where he took command of the Continental Army on July 3, 1775.

The British won the Battle of Bunker Hill (actually fought on Breed's Hill) in Charlestown on June 17, 1775, but at the cost of half their forces. They abandoned Boston the following March 17. On July 4, 1776, the Continental Congress adopted the Declaration of

Independence. Although many Bostonians fought in the six-year war that followed, no more battles were fought in Boston.

After the war, Boston again became a center of commerce—fishing, whaling and trade with the Far East dominated the economy. Exotic spices and fruits, textiles and porcelain were familiar luxuries in Boston and nearby Salem. The influential merchant families became known as "Boston Brahmins," and they spearheaded the cultural renaissance that continued long after the effects of the War of 1812 ravaged international shipping, and banking and manufacturing rose in importance. Boston took a back seat to New York and Philadelphia in size and influence, but became known for fine art and architecture, including the luxurious homes on Beacon Hill, and a flourishing intellectual community.

By the mid–19th century, Ralph Waldo Emerson, Oliver Wendell Holmes, Henry Wadsworth Longfellow, Nathaniel Hawthorne, Bronson and Louisa May Alcott, John Greenleaf Whittier, Walt Whitman, Henry David Thoreau, even Charles Dickens (briefly) and Mark Twain (more briefly) had appeared on the local literary scene. William Lloyd Garrison published the weekly *Liberator* newspaper, a powerful voice in the antislavery and social reform movements. Boston became an important stop on the Underground Railroad, the secret network developed by the abolitionists to smuggle slaves into Canada.

During the Civil War (1861–65), abolitionist sentiment was the order of the day—to such a degree that the rolls listing the names of the war dead in Harvard's Memorial Hall include only members of the Union Army. Massachusetts' contributions to the war effort included enormous quantities of firearms, shoes, blankets, tents, and men. The famed black abolitionist Frederick Douglass, a former member of the Massachusetts Anti-Slavery Society, helped recruit the 54th and 55th Massachusetts Colored Regiments. The story of the 54th, the first all-black army unit, and its commander, Col. Robert Gould Shaw, is told in the movie *Glory*.

By 1822, Boston town had become a city. From 1824–26, Mayor Josiah Quincy oversaw the landfill project that moved the waterfront away from Faneuil Hall. The market building

corner of Foster and Commercial streets ruptures. Two million gallons of raw molasses spill into the streets of the North End, killing 21 people.

- **1930s** The Great Depression devastates what remains of New England's industrial base.
- **1940s** The Second World War and the accompanying industrial frenzy restore some vitality to the economy, particularly the shipyards.
- **1942** A fire at the Cocoanut Grove nightclub kills 491 people.
- **1946** John F. Kennedy is elected to Congress from Boston's First Congressional District.
- **1954** The first successful human-to-human organ transplant (of a kidney) is performed at Brigham and Women's Hospital.
- **1957** The Boston Celtics win the first of their 16 NBA championships.
- **1958** The Freedom Trail is mapped out and painted.
- **1959** Construction of the Prudential Center begins, and with it, the transformation of the skyline.
- **1962** Scollay Square is razed to make room for Government Center.
- **1966** Massachusetts Attorney General Edward Brooke, a Republican, becomes the first black elected to the U.S. Senate in the 20th century.
- **1969** Students protesting the Vietnam War occupy University Hall at Harvard.
- **1974** In September, school busing begins citywide (a full 20 years after the U.S. Supreme Court made school segregation illegal), sparking tension in Roxbury and Charlestown.
- **1976** The restored Faneuil Hall Marketplace opens.
- **1988** The Central Artery/Third Harbor Tunnel Project is approved.

continues

- **1990** The Women's Heritage Trail, celebrating 20 women who have been influential in Boston and the nation, is established.
- **1993** Thomas Menino is elected mayor, becoming the first Italian-American to hold the office.
- **1995** The New England Holocaust Memorial is dedicated.
- **1995** The FleetCenter opens, replacing Boston Garden as the home of the basketball Celtics and the hockey Bruins.
- **1996** Mayor Menino announces plans for a $45 million renovation of the buildings along the Freedom Trail.

constructed at that time was named in his honor. The undertaking was one of many, all over the city, in which hills were lopped off and deposited in the water, transforming the coastline and skyline. For example, the filling of the Mill Pond, now the area around North Station, began in 1807 and in 25 years consumed the summits of Copp's and Beacon hills. The largest project, started in 1835 and completed in 1882, was the filling of the Back Bay, the body of mud flats and marshes that gave its name to the present-day neighborhood. Beginning in 1857, much of the fill came by railroad from Needham. In the 19th century the city tripled in area, creating badly needed space.

The railroad boom of the 1820s and '30s and the flood of immigration that began soon after made New England an industrial center, and Boston, then as now, was its unofficial capital. Thousands of immigrants from Ireland settled in the city, the first ethnic group to do so since the French Huguenots in the early 18th century. Signs reading "No Irish need apply" soon became scarce as the new arrivals gained political power: The first Irish mayor was elected in 1885.

By this time the class split in society was a chasm, with the influx of immigrants who swelled the ranks of the local working class adding to the social tension. The Irish led the way and were followed by eastern European Jewish, Italian, and Portuguese immigrants, who had their own neighborhoods, churches, schools, newspapers, and livelihoods that intersected only occasionally with "proper" society. Even as the upper crust was sowing seeds that would wind up enriching everyone—the Boston Symphony, Boston Public Library, and the Museum of Fine Arts were founded in the second half of the 19th century—it was engaging in behavior that gained Boston a reputation for making snobbery an art form. In 1889 the private St. Botolph Club removed John Singer Sargent's portrait of Isabella Stewart Gardner from public view (it's now at the museum that bears her name) because her dress was too tight.

The St. Botolph Club was and is in the Back Bay, a fashionable address from day one. The South End is roughly the same age but became an immigrant enclave by the turn of the century and was considered literally the wrong side of the tracks until gentrification swept through in the 1970s. The Boston Brahmins could keep their new neighbors out of many areas of their lives, but not politics. The forbearers of the Kennedy clan had by now appeared on the scene—John F. "Honey Fitz" Fitzgerald, Rose Kennedy's father, was elected mayor in 1910—and the world was changing.

Though World War II bolstered Boston's Depression-ravaged industrial economy, the war's end prompted an economic transformation. Shipping declined, along with New England's textile, shoe and glass industries, at the same time that students on the G.I. Bill were pouring into area colleges and universities. The rise of high technology led to new construction, changing the look of the city yet again. The 1960s saw the beginning of a building boom that continues to this day, stalled but not stopped by the recession of the late '80s.

For we must consider that we shall be as a city upon a hill. The eyes of all people are upon us . . .

—John Winthrop, *A Model of Christian Charity* (sermon) (1630)

I do not speak with any fondness, but the language of coolest history, when I say that Boston commands attention as the town which was appointed in the destiny of nations to lead the civilization of North America.

—Ralph Waldo Emerson, *The Natural History of the Intellect* (1893)

I shall enter no encomium upon Massachusetts; she needs none. There she is. Behold her, and judge for yourselves. There is her history; the world knows it by heart. The past, at least, is secure. There is Boston and Concord and Lexington and Bunker Hill; and there they will remain forever.

—Daniel Webster, speech (1830)

The mid-'70s were scarred by the incidents surrounding the Boston busing crisis, sparked by a court-ordered school desegregation plan enacted in 1974 that touched off riots, violence and a white boycott. Because of "white flight," Boston is now what urban planners call a "doughnut city"—one with a relatively large black population (25% of Boston residents are black, compared to 11% of the U.S. population) surrounded by many lily-white suburbs—and has battled its reputation for racism with varying degrees of success. One of the most integrated neighborhoods, Jamaica Plain, is linked to the least integrated, Charlestown—but only by the Orange Line of the subway. The school system has yet to fully recover from the traumatic experience of busing, but every year it sends thousands of students on to the institutions of higher learning that continue to be Boston's greatest claim to fame.

To get a sense of what Boston is (and is not) like today, hit the streets. The puritanical Bostonian is virtually extinct, but you can still see traces of the various groups, institutions, and events that have shaped Boston history to make it the complex city it is today.

4 Famous Bostonians

Samuel Adams (1722–1803)   Perhaps best known today as the namesake of the excellent local brew, Adams was a leader of the American Revolution, and often spoke at the "Cradle of Liberty," Faneuil Hall, where his statue stands. An organizer of the Sons of Liberty and the Boston Tea Party, he later served as governor (1794–97).

Larry Bird (b. 1956)   The "hick from French Lick (Indiana)" joined the Celtics in 1979 and led them to three National Basketball Association titles by 1986. Whether he was the best player in team history is open to (lengthy, contentious) debate, but he's certainly the most famous. Although he retired after the 1992 Olympics, you'll still see his Number 33 jersey around town.

Louis D. Brandeis (1856–1941)   The first Jewish justice on the United States Supreme Court, Brandeis was a public advocate for consumers and labor unions. A graduate of Harvard Law School, he practiced in Boston before his appointment to the court. Brandeis University in suburban Waltham is named for him.

Charles Bulfinch (1763–1844)   The foremost practitioner of the Federal style of architecture, Bulfinch designed the State House, St. Stephen's Church in the North End, Massachusetts Hall at Harvard, the central part of Massachusetts General Hospital, and many Beacon Hill mansions. He also completed the U.S. Capitol and supervised the expansion of Faneuil Hall.

Sarah Caldwell (b. 1929)   Caldwell founded the Opera Company of Boston in 1957 and brought first-rate opera, which has had a checkered past in Boston, back to the city. As stage director and operatic conductor, she has supervised more than 45 productions of traditional and contemporary works.

Julia Child (b. 1912)   A Cambridge resident, "The French Chef" has been a TV star since 1963. A respected author and teacher, she helped put Boston on the gastronomical map even before she was immortalized on "Saturday Night Live."

John Singleton Copley (1738–1815)   Considered the first great portrait painter in North America, Copley made his reputation in Boston before relocating to London in 1775. Many of his best-known works are in the collection of the Museum of Fine Arts.

James Michael Curley (1874–1958)   A legend in Boston politics, the colorful Democratic boss served as mayor (four times), governor, U.S. congressman, and even as a federal prisoner (he was arrested for fraud but was later pardoned). He is captured in bronze twice (sitting and standing) in a small park near Dock Square, across from Faneuil Hall.

Dorothea Dix (1802–87)   An early investigative reporter, she persuaded the Massachusetts State Legislature to improve conditions for the mentally ill in state hospitals and mounted a national campaign on their behalf, prompting 15 other states and Canada to improve treatment in state hospitals.

Mary Baker Eddy (1821–1910)   The founder of Christian Science (1879) and the *Christian Science Monitor* (1908), and the author of the Christian Science textbook, *Science and Health with Key to the Scriptures*, Eddy developed her beliefs during years of studying the New Testament. The Mother Church Building, one of Boston's most imposing structures, was built in 1894 and expanded in 1904.

Ralph Waldo Emerson (1803–82)   A central figure in the mid–19th century literary and philosophical "flowering of New England," Emerson was born in Boston and in his later years was known as "the sage of Concord." An ordained minister, he gained fame as a philosopher, poet, essayist, lecturer, and leader of the transcendentalist movement. He befriended and influenced, among others, Thoreau, Hawthorne, Holmes, Whitman, Amos Bronson Alcott, Louisa May Alcott, Longfellow, and Lowell.

Fannie Farmer (1857–1915)   The author of *The Boston Cooking School Cook Book* helped revolutionize the culinary arts by including measurements and precise directions in recipes. Her 1896 master work, available in a facsimile edition, is in use to this day (in revised form) as *The Fannie Farmer Cookbook*.

Arthur Fiedler (1894–1979)   The organizer of the free concert series that began on the Esplanade on July 4, 1929, Fiedler was the conductor of the Boston Pops Orchestra for 50 years. An aluminum rendering of his head is at the Esplanade end of the Arthur Fiedler Footbridge.

William Lloyd Garrison (1805–79) An early leader in the antislavery movement and the publisher of the weekly newspaper the *Liberator* at a time when slavery was widely condoned, Garrison faced great opposition for his beliefs and activities, and at one point a mob dragged him through the streets. Eventually he was honored by President Abraham Lincoln and others for his fight to abolish slavery.

John Hancock (1737–93) The first to sign the Declaration of Independence and president of the Continental Congress, Hancock, a wealthy merchant, played a crucial role in financing and organizing the efforts of the colonists during the Revolution. He later served as governor of Massachusetts and mayor of Boston.

John F. Kennedy (1917–63) Born in Brookline and educated at Harvard, Kennedy represented Boston in the U.S. House and Massachusetts in the Senate before being elected president in 1960. The youngest man and first Catholic to hold the office, he was a liberal Democrat who had many admirers and enemies. The Kennedy Library in Dorchester and the Kennedy School of Government at Harvard celebrate his life and accomplishments.

Frederick Law Olmsted (1822–1903) Best known as the co-designer of New York's Central Park, Olmsted coined the term "landscape architect" to describe his work creating city gardens and parks. He conceived Boston's "Emerald Necklace," a 7-mile network of parks that includes Boston Common, the Public Garden, the Commonwealth Avenue mall, the Charles River Esplanade, the Back Bay Fens, the Arnold Arboretum, and Franklin Park.

Bobby Orr (b. 1948) Considered the National Hockey League's best defenseman ever, Orr played for the Bruins from 1967–76. A brilliant skater and defender as well as a potent scoring threat, he led the team to its most recent Stanley Cup championship, in 1972.

Paul Revere (1735–1818) Immortalized in Henry Wadsworth Longfellow's poem "Paul Revere's Ride," the patriot and soldier was trained as a silversmith and also worked as a dentist, printer, engraver, and bell manufacturer. His silver, the finest of the period, is on view in many area museums and at his home in the North End, which is open to visitors.

Ted Williams (b. 1918) The legendary Red Sox slugger is a native of San Diego and a resident of Florida, but it was in Boston that he achieved his stated goal: "All I want out of life is that when I walk down the street folks will say, 'There goes the greatest hitter who ever lived.'"

Malcolm X (1925–1965) In the 1940s the controversial civil rights leader and outspoken Muslim minister lived in the Roxbury section of Boston for several formative years in which he frequented the dance halls, worked briefly at the Omni Parker House, and ran a burglary ring near Harvard Square. He also served jail time in Charlestown prison and a penal colony in Norfolk, Massachusetts, where he had his famous religious awakening and educated himself by copying the dictionary.

5 The Architectural Landscape

Surveying the Boston skyline and waterfront from Charlestown, the eye is irresistibly drawn to one structure. It's small compared to the glittering office towers and harbor-view condo complexes nearby, but it dwarfs its closest neighbors, as it has for hundreds of years. It's the Old North Church, which opened in 1723.

From just about anywhere else along the harbor, the eye repeatedly returns to a vastly different place. A dramatic archway allows a peek of downtown and, often, of a flag or banner flapping in the courtyard under the huge dome. It's the Boston Harbor Hotel, which opened in 1987.

The wide and wild variety of architecture makes Boston a visual treat. Fashions change, buildings disappear, urban renewal leads to questionable decisions, but everywhere you go, there's something interesting to look at.

Built around 1680, Paul Revere's brown, wooden house on North Square is a reminder that for its first two centuries, Boston buildings were mostly made of wood and huge portions of the town regularly burned to the ground. The house is colonial in age but Tudor, rather than typically "colonial," in style. The casement windows and overhanging second floor are medieval features, and when the Reveres moved in, in 1770, the house was no longer fashionable. The one next door would have been: The Pierce/Hichborn House, constructed of brick around 1711, is a good example of the Georgian architecture that was the rage in 18th century Boston.

The next era in Boston architecture, a period dominated by the federal style, had its heyday from 1780 to 1820, and was identified with a single architect: Charles Bulfinch. Two of Boston's most historic buildings, the Old North Church and Faneuil Hall, opened in 1742, look the way they do today because of Bulfinch, and both bear the distinctive stamp of the architectural style he helped to create. He designed the church's steeple after the old one was destroyed in a hurricane in 1804 (the one where Paul Revere saw the lanterns, as described in the famous Longfellow poem, was 16 feet taller), and planned the 1805 enlargement of Faneuil Hall, which is now three times its original size.

Bulfinch's work can be seen all over Boston, most conspicuously in the State House (1797) and in many Beacon Hill residences. The new Americans rejected British influence after the war and turned to classical antiquity (filtered through the Scottish architect Robert Adam) for the austere features that characterize the style: Ionic and Corinthian detailing, frequently in white against red brick or clapboard; fanlights over doors; and an almost maniacal insistence on symmetry. At 141 Cambridge St. (1796), the first residence Bulfinch designed for Harrison Gray Otis, this obsession with symmetry resulted in the inclusion of a room with one false door (to balance out the real one).

No other architect is as closely associated with Boston as Bulfinch, but in a brief visit you're likely to see just as much of the work of several others. Quincy Market (1826), the Greek Revival centerpiece of Faneuil Hall Marketplace, was designed by Alexander Parris. It was renovated and reopened in 1976, for the Bicentennial celebration. Across town, Trinity Church (1877), a Romanesque showpiece in Copley Square, is H. H. Richardson's masterwork. Facing it is Charles Follen McKim's Boston Public Library (1885–95), a large and imposing structure with columns and majestic staircases influenced by the Bibliotheque Nationale in Paris.

Fascinating architectural areas lie north and south of Copley Square. Heading north, you come to the Back Bay, whose origins allow for a logical street pattern. The grid was planned in the 1860s and '70s mostly by Arthur Gilman, and the Parisian flavor of the boulevards reflects his interest in the French Second Empire style. It's also evident in Gilman's design (with Gridley J. F. Bryant) of Old City Hall (1862) on School Street, whose mansard roof was an early example of a style duplicated on hundreds of townhouses in the Back Bay. The neighborhood's lavish Victorian mansions are for the most part no longer single-family residences, but are divided into apartments or used as businesses, schools, or public buildings. Heading south from Copley Square, you come to the South End, another trove of Victoriana whose park-studded layout owes more to London than Paris.

On Commonwealth Avenue in the Back Bay, you may notice a feature that's repeated all over town: public art. Boston's first "portrait sculpture," of Benjamin Franklin, is in front of Old City Hall. Washington is in the Public Garden, and Christopher Columbus can be found in the park that bears his name. You can talk politics with a bronze James Michael Curley at Congress and North streets, or plunge into Faneuil Hall Marketplace to talk basketball with Arnold "Red" Auerbach, founder of the Boston Celtics. The lawns around the State House are practically full of stone people, and across the street, Boston Common is littered with monuments and memorials. And in Copley Square, a statue of a tortoise and a hare greets runners crossing the finish line of the Boston Marathon.

The architecture of the building boom that started in the 1960s owes much to the fertile mind of a former Harvard instructor, I. M. Pei. His firm was responsible for much of the new construction, which has had varying degrees of success. The Christian Science Center (1973), the John F. Kennedy Library (1979), and the West Wing of the Museum of Fine Arts (1981) are rousing successes. The John Hancock Tower (1974) is the most dramatic point in the skyline, a signature of Boston, but began its life by shedding panes of glass onto the street below (the problem has been corrected). Government Center dates to the early '60s and is resented by many Bostonians less for its inelegant concrete-block plainness than because it replaced Scollay Square, a gritty, congested area once filled with shops and burlesque houses. The Square's decrepitude and appeal are recalled with equal affection.

Government Center's greatest offense is that it surrounds City Hall, a utilitarian monstrosity whose numerous sins are just starting to be corrected. The vast brick wasteland of City Hall Plaza has been broken up by a small park, and there's talk of a hotel and a music hall on the plaza and a restaurant on the roof of City Hall. Until that happens, it's still possible to do a little trick: Facing the building from the plaza or from Faneuil Hall, hold up the "tails" side of a nickel, upside-down. The resemblance to an inverted Monticello (Thomas Jefferson's Virginia estate) is eerie.

6 Boston Cuisine: A Gift from the Sea (and Land)

SEAFOOD Nutritionists have recently taken to reminding us of what Bostonians have known all along: Fish is good for you. It has become a staple on restaurant menus across the country, but Boston is one of the very best places to try some.

Fishing has been a staple of the local economy for as long as there's been a local economy, and although the industry is in decline, it's still important for financial and culinary reasons. Chefs and owners of the city's best restaurants visit the docks and markets before dawn to make sure the day's specials are just that. If you've never had fresh fish or shellfish, you're in for a treat.

A few unfamiliar terms will probably jump out at you. "Scrod" or "schrod" is a generic term for whatever white-fleshed fish looked good that day, almost always served in fillets. Some people claim that "schrod" (with an "h") is haddock and "scrod" is cod, pollock, or hake, but it's such a fine distinction that you should ask if you're curious. Scrod is served fried (often in fish and chips), broiled, poached, and even roasted. If haddock manages to stay off the schrod platter, it's sometimes smoked and turned into "finnan haddie," a rich, briny, decadent treat usually served in a cream sauce.

Other species of fish often seen on local menus (not always locally caught, but always skillfully prepared) include salmon, tuna, swordfish, bluefish, flounder, sole, tilefish (another white-fleshed fish), striped bass, and monkfish. Local shellfish include scallops, mussels, shrimp, and oysters.

You'll often see fish cooked in chowder, but more often you'll see clam chowder, a staple at restaurants in every price range. New England clam chowder, as it's called, consists of chopped hard-shell clams, potatoes, cream, salt pork (usually), onions (usually), celery (sometimes), milk (sometimes), and never, ever, tomatoes, which would make it Manhattan clam chowder, a New York favorite that is almost impossible to find in restaurants north of Connecticut.

If you want clams but you don't want soup, at many places you can order "steamers" (soft-shell clams cooked in the shell) as an appetizer or main dish. More common on the appetizer menu are hard-shell clams—littlenecks (small), or cherrystones (medium-size)—served raw, like oysters. If you happen to find yourself at a place with a "raw bar," you can order clams and oysters singly or by the half- or full dozen. They're opened (a fascinating procedure you may be allowed to watch) and served on a bed of ice with a wedge of lemon, hot sauce, and sometimes a dish of horseradish. Technically, all hard-shell clams are quahogs (say "co-hogs"), but that term is usually reserved for large specimens. They're often served stuffed—the flesh is chopped, seasoned, mixed with bread crumbs, and cooked in the shells.

New England fried clams are also especially good. Fresh, not frozen, they come whole (with the plump belly) or in "strips" (without), lightly battered and served with french fries and cole slaw. Even greasy fried clams are ambrosial, and prepared correctly, they're a delicacy. You'll probably also see the clam "roll," a portion of fried clams served on a hot dog bun. A roll is perfect if you're a light eater—or if you're on a budget; the other popular fillings for rolls are the more expensive seafood salad and lobster.

Mmm, lobster. Lobster was once so abundant off the Massachusetts coast that the resident Indians showed the Pilgrims how to use the ugly crustaceans as fertilizer. Today the supply fluctuates by the day, boosting or depressing the price in the market and on the menu. It's usually expensive (and worth it), so many Bostonians wait for a special occasion to have it. Order lobster boiled or steamed, and you'll get a plastic bib, nutcrackers (for the claws and tail), picks (for the legs), drawn butter (for dipping), and a big bowl (for the residual wreckage). Your server can give you pointers. If you want someone else to do the dirty work, lobster is also available stuffed, broiled, baked, in a "pie" (usually a casserole), over pasta, or in salad. If your cholesterol level can stand it, try lobster Newburg (cooked in butter, simmered in sherry, and mixed with a cream and egg yolk sauce) and lobster thermidor (boiled and cooked in cream sauce seasoned with mustard, sherry, and cayenne).

Lobsters are sometimes part of a New England clambake, traditionally prepared in a pit dug on the beach. A fire is lit in the pit and covered with a layer of stones, and when the fire dies down, the smoking-hot stones are covered with layers of clams, corn, potatoes, lobster and chicken, separated by layers of wet seaweed. A clambake in a restaurant might consist of the elements prepared separately (without the seaweed). Hold out for a clambake where all the ingredients are cooked in a big pot on the stove—lobster with all the trimmings cooked together has a different (better) flavor than separately prepared ingredients combined after they're already done.

BAKED BEANS & SWEETS   Traditional Boston baked beans originated in the days when church was an all-day affair and cooking on the Sabbath was forbidden. Typically, a crock of beans was set in a brick oven (next to a huge, walk-in cooking fireplace) on Saturday to cook in the retained heat until Sunday dinner at noon the next day.

Boston baked beans are prepared by soaking dried pea beans or navy beans in water overnight and then boiling them briefly. The cooked beans then go into a

Sports, Politics and Revenge

As noted, Boston is in a fallow period for sports, and as for revenge . . . well, let's just say that revenge is a staple. Politics, the third of the traditional Boston obsessions is arguably the most interesting. In a city where anything and everything can lead to a lively debate, that shouldn't come as a surprise. Boston has produced leaders of the Revolution (Samuel Adams, John Hancock), a leader of the loyalists (Gov. Thomas Hutchinson, who died in exile in England), a revered president (John F. Kennedy) and a presidential nominee (Michael Dukakis).

The local political legacy is less distinguished but far more colorful. In fact, after the burst of Irish immigration led to the election of the first Irish mayor in 1885, the word "colorful" started cropping up a lot. "Machine" politics and patronage were the order of the day. In 1910, John F. "Honey Fitz" Fitzgerald was elected mayor, thrilling his daughter Rose, who is better known as John F. Kennedy's mother. Honey Fitz was known for singing "Sweet Adeline" and dancing as the returns came in after a successful campaign.

Fitzgerald's successful opponent in the 1913 election was James Michael Curley, who was mayor four times over four decades. Curley spent part of his last term in a federal prison, doing time for fraud before being pardoned by President Truman. His final, unsuccessful mayoral campaign was the subject of Edwin O'Connor's novel *The Last Hurrah*. The reform politics of the 1960s bleached many of the "colorful" details out of Boston government, and the Brahmin—Irish stranglehold on the mayor's office was finally broken in 1993, with the election of Thomas M. Menino, an Italian-American.

Other well-known Boston politicians include Sen. Edward Kennedy and former Speakers of the House John W. McCormack and Thomas P. "Tip" O'Neill, who both have buildings named after them. As a rule, if you can't figure out where the name of a building or other public place in Boston came from, you can assume it's named after a politician.

crock with dry mustard, brown sugar or molasses, some cooking water or beer, and sometimes onions, ketchup, or vinegar. The mixture is topped with strips of salt pork and cooked for about eight hours. Made correctly, they're wonderful. In the sort of restaurant that serves real baked beans, you'll probably also see cornbread and brown bread, which is really more of a steamed pudding of whole wheat and rye flour, cornmeal, molasses, buttermilk, and, usually, raisins.

If you're getting the idea that molasses is important in traditional New England cooking, you're right. If you're a molasses fiend (this isn't for amateurs), try "Indian pudding," a heavy dish that's basically very sweet cornmeal mush topped with whipped cream or ice cream.

For ice cream on its own, you couldn't have come to a better place. Although the ice cream mania of 10 years ago has passed, people still gobble anything chilly year-round—frozen yogurt in a snowbank, anyone? Be aware that a milk shake in Boston (and other parts of New England) is exactly that: milk, shaken, with some flavored syrup. The concoction the rest of the world considers a milkshake is a frappé (say "frap") to Bostonians, and with extra ice cream it's sometimes called a "Western frappé." And you know those sweet little bits of colorful candy that ice cream parlors scatter on top of ice cream cones? Most people call them "sprinkles." In New England, ask for "jimmies."

7   Recommended Books and Films

BOOKS   A list of authors with ties to Boston could fill a book of its own and still only scratch the surface. To get in the mood for Boston before visiting, let the impulse that inspired you to make the trip guide you around the library or bookstore. Here are a few suggestions.

For children, *Make Way for Ducklings,* by Robert McCloskey, is the quintessential Boston classic. It tells the story of Mrs. Mallard and her babies on the loose in the Back Bay. In honor of the famous book, the duck family is cast in bronze at the Public Garden. A good historical title for kids is *Johnny Tremain,* by Esther Forbes, a fictional boy's-eye-view account of the Revolutionary War era.

For adults, two Pulitzer Prize winners have chronicled the city's history. *Paul Revere and the World He Lived In* is Esther Forbes' look at Boston before, during, and after the Revolution, and J. Anthony Lukas' *Common Ground: A Turbulent Decade in the Lives of Three American Families* is the definitive account of the Boston busing crisis of the 1970s.

Architecture buffs will enjoy *Cityscapes of Boston,* by Robert Campbell and Peter Vanderwarker, and *Lost Boston,* by Jane Holtz Kay. *The Proper Bostonians,* by Cleveland Amory, and *The Friends of Eddie Coyle,* by George V. Higgins, offer fictional looks at wildly different strata of Boston society.

"Paul Revere's Ride," Henry Wadsworth Longfellow's classic but historically questionable poem about the events of April 18–19, 1775, is collected in many anthologies.

FILMS   Television has done more than any movie to make Boston familiar to international audiences. *Cheers* (no, the bar isn't anything like the set), *St. Elsewhere,* and *Spenser: For Hire* all used the city as a backdrop. For a complete TV tribute to the city, play the montage at the beginning of the 1995 sitcom "Boston Common" in slow motion.

In the film category, *Blown Away,* starring Jeff Bridges, makes the city look spectacular, especially in the opening scenes. *Celtic Pride* (Dan Aykroyd, Damon Wayans) and *Mrs. Winterbourne* (Shirley MacLaine, Ricki Lake), filmed in and around Boston and released in 1996, added nothing to the area's cinematic reputation, but should be available on video by the time you read this. Classic movies that can give you a taste of the flavor of the region include *The Witches of Eastwick* (Jack Nicholson, Cher, Susan Sarandon), *Glory* (Denzel Washington, Matthew Broderick), *The Verdict* (Paul Newman, James Mason), *Housesitter* (Goldie Hawn, Steve Martin), and the sentimental favorite, *Love Story* (Ryan O'Neal, Ali MacGraw).

Planning a Trip to Boston

This chapter addresses the practical issues that arise when traveling to a new place. Now that you've decided to visit Boston, how do you get there? How much will it cost? When should you go? How can you learn more? You'll find answers to these questions here, along with information about the climate and the events, festivals, and parades you might want to see when you get there.

1 Visitor Information & Money

VISITOR INFORMATION

The **Greater Boston Convention & Visitors Bureau** (P.O. Box 990468, Prudential Tower, Suite 400, Boston, MA 02199; ☎ **617/536-4100** or 800/888-5515 outside MA; fax 617/424-7664) offers a free travel planner, a comprehensive guidebook ($4.95) and a *Kids Love Boston* guidebook. It operates **Boston by Phone** (☎ **800/374-7400**), which provides information on attractions, dining, performing arts and nightlife, shopping, and travel services.

You can also contact the **Massachusetts Office of Travel and Tourism** (100 Cambridge St., 13th floor, Boston, MA 02202; ☎ **617/727-3201** or 800/447-6277; fax 617/727-6525; e-mail vacationinfo@state.ma.us); they'll send you a free "Getaway Guide" magazine that includes information about attractions and lodgings, a map, and a seasonal calendar.

For information about Cambridge, contact **Cambridge Discovery, Inc.** (P.O. Box 1987, Cambridge, MA 02238; ☎ **617/497-1630**).

Information about Boston is also available on the internet. A good place to start is http://www.city.net/countries/united_states/massachusetts/boston; or http://www.city.net/countries/united_states/massachusetts/cambridge.

Both are packed with information and links to other sites. The Convention & Visitors Bureau offers listings of visitor services that can be reached through toll-free numbers (http://www.dvm.com/users/dvm/boston). When you're ready to start planning activities, check out Boston.com (http://www.boston.com), which has links to publications, including the *Boston Globe,* museums and other arts resources, including the Museum of Fine Arts, and an interactive tour of the Freedom Trail.

What Things Cost in Boston	U.S. $
Taxi from airport to downtown Boston	16.00–22.00
Bus from airport to downtown Boston	8.00
MBTA subway token	.85
Double at Four Seasons Hotel (deluxe)	320.00–495.00
Double at Boston Park Plaza Hotel & Towers (moderate)	175.00–225.00
Double at Chandler Inn Hotel (budget)	99.00
Lunch for one at Zuma's Tex-Mex Café (moderate)	6.95–17.95
Lunch for one at Bob the Chef's (budget)	3.00–10.50
Dinner for one, without wine, at Aujourd'hui (deluxe)	26.00–35.50
Dinner for one, without wine, at Lo Conte's (moderate)	9.95–24.00
Dinner for one, without wine, at Jimbo's Fish Shanty (budget)	6.00–16.00
Glass of beer	2.75–4.00
Coca-Cola	.75–1.00
Cup of coffee	1.00–1.50
Roll of ASA 100 Kodacolor film, 36 exposures	6.75–8.00
Admission to the Museum of Fine Arts, Boston	8.00
Movie ticket	4.75–7.50
Theater ticket	30.00–90.00

MONEY

In addition to the details below, foreign travelers should see Chapter 3 for monetary descriptions and currency-exchange information.

U.S. dollar **traveler's checks** are the safest way to carry currency. They're as good as cash in most places and can be replaced if they are lost or stolen. However, some establishments restrict the amount they will accept or cash, so purchase some in small denominations for convenience. Before you leave home, make a list of the serial numbers and keep it separate from the checks in case you need to replace them.

If you prefer not to carry too much cash at one time, there are **Automated Teller Machines (ATMs),** also known simply as cash machines, all over Boston. Most are located at banks, shopping malls, and supermarkets. Call your ATM network before you leave home to check out its Boston locations. Cirrus (☎ **800/424-7787**) and PLUS Global ATM Locator Service (☎ **800/843-7587**) are international networks that connect with most other ATM institutions. They supply locations of machines over the phone.

2 When to Go

Boston attracts and entertains large numbers of visitors year-round, and hotel rooms can occasionally be difficult to find. Foliage season (mid-September to early November), when the trees are aflame with autumn color, has become a huge draw in recent years, and the periods around college graduation (mid- to late May and early June) and the major citywide events (listed below) have high hotel occupancy rates. Try to reserve a room early if you know you'll be traveling at busy times. Hotel rates are usually lower during the winter.

Boston's Average Temperatures & Rainfall

	Jan	Feb	Mar	Apr	May	June	July	Aug	Sept	Oct	Nov	Dec
Temp (°F)	30	31	38	49	59	68	74	72	65	55	45	34
Rain (inches)	4.0	3.7	4.1	3.7	3.5	2.9	2.7	3.7	3.4	3.4	4.2	4.9

CLIMATE

You've probably already heard the saying about New England weather—"If you don't like it, wait 10 minutes." It's not as changeable as all that, but variations from day to day can be enormous, and dressing in layers is always a good idea. Fall and spring are the best times to visit if you're hoping for moderate temperatures, but spring is brief (it doesn't really settle in until early May). Summers tend to be hot and sticky, especially in July and August, and winters are cold and usually snowy— bring a heavy coat. But you can roast in May and freeze in June, shiver in July and wish you'd packed shorts in March.

Once in Boston, you can check the weather by looking up at the short column of lights on top of the old John Hancock building in the Back Bay. (The new Hancock building is the glass tower next door.) A steady blue light means clear; flashing blue, cloudy; steady red, rain; flashing red, snow—except during the summer, when flashing red means the Red Sox game has been canceled.

BOSTON CALENDAR OF EVENTS

The **City of Boston Special Events Line** (☎ 800/822-0038) has a recording listing cultural and educational happenings for the current month. The **Office of Special Events** (☎ 617/635-3911) can answer questions about specific activities.

January

- **Chinese New Year,** Chinatown. Dragon parade, fireworks, and many raucous festivals. Special programs at the Children's Museum. Depending on the Chinese lunar calendar, the holiday falls between January 21 and February 19.
- **Martin Luther King Jr. Birthday Celebration.** Various locations. Events include speeches, musical tributes, and gospel celebrations. Third Monday of the month.

February

- **Black History Month.** Various locations. Activities include tours of the Black Heritage Trail led by National Park Service rangers (617/742-5415). All month.
- **Beanpot Hockey Tournament,** FleetCenter (617/624-1000). Boston College, Boston University, Harvard University, and Northeastern University vie for bragging rights and a trophy shaped like, yes, a beanpot. First two Mondays of the month.
- **School Vacation Week.** More of an occasion than an event. The slate of activities for children is truly impressive, including plays, special exhibitions and programs, and tours. Contact individual attractions for information on special programs. Third week of the month.

March

- **St. Patrick's Day/Evacuation Day.** Parade, South Boston. Celebration, Faneuil Hall Marketplace. The five-mile parade salutes the city's Irish heritage and the day British troops left Boston in 1776. Head to Faneuil Hall Marketplace for music, dancing, and food. March 17.
- **New England Spring Flower Show,** Bayside Expo Center, Dorchester. This annual harbinger of spring presented by the Massachusetts Horticultural Society (617/536-9280) draws huge crowds starved for a glimpse of green. Second or third week of the month.

April

❷ **Patriots Day.** The events of April 18–19, 1775, which signified the start of the Revolutionary War, are commemorated and re-enacted. Lanterns are hung in the steeple of the Old North Church; Participants dressed as Paul Revere and William Dawes ride to Lexington and Concord to warn the Minutemen that "the regulars are out" (not that "the British are coming"—most colonists considered themselves British); battles are fought at Lexington and then Concord.

> **Where:** Paul Revere House, Old North Church, Lexington Green, Concord's North Bridge. **When:** The third Monday of the month, which is a state holiday. **How:** Contact the Paul Revere House (617/523-2338), the Lexington Chamber of Commerce's Visitor Center (1875 Massachusetts Ave., Lexington, MA 02173; 617/862-1450), or the Concord Chamber of Commerce (2 Lexington Rd., Concord, MA 01742; 508/369-3120).

• **Boston Marathon,** from Hopkinton, Massachusetts, to Boston. International stars and local amateurs join in the world's oldest and most famous marathon. The noon start means that the fastest runners hit Boston about two hours later; weekend runners stagger across the Boylston Street finish line as long as six hours after that. Third Monday of the month.

• **Swan Boats Return** to the Public Garden. Since their introduction in 1877, the swan boats have been a symbol of Boston. Like real swans, they go away for the winter. Saturday before Patriots Day.

May

• **Museum-Goers' Month,** various locations. Contact individual museums for details and schedules of special exhibits, lectures, and events. All month.

• **Boston Kite Festival,** Franklin Park (617/635-4505). Kites of all shapes and sizes take to the air above a celebration that includes kite-making clinics, music, and other entertainment. Mid-month.

• **Lilac Sunday,** Arnold Arboretum, Jamaica Plain (617/524-1717). The only day of the year that picnicking is permitted at the arboretum. From sunrise to sunset, you may wander the grounds and enjoy the sensational spring flowers, including more than 400 varieties of lilacs in bloom. Usually held on the third Sunday of the month.

• **Street Performers Festival,** Faneuil Hall Marketplace. Everyone but the pigeons seems to get into the act as sword-swallowers, jugglers, musicians, magicians and artists strut their stuff. Late May.

• **Art Newbury Street,** Newbury Street. Twice a year, more than 30 galleries are open and the street is closed to traffic from the Public Garden to Massachusetts Avenue as art-lovers wander through the special exhibits and enjoy the outdoor entertainment. Late May.

June

• **Boston Dairy Festival,** Boston Common. Cows were allowed to graze on Boston Common for 200 years; now they return once a year, accompanied by other farm animals, milking contests and children's activities. The "Scooper Bowl," or ice cream extravaganza, takes place simultaneously on City Hall Plaza. First week of June.

• **Bunker Hill Parade,** Charlestown. An observation of the Battle of Bunker Hill, June 17, 1775, which the Americans lost. The parade winds through Charlestown to the monument and ends at the Navy Yard. Sunday closest to June 17.

❷ *Boston Globe* **Jazz Festival.** Big names and rising stars of the jazz world appear at lunchtime, after-work, evening, and weekend events, some of which are free.

Where: Various locations, indoors and outdoors. **When:** Third week of June. **How:** Contact the *Globe* (617/929-2000) or pick up a copy of the paper for a schedule when you arrive in town. Some events require tickets purchased in advance.

July

✪ **Boston Harborfest.** The city puts on its Sunday best for Fourth of July, which has become a gigantic weeklong celebration of Boston's maritime history and an excuse to just get out and have fun. Events include concerts, guided tours, talks, cruises, fireworks, the Boston Chowderfest, and the annual turnaround of the USS *Constitution,* usually executed by tugboats. In 1997, in celebration of her 200th birthday, the *Constitution* will be under sail for the first time in more than a century.

Where: Downtown, along Boston Harbor, and the Harbor Islands. **When:** First week in July. **How:** Contact Boston Harborfest (45 School St., Boston, MA 02108-3204; 617/227-1528 or fax 617/227-1886).

* **Boston Pops Concert and Fireworks Display,** Hatch Memorial Shell on the Esplanade. Overnight camping is no longer permitted, but people wait from dawn till dark for the music to start. They also show up at the last minute—the Cambridge side of the river, near Kendall Square, is a good spot to watch the spectacular aerial show. The program includes the *1812 Overture* with actual cannon fire that coincides with the pyrotechnics. July 4.

August

* **Italian-American Feasts,** North End. These weekend street fairs begin in July, but the two biggest are saved for last, the Fishermen's Feast and the Feast of St. Anthony. The sublime (fresh seafood prepared while you wait; live music and dancing in the street) mingles with the ridiculous (carnival games and fried-dough stands) to leave a lasting impression of fun and indigestion. Last two weekends in August.
* **Salem's Heritage Days.** Various locations, Salem. A week-long event with entertainment, food, and programs highlighting Salem's multicultural heritage. Contact the Salem Office of Tourism & Cultural Affairs (800/777-6848) for specifics. Second or third week of August.

September

* **Cambridge River Festival,** on Memorial Drive from Kennedy Street to Western Avenue. A salute to the arts, with music, dancing, children's activities, and international food in an outdoor setting. Early September.
* **Boston Film Festival.** Various locations. Alternative and art films continue their turn around the festival circuit or make their premiere, sometimes accompanied by a talk by an actor or filmmaker. Middle of the month.
* **Art Newbury Street,** Newbury Street. As it does for the May event, Newbury Street closes from the Public Garden to Massachusetts Avenue and the galleries throw their doors open. Late September.

October

* **Columbus Day Parade,** downtown and the North End. Beginning with a ceremony on City Hall Plaza at 1pm, the parade, appropriately enough, winds up in the city's Italian neighborhood, following Hanover Street to the Coast Guard station on Commercial Street. Second Monday of the month.
* **Ringling Brothers and Barnum & Bailey Circus,** FleetCenter. The Greatest Show on Earth makes its annual two-week visit. Middle of the month.
✪ **Head of the Charles Regatta,** Boston and Cambridge. High school, college and post-collegiate rowing teams and individuals—some 4,000 in all—race in front of hordes of fans along the banks of the Charles River and on the bridges spanning it. Long a

magnet for party-hearty preppies, the race became more enjoyable for most spectators when strict enforcement of laws banning open alcohol containers began. This event always seems to fall on the crispest, most picturesque Sunday of the season.

Where: Along both sides of the river from the basin to the Eliot Bridge in west Cambridge. **When:** Late October. **How:** Sit, stroll, or perch on a bridge. **Tip:** The boats (called "shells") are numbered sequentially and race against the clock from a staggered start. If a higher-numbered team is ahead of one with a lower number, it's making good time. You can call the **Metropolitan District Commission** Harbor Master (617/727-0537) for information.

- **Salem Haunted Happenings.** Various locations. Parades, parties, fortune-telling, cruises, and tours lead up to a ceremony on the big day. Contact the Salem Office of Tourism & Cultural Affairs (800/777-6848) for specifics. Last two weeks of the month.

November

- **An Evening with Champions,** at Harvard's Bright Athletic Center, Allston. World-class ice skaters and local students (who once upon a time included 1994 Olympic silver medalist Nancy Kerrigan) stage three performances to benefit the Jimmy Fund, the children's fund-raising arm of the Dana-Farber Cancer Institute. Sponsored by Harvard's Eliot House (617/493-8172).

- **Thanksgiving Celebration,** Plymouth (800/USA-1620). The holiday that put Plymouth on the map is observed with a "stroll through the ages," showcasing 17th- and 19th-century Thanksgiving preparations in historic homes. Plimoth Plantation, where the colony's first years are re-created, wisely offers a Victorian Thanksgiving feast, for which reservations are required (508/746-1622). Thanksgiving Day.

December

- **Christmas Tree Lighting,** Prudential Center. Carol singing precedes the lighting of a magnificent tree from Nova Scotia—an annual expression of thanks from the people of Halifax for Bostonians' help in fighting a devastating fire more than 70 years ago. First Saturday of December.

- **Boston Tea Party Reenactment,** at the Tea Party Ship and Museum, Congress Street Bridge (617/338-1773). Chafing under British rule, the colonists rose up on December 16, 1773, to strike a blow where it would cause real pain—in the pocketbook. Mid-December.

- ✪ **First Night.** The concept is spreading all over the country, but the original, and still the best, arts-oriented, no-alcohol, city-wide New Year's Eve celebration is in Boston. Events start in the early afternoon and include a parade, ice sculptures, art exhibitions, theatrical performances, and indoor and outdoor entertainment. It all wraps up at midnight with a spectacular fireworks display over the harbor.

Where: Back Bay and the waterfront. **When:** December 31. **How:** Contact First Night (617/542-1399).

3 Health & Insurance

Before you leave, be sure you are protected with adequate health insurance coverage, and that you understand your insurance provider's procedures for medical treatment when you're away from home.

INSURANCE   Most travel agents sell low-cost health, loss, and trip-cancellation insurance to their vacationing clients. Rates for these short-term policies are generally reasonable, and the policies allow you to supplement existing coverage with a minimum of complications. Other forms of travel-related insurance are also available, including coverage for lost or damaged baggage. Often a single policy provided by your travel agent will protect you in all of these areas and also will provide supplementary medical coverage.

4 Tips for Travelers with Special Needs

FOR TRAVELERS WITH DISABILITIES   Boston, like all other U.S. cities, has taken the required steps to provide access for the disabled. Hotels must provide accessible rooms; museums and street curbs have ramps for wheelchairs. The Americans with Disabilities Act (ADA), effective in 1992, requires all forms of public transportation to provide special services to persons with disabilities. All MBTA buses have lifts or kneelers (call ☎ 800/LIFT-BUS for more information). While some bus routes are wheelchair-accessible at all times, you might have to make a reservation as much as a day in advance for others. Some taxis are now equipped to handle wheelchairs—call individual taxi services to find out if they are. In addition, there is now an Airport Handicap Van (☎ 617/561-1769). For reduced fares in public transportation, persons with disabilities can apply to purchase a Transportation Access Pass (TAP) from the MBTA Access Pass Office (10 Boylston Pl., Boston, MA 02116; ☎ 617/222-5438). The application must be completed by a licensed healthcare professional. *Note:* Although Boston has made progress, some wheelchair-dependent travelers have recently reported difficulty negotiating curbs and buses. Please do some research before you leave home. An excellent source of information for the disabled is the **Information Center for Individuals with Disabilities** (29 Stanhope St., 4th floor, P.O. Box 256, Boston, MA 02117; ☎617/450-9888 or 800/462-5015 in MA; TDD 617/424-6855.) Hours are 8:30am to 4:30pm. They can answer questions and also publish helpful fact sheets and a newsletter. The **Massachusetts Coalition for Citizens with Disabilities** (20 Park Plaza, Suite 603, Boston, MA 02116; ☎ 617/482-1336 or 800/ 55VOTER, voice or TDD) is also helpful.

FOR GAY & LESBIAN TRAVELERS   The **Gay and Lesbian Helpline** offers information (☎ 617/267-9001) Monday through Friday from 4 to 11pm, Saturday 6 to 8:30pm, and Sunday 6 to 10pm. You can also contact the **Boston Alliance of Gay and Lesbian Youth,** or BAGLY (☎ 800/422-2459). *In Publications* (258 Shawmut Ave., Boston, MA 02118; ☎ 617/426-8246) and *Bay Windows* (1523 Washington St., Boston, MA 02118; ☎ 617/266-6670), publish weekly newspapers that concentrate on upcoming gay-related events, news and features.

FOR SENIORS   Boston offers many discounts to seniors with identification. Hotels, restaurants, museums and movie theaters offer special deals. Discounts are usually offered in restaurants and theaters only at off-peak times, but museums and other attractions offer reduced rates at all times. Seniors can ride the MBTA subways for 20¢ (85¢ for others), and local bus fares for seniors are 15¢. On zoned and express buses and on the commuter rail, the senior citizen fare is half the regular fare. On the commuter rail, all you need as proof of age is a valid driver's license or passport, but for the subway and buses you have to have an MBTA senior citizen card. Call in advance for information on purchasing the senior citizen card, which is available at the Downtown Crossing MBTA station (☎ 617/722-5438) weekdays from 8:30am to 4:15pm.

The **American Association of Retired Persons,** or AARP (601 E St. NW, Washington, D.C., 20049; ☎ 202/434-2277), offers discounts on car rentals, accommodations, airfares, and sightseeing. **Grand Circle Travel** (347 Congress St., Boston, MA 02210; ☎ 617/350-7500 or 800/221-2610) organizes escorted tours and cruises for retired persons.

A Golden Age Passport will give you free lifetime admission to all recreation areas run by the federal government, including parks and monuments.

You might also be interested in the programs for those 60 and older organized by **Elderhostel, Inc.** (75 Federal St., Boston, MA 02110; ☎ 617/426-8056). Participants generally live in a dorm at one of the area's colleges, take courses at the college in the morning, and explore the city in the afternoon.

FOR FAMILIES   Children (usually under 17) can stay free in their parents' hotel room, when using existing bedding. Many hotels have package deals for families that offer a suite or breakfast for the kids, plus discount coupons for museums and restaurants. The **Greater Boston Convention & Visitors Bureau** (P.O. Box 990468, Prudential Tower, Suite 400, Boston, MA 02199; ☎ 617/536-4100 or 800/888-5515 outside MA; fax 617/424-7664) publishes a brochure listing family-friendly hotel packages and discounts.

FOR STUDENTS   Students don't actually rule Boston—it just feels that way sometimes. Museums, theaters, concert halls and other attractions often offer discounts for college and high school students with valid identification. During the summer months students can rent rooms in college dorms on some of the campuses. Check with the schools for information. Visiting students should check the bulletin boards at Boston University, Harvard, and MIT; many events will be open to them. The weekly *Boston Phoenix* lists many activities for students.

5 Getting There

BY PLANE

The major domestic carriers flying into Boston's **Logan International Airport** are **American** (☎ 800/433-7300), **Continental** (☎ 800/523-3273), **Delta** (☎ 800/221-1212), **Northwest** (☎ 800/225-2525), **TWA** (☎ 800/221-2000), **United** (☎ 800/241-6522), and **USAir** (☎ 800/428-4322). Most of the major international carriers also fly into Boston. Be prepared to show identification that matches the name on your ticket when you board.

FINDING THE BEST AIRFARE   To purchase a ticket quickly and without much hassle, go through your travel agent. To get the best price, you need to shop around, probably on your own. Fares change constantly; they vary from airline to airline and even from day to day at the same airline. Try to schedule your travel for weekdays during the busy summer season and avoid major holiday periods, when fares go up. Staying over a Saturday night usually means a lower price. Call around, or ask your travel agent to call around, as far in advance of your trip as possible. And be flexible, if you can—shifting a day or two can sometimes mean great savings, but you have to ask.

In general, the lowest fares are economy (also known as tourist) or APEX (Advance Purchase Excursion fare). The former has no restrictions, while the latter requires you to reserve and pay for the ticket seven, 14, 21 or 30 days in advance and stay for a minimum number of days. As a rule, the lower the price, the more trouble and expense it is to change plans. APEX fares are usually nonrefundable, and there is a charge for changing dates. However, the savings are considerable. If you have access to America Online (AOL), go to keyword "travel" and look for

EAASY SABRE. There you can look up all available flights and fares to Boston for the dates you intend to travel. You can also make reservations though this service.

A **charter** flight can be a good option if you choose the company carefully. Tour operators book a block of seats and then offer them at substantial reductions. You must book and pay in advance, and may lose your full payment or be hit with a penalty if you cancel—or if the company goes out of business. Check with the Better Business Bureau before you pay to make sure the company is reliable. **Consolidators** (also known as "bucket shops") buy blocks of tickets from airlines and resell them, often at rates below the official ones. As with charter companies, check with the Better Business Bureau. To fly **standby,** you wait at the airport for an empty seat on your flight. After all reserved seats are accounted for, you may be able to board at great savings. If not, you go home and try again, or book a regular flight.

LOGAN INTERNATIONAL AIRPORT   Boston's airport, in East Boston at the end of the Sumner, Callahan and Ted Williams tunnels, is one of the most accessible in the country, situated just 3 miles across the harbor from the downtown area. Access to the city is by cab, bus and subway via underwater tunnels, or by boat. The **subway** is fast and cheap—10 minutes (to Government Center) and 85¢. Free **shuttle buses** run from each terminal to the Airport station on the MBTA Blue Line from 5:30am to 1am every day of the year. The Blue Line stops at Aquarium (for the waterfront) and at State Street and Government Center, downtown points where you can exit or transfer to the other lines.

Some hotels have their own **limos**; ask about them when you make your reservations. A **cab** from the airport to downtown costs between $16 and $22. (See "Getting Around," in Chapter 4, for more information on taxis.) The ride into town takes from 10 minutes to a half hour, depending on the time of day and how congested the approach to the tunnel is. If you must travel during rush hour or on Sunday afternoon, allow extra time, or plan to take the subway and pack accordingly.

To cruise to Rowes Wharf on Atlantic Avenue (perfect for the Boston Harbor Hotel, Marriott Long Wharf, or for getting a cab elsewhere) in just seven minutes, dock to dock, try the **Airport Water Shuttle.** Courtesy buses from all terminals connect with the weather-protected, heated boats, which sail every 15 minutes from 6am to 8pm on weekdays, and every half hour on Friday until 11pm, Saturday from 10am to 11pm, and Sundays and national holidays (except Thanksgiving Day, Christmas, New Year's Day, and Fourth of July) from 10am to 8pm. The one-way fare is $8 for adults and children 12 and up, and $4 for senior citizens; children under 12 travel free.

If you're headed for the suburbs, the Massachusetts Port Authority coordinates **bus service** (☎ 800/23LOGAN) from the airport to suburban hubs in Braintree, Framingham, and Woburn. You can also try the **Share-A-Cab booths** at each terminal and save up to half the fare. **Limousine** and bus service north, south, and west of the city is available, usually by pre-arrangement. Call **Carey Limousine Boston** (☎ 617/623-8700 or 800/743-2282) or **Stagecoach Executive Sedan Services, Inc.** (☎ 617/723-9393 or 800/922-9500).

If you prefer to rent (hire) a car, the following agencies offer shuttle service from the airport to their offices: **Alamo** (☎ 800/327-9633), **Avis** (☎ 800/831-2847), **Budget** (☎ 800/527-0700), **Enterprise** (☎ 800/325-8007), **Hertz** (☎ 800/654-3131), **National** (☎ 800/227-7368) and **Thrifty** (☎ 800/367-2277).

FLYING WITH FILM AND LAPTOPS   Traveling with electronic devices and film (exposed or not) can take a little extra time in this age of heightened security.

X-ray machines won't affect film up to ASA 400, but you might want to request a visual check (in which the camera is checked for inappropriate equipment) anyway. A visual check for computers is standard practice in most airports—you'll probably be asked to switch it on, so be sure the batteries are charged. You may use your computer in flight, but not during take-off and landing because of possible interference with cockpit controls. In many cases, airport security guards will also ask you to turn on electronic devices (including camcorders and personal stereos) to prove that they are what they appear to be, so make sure batteries are charged and working for these items as well.

BY CAR

Driving to Boston is not difficult. The major highways leading to and from Boston are I-95 (Massachusetts Route 128), which connects Boston to highways in Connecticut and New York; I-90, the Massachusetts Turnpike, an east-west toll road that links up with the New York State Thruway; I-93/U.S. 1, extending north to Canada and leading to the Northeast Expressway, which enters downtown Boston; and I-93/Route 3, the Southeast Expressway, which connects Boston with the south, including Cape Cod.

The Massachusetts Turnpike ("Mass Pike") extends into the center of the city and connects with the Central Artery (the John F. Fitzgerald Expressway), which is linked to the Northeast Expressway. If you want to avoid Central Artery construction, exit at Prudential Center in the Back Bay. The Southeast Expressway is a busy commuter route, so try to avoid it at rush hour.

The approach to Cambridge is either Storrow Drive or Memorial Drive, one on each side of the Charles. Storrow Drive has a Harvard Square exit that leads you across the Anderson Bridge to John F. Kennedy Street and into the square; Memorial Drive intersects with Kennedy Street; turn away from the bridge to reach the square.

Since Boston is 208 miles from New York, the driving time is about 4 1/2 hours. The 992-mile drive from Chicago to Boston should take around 21 hours; from Washington, D.C., it takes about 8 hours to cover the 468 miles.

The **American Automobile Association** (☎ 800/AAA-HELP) provides its members with maps, itineraries and other travel information, and arranges free towing if you break down. Be aware that the Mass Pike is a privately operated road that arranges its own towing; if you break down there, wait in the car until one of the regular patrols arrives.

A word of caution about driving in the city: The Central Artery/Third Harbor Tunnel project, or "Big Dig," has begun, and while the Central Artery (the John F. Fitzgerald Expressway) is being moved underground, traffic patterns in the area change almost daily. Paradoxically, this means that streets, attractions and businesses are well labeled, but that's because they're sometimes impossible to find in the maze of jersey barriers and construction sites. If possible, avoid the Central Artery altogether by choosing alternate routes. The Ted Williams Tunnel part of this undertaking, which will eventually connect the Pike to the airport, is complete; the connection is part of the rest of the project, and until it's finished, the tunnel is open only to commercial traffic (at the risk of a hefty fine).

It's impossible to say this often enough: When you reach your hotel, leave your car in the garage and walk or use public transportation. Use the car for trips to the suburbs, the North Shore, or Plymouth; if you must drive in town, ask at the front desk for a route around or away from the construction area.

BY TRAIN

Boston has three rail centers: **South Station** on Atlantic Avenue, **Back Bay Station** at 145 Dartmouth Street, and **North Station** on Causeway Street. **Amtrak** (☎ 617/482-3660) has arrival and departure points at South Station and Back Bay Station. At South Station you can take the Red Line to Cambridge or get off at Park Street, the central hub of the **MBTA** (☎ 617/222-3200), where you can make connections to the Green, Blue and Orange lines. The Orange Line connects Back Bay Station with Park Street and other points. The MBTA operates trains to Ipswich, Rockport and Fitchburg from North Station, and commuter lines to points south of Boston from South Station.

Amtrak (☎ 800/USA-RAIL) runs to South Station from New York, with stops at Route 128 and Back Bay Station. Express trains make the trip in about 4 hours; others take $4^1/_2$ to 5 hours or longer. All-reserved Northeast Direct service predominates; fares range from $86 to $128 round trip. The round-trip unreserved fare is about $86. From Washington, D.C., count on $8^1/_2$ hours; Northeast Direct fares run from $132 to $172 round trip. Unreserved fares range from $122 to $156. Traveling time from Chicago is 22 hours (sleepers are available), and the fares range from $128 to $198 round trip. All of these fares are subject to change and may fluctuate depending on the time of year. During slow times, excursion fares may be available. Discounts are not available Friday and Sunday afternoon. Always remember to ask for the discounted rate.

Once a somewhat scary destination, South Station was extensively renovated and restored in the late 1980s, and it's now a beautiful, airy facility with a newsstand, bookstore kiosk, florist, bakery and a wide range of food choices. The one-ton clock above the main entrance is the only remaining hand-wound tower clock in New England. It is wound once a week from a small room behind the 14-foot-diameter clock face.

BY BUS

The brand new South Station Transportation Center (a fancy name for the bus terminal) is at 700 Atlantic Avenue, right next to the train station, and it's the city's bus-service hub. It's served by the following bus lines: **Greyhound** (☎ 617/526-1810 or 800/231-2222), **American Eagle** (☎ 508/993-5040 or 800/453-5040), **Bonanza** (☎ 617/720-4110 or 800/ 556-3815), **Brush Hill** (☎ 617/986-6100), **Concord Trailways** (☎ 617/426-8080 or 800/639-3317), **Peter Pan** (☎ 617/426-7838 or 800/343-9999), **Plymouth & Brockton** (☎ 617/773-9401) and **Vermont Transit** (☎ 800/451-3292).

Sample fares and times on Greyhound (and Peter Pan, which serves some of the same destinations) to Boston from other major cities are as follows: From New York, $48 round trip, 4 to 5 hours. From Washington, D.C., $92 round trip, 11 hours. From Chicago, $210 round trip, 24 to 27 hours. These fares are all subject to change. Greyhound will occasionally discount tickets purchased several weeks in advance.

3 For Foreign Visitors

Although American fads and fashions have spread across Europe and other parts of the world, making the United States seem like familiar territory before your arrival, there are still many peculiarities and uniquely American situations that any foreign visitor will encounter.

1 Preparing for Your Trip

ENTRY REQUIREMENTS

DOCUMENT REGULATIONS   Canadian citizens may enter the United States without visas; they need only proof of residence.

Citizens of the United Kingdom, New Zealand, Japan, and most western European countries traveling with valid passports may not need a visa for fewer than 90 days of holiday or business travel to the United States, providing that they hold a round-trip or return ticket and enter the United States on an airline or cruise line participating in the visa waiver program. (Note that citizens of these visa-exempt countries who first enter the United States may then visit Mexico, Canada, Bermuda, and/or the Caribbean islands and then reenter the United States, by any mode of transportation, without needing a visa. Further information is available from any U.S. embassy or consulate.)

Citizens of countries other than those stipulated above, including citizens of Australia, must have two documents: a valid passport, with an expiration date at least six months later than the scheduled end of the visit to the United States; and a tourist visa, available without charge from the nearest U.S. consulate. To obtain a visa, the traveler must submit a completed application form (either in person or by mail) with a $1^1/_2$-by-$^1/_2$ inch-square photo and demonstrate binding ties to the residence abroad.

Usually you can obtain a visa at once or within 24 hours, but it may take longer during the summer rush from June to August. If you cannot go in person, contact the nearest U.S. embassy or consulate for directions on applying by mail. Your travel agent or airline office may also be able to provide you with visa applications and instructions. The U.S. consulate or embassy that issues your visa will determine whether you will be issued a multiple- or single-entry visa and any restrictions regarding the length of your stay.

MEDICAL REQUIREMENTS   No inoculations are needed to enter the United States unless you are coming from, or have stopped over in, areas known to be suffering from epidemics, particularly cholera or yellow fever.

If you have a disease requiring treatment with medications containing narcotics or drugs requiring a syringe, you should carry a valid signed prescription from your physician to allay any suspicions that you are smuggling drugs.

CUSTOMS REQUIREMENTS   Every adult visitor may bring in, free of duty: 1 liter of wine or hard liquor; 200 cigarettes or 100 (non-Cuban) cigars or 3 pounds of smoking tobacco; and $100 worth of gifts. These exemptions are offered to travelers who spend at least 72 hours in the United States and who have not claimed them within the preceding six months. It is altogether forbidden to bring into the country foodstuffs (particularly cheese, fruit, cooked meats, and canned goods) and plants (vegetables, seeds, tropical plants, and so on). Foreign tourists may bring in or take out up to $10,000 in U.S. or foreign currency with no formalities; larger sums must be declared to Customs upon entering or leaving.

INSURANCE

There is no national health system in the United States. Because the cost of medical care is extremely high, we strongly advise every traveler to secure health coverage before setting out.

You may want to take out a comprehensive travel policy that covers (for a relatively low premium) sickness or injury costs (medical, surgical, and hospital); loss or theft of your baggage; trip-cancellation costs; guarantee of bail in case you are arrested; and costs of accident, repatriation, or death. Such packages (for example, "Europe Assistance" in Europe) are sold by automobile clubs at attractive rates, as well as by insurance companies and travel agencies.

MONEY

CURRENCY & EXCHANGE   The U.S. monetary system has a decimal base: one American dollar ($1) = 100 cents (100¢).

Dollar bills commonly come in $1 (a "buck"), $5, $10, $20, $50, and $100 denominations (the last two are not welcome when paying for small purchases and are not accepted in taxis or at subway token booths). There are also $2 bills (seldom encountered).

There are six denominations of coins: 1¢ (one cent or a penny), 5¢ (five cents or a nickel), 10¢ (ten cents or a dime), 25¢ (twenty-five cents or a quarter), 50¢ (fifty cents or a half dollar), and the rarely seen $1 piece.

The foreign-exchange bureaus so common in Europe are rare even at airports in the United States and nonexistent outside major cities. Try to avoid having to change foreign money, or traveler's checks in currency other than U.S. dollars, at a small-town bank, or even a branch in a big city.

TRAVELER'S CHECKS   Traveler's checks denominated in U.S. dollars are readily accepted at most hotels, motels, restaurants, and large stores. But the best place to change traveler's checks is at a bank. Do not bring traveler's checks denominated in other currencies.

CREDIT CARDS   The method of payment most widely used is the credit card: Visa (BarclayCard in Britain), MasterCard (EuroCard in Europe, Access in Britain, Chargex in Canada), American Express, Diners Club, Discover, and Carte Blanche. You can save yourself trouble by using "plastic money" rather than cash or traveler's checks in most hotels, motels, restaurants, and retail stores (a growing number of food and liquor stores now accept credit cards). You must have a credit card to rent a car. It can also be used as proof of identity (often carrying more weight than a passport), or as a "cash card," enabling you to draw money from banks that accept them.

SAFETY

GENERAL   While tourist areas are generally safe, crime is on the increase everywhere, and U.S. urban areas tend to be less safe than those in Europe or Japan. Visitors should always stay alert. This is particularly true of large U.S. cities like Boston. It is wise to ask the city's or area's tourist office if you're in doubt about which neighborhoods are safe. Avoid deserted areas, especially at night. Don't go into any city park at night unless there is an event that attracts crowds—for example, Boston's concerts on the Esplanade. Generally speaking, you can feel safe in areas where there are many people and many open establishments.

Avoid carrying valuables with you on the street, and don't display expensive cameras or electronic equipment. Hold on to your pocketbook, and place your billfold in an inside pocket. In theaters, restaurants and other public places, keep your possessions in sight.

Remember also that hotels are open to the public, and in a large hotel security may not be able to screen everyone entering. Always lock your room door—don't assume that once inside your hotel you are automatically safe and no longer need to be on your guard.

DRIVING   The best way to protect yourself is to be aware of your surroundings. Question your rental agency about personal safety, or ask for a brochure of traveler safety tips when you pick up your car. Obtain from the agency written directions, or a map with the route clearly marked, showing how to get to your destination. And, if possible, arrive and depart during daylight hours.

Recently more and more crime in all U.S. cities has involved cars and drivers, most notably, what is called "carjacking." If you drive off a highway into a doubtful neighborhood, be sure to keep the doors locked and the windows rolled up, and leave the area as quickly as possible. If you have an accident, even on the highway, stay in your car with the doors locked until you assess the situation or until the police arrive. If you are bumped from behind on the street or are involved in a minor accident with no injuries and the situation appears to be suspicious, motion to the other driver to follow you to the nearest police precinct, well-lighted service station, or all-night store. *Never* get out of your car in such situations.

If you see someone on the road who indicates a need for help, do *not* stop. Take note of the location, drive on to a well-lighted area, and telephone the police by dialing 911. This is a free call, even from pay phones.

Park in well-lighted, well-traveled areas if possible. Always keep your car doors locked, whether attended or unattended. Look around you before you get out of your car, and never leave any packages or valuables in sight. If someone attempts to rob you or steal your car, do *not* try to resist the thief/carjacker—report the incident to the police department immediately.

You may wish to contact the Greater Boston Convention & Visitors Bureau before you arrive. They can provide you with a safety brochure.

2   Getting to the U.S.

Travelers from overseas can take advantage of the **APEX (Advance Purchase Excursion) fares** offered by all the major U.S. and European carriers. Most itineraries will take you through another American city, but some airlines do serve Boston directly: **American** and **TWA** from Paris, **British Airways, Virgin Atlantic** and **Delta** from London, **Lufthansa** from Frankfurt, **Northwest** from Amsterdam, and **Swissair** from Geneva and Zurich. Sale times depend on market activity, and fares between October and March are almost always lower than in the summer.

Some large American airlines (for example, TWA, American Airlines, Northwest, United, and Delta) offer travelers on their trans-Atlantic or trans-Pacific flights special discount tickets under the name **Visit USA,** allowing travel between any U.S. destinations at minimum rates. They are not on sale in the United States, and must be purchased before you leave your foreign point of departure. This system is the best, easiest, and fastest way to see the United States at low cost. You should obtain information well in advance from your travel agent or the office of the airline concerned, since the conditions attached to these discount tickets can be changed without advance notice.

The visitor arriving by air, no matter what the port of entry, should cultivate a good measure of patience and resignation before setting foot on U.S. soil. Getting through Immigration control may take as long as two hours on some days, especially on summer weekends. Add the time it takes to clear Customs and you'll see that you should make very generous allowance for delay in planning connections between international and domestic flights—an average of two to three hours at least.

In contrast, travelers arriving by car or by rail from Canada will find border-crossing formalities streamlined to the vanishing point. And air travelers from Canada, Bermuda, and some places in the Caribbean can sometimes go through Customs and Immigration at the point of departure, which is much quicker and less painful.

For further information about travel to and arrival in Boston, see "Getting There" in Chapter 2.

3 Getting Around the U.S.

Flying is the fastest, and most expensive, mode of travel within the U.S. For a list of carriers that serve Boston, see "Getting There," in Chapter 2.

Travel **by car** (or perhaps bicycle) is the best way to see the country outside of the major cities, especially if you have time to explore. The major roads are excellent, and the secondary routes that branch off of them can lead you to the small towns and natural wonders that help make the U.S. such a multifaceted destination.

International visitors can buy a **USA Railpass,** good for 15 or 30 days of unlimited travel on Amtrak (☎ 800/USA-RAIL). The pass is available through many foreign travel agents. Prices in 1996 for a 15-day pass were $245 off-peak and $355 during peak travel periods; a 30-day pass costs $350 off-peak and $440 in peak months. (With a foreign passport, you can also buy passes at some Amtrak offices in the United States, including locations in Boston, San Francisco, Los Angeles, Chicago, New York, Miami, and Washington, D.C.) Reservations are generally required and should be made for each part of your trip as early as possible.

Visitors should be aware of the limitations of long-distance rail travel in the United States. With a few notable exceptions (for instance, the Northeast Corridor between Boston and Washington, D.C.), service is rarely up to European standards: Delays are common, routes are limited and often infrequently served, and fares are rarely significantly lower than discount airfares. Thus, cross-country train travel should be approached with caution.

The cheapest way to travel in the United States is by bus. **Greyhound,** the country's nationwide bus line, offers an Ameripass for unlimited travel for 7 days (for

$179), 15 days (for $289), 30 days (for $399), and 60 days (for $599). Bus travel in the United States can be both slow and uncomfortable, so this option is not for everyone.

FAST FACTS FOR THE FOREIGN TRAVELER

Automobile Organizations   Auto clubs will supply maps, suggested routes, guidebooks, accident and bail-bond insurance, and emergency road service. The major auto club in the United States, with 955 offices nationwide, is the **American Automobile Association (AAA)**. Members of some foreign auto clubs have reciprocal arrangements with the AAA and enjoy its services at no charge. If you belong to an auto club, inquire about AAA reciprocity before you leave. The AAA can provide you with an International Driving Permit that validates your foreign license, and you may be able to join the AAA even if you are not a member of a reciprocal club. To inquire, call **800/222-4357**. In addition, some automobile rental agencies now provide these services, so you should inquire about their availability when you rent your car.

Business Hours   Banks are open weekdays from 8:30 or 9am to 3 or 4pm, and sometimes Saturday morning; most offer 24-hour access to Automated Teller Machines (ATMs). Business offices generally are open weekdays from 9am to 5pm. Stores and other businesses are open six days a week, with most open on Sunday as well; department stores usually stay open until 9pm at least one night a week.

Climate   See "When to Go," in Chapter 2.

Currency   See "Preparing for Your Trip," earlier in this chapter.

Currency Exchange   A reliable choice is **Thomas Cook Currency Services, Inc.** (160 Franklin St., Boston, MA; ☎ **800/287-7362**), which has been in business since 1841 and offers a wide range of services. They sell commission-free foreign and U.S. traveler's checks, drafts, and wire transfers; they also do check collections (including Eurochecks). Their rates are competitive, and their service is excellent. Other places in Boston at which to change money are the **Boston Bank of Commerce,** 133 Federal St. (☎ **617/457-4400**); **Ruesch International,** 45 Milk St. (☎ **617/482-8600**); and **BayBank,** at Logan Airport, Terminal C (☎ **617/569-1172** and Terminal E (☎ **617/567-2312**), and in Cambridge, 1414 Massachusetts Ave. (☎ **617/556-6050**).

Drinking Laws   The legal drinking age in Boston is 21. Liquor sales are not allowed on Sunday in stores only, but bars, taverns, and restaurants take up the slack.

Electric Current   The U.S. uses 110–120 volts, 60 cycles, compared to 220–240 volts, 50 cycles, in most of Europe. Besides a 100-volt converter, small appliances of non-American manufacture, such as hair dryers or shavers, will require a plug adapter, with two flat, parallel pins.

Embassies/Consulates   All embassies are located in the national capital, Washington, D.C.; some consulates are located in major cities, and most nations have a mission to the United Nations in New York City.

Listed here are the embassies and New York or Boston consulates of Australia, Canada, Ireland, New Zealand, and Britain. If you are from another country, you can get the telephone number of your embassy by calling "Information" in Washington, D.C. (☎ **202/555-1212**).

The **Australian embassy** is at 1601 Massachusetts Ave. NW, Washington, DC 20036 (☎ **202/797-3000**). The **consulate in New York** is located at the International Building, 630 Fifth Ave., Suite 420, New York, NY 10111 (☎ **212/408-8400**). The **consulate in Los Angeles** is located at Century Plaza Towers, 19th floor, 2049 Century Park East, Los Angeles, CA 90067 (☎ 310/229-4800).

The **Canadian embassy** is at 501 Pennsylvania Ave. NW, Washington, DC 20001 (☎ **202/682-1740**). The **consulate in New York** is located at 1251 Avenue of the Americas, New York, NY 10020 (☎ **212/596-1600**); the **consulate in Boston** is at 3 Copley Place, Suite 400, Boston, MA 02116 (☎ **617/262-3760**). A third **consulate, in Los Angeles,** is located at 300 Santa Grand Ave., Suite 1000, Los Angeles, CA 90071 (☎ **213/346-2700**).

The **Irish embassy** is at 2234 Massachusetts Ave. NW, Washington, DC 20008 (☎ **202/462-3939**). The **consulate in New York** is located at 345 Park Ave., 17th floor, New York, NY 10022 (☎ **212/319-2555**). The **consulate in San Francisco** is located at 655 Montgomery St., Suite 930, San Francisco, CA 94111 (☎ **415/392-4214**).

The **New Zealand Embassy** is at 37 Observatory Circle NW, Washington, DC 20008 (☎ **202/328-4800**). The **consulate in New York** is located at 780 3rd Ave., Suite 1904, New York, NY 10017-2024 (☎ **212/832-4038**). The **consulate in Los Angeles** is located at 12400 Wilshire Blvd., Suite 1150, Los Angeles, CA 90025 (☎ **310/207-1605**).

The **British embassy** is at 3100 Massachusetts Ave. NW, Washington, DC 20008 (☎ **202/462-1340**). The **consulate in Boston** is located at 600 Atlantic Ave., Federal Reserve Plaza, 25th floor, Boston, MA 02210 (☎ **617/248-9555**). The **consulate in New York** is located at 845 Third Ave., New York, NY 10022 (☎ **212/745-0200**). The **consulate in Los Angeles** is located at 11766 Wilshire Blvd., Suite 400, Los Angeles, CA 90025 (☎ **310/477-3322**).

Emergencies   Call **911** for fire, police, and ambulance. If you encounter such travelers' problems as sickness, accident, or lost or stolen baggage, call the **Travelers Aid Society,** an organization that specializes in helping distressed travelers, whether American or foreign. In Boston the number is **617/542-7286** (they are open Monday through Friday from 8:30am to 4:30pm).

Gasoline (Petrol)   One U.S. gallon equals 3.75 liters, while 1.2 U.S. gallons equal one Imperial gallon. You'll notice there are several grades (and price levels) of gasoline available at most gas stations. And you'll also notice that their names change from company to company. Unleaded gas with the highest octane is the most expensive. Each gas company has a different name for the various levels of octane, but most fall into the "regular," "super," and "plus" categories (most rental cars take the least expensive "regular" unleaded).

Holidays   On the following legal national holidays, banks, government offices, post offices, and many stores, restaurants, and museums are closed: January 1 (New Year's Day), third Monday in January (Martin Luther King Day), third Monday in February (Presidents' Day, Washington's Birthday), last Monday in May (Memorial Day), July 4 (Independence Day), first Monday in September (Labor Day), second Monday in October (Columbus Day), November 11 (Veterans Day/Armistice Day), fourth Thursday in November (Thanksgiving Day), and December 25 (Christmas Day).

In Massachusetts, the third Monday in April is Patriot's Day, and March 17 is Evacuation Day. State offices are closed.

Finally, the Tuesday following the first Monday in November is Election Day, and is a legal holiday in presidential election years.

Legal Aid The well-meaning foreign tourist will probably never become involved with the American legal system. However, there are a few things you should know just in case. If you are "pulled over" for a minor infraction (for example, of the highway code, such as speeding), never attempt to pay the fine directly to a police officer; you may wind up arrested on the much more serious charge of attempted bribery. Pay fines by mail, or directly into the hands of the clerk of the court. If accused of a more serious offense, it's wise to say and do nothing before consulting a lawyer. Under U.S. law, an arrested person is allowed one telephone call to a party of his or her choice. Call your embassy or consulate.

Mail If you want your mail to follow you on your vacation and you aren't sure of your address, your mail can be sent to you, in your name, **c/o General Delivery** at the McCormack Post Office in Boston (☎ **617/654-5684**). The addressee must pick it up in person and produce proof of identity (driver's license, credit card, passport, etc.).

Generally to be found at intersections, mailboxes are blue with a red-and-white stripe and carry the inscription "U.S. Mail." If your mail is addressed to a U.S. destination, don't forget to add the five-figure postal code, or ZIP (Zone Improvement Plan) Code, after the two-letter abbreviation of the state to which the mail is addressed (MA for Massachusetts).

Medical Emergencies If you become ill, consult your hotel desk staff or concierge for referral to a physician. For an ambulance, dial 911.

Newspapers/Magazines National newspapers include the *New York Times*, *USA Today*, and the *Wall Street Journal*. National news weeklies include *Newsweek*, *Time*, and *U.S. News & World Report*. The major newspapers in Boston are the *Boston Globe* and *Boston Herald*.

Radio/Television Audiovisual media, with four coast-to-coast networks—ABC, CBS, NBC and Fox—joined in recent years by the Public Broadcasting System (PBS) and the cable news network CNN, play a major part in American life. In big cities, televiewers have a choice of a few dozen channels (including basic cable), most of them transmitting 24 hours a day, without counting the pay-TV channels showing recent movies or sports events. For the major stations in Boston, see "Fast Facts: Boston," Chapter 4.

Safety See "Safety" in "Preparing for Your Trip," above.

Taxes In the United States there is no VAT (value-added tax) or other indirect tax at a national level. Every state, and each city in it, is allowed to levy its own local tax on all purchases, including hotel and restaurant checks, airline tickets and so on.

Telephone/Telegraph/Telex The telephone system in the United States is run by private corporations, so rates, especially for long-distance service, can vary widely—even on calls made from public telephones. Local calls in Boston (in area codes 617 and sometimes 508) usually cost 10¢.

Generally, hotel surcharges on long-distance and local calls are astronomical. You are usually better off using a **public pay telephone**, which you will find clearly marked in most public buildings and private establishments as well as on the street. Outside metropolitan areas, public telephones are more difficult to find. Stores and gas stations are your best bet.

Most long-distance and international calls can be dialed directly from any phone. For calls to Canada and other parts of the United States, dial 1 followed by the area code and the seven-digit number. For international calls, dial 011 followed by the country code, city code, and the telephone number of the person you wish to call.

For **reversed-charge** or **collect** calls, and for **person-to-person calls,** dial 0 (zero, not the letter "O") followed by the area code and number you want; an operator will then come on the line and you should specify that you are calling collect, or person to person, or both. If your operator-assisted call is international, ask for the overseas operator.

For local directory assistance ("Information"), dial 411; for long-distance information dial 1, then the appropriate area code and 555-1212.

Like the telephone system, **telegraph** and **telex** services are provided by private corporations like ITT, MCI, and above all Western Union. You can bring your telegram in to the nearest Western Union office (there are hundreds across the country), or dictate it over the phone (a toll-free call, ☎ **800/325-6000**). You can also telegraph money, or have it telegraphed to you very quickly over the Western Union system.

Telephone Directory There are two kinds of telephone directories available to you. The general directory is the so-called **white pages,** in which private and business subscribers are listed in alphabetical order. The inside front cover lists the emergency number for police, fire, and ambulance, and other vital numbers (like the Coast Guard, poison-control center, crime victims hotline, and so on). The first few pages are devoted to community-service numbers, including a guide to long-distance and international calling, complete with country codes and area codes.

The second directory, printed on yellow paper (hence its name, **yellow pages**), lists all local services, businesses and industries by type of activity, with an index at the back. The listings cover not only such obvious items as automobile repairs by make of car, or drugstores (pharmacies), often by geographical location, but also restaurants by type of cuisine and geographical location, bookstores by special subject and/or language, places of worship by religious denomination, and other information that the tourist might otherwise not readily find. The yellow pages also include city plans or detailed area maps, often showing postal ZIP Codes and public transportation routes.

Time The United States is divided into four time zones (six, if you include Alaska and Hawaii). From east to west, these are: Eastern Standard Time (EST), Central Standard Time (CST), Mountain Standard Time (MST), Pacific Standard Time (PST), Alaska Standard Time (AST) and Hawaii Standard Time (HST). Always keep time zones in mind if you are traveling (or even telephoning) long distances in the United States. For example, noon in New York City (EST) is 11am in Chicago (CST), 10am in Denver (MST), 9am in Los Angeles (PST), 8am in Anchorage (AST), and 7am in Honolulu (HST).

"Daylight saving time" is in effect from the first Sunday in April through the last Saturday in October (actually, the change is made at 2am on Sunday) except in Arizona, Hawaii, part of Indiana, and Puerto Rico. Daylight Saving Time moves the clock one hour ahead of standard time.

Tipping   This is part of the American way of life, based on the principle that you should pay for any special service you receive. Here are some rules of thumb: bartenders: 10% to 15%; bellhops: at least 50¢ per piece, $2 to $3 for a lot of baggage; cab drivers: 15% of the fare; cafeterias, fast-food restaurants: no tip; chambermaids: $1 a day; checkroom attendants (restaurants, theaters): $1 per garment; cinemas, movies, theaters: no tip; doormen (hotels or restaurants): not obligatory; gas station attendants: no tip; hairdressers: 15% to 20%; redcaps (airport and railroad station): at least 50¢ per piece, $2 to $3 for a lot of baggage; restaurants, nightclubs: 15% to 20% of the check; sleeping-car porters: $2 to $3 per night; valet parking attendants: $1.

Toilets   Foreign visitors often complain that public toilets are hard to find in most U.S. cities. True, there are none on the streets, but the visitor can usually find one in a bar, restaurant, hotel, museum, department store, or service station—and it will probably be clean (although the last mentioned sometimes leaves much to be desired). Note, however, a growing practice in some restaurants and bars of displaying a sign saying toilets are for the use of patrons only. You can ignore this sign, or better yet, avoid arguments by paying for a cup of coffee or soft drink, which will qualify you as a patron. The cleanliness of toilets at railroad stations and bus depots may be open to question. Some public places are equipped with pay toilets, which require you to insert one or more coins into a slot on the door before it will open.

Getting to Know Boston

Boston bills itself as "America's Walking City," and walking is by far the easiest way to get around. Legend has it that the streets were laid out along cowpaths, but the layout owes more to 17th-century London and to Boston's original shoreline. To orient yourself, it helps to look at the big picture. This chapter will give you an overview of the city's layout and neighborhoods. It also lists information and resources you might need while you're away from home. As you familiarize yourself with Boston's geography, it might help to identify the various neighborhoods and landmarks on the free map provided with this guide.

1 Orientation

VISITOR INFORMATION

You'll probably want to begin exploring at one of the city's visitor information centers. The staff members are knowledgeable and helpful, and you can pick up free maps, brochures, listings of special exhibits, and schedules and find out the admission fees for the historic attractions.

The **Boston National Historic Park Visitor Center,** at 15 State St. (☎ **617/242-5642**), across the street from the Old State House and the State Street "T" station, is a good place to start your excursion. National Park Service rangers staff the center, dispense information, and lead free tours of the Freedom Trail. The audiovisual show about the trail provides basic information on 16 historic sites. The center is accessible by stairs and ramps and has restrooms and comfortable chairs. Open daily from 9am to 5pm except Thanksgiving Day, Christmas, and New Year's Day.

The Freedom Trail, a line of red paint or red brick on or in the sidewalk, begins at the **Boston Common Information Center,** at 146 Tremont St. on the Common. The center is open Monday to Saturday from 8:30am to 5pm and Sunday from 9am to 5pm. It's run by the Greater Boston Convention and Visitors Bureau (☎ **617/536-4100**), as is the **Prudential Information Center,** in Center Court on the main level of the Prudential Center. It's open from 9am to 6pm Monday through Friday, 10am to 6pm Saturday, and Sunday from 11am to 6pm.

In Cambridge, **Cambridge Discovery** (☎ **617/497-1630**) operates an information kiosk in the heart of Harvard Square, near the "T" entrance at the intersection of Massachusetts Avenue, John F. Kennedy Street, and Brattle Street. It's open Monday to Saturday 9am to 5pm and Sunday 1 to 5pm.

Impressions ──

And this is good old Boston,
The home of the bean and the cod,
Where the Lowells talk to the Cabots,
And the Cabots talk only to God

> —John Collins Bossidy, toast at the Holy Cross College alumni dinner (1910)

Boston State-House is the hub of the solar system. You couldn't pry that out of a Boston man, if you had the tire of all creation straightened out for a crowbar.

> —Oliver Wendell Holmes, *The Autocrat of the Breakfast-Table* (1858)

The Bostonians are really, as a race, far inferior in point of anything beyond mere intellect to any other set upon the continent of North America. They are decidedly the most servile imitators of the English it is possible to conceive.

> —Edgar Allan Poe, letter (1849)

PUBLICATIONS   The city's newspapers offer the most up-to-date information about events in the area. The "Calendar" section of the Thursday *Boston Globe* lists festivals, street fairs, concerts, films, speeches, and dance and theater performances. The Friday *Boston Herald* has a similar, smaller insert called "Scene." Both papers briefly list weekend events in their Saturday editions. The arts-oriented *Boston Phoenix,* published on Thursday, has extensive entertainment and restaurant listings.

Where, a monthly magazine available free at most hotels throughout the city, gives information about shopping, nightlife, attractions, and current shows at museums and galleries. Another freebie, *Quick Guide,* is published four times a year and offers entertainment and shopping listings, a restaurant guide, and maps.

The weekly *Tab,* which lists neighborhood-specific events information, the twice-monthly *Improper Bostonian,* with extensive event and restaurant listings, and the "Styles" section of the *Phoenix,* are all available free from newspaper boxes around the city. *Boston* magazine (☎ **617/262-9700**) is a lifestyle-oriented monthly with general-interest stories on the city and listings on entertainment and dining.

CITY LAYOUT

When it was established as the first permanent European settlement in the region in 1630, Boston was one-third the size it is now. Parts of the city still reflect its original layout, a seemingly haphazard plan that leaves even longtime residents tearing out their hair. Old Boston is littered with alleys, dead ends, one-way streets, streets that change names, and streets named after extinct geographical features. On the plus side, every "wrong" turn downtown, in the North End or on Beacon Hill is a chance to see something interesting that you might otherwise have missed.

Much of the city's landscape was transformed by landfill projects of the 19th century, which altered the shoreline and created the Back Bay, where the streets proceed in orderly, parallel lines. After some frustrating time in the older part of the city, this simple plan will seem ingenious.

The most "main" street downtown is Washington Street. The causeway that connected the Boston peninsula to the mainland in the 17th and 18th centuries ran along this street, then called Orange in honor of the British royal family. By 1824 it had been renamed after George Washington; as another tribute, streets (except Massachusetts Avenue) change their names when they cross Washington Street: Bromfield becomes Franklin, Winter becomes Summer, Stuart becomes Kneeland. Off Washington Street in Chinatown, several blocks inland, is Beach Street, which used to be harborfront property.

Vestiges of the old waterfront crop up in other odd places. For example, Dock Square, at Congress and North streets, is a reminder of the days when ships could deliver their cargo directly to the market on the first floor of Faneuil Hall. Then there's Commercial Wharf North and South, between Commercial Street and Atlantic Avenue in the North End, and quite landlocked.

Beacon Hill is also named after a long-ago topographical feature. It seems like a big enough hill today—until you see the pillar behind the State House that rises 60 feet into the air, a reminder of its original height, before earth was taken from the top of the hill to be used as landfill. In their loftier days, Beacon, Copp's, and Fort hills gave the Shawmut peninsula the name Trimountain, known today as Tremont. Copp's and Fort hills sloped down to the town dock at Dock Square. Today, Copp's Hill is smaller, but still overlooks the North End; Fort Hill, which extended through downtown toward South Station, was leveled between 1869 and 1872. High Street, now quite flat, was once actually high.

When the hills were pulled down to fill in the coves that made up the shoreline, the layout of some new streets was somewhat willy-nilly. Not so in the Back Bay, where the streets not only line up but even go in alphabetical order, starting at the Public Garden with Arlington, then Berkeley, Clarendon, Dartmouth, Exeter, Fairfield, Gloucester, and Hereford (and then Massachusetts). In the South End, also mostly landfill, the grid is less pristine but still pretty logical. Streets change from West to East when they cross Washington Street, and many of the names are those of the towns with train service from South Station (e.g., Concord, Worcester, and Springfield), which was new when the streets were being christened.

MAIN ARTERIES AND STREETS   The most prominent feature of downtown Boston is Boston Common, whether in person, on a map, or from atop the John Hancock Tower or the Prudential Center (see Chapter 7, "What to See & Do in Boston"). The land for the Common was set aside in 1640, when it had only three trees. The Common is bordered by Park Street, which is one block long (but looms large in the geography of the "T"), and four important thoroughfares. Tremont Street originates at Government Center and runs through the Theater District into the South End and Roxbury. Beacon Street branches off Tremont at School Street and curves around, passing the golden dome of the State House at the apex of Beacon Hill and the Public Garden at the foot, and slicing through the Back Bay and Kenmore Square on its way into Brookline. At the foot of the hill Beacon crosses Charles Street, the fourth side of the Common and the main street of Beacon Hill. Near Massachusetts General Hospital, Charles crosses Cambridge Street, which loops around to Government Center and turns into Tremont Street.

On the far side of Government Center, I-93 (a.k.a. the Fitzgerald Expressway) separates the North End from the rest of the city. Hanover Street is the main street of the North End; at the harbor it intersects with Commercial Street, which runs along the waterfront from the North Washington Street bridge (the route to Charlestown, a.k.a. the Charlestown bridge) until it gives way to Atlantic Avenue at Fleet Street. Atlantic Avenue completes the loop around the North End and runs more or less along the waterfront past South Station.

Boylston Street is the fifth side of the Common. It runs next to the Public Garden, through Copley Square and the Back Bay, and on into the Fenway. To get there it has to cross Massachusetts Avenue, or "Mass. Ave.," as it's almost always called (you might as well get into the habit now). Mass. Ave. originates 9 miles away in Lexington, cutting through Arlington and Cambridge before hitting Boston at

Storrow Drive, then Beacon Street, Marlborough Street, and Commonwealth Avenue. "Comm. Ave." starts at the Public Garden and runs through Kenmore Square, past Boston University, and into the western suburbs. Farther along Mass. Ave., Symphony Hall is at the corner of Huntington Avenue. Huntington begins at Copley Square and passes Symphony Hall, Northeastern University, and the Museum of Fine Arts before crossing into Brookline and becoming Mass. Route 9.

FINDING AN ADDRESS   There's no rhyme or reason to the street pattern, compass directions are virtually useless, and there aren't enough street signs. The best way to find an address is to call ahead and ask for directions, including landmarks, or leave extra time for wandering around. If the directions involve a "T" stop, be sure to ask which exit to use—most stations have more than one.

STREET MAPS   In addition to the map provided with this guide, free maps of downtown Boston and the rapid transit lines are available at visitor information centers around the city. The Prudential Life Insurance Company (800 Boylston St.; ☎ 617/236-3318) distributes a neighborhood map of Boston at the Skywalk viewing platform, open daily, 10am to 10pm. It's helpful for walking trips of Beacon Hill, the North End, Chinatown, the South End, Charlestown, and Harvard Square. You can also write to the Greater Boston Convention & Visitors Bureau (P.O. Box 990468, Prudential Tower, Suite 400, Boston, MA 02199) for a visitor information kit that includes a city/subway/Freedom Trail map. Enclose a $4.95 check or money order.

The Metropolitan District Commission (MDC) has an excellent map of the reservations, parks, and recreation areas in Greater Boston. It tells where to find salt- and freshwater beaches, swimming and wading pools, picnic areas, foot trails and bridge paths, playgrounds, tennis and golf courses, fresh- and saltwater fishing, bicycle paths, and outdoor ice-skating rinks. Contact Community Affairs at the MDC, 20 Somerset St., Boston, MA 02108 (☎ 617/727-5114 ext. 530) for a copy.

Gousha's Boston Fast Map ($4.95), Streetwise Boston ($5.95), and Artwise Boston ($5.95) are sturdy, laminated maps available at most bookstores. Less detailed but more fun is MapEasy's GuideMap to Boston ($5.50), a hand-drawn map of the central areas and major attractions.

NEIGHBORHOODS IN BRIEF

The Waterfront   Boston's harbor gained its excellent reputation from the fact that it's sheltered; this neighborhood faces not the ocean but the Inner Harbor. Although for purposes of city government (notably parking regulations) it's considered part of the North End, the Waterfront neighborhood has a different feel. The narrow area along Atlantic Avenue and Commercial Street, once filled with wharves and warehouses, now boasts luxury condos, marinas, restaurants, offices, and two hotels. Also on the waterfront are the New England Aquarium and piers, where you can set out on harbor cruises and whale-watching expeditions.

The North End   Crossing under I-93 from downtown on the way to the waterfront brings you to one of the city's oldest neighborhoods, the North End. Home to waves of immigrants in the course of its history, it's been predominantly Italian for 70 years or so, but the balance is shifting. The best estimates say it's now about half Italian-American and half newcomers, many of them young professionals who walk to work in the Financial District. Nevertheless, you'll hear Italian spoken in the streets and find a wealth of Italian restaurants, caffès, and shops. Nearby, and technically part of the North End, is the North Station area. With the September 1995 opening of the FleetCenter to replace Boston Garden (which is slated for demolition but was still standing at press time), the restaurants and clubs in the part of the North End near Beacon Hill really started jumping. This commercial area is, at the moment, not a place to wander around alone at night.

Faneuil Hall Marketplace/Haymarket   Employees aside, actual Boston residents tend to be in short supply at Faneuil Hall Marketplace (also called Quincy Market after the central building). An irresistible draw for out-of-towners and suburbanites, the cluster of restored market buildings bounded by Government Center, State Street, the waterfront, and the North Station area is the city's most popular attraction. You'll find restaurants, bars, a food court, specialty shops, and Faneuil Hall itself. Haymarket, just off the Central Artery, is home to an open-air produce and fish market on Fridays and Saturdays.

Government Center   Love it or hate it, Government Center introduces modern design into the redbrick facade of traditional Boston architecture. Flanked by Beacon Hill, Downtown Crossing, and Faneuil Hall Marketplace, it is home to state and federal office towers and to Boston City Hall.

Financial District   Bounded loosely by State Street, Downtown Crossing, Summer Street, and Atlantic Avenue, the Financial District is the banking, insurance, and legal center of the city. You'll find it frantic during the day and practically empty in the evening. Several impressive office towers now loom over the Custom House, once famous for its observation deck tower and now undergoing extensive renovations.

Beacon Hill   The tiny residential area in the shadow of the golden dome of the State House is made up of narrow, tree-lined streets and architectural showpieces, mostly in Federal style. Louisburg Square and Mount Vernon Street, two of the loveliest (and most exclusive) spots in Boston, are on Beacon Hill. Bounded by Government Center, Boston Common, and the river, it's also popular with employees of Massachusetts General Hospital, on the nominally less fashionable north side of the neighborhood.

Downtown Crossing   The intersection that gives Downtown Crossing its name is at Washington Street where Winter Street becomes Summer Street, and Filene's and Macy's face off across the pedestrian mall. The name applies roughly to the shopping and business district between the Common, the Theater District, the Financial District, and Government Center. It hops during the day and slows down considerably at night, after business hours.

Chinatown   The third-largest Chinese community in the country resides in a small but growing area near the Theater District. The narrow streets—jammed with Chinese and Vietnamese restaurants, groceries, and gift shops—have a real neighborhood feel. As the "Combat Zone," or red-light district, shrinks under pressure from the business community, Chinatown is expanding to fill the area between Downtown Crossing and the Mass. Turnpike extension. This is the only part of the city where you can definitely find food after midnight—some restaurants are open until 3 or 4am.

Back Bay   Perpetually fashionable since its creation out of landfill a century ago, the Back Bay overflows with gorgeous architecture and chic shops. It is bounded by the Public Garden (to the west), Massachusetts Avenue (to the east), the river (to the north) and Huntington Avenue (to the south), or St. Botolph Street, by some accounts. Students dominate the area near Mass. Ave. and grow scarce as property values rise the closer you get to the Public Garden. Commonwealth Avenue is largely residential, and Newbury Street is largely commercial; both are excellent places to walk around. In the Back Bay you'll find Trinity Church, the Boston Public Library, the John Hancock Tower, Copley Place, the Prudential Center, and the Hynes Convention Center.

Huntington Avenue   Not an actual neighborhood, but not an area you'll want to miss, Huntington Avenue starts at Copley Square, and separates Copley Place from the Prudential Center before heading south into the suburbs. A number of important landmarks are situated along it, including the Christian Science Center, Symphony Hall (at the corner of Massachusetts Avenue), Northeastern University, and the Museum of Fine Arts. Parts of Huntington can sometimes be a little risky, so if you're leaving the museum at night, stick to the car or the Green Line, travel in a group, or both.

The South End   Cross Stuart Street or Huntington Avenue heading south and you'll soon find yourself in a landmark district packed with Victorian row houses and little parks. Known for its ethnic, economic, and cultural diversity, galleries, and boutiques, the South End has a large gay community and some of the best restaurants in the city. With the gentrification of the 1980s, Tremont Street (particularly the end closest to downtown) gained a cachet it hadn't known for almost a century. Note: Don't confuse the South End with South Boston, a predominantly Irish-American residential neighborhood.

Kenmore Square   The white-and-red Citgo sign that dominates the skyline above the intersection of Commonwealth Avenue, Beacon Street, and Brookline Avenue tells you you're approaching Kenmore Square. Its shops, bars, restaurants, and clubs are a magnet for students from adjacent Boston University. The college-town atmosphere goes out the window when the Red Sox are in town and baseball fans pour into the area on the way to historic Fenway Park, three blocks away (just follow the crowds).

Charlestown   One of the oldest areas of Boston, this is where you'll see the Bunker Hill Monument and U.S.S. *Constitution* ("Old Ironsides"), as well as one of the city's best restaurants, Olives. Off the beaten track, Charlestown is an almost entirely white residential neighborhood with a well-deserved reputation for insularity.

Cambridge   Though an independent city, Cambridge is often regarded as a Boston neighborhood, and it does often feel like one since it is so readily accessible from Boston. It's a diverse community with important historical sites, and many excellent stores, restaurants and cultural institutions. For Ivy League opulence in a relaxed but expensive student environment, visit Harvard Square. For a more gritty urban and multi-ethnic feel, and budget record stores, restaurants and secondhand clothing stores, check out Central Square.

2 Getting Around

BY PUBLIC TRANSPORTATION

The Massachusetts Bay Transportation Authority, or MBTA (☎ 617/222-3200), is known as the "T," and its logo is the letter in a circle. It runs the subways, trolleys, and buses in Boston and many suburbs, as well as the commuter rail. The "T" has a web site (http://www.mbta.com) that gives you access to maps, schedules, and other information.

Directional Signals

Maps of Boston show the North End and the South End; more study reveals that if there were an East End, it would be either in the harbor or (geography be hanged) in South Boston. Where's the West End?

Good question. The West End was a neighborhood much like the North End, with narrow, crowded streets, a large immigrant population, and a desirable location. It filled the area between Beacon Hill, the river, North Station, and what's now Government Center. The high-rise condo and apartment buildings of the Charles River Park complex take up that space today. Urban renewal fever swept over Boston and first began to sweep the West End away in 1958, displacing the residents and leaving precious few reminders that it ever existed. On Cambridge Street you'll find the Old West Church and the West End branch of the Boston Public Library, and that seems to be all. But if your travels take you to the area around North Station and the FleetCenter, leave five minutes extra to walk to the low-numbered end of Causeway Street. On Lomasney Way, on a traffic island under the elevated Green Line tracks, stands one lonely four-story brick residential building. Anywhere else in the city, it would be absolutely unremarkable. It's the last house in the West End.

DISCOUNT PASSES   The Boston Visitor Passport (☎ **617/222-5218**) is one of the best deals in town. You get unlimited travel for a one-, three-, or seven-day period on all subway lines and local buses and Zones 1A and 1B of the commuter rail system, plus discounts on museums, restaurants, and entertainment. The cost is $5 for one day, $9 for three days, and $18 for seven days. Passes are for sale at the Airport "T" station, North Station, South Station, and Back Bay Station, at the Government Center, Harvard, and Riverside "T" stations, the Boston Common information center, and Quincy Market. Your hotel might also be able to provide you with the Visitor Passport.

BY SUBWAY   The subways and Green Line trolleys will take you around Boston faster than any other mode of transportation except walking. You might find this hard to believe when you're trapped in a tunnel during rush hour, but it's true. The oldest system in the country, it dates to 1897, and recent and ongoing improvements have made it quite reliable. It's also packed with art—if your travels take you through the Kendall/MIT Red Line station and you're not in a hurry, hop off and play with the handles on either platform that control the "kinetic sculptures" between the sets of tracks. You'll be rewarded with the sound of thunder on the outbound side and the bell-like peal of a hammer striking metal on the other side.

The subways are color-coded and called the Red, Green, Blue, and Orange lines. The commuter rail to the suburbs shows up on system maps in purple (but it's rarely called the Purple Line). The local fare is 85¢ (you'll need a token) and can be as much as $2.25 for some surface line extensions on the Green and Red lines. Route and fare information and timetables are available at Park Street station (under the Common), which is the center of the system. Signs reading "inbound" and "outbound" refer to the location in relation to Park Street.

Note that service begins at around 5am and shuts down between 12:30 and 1am, systemwide. The only exception is New Year's Eve, or First Night, when closing time is 2am.

Token vending machines are gaining popularity and can currently be found at Airport (Blue Line); Back Bay and Downtown Crossing (Orange Line); Prudential (Green Line); and South Station, Downtown Crossing, and Harvard (Red Line).

The Green Line is not wheelchair accessible, but most stations on other lines are. They are indicated on system maps. To learn more, call the Office for Transportation Access (☎ **800/533-6282** or 617/222-5123; TDD for the hearing impaired 617/222-5415).

BY BUS   The MBTA (☎ **617/222-3200**) runs buses and "trackless trolleys" (identifiable by their electric antennae but otherwise indistinguishable from buses) that provide service crosstown and to and around the suburbs. The local bus fare is 60¢; express buses are $1.50 and up. Exact change is required. Many buses are equipped with lifts for wheelchairs (☎ **800/LIFT-BUS**).

BY CAR

If you plan to confine your visit to Boston proper, there's absolutely no reason to have a car, and in fact, it's probably more trouble than it's worth. If you're driving to Boston, leave the car in the hotel garage and use it for day trips or to visit Cambridge, if you're feeling flush—you'll probably wind up paying to park there, too. If you're not motoring and you decide to take a day trip (see Chapter 11, "Easy Excursions"), you'll probably want to rent a car. Here's the scoop.

RENTALS   The major car-rental firms have offices in Boston and at Logan Airport. (Be aware that a hefty drop-off charge is standard for most companies if you rent in one city and return in another.) If you're traveling at a busy time, reserve a car well in advance. Companies with offices at the airport include: Alamo (☎ **800/327-9633**), Avis (☎ **800/831-2847**), Budget (☎ **800/527-0700**), Enterprise (☎ **800/325-8007**), Hertz (☎ **800/654-3131**), National (☎ **800/ 227-7368**), and Thrifty (☎ **800/367-2277**). Most companies have cars for non-smokers, but you have to ask.

To reserve a car once you're in town, call the toll-free number or try the local office. Most companies have several outlets in the area; ask for the one nearest your hotel. They include: Alamo (☎ 617/561-4100), Avis (☎ 617/561-3500), Budget (☎ 617/497-1800), Dollar (☎ 617/523-0518), Enterprise (☎ 617/561-4488), Hertz (☎ 617/338-1503), National (☎ 569-6700), and Thrifty (☎ 617/ 569-6500).

Expect to pay at least $35 a day for a midsize car from a national chain. To cut costs, you might look in the yellow pages for a smaller local company or (for a weekly rental) an auto dealership.

To rent from the major national chains, you must be at least 25 years old and have a valid driver's license and credit card. If you don't have a credit card, you'll probably have to make alternative arrangements in advance; some companies require that you meet strict eligibility stipulations before they'll give you a car. Read the rental agreement carefully, and know what your obligations are (for example, returning the car with a full tank, or paying the company to refill it).

Your rental fee does not include insurance, but you may be covered under the insurance on your car at home, and many credit cards offer automatic coverage. Check before you pick up the rental car. Otherwise be prepared to pay for Collision Damage Waiver or Loss Damage Waiver. Without coverage you could be liable for the full retail price of the car if it is damaged or stolen.

PARKING   It's difficult to find your way around Boston and practically impossible to find parking in some areas. Most spaces on the street are metered (and patroled

Boston MBTA Rapid Transit Lines

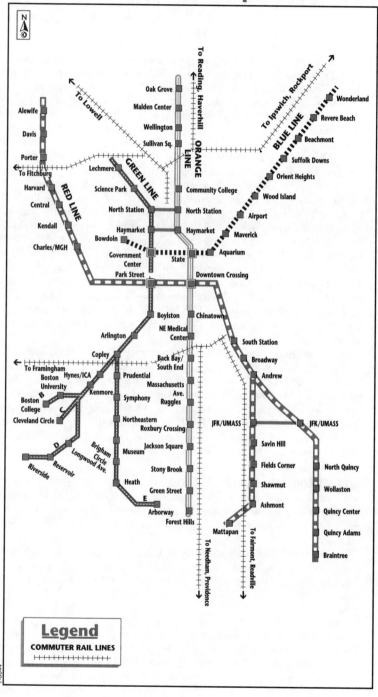

until 6pm on the dot every day except Sunday), open to nonresidents for exactly two hours or less between 8am and 6pm. The penalty is a $20 ticket, but should you blunder into a tow-away zone, retrieving the car will take at least $50 and a lot of running around. Read the sign or the meter carefully. In some areas parking is allowed only at certain hours. Rates vary in different sections of the city (usually $1 an hour downtown), so bring plenty of quarters and dimes. Time limits range from 30 minutes to two hours. Tip: During the day, if you're visiting the eastern part of Cambridge, near MIT, parking on Memorial Drive is free and usually not terribly hard to find.

To save yourself a lot of aggravation, leave the car in a garage or lot and walk. Most will cost no more than $20 for a full day, and there's often a lower flat rate if you enter and exit before certain times or if you park in the evening. Some restaurants offer reduced rates at nearby garages; ask when you call for reservations.

The two largest garages are under Boston Common and under the Prudential Center. The reasonably priced city-run garage under the Common (☎ 617/954-2096) at Charles Street was renovated recently and is limited to vehicles less than 6 feet, 3 inches tall. The garage at the Prudential Center (☎ 617/267-1002) has entrances on Boylston Street, Huntington Avenue, and Exeter Street, and at the Sheraton Boston Hotel & Towers. Parking is discounted if you make a purchase at the Shops at Prudential Center. A similar deal is offered at the garage at Copley Place (☎ 617/375-4488), off Huntington Avenue. The All Right lot off North Street under the Expressway (☎ 617/523-1719) offers a discount to patrons of many North End restaurants and shops—look for a sign in the window of the business.

Good-sized garages can be found at Government Center off Congress Street (☎ 617/227-0385), at the New England Aquarium (☎ 617/723-1731), at 75 State Street (☎ 617/742-7275), and near the Hynes Convention Center on Dalton Street (☎ 617/247-8006). There's also parking under the lovely park in Post Office Square, where another garage once stood. It's at Zero Post Office Square (☎ 617/423-1430), bounded by Milk, Pearl, Franklin, and Congress Streets, across the street from Hotel Le Meridien, and near Faneuil Hall Marketplace and the New England Aquarium. It is open 24 hours with entrances on Pearl and Congress streets and is safe and easy to use.

SPECIAL DRIVING RULES   A right turn is allowed at a red light after stopping when traffic permits, unless a sign is posted saying otherwise (as it often is downtown). Seat belts are not mandatory for adults, but they are required for children, and infants and toddlers must be strapped into car seats. These laws are strictly enforced.

Two state laws to be aware of, if only because the frequency with which they're broken will take your breath away: Pedestrians in the crosswalk have the right of way, and vehicles already in a rotary (traffic circle or roundabout) have the right of way.

BY TAXI

Taxis are expensive and not always easy to find—try a hotel, or call a dispatcher. The fare structure is as follows: the first one-quarter of a mile (when the flag drops) costs $1.50, and each additional one-eighth of a mile is 20¢. "Wait time" is extra, and the passenger pays all tolls as well as the $1.50 airport fee (on trips leaving Logan only). Charging a flat rate is not allowed within the city; the Police Department publishes a list of distances to the suburbs that establishes the flat rate

Cab drivers have a dress code established and enforced by the city. They must wear a shirt with a collar, be clean, and keep their beards neatly trimmed.

If you want to report a problem or have lost something in a cab, the Police Department runs a Hackney Hotline (☎ **617/536-8294**).

To call ahead for a cab, try the Independent Taxi Operators Association, or ITOA (☎ **617/426-8700**), Town Taxi (☎ **617/536-5000**), or Checker Taxi (☎ **617/536-7000**).

BY BICYCLE

Bring your own bike or rent one—you'll fit right in. Unless you're a real pro, though, you'll probably want to stay off the streets until you're comfortable with the city layout and traffic patterns. Boston has more than 50 miles of marked bike paths, including the 17-mile Dr. Paul Dudley White loop around the Charles River from the Museum of Science to Watertown and back.

A convenient place to rent a bike is Earth Bikes, at 35 Huntington Avenue, near Copley Square (☎ **617/267-4733**). Bike rentals start at $12 for four hours and include free use of helmets and complimentary maps. Earth Bikes is open from April to October, 10am to 7pm, Tuesday through Sunday, and Monday holidays. Call for hours on rainy days. A deposit (cash or by American Express, Visa, or MasterCard) is required, as is a driver's license or passport. If you bring or rent a bike, be sure to lock it properly when leaving it unattended, as bicycles are often targeted by thieves eager to make off with any bikes or bike parts that are not chained down.

FAST FACTS: Boston

Airport   See "Getting There" in Chapter 2.

American Express   The main local office is at 1 Court St. (☎ 617/723-8400), close to the Government Center MBTA stop. It's open Monday through Friday from 8:30am to 5:30pm. The Cambridge office, just off Harvard Square at 39 John F. Kennedy St. (☎ **617/661-0005**), is open Monday through Friday 9am to 5pm and Saturday 11am to 3pm.

Area Code   For Boston and the immediate suburbs, it's 617; for other suburbs, it's 508. You sometimes must dial "1" and the area code before a number in the same area code (for example, when calling Marblehead from Boston).

Baby-sitters   Check with the desk staff or concierge at your hotel. Many maintain lists of reliable sitters.

Business Hours   Banks are open weekdays from 8:30 or 9am to 3 or 4pm, and sometimes Saturday morning; most offer 24-hour access to Automated Teller machines (ATMs). Business offices generally are open weekdays from 9am to 5pm. Stores and other businesses are open six days a week, with most open on Sunday as well; department stores usually stay open until 9pm at least one night a week. By law, most bars close at 1am (a few are open until 2am).

Camera Repair   Try Bromfield Camera & Video at 10 Bromfield St. (☎ **617/426-5230**) or the Camera Center at 107 State St. (☎ **800/924-6899** or 617/227-7255).

Car Rentals   See "Getting Around" earlier in this chapter.

Climate   See "When to Go" in Chapter 2.

Dentists   The desk staff or concierge at your hotel may be able to provide the name of a dentist. The Metropolitan District Dental Society (☎ **508/651-3521**) can point you toward a member of the Massachusetts Dental Society.

Doctors   The desk staff or concierge at your hotel will probably be able to direct you to a doctor, but you can also try one of the many referral services run by Boston hospitals. Among them are: Beth Israel Healthcare Physician Referral (☎ **617/667-5356**), Brigham and Women's Hospital Physician Referral Service

(☎ **800/294-9999**), Deaconess Hospital MediCall (☎ **800/472-4800**), Massachusetts General Hospital Physician Referral Service (☎ **617/726-5800**), and New England Medical Center Physician Referral Service (☎ **617/ 636-9700**).

Driving Rules   See "Getting Around" earlier in this chapter.

Drugstores   See "Pharmacies" below.

Emergencies   Call 911 for fire, ambulance, or the Boston, Brookline, or Cambridge police. This is a free call from pay phones. For the state police, call **617/523-1212**.

Eyeglass Repair   Cambridge Eye Doctors has offices in downtown Boston at 100 State St. (☎ 617/742-2076) and 300 Washington St. (☎ 617/426-5536). In Cambridge, For Eyes Optical has a branch at 56 John F. Kennedy St. (☎ 617/876-6031).

Hospitals   Here's hoping you won't need to evaluate Boston's reputation for excellent medical care. In case you do: Massachusetts General Hospital (55 Fruit St.; ☎ **617/726-2000**, or 617/726-4100 for children's emergency services) and New England Medical Center (750 Washington St; ☎ **617/636-5000**, or 617/636-5566 for emergency services) are closest to downtown Boston. At the Harvard Medical Area on the Boston-Brookline border are, among others, Beth Israel Hospital (330 Brookline Ave.; ☎ **617/667-8000**, or 617/667-3337 for emergency services), Brigham and Women's Hospital (75 Francis St.; ☎ **617/732-5500**), and Children's Hospital (300 Longwood Ave.; ☎ **617/ 355-6000**, or 617/355-6611 for emergency services). In Cambridge are Cambridge Hospital (1493 Cambridge St.; ☎ **617/498-1000**, or 617/498-1429 for emergency services) and Mount Auburn Hospital (330 Mount Auburn St.; ☎ **617/492-3500**, or 617/499-5025 for emergency services).

Hotlines   AIDS Hotline (☎ **800/235-2331** or 617/536-7733), Poison Information Center (☎ **800/682-9211** or 617/232-2120), Rape Crisis (☎ **617/ 492-7273**), Samaritans Suicide Prevention (☎ **617/247-0220**), Samariteens (☎ **800/252-8336** or 617/247-8050).

Information   See "Visitor Information" earlier in this chapter.

Libraries   The main branch of the Boston Public Library is at Copley Square. (See Chapter 7, "What to See & Do in Boston.")

Liquor Laws   The legal drinking age is 21. In many bars, particularly near college campuses, you may be asked for ID if you appear to be under 30 or so. At sporting events, everyone purchasing alcohol is asked to show ID. Alcohol is sold in liquor stores and a few supermarkets and convenience stores. Liquor stores (and the liquor sections of supermarkets) are closed on Sundays, but alcohol may be served in restaurants. Some suburban towns are "dry."

Lost Property   The "T" divides its Lost and Found into buses (☎ **617/ 222-5607**), commuter rail (☎ **617-222-3600**), and individual subway lines: Blue (☎ **617/222-5533**), Green (☎ **617/222-5221**), Orange (☎ **617/ 222-5403**), and Red (☎ **617/222-5317**). If you lose something in a taxi, call the cab company or the Police Department's Hackney Hotline (☎ **617/536-8294**).

Luggage Storage/Lockers   The desk staff or concierge at your hotel may be able to arrange storage for you. Lockers are available at the airport but not at South Station.

Maps   See "City Layout" earlier in this chapter.

Newspapers/Magazines   The *Boston Globe* (☎ **617/929-2000**) and *Boston Herald* (☎ **617/426-3000**) are published daily. The *Boston Phoenix* (☎ **617/ 536-5390**), a weekly, emphasizes arts coverage and publishes extensive entertainment and restaurant listings. *Boston* magazine (☎ **617/262-9700**) is a lifestyle-oriented monthly.

Pharmacies (Late-Night)   The pharmacy at the CVS in the Porter Square Shopping Center, off Massachusetts Avenue in Cambridge (☎ **617/876-5519**), is open 24 hours, seven days a week. The pharmacy at the CVS at 155–157 Charles Street in Boston (☎ **617/523-1028**), next to the Charles "T" stop, is open until midnight. Some emergency rooms can fill your prescription at the hospital's pharmacy.

Police   Call 911 for emergencies.

Post Office   The main post office at 25 Dorchester Ave. (☎ **617/654-5326**), behind South Station, is open 24 hours, seven days a week.

Radio   AM stations include: WBZ (news, Bruins games), 1030; WEEI (sports, Red Sox games), 850; WRKO (talk, sports, Celtics games), 680; WILD (urban contemporary, soul), 1090. FM stations include: WBCS (country), 96.9; WBOS (soft rock), 92.9; WBCN (rock, Patriots games), 104.1; WBUR (public radio, classical music), 90.9; WCRB (classical music), 102.5; WGBH (public radio, classical music, jazz), 89.7; WODS (oldies), 103.3; WJMN (pop, urban contemporary), 94.5, MFNX (alternative rock), 101.7, and WZLX (classic rock), 100.7.

Restrooms   The visitor center at 15 State St. has a public restroom, as do most hotels, department stores, and public buildings. There are restrooms at the CambridgeSide Galleria, Copley Place, Prudential Center, and Quincy Market shopping areas, and one of the few public restrooms in Harvard Square is in the Harvard Coop department store. Some public places are equipped with pay toilets, usually costing 10¢.

Safety   On the whole, Boston is a safe city for walking. As in any large city, stay out of the parks at night unless you're in a crowd, and in general, trust your instincts—a dark, deserted street is probably deserted for a reason. Specific areas to avoid at night include Boylston Street between Tremont Street and Washington Street, and Tremont Street from Stuart Street to Boylston Street. The "Combat Zone," or red-light district, has almost shrunk out of existence, but the neighborhood still isn't great. Public transportation in the areas you're likely to be is busy and safe, but service stops between 12:30 and 1am. Always be aware of your surroundings, keep a close eye on your possessions, and be particularly careful with cameras, purses, and wallets, all favorite targets of thieves and pickpockets.

Taxes   The 5% sales tax is not levied on food, prescription drugs, newspapers, or clothing worth less than $175, but there seems to be a tax on almost everything else. The lodging tax is 9.7%; the meal tax (which also applies to take-out food) is 5%; the gasoline tax (included on the price at the pump) is 10%. There is also a tax on alcohol based on alcoholic content.

Taxis   See "Getting Around" earlier in this chapter.

Television   Stations include: Channel 2 (WGBH), public television; Channel 4 (WBZ), CBS; Channel 5 (WCVB), ABC; Channel 7 (WHDH), NBC; Channel 25 (WFXT), Fox; Channel 38 (WSBK), UPN; and Channel 56 (WLVI), WB. Cable TV is available throughout Boston and the suburbs.

Time Zone   Boston is in the Eastern time zone. Daylight saving time is in effect from the first Sunday in April through the last Sunday in October.

Useful Telephone Numbers   Travelers Aid Society (☎ **617/542-7286**). Greater Boston Convention & Visitors Bureau (☎ **617/536-4100**). Information Center for Individuals with Disabilities (☎ **617/450-9000** or 800/462-5015, MA only). General Postal Service information (☎ **617/451-9922**). The correct time (☎ 617/637-1234).

Weather   Call **617/936-1234** for forecasts.

5 Accommodations

Whether you're traveling on an expense account or a tight budget (or both), you'll have little difficulty finding a suitable place to stay in or near Boston. Getting a room shouldn't be a problem, but it's always a good idea to make a reservation, especially during the busy spring and fall convention seasons, the vacation months of July and August, and the college graduation season of May–June. Even at the busiest times, if you're in search of a good deal and willing to chase it down, you can usually find one.

Rates at most area hotels are lower on weekends than on week-nights, when business and convention travelers fill rooms. Bargain-hunters who don't mind cold and the possibility of snow (sometimes *lots* of snow) will want to aim for January through March, when some great deals are offered, especially on weekends. As with travel plans, it helps to be flexible when you're selecting dates—a hotel that's full of conventioneers one week may be courting business a few days later.

When selecting a hotel, ask a lot of questions about rates and amenities. Members of professional organizations, frequent-flyer programs, and auto clubs may be eligible for discounts or other perks such as free parking, but they generally won't be offered unless you ask. The same goes for the special rates that some hotels offer to senior citizens and students with ID cards. If you have allergies or special requests—for a bed board, a room that faces in a particular direction, or accommodations for your pet, for example—make arrangements in advance.

Most hotels do not charge for children sharing rooms with their parents. Parking is available at most hotels (usually for a fee) and motels, while others have arrangements with nearby garages. Just about every hotel sets aside rooms, and often entire floors, exclu-sively for nonsmokers.

In this chapter, the hotels are divided into the following price categories, using the lowest price for a double room during the summer as a yardstick: **Very Expensive,** $225 and up; **Expensive,** $160–$225; **Moderate,** $100–$160; and **Inexpensive,** less than $100. Prices are per night and do not include taxes. If you're travel-ing alone, rates are almost always lower. And remember that week-end and other package deals can knock the price down considerably.

Boston charges a 9.7% tax on all hotel rooms (5.7% for the state, 4% for the city). Not all suburban cities have a local tax, so you may have to pay only the 5.7% state tax in some towns.

To help you choose a hotel, the recommendations that follow are listed by location and then by price; within these categories the hotels are listed alphabetically. This chapter concentrates on hotels that are convenient to historic areas and transportation, those that provide special touches of luxury or service, and those that offer good value for the money. The listings cover Boston, Cambridge, and several nearby suburbs, along with a few resort hotels with easy access to the city and points of interest.

MORE SUGGESTIONS   The **Greater Boston Convention and Visitors Bureau** (☎ **800/888-5515** outside MA. or 617/536-4100; fax 617/424-7664) publishes a free travel-planning guide, a comprehensive guidebook, and another children-focused guide called *Kids Love Boston;* all three are helpful in finding accommodations that will suit your needs and can offer substantial savings. To get the guidebook in advance of your trip, send $4.95 to the Greater Boston Convention & Visitors Bureau, P.O. Box 990468, Prudential Tower, Dept. TPO, Boston, MA 02199-0468. Also contact the **Massachusetts Office of Travel and Tourism** (100 Cambridge St., 13th floor, Boston, MA 02202; ☎ **800/447-6277** or 617/727-3201; fax 617/727-6525; e-mail vacationinfo@state.ma.us), which publishes a free "Getaway Guide" magazine. It's divided into six regional sections that list accommodations and attractions, and includes a map and a seasonal calendar.

BED & BREAKFASTS   Whether you're uncomfortable with the idea of a big, impersonal chain hotel or just can't afford one, a B&B can be a good option. Accommodations offered in the homes of local families are usually as inexpensive as a budget hotel and often more comfortable. In most cases breakfast is included in the room rate. The following organizations can help match you with a suitable host:

Bed and Breakfast Associates Bay Colony Ltd. (P.O. Box 57-166, Babson Park Branch, Boston, MA 02157; ☎ **800/347-5088** or 617/449-5302; fax 617/449-5958) lists more than 150 bed-and-breakfasts and inns in the metropolitan Boston area and throughout eastern Massachusetts, including the North Shore, South Shore, and Cape Cod. They also arrange long-term lodging and list furnished apartments and house-sharing opportunities. A member of the B&B National Network, they can also help arrange reservations elsewhere in the United States and in Canada.

Bed and Breakfast Agency of Boston (47 Commercial Wharf, Boston, MA 02110; ☎ **800/CITY-BNB** or 617/720-3540; fax 617/523-5761; from the United Kingdom, call 0800/89-5128) offers accommodations in waterfront lofts and historic homes (including Federal and Victorian townhouses) in Boston and Cambridge. Nightly, weekly, monthly, and special winter rates are available. Listings include 155 rooms and 60 suites as well as furnished studios and apartments, all within walking distance of downtown. Trolley tour discounts are available.

New England Bed and Breakfast (P.O. Box 9100, Suite 176, Newton Centre, MA 02159; ☎ **617/244-2112**) offers home accommodations in the suburbs that are a short drive from Boston but within walking distance of public transportation. They have residences for nonsmokers, and will make an appropriate match if you have allergies.

Host Homes of Boston (P.O. Box 117, Waban Branch, Boston, MA 02168; ☎ **617/244-1308;** fax 617/244-5156) lists 45 homes offering personalized hospitality and clean, comfortable accommodations. Many hosts speak foreign languages, and all provide breakfast. A two-night minimum stay is required.

Bed & Breakfast Reservations North Shore/Greater Boston/Cape Cod (P.O. Box 35, Newtonville, MA 02160; ☎ **800/832-2632** outside MA or 617/964-1606; fax 617/332-8572; e-mail bnbinc@ix.netcom.com) matches visitors with carefully

Boston Accommodations

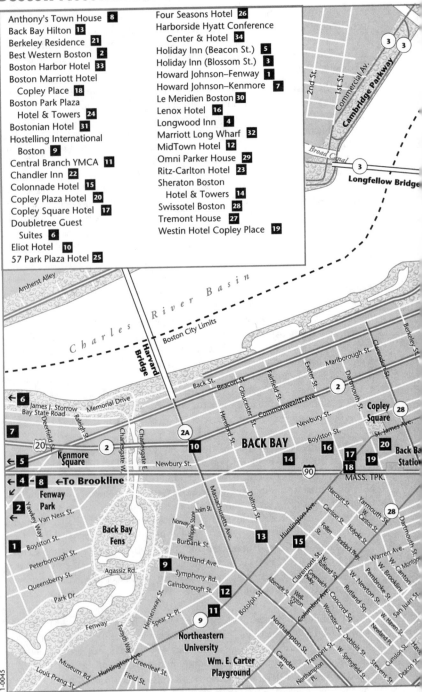

Anthony's Town House **8**
Back Bay Hilton **13**
Berkeley Residence **21**
Best Western Boston **2**
Boston Harbor Hotel **33**
Boston Marriott Hotel
  Copley Place **18**
Boston Park Plaza
  Hotel & Towers **24**
Bostonian Hotel **31**
Hostelling International
  Boston **9**
Central Branch YMCA **11**
Chandler Inn **22**
Colonnade Hotel **15**
Copley Plaza Hotel **20**
Copley Square Hotel **17**
Doubletree Guest
  Suites **6**
Eliot Hotel **10**
57 Park Plaza Hotel **25**

Four Seasons Hotel **26**
Harborside Hyatt Conference
  Center & Hotel **34**
Holiday Inn (Beacon St.) **5**
Holiday Inn (Blossom St.) **3**
Howard Johnson–Fenway **1**
Howard Johnson–Kenmore **7**
Le Meridien Boston **30**
Lenox Hotel **16**
Longwood Inn **4**
Marriott Long Wharf **32**
MidTown Hotel **12**
Omni Parker House **29**
Ritz-Carlton Hotel **23**
Sheraton Boston
  Hotel & Towers **14**
Swissotel Boston **28**
Tremont House **27**
Westin Hotel Copley Place **19**

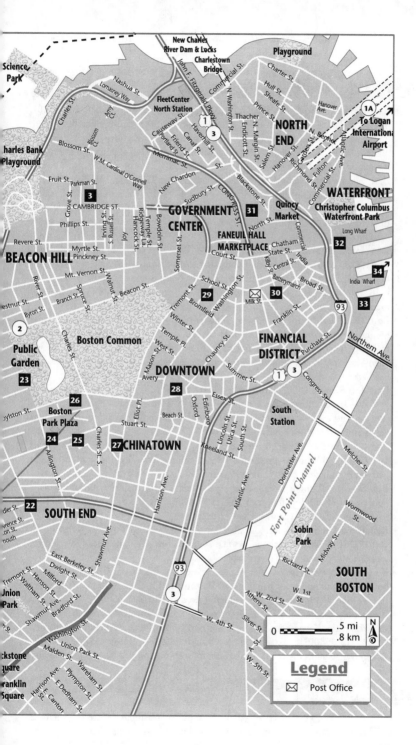

inspected accommodations in Greater Boston and areas north of Boston, and on Cape Cod.

1 Best Bets

- **Best Historic Hotel:** The Copley Plaza (138 St. James Ave. ☎ 617/267-5300), built in 1912 on the original site of the Museum of Fine Arts, has entertained every president since William Howard Taft, including President Kennedy, who visited regularly for the fish chowder. There's a display of historic memorabilia in a cabinet in the majestic main lobby.
- **Best for Business Travelers:** Le Meridien Boston (250 Franklin St., ☎ 617/451-1900), located in the heart of the Financial District, has a full-service business center with currency exchange, as well as a great health club. And, so you'll know what to wear without leaving the hotel, a weather report is delivered to your room every evening.
- **Best for a Romantic Getaway:** The Eliot Hotel's (370 Commonwealth Ave., ☎ 617/267-1607) intimate atmosphere and elegant furnishings make it a great spot for trysting. And if you and your beloved need a break from one another, most of the units are suites—with French doors, so you can slip into separate rooms but still maintain eye contact.
- **Best Hotel Lobby for Pretending That You're Rich:** As you walk around the ground floor of the Boston Harbor Hotel (70 Rowes Wharf, ☎ 617/439-7000), make believe you just tied up your yacht out front and are keeping an eye on it. Then feign a hurried exit to a fictitious important meeting in the Financial District and head across the street.
- **Best for Families:** The Boston Park Plaza Hotel & Towers (64 Arlington St., ☎ 617/426-2000) offers great family services. Kids are treated to gifts and Red Sox sundaes, and there's a story hour complete with milk and cookies. Movie screenings are given for the whole family.
- **Best Moderately Priced Hotel:** The Copley Square Hotel (47 Huntington Ave., ☎ 617/536-9000) offers excellent service, comfortable rooms, and a great location without breaking the bank. And every afternoon, guests are treated to tea.
- **Best Service:** Without a doubt, the hotel offering the best service in Boston is the Four Seasons (200 Boylston St., ☎ 617/338-4400). Standards are sky-high, and the friendly and efficient staff meets and exceeds them.
- **Best Hotel Pool:** The enormous Sheraton Boston Hotel & Towers (39 Dalton St., ☎ 617/236-2000) is a little impersonal because of its size, but it does have a great indoor/outdoor pool with a retractable dome.
- **Best Views:** Several hotels offer impressive views of their immediate surroundings, but for a picture-postcard panorama of Boston and Cambridge, head to the upper floors of the Westin Hotel (10 Huntington Ave., ☎ 617/262-9600).
- **Best Hotels for Baseball Fans:** Devotees of the national pastime can rub shoulders with real major leaguers at the Boston Marriott Copley Place (110 Huntington Ave., ☎ 617/236-5800) and the Sheraton Boston Hotel & Towers (39 Dalton St., ☎ 617/236-2000), the standard addresses for teams in town to take on the Red Sox.

2 Downtown

The downtown area extends from Atlantic Avenue to Washington Street. It includes the Freedom Trail and the historic neighborhoods defined in Chapter 4 as the

Waterfront, Faneuil Hall, the Financial District, Downtown Crossing, and Beacon Hill.

VERY EXPENSIVE

✪ Boston Harbor Hotel

70 Rowes Wharf (entrance on Atlantic Ave.), Boston, MA 02110. ☎ **800/752-7077** or 617/439-7000. Fax 617/330-9450. 230 rms, 26 suites. A/C MINIBAR TV TEL. $235–$385 double; from $350 suite. Children under 18 stay free in parents' room. Extra person $50. Weekend packages available. AE, DC, DISC, MC, V. Self-parking $21 weekdays; valet parking $23 daily. MBTA: Blue Line to Aquarium or Red Line to South Station.

The Boston Harbor Hotel is the prettiest in town, whether you approach from land or sea (the Airport Water Shuttle stops here). A dazzling six-story-high archway links the harbor and the city, and you'll forget about the Central Artery construction raging out front as soon as you glimpse the water. The hotel is within walking distance of downtown and the waterfront attractions, and it prides itself on offering top-notch service to travelers pursuing both business and pleasure. A museum-quality collection of paintings, drawings, and prints enhances the grand public spaces of the hotel, a 16-story redbrick structure that's part of a 10-year-old hotel-office-retail-condominium complex.

Guest rooms have a view of the harbor or the Boston skyline (rooms with city views are cheaper), and all have windows that open. Each is a luxurious bed- and living-room combination, decorated with mahogany furnishings that include armoire, desk, and comfortable chairs. Some suites have private terraces. Standard guest room amenities include hair dryers, bathrobes, slippers, and umbrellas.

Dining/Entertainment: Overlooking the harbor, the Rowes Wharf Restaurant serves fresh seafood and American cuisine at breakfast, lunch, dinner, and Sunday brunch, and the Harborview Lounge offers afternoon tea and evening cocktails. The Rowes Wharf Bar serves cocktails and light fare from 11:30am to midnight. The Rowes Wharf Cafe offers outdoor dining from May to September.

Services: Concierge; 24-hour room service; valet service; nightly turndown; twice-daily maid service; baby-sitting; valet parking.

Facilities: Pay-per-view movies; health club and spa with 60-foot lap pool; whirlpool; sauna, steam, and exercise rooms; and a salon for facials, massage, pedicures, and manicures. State-of-the-art business center with professional staff. Three floors for nonsmokers; 18 rooms for the disabled.

The Bostonian Hotel

40 North St., Boston, MA 02109. ☎ **800/343-0922** or 617/523-3600. Fax 617/523-2454. 152 rms, 16 suites. A/C MINIBAR TV TEL. $245–$325 double; $335–$355 honeymoon or executive room; $450–$725 suite. Children under 12 stay free in parents' room. Extra person $20. Special weekend rates and other packages available. AE, DC, JCB, MC, V. Parking $20. MBTA: Green or Blue Line to Government Center, or Orange Line to Haymarket.

Across the street from Faneuil Hall Marketplace, the relatively small Bostonian Hotel is big on service and amenities that make it competitive with the city's larger hotels. It's a unique building, with a round, cobbled parking area in a tiny court-yard outside the small but plush glass-walled lobby. The four- and seven-story red-brick hotel consists of two wings—one, an old warehouse building, dates from 1824, the other from 1890. One wing is furnished in contemporary style, the other more traditionally. The interior is a pleasant agglomeration of architectural styles, with lots of glass and brass, and public spaces are decorated with artwork on loan from the Bostonian Society.

Guest rooms are furnished with armoires and tables, and many have French doors that open onto private balconies. Some suites have double vanities and separate dressing areas (terrycloth robes are provided), working fireplaces, or Jacuzzis. All rooms have stereo VCRs, 26-inch TVs, safes and two-line phones with dataports. Bathrooms are equipped with hair dryers, heat lamps, and both overhead and European-style hand-held shower sprays. This is one hotel where, in the interests of noise evasion, you really want to be as high up as you can afford, and away from the street if you can stand not having a nice view. Faneuil Hall Marketplace is busy from early till late, the Central Artery construction is nearby (and will be closer before it's farther away), and on Friday and Saturday, the noisy Haymarket vendors are in place by 7am.

Dining/Entertainment: On the fourth-floor rooftop is the glass-enclosed Seasons restaurant, one of Boston's finest.

Services: Concierge; 24-hour room service; newspaper delivery; nightly turndown; express checkout; limousine service to Logan Airport.

Facilities: VCRs; complimentary health club privileges at the excellent Sky Club four blocks away; rooms for nonsmokers available.

✪ Le Meridien Boston

250 Franklin St. (at Post Office Sq.), Boston, MA 02110. ☎ **800/543-4300** or 617/451-1900. Fax 617/423-2844. 326 rms, 22 suites. A/C MINIBAR TV TEL. $285–$335 double; $450–$800 suite. Extra person $25. Weekend rates from $145 per night, including use of pool and health club plus parking. AE, CB, DC, MC, V. Parking $24. MBTA: Blue or Orange Line to State or Red Line to Downtown Crossing.

Located in the old Federal Reserve Bank building, which was designed by R. Clipston Sturgis in 1922 in the style of a 16th-century Roman palace, this nine-story granite-and-limestone hotel is an architectural marvel. You'll see the bank's original grand marble staircase, which now leads to the dining areas; two murals by N. C. Wyeth on the walls of the bar; and ornately carved marble fireplaces and floor-to-ceiling arched windows. The location, in the heart of the Financial District, is perfect for business travelers, and vacationing visitors will be near the waterfront and downtown attractions. Whatever your mission, you'll find the service by the multilingual staff superb.

Guest rooms are arranged in 153 different configurations, including dramatic loft suites with first-floor living rooms, a bedroom in the loft area, and bathrooms on both levels. The glass mansard roof (not part of the original design) surrounds the top three stories, where a number of rooms have large, sloped windows and extraordinary views. The already-plush guest rooms underwent a $5.5 million renovation in 1995. Each has two telephones (one in the bathroom).

Dining/Entertainment: The award-winning Julien restaurant serves lunch and dinner. The Julien Bar features live piano music six nights a week. A six-story glass atrium rises above the Café Fleuri, which serves breakfast, lunch, dinner, the Saturday "Chocolate Bar Buffet" (September through May), and Sunday jazz brunch. La Terrasse is the seasonal outdoor cafe.

Services: Concierge; 24-hour room service; dry cleaning and laundry service; weekday newspaper delivery; daily weather report.

Facilities: Pay-per-view movies; forty-foot indoor pool; well-equipped health club with whirlpool and sauna; full-service business center with library and full-time staff; conference rooms. Six floors for nonsmokers; 15 rooms for the disabled.

Swissôtel Boston (The Lafayette)

1 Avenue de Lafayette, Boston, MA 02111. ☎ **800/621-9200** or 617/451-2600. Fax 617/451-0054. 454 rms, 46 suites. A/C MINIBAR TV TEL. $255–$320 double. $370–$2,500 suite or

Swiss Butler Executive Level. Children under 18 stay free in parents' room. Extra person $25. Weekend packages available. AE, CB, DC, DISC, JCB, MC, V. Valet parking $22 weekdays, $8 weekends. MBTA: Red Line to Downtown Crossing.

Adjacent to a dreary stretch of Washington Street, this 22-story hotel presents a plain white facade that belies the opulence within. Elevators transport guests *up* to the luxurious, wood-paneled lobby, where European style takes over. The hotel is decorated with both antique and contemporary furnishings, and elegant touches such as Waterford crystal chandeliers and imported marble columns accent the lavish setting.

Guest rooms are grouped around four atriums with semiprivate lobbies, creating the effect of several small hotels within the hotel Each room features a sitting area with desk, settee, and king- or twin-size beds. The suites have either L-shaped rooms with sitting areas or living rooms with connecting bedrooms. All rooms have three telephones with dataports. On the Executive Level, guests are pampered from check-in to express checkout, and a Swiss Butler on this level performs traditional valet functions, acts as a private concierge, and even runs errands.

The hotel's Downtown Crossing location and business amenities make it popular with conventioneers and corporate travelers during the week, so the weekend packages can be great deals.

Dining/Entertainment: Café Suisse serves breakfast, lunch, dinner, and Sunday brunch featuring both Swiss and American favorites. The Lobby Lounge, located in the atrium lobby, offers cocktails and light meals.

Services: 24-hour room service; dry cleaning; valet service; nightly turndown.

Facilities: Pay-per-view movies; 52-foot indoor pool; health club; exercise room; saunas; sun terrace; high-tech business center; conference rooms. Six floors for nonsmokers.

EXPENSIVE

Boston Marriott Long Wharf

296 State St., Boston, MA 02109. ☎ **800/228-9290** or 617/227-0800. Fax 617/227-2867. 400 rms, 12 suites. A/C TV TEL. Apr–Nov $189–$269 double; Dec–Mar $159–$229 double. Extra person free. Weekend packages from $189 double; $450–$490 suite. AE, DC, DISC, JCB, MC, V. Parking $22. MBTA: Blue Line to Aquarium.

The terraced red-brick exterior of this long, narrow seven-story hotel looks nothing like the ocean liner it supposedly resembles, but it is one of the most recognizable sights on the harbor. A stone's throw from the New England Aquarium, it's convenient to all the downtown and waterfront attractions, and just two subway stops from the airport. A Rufus Porter harbor scene, one of the few remaining original frescoes painted by the 19th-century artist, dominates the lobby wall near the escalator. Although the locale is not identified, it is thought to be Boston Harbor in the early 1800s. It's worth seeing even if you're not a hotel guest.

Rooms face either side of Long Wharf, with views of Central Wharf and the aquarium or Mercantile Wharf and Waterfront Park. Rooms are large and decor varies, but all have in-room movies, a choice of king-size or double beds, and a table and chairs in front of the window.

The seventh floor is the Concierge Level, with fresh flowers in the guest rooms; complimentary continental breakfast, cocktails, and hors d'oeuvres served in a private lounge; and private exercise facilities.

Dining/Entertainment: The atrium-style Palm Garden, a cafe and lounge used for Sunday brunch, has a magnificent 420-foot ceiling mural; Oceana Restaurant features a 180-degree expanse of glass wall fronting the harbor; Waves Bar & Grill serves cocktails and light fare.

Services: Concierge; valet laundry; valet parking.

Facilities: Pay-per-view movies; indoor pool with an outdoor terrace; exercise room; whirlpools; saunas; game room; business center; conference rooms; 18 rooms for the disabled.

Holiday Inn

5 Blossom St., Boston, MA 02114. ☎ **800/HOLIDAY** or 617/742-7630. Fax 617/742-4192. 303 rms, 2 suites. A/C TV TEL. $199 double. $15 for rollaway. Extra person $20. Children under 18 stay free in parents' room. 10% senior discount with AARP card. Weekend and corporate packages available. AE, DC, DISC, JCB, MC, V. Parking $16 in covered lot adjacent to hotel. MBTA: Red Line to Charles/MGH.

At the base of Beacon Hill, near Massachusetts General Hospital, this utilitarian hotel rises 14 stories above a shopping plaza where you'll find a supermarket, shops, and several fast-food restaurants. As you would expect at a Holiday Inn, the rooms have modern, functional furniture and simple decor. The furnishings date to a $10 million renovation of all guest rooms and public spaces completed in 1995. Each room has a picture-window view of the city (or the parking lot—ask to be as high up as possible).

Dining/Entertainment: Foster's Bar & Grill Restaurant serves breakfast, lunch, and dinner.

Services: In-room coffee and tea service on executive floor; newspaper delivery; secretarial services available.

Facilities: Pay-per-view movies; outdoor heated pool; small exercise room; laundry room; rooms for nonsmokers available.

Omni Parker House

60 School St., Boston, MA 02108. ☎ **800/THE-OMNI** or 617/227-8600. Fax 617/742-5729. 535 rms, 12 suites. A/C TV TEL. $185–$325 double; $260 minisuite; $295–$600 large suite. Children under 16 stay free in parents' room. Weekend packages available. AE, CB, DC, DISC, MC, V. Valet parking $22; self-parking $15. MBTA: Green Line to Government Center or Red Line to Park Street.

Built in 1855, the Parker House is the oldest continuously operating hotel in America, and has entertained many famous guests (and, interestingly, has had some famous employees as well—Malcolm X and Ho Chi Minh both worked here as young men). The best-known group of guests consisted of Henry Wadsworth Longfellow, Oliver Wendell Holmes, Ralph Waldo Emerson, Nathaniel Hawthorne, and sometimes even Charles Dickens, who regularly met at the hotel as a literary salon called the Saturday Club. Those 19th-century luminaries would probably feel at home today in the 14-story hotel's beautifully maintained public areas, where walls have the original American oak paneling and doors are accented with burnished bronze. The downstairs decorations are echoed in the comfortable guest rooms. Some rooms are quite small and have bathrooms equipped with showers only. Rooms have views of Old City Hall or Government Center.

Dining/Entertainment: Parker's Restaurant serves breakfast and lunch (including the famous Parker House rolls, which were invented here). Parker's Bar is on the site of the Saturday Club's former meetingplace. The Last Hurrah Bar & Grill, on the lower level, is a fun spot for lunch, dinner, drinks and dancing. Also on the premises are a deli and a cafe.

Services: Concierge; room service until 11pm; secretarial services available.

Facilities: Use of nearby health club; conference rooms. Rooms for nonsmokers and the disabled available.

3   Back Bay

Many hotels are clustered in the upscale Back Bay. The listings in this area are split into two sections, the first including hotels near Boston Common, the Public Garden, and the Theater District, and the second those closer to Copley Square, the Hynes Convention Center, and Massachusetts Avenue. The first group is closer to downtown, but nothing in central Boston is particularly far from anything else.

BOSTON COMMON/PUBLIC GARDEN/THEATER DISTRICT

VERY EXPENSIVE

○ Four Seasons Hotel

200 Boylston St., Boston, MA 02116. ☎ **800/332-3442** or 617/338-4400. Fax 617/423-0154. 288 rms, 80 suites. A/C MINIBAR TV TEL. $320–$495 double; from $650 one-bedroom suite; from $1,100 two-bedroom suite. Weekend packages available. AE, CB, DC, DISC, JCB, MC, V. Valet parking $22. MBTA: Green Line to Arlington.

Many other hotels offer exquisite service, beautiful locations, elegant guest rooms and public areas, a health club, and wonderful restaurants; but no other hotel in Boston combines every element you expect from a luxury hotel quite so seamlessly and pleasingly as the Four Seasons has since it opened in 1985. Overlooking the Public Garden, the 16-story redbrick-and-glass hotel combines traditional with contemporary, architecturally and in terms of attitude. Each room is elegantly appointed and has a striking view. Beds are large and comfortable, and breakfronts conceal the 19-inch remote-control TV and refrigerated minibar. The suites range from Four Seasons Executive Suites, which have enlarged alcove areas for entertaining or business meetings, to luxurious one-, two-, and three-bedroom deluxe suites, which are the utmost in elegance, privacy, and comfort. All rooms have bay windows that open, individual climate control, three two-line phones with computer and fax capability, hair dryers, terrycloth bathrobes, and a safe. Children receive bedtime snacks and toys. Small pets are accepted and treated as well as their traveling companions, with a special menu and amenities.

Dining/Entertainment: The elegant restaurant Aujourd'hui, one of Boston's best, serves fine French cuisine; the Bristol Lounge is open for lunch, afternoon tea, dinner, and breakfast on Sunday, and features live entertainment nightly.

Services: In general, if you want it, you'll get it. Concierge; 24-hour room service; valet service; twice-daily maid service; valet parking; complimentary limousine service to downtown Boston addresses. If you lose your luggage en route, the staff will purchase new items and provide you with a full set of toiletries and other necessities.

Facilities: Pay-per-view movies; indoor heated pool and whirlpool with a view of the Public Garden; health spa with weight machines, StairMasters, treadmills, private masseuse, and sauna. (The pool and spa are shared with residents of the condominiums on the upper floors of the hotel.) Excellent business center; conference rooms. Five no-smoking floors; rooms for the disabled available.

The Ritz-Carlton

15 Arlington St., Boston, MA 02117. ☎ **800/241-3333** or 617/536-5700. Fax 617/536-1335. 237 rms, 48 suites. A/C MINIBAR TV TEL. $270–$370 double; $500–$2,000 one-bedroom suite, $720–$2,100 two-bedroom suite. Ritz-Carlton Club $565–$795 one-bedroom suite, $830–$1,175 two-bedroom suite. Weekend packages available. AE, CB, DC, DISC, JCB, MC, V. Valet parking $20. MBTA: Green Line to Arlington.

Overlooking the Public Garden, the Ritz-Carlton has a tradition of gracious service that has made it famous since it opened in 1927, attracting both the "proper Bostonian" and the celebrated guest. The service and attention to detail are legendary. The 17-story hotel has the highest staff-to-guest ratio in the city, including white-gloved elevator operators.

The guest rooms have classic French provincial furnishings accented with imported floral fabrics and crystal chandeliers. Each room has two telephones (one in the bathroom), a refrigerator, a well-stocked honor bar, a safe, and an individual climate-control unit. The bathrooms are finished in Vermont marble, and terry-cloth robes are provided. All the guest rooms have closets that lock, and some have windows that open. Fresh flowers are provided in all suites. Many suites have wood-burning fireplaces.

The rooms on the top three floors have a panoramic view of the Public Garden and the city. Guests on those floors are invited to use the Ritz-Carlton Club, a pleasant lounge that has its own concierge and is open from 7am to 11pm, serving complimentary breakfast, afternoon tea, hors d'oeuvres, and after-dinner sweets.

Dining/Entertainment: The superb Dining Room is described in Chapter 6, and the popular Ritz Bar, located off the street-level lobby, is covered in Chapter 10. The second-floor Lounge is famous for afternoon tea, and from 5:30pm until midnight cigar and pipe smokers can relax over cognac, rare cordials, caviar, and desserts. The Café is open for breakfast, lunch, and dinner from 7am to midnight. The Roof, located on the 17th floor and open seasonally, offers a splendid view of the city with dinner and dancing to the Ritz-Carlton Orchestra. A famously strict dress code (the mayor of Boston was once turned away from the bar) is enforced.

Services: Concierge, 24-hour room service, dry cleaning and laundry service, complimentary newspaper delivery, nightly turndown, twice-daily maid service, babysitting available, secretarial services arranged, complimentary limousine service available, and complimentary shoeshine.

Facilities: Well-equipped fitness center with sauna and massage room; use of pool at nearby Le Pli Health Spa; conference rooms; beauty salon; flower and gift shop.

EXPENSIVE

Boston Park Plaza Hotel & Towers

64 Arlington St. (at Park Plaza), Boston, MA 02116. ☎ **800/225-2008** or 617/426-2000. Fax 617/426-1708. 960 rms, 10 suites. A/C TV TEL. Main hotel $175–$265 double; Towers $195–$245 double; $375–$2,000 suite. Extra person $20. Senior discounts and special packages available. Children 17 and under stay free in parents' room. AE, DC, MC, V. Valet parking $18. MBTA: Green Line to Arlington.

Built as the great Statler Hilton in 1927, the hotel is proud of its history and equally proud of its renovations. The lovely old features—such as the spacious lobby with its crystal chandelier, gilt trim, and red-carpeted corridors—have been retained, but the rooms have been updated with modern comforts. Room size and decor vary greatly (some rooms are quite small). The superior rooms offer extra services and access to a hospitality suite serving complimentary continental breakfast and evening wine and cheese. The location is central—just a block from Boston Common and the Public Garden, and about the same distance from the Theater District. The hotel lobby is a little commercial hub, with a travel agency, foreign currency exchange, Amtrak and airline ticket offices, and a pharmacy.

Environmentally conscious guests will be pleased to know that the Boston Park Plaza Hotel has initiated an environmental policy that is a model for the industry. All nonbiodegradable products have been eliminated from guest rooms, recycling programs are in effect, and stationery and forms are printed on dioxin-free recycled paper. A "Green Team" of hotel employees is attempting to conserve energy and water and to eliminate hazardous waste.

Dining/Entertainment: Guests can choose from the Cafe Rouge, which serves healthful cuisine prepared in consultation with the natural-foods supermarket chain Bread & Circus; the famous Legal Sea Foods restaurant; the Captains Bar; Cafe Eurosia; and Swans Court in the Grand Lobby.

Services: Concierge; 24-hour room service; valet laundry; secretarial services; valet parking.

Facilities: Pay-per-view movies; health club; kids' video/game room; hairdresser; beauty salon. Rooms for nonsmokers available.

MODERATE

57 Park Plaza Hotel

200 Stuart St. (at Park Sq.), Boston, MA 02116. ☎ **617/482-1800.** Fax 617/451-2750. 354 rms, 10 suites. A/C TV TEL. $140–$200 double; suite $155 and up. Extra person or cot $15. Children under 18 stay free in parents' room. Cribs free. Weekend and family packages available. AE, DC, MC, V. Discounted indoor parking with direct access to your floor. MBTA: Green Line to Boylston.

In preparation for a franchise change from Howard Johnson to Radisson (scheduled for April 1997), the 57 Park Plaza Hotel underwent a major renovation of its guest rooms and public areas in 1996. The hotel was already quite nice; call to see if a change in rates accompanied the change in management.

Rooms in the modern, 24-story hotel have private balconies (with great views from the higher floors), king-size beds or two double beds, and a sitting area. Also available are minisuites with one king-size bed and a parlor area with a sofa, table, and chairs. Three-quarters of the rooms are set aside for nonsmokers.

You can swim year-round in the heated pool on the seventh floor, use the outdoor sundeck (seasonally), or take a sauna. This centrally located downtown hotel is part of a complex that includes the 57 Restaurant.

⑤ Tremont House

275 Tremont St., Boston, MA 02116. ☎ **800/331-9998** or 617/426-1400. Fax 617/482-6730. 281 rms, 34 suites. A/C TV TEL. $139–$199 double; $170–$270 suite. Children under 16 stay free in parents' room. Extra person $10. Weekend packages and 10% AAA discount available. AE, CB, DC, DISC, MC, V. Parking $15 in nearby garage or lot. MBTA: Green Line to Boylston or Orange Line to New England Medical Center.

The Tremont House is as close to Boston's theaters as you can be without actually attending a show, and is convenient to downtown and the Back Bay.

This 15-story brick building, formerly the landmark Hotel Bradford, has been completely renovated to preserve the style that prevailed when the hotel was built in 1924. The original gold-leaf decorations and crafted ceilings in the huge lobby and ballrooms have been restored, the original marble walls and columns refurbished, and elegant, sparkling-new chandeliers installed.

The hotel, which has affordable rates and modern furnishings, is geared to travelers on a modest budget. That's not to say that there are no services—conference rooms, secretarial services, and valet laundry are available. There are three top-of-the-line units that feature kitchenettes with a range, sink, and refrigerator (great for families who want to eat in). Four floors are reserved for nonsmokers, and there are 14 rooms for the disabled.

Weekend clubgoers have two options in the hotel. The upscale Roxy nightclub features Top 40 and international music, and the Jukebox club is a favorite with suburbanites. The Tremont Deli serves a casual menu at breakfast, lunch, and dinner.

COPLEY SQUARE/CONVENTION CENTER/ MASSACHUSETTS AVENUE

VERY EXPENSIVE

The Colonnade Hotel

120 Huntington Ave., Boston, MA 02116. ☎ **800/962-3030** or 617/424-7000. Fax 617/ 424-1717. 285 rms, 10 suites. A/C MINIBAR TV TEL. $240 standard double; $250 superior double; $270 deluxe double; suites $450–$1,400. Children under 12 stay free in parents' room. AE, CB, DC, MC, V. Parking $20. MBTA: Green Line, E train to Prudential.

With Copley Place on one side and the Prudential Center across the street, the independently owned Colonnade is a slice of Europe in the all-American shopping mecca of the Back Bay. You might hear a dozen languages spoken by the guests and employees of this 10-story concrete-and-glass hotel, where the friendly, professional staff is known for giving every patron personalized VIP service. The elegance of the quiet, high-ceilinged public spaces is reflected in the guest rooms, which feature contemporary oak or mahogany furnishings, marble baths, pedestal sinks, bathrobes, and hair dryers. The newly designed suites have dining rooms and sitting areas, and the "author's suite" features autographed copies of the work of celebrated (or at least published) literary guests. And there's a pool on the roof.

Dining/Entertainment: Extremely popular before and after the Symphony, the Cafe Promenade features seasonal menus and gourmet pizzas in a bistro setting. Every Friday and Saturday night, there's live entertainment and dancing in Zachary's Bar.

Services: Concierge; 24-hour room service; nightly turndown; valet parking.

Facilities: Seasonal "rooftop resort" with heated outdoor pool and fitness room; car-rental desk.

The Copley Plaza Hotel

138 St. James Ave., Boston, MA 02116. ☎ **800/WYNDHAM** or 617/267-5300. Fax 617/ 247-6681. 373 rms, 61 suites. A/C MINIBAR TV TEL. $275–$374 double; $395–$1,400 suite. Extra person $25. AE, CB, DC, JCB, MC, V. Valet parking $22. MBTA: Green Line to Copley or Orange Line to Back Bay.

Built in 1912, the Copley Plaza faces Copley Square, with Trinity Church on one side and the Boston Public Library on the other. The Renaissance revival hotel has been synonymous with elegance since it opened. Renowned for its opulent decorative features, including crystal chandeliers, Italian marble columns, gilded vaulted ceilings, mirrored walls, and mosaic tile floors, the hotel has entertained royalty, statesmen, and celebrities, and every United States president since William Howard Taft. Guest rooms and suites reflect the elegance of the public spaces and are furnished with reproduction Edwardian antiques. Additional in-room features include coffeemakers, phones with computer dataports, and movies. Bathrooms are equipped with hair dryers and heat lamps. After you settle into your room, you can go on a walking tour that focuses on the hotel's art, architecture, and history with a member of the multilingual staff.

In 1996 the Fairmont hotel group announced plans to acquire the Copley Plaza. Fittingly, Fairmont's best-known property is the Plaza in New York, which had the same architect as the Copley Plaza, Henry Janeway Hardenbergh.

Dining/Entertainment: Options include the distinguished Plaza Dining Room, serving classic American cuisine; the Library Bar; the Plaza Bar, which serves light meals and features live entertainment; Copley's Restaurant (breakfast, lunch, after-noon tea, and dinner); and Copley's Bar.

Services: Concierge, 24-hour room service, dry cleaning and laundry service, nightly turndown, twice-daily maid service.

Facilities: Pay-per-view movies; fitness center; complimentary use of the nearby Le Pli Spa (with pool and sauna) at the Heritage; conference rooms; beauty salon. Four floors are reserved for nonsmokers, and rooms for the disabled are available.

EXPENSIVE

Boston Back Bay Hilton

40 Dalton St., Boston, MA 02115. ☎ **800/874-0663**, 800/HILTONS or 617/236-1100. Fax 617/867-6104. 330 rms, 5 suites. A/C TV TEL. $195–$225 double; $410 one-bedroom suite; $800 two-bedroom suite. Packages and AAA discount available. Extra person $20. AE, CB, DC, DISC, MC, V. Parking $15. MBTA: Green Line, B, C, or D train to Hynes/ICA or E train to Prudential.

The motto at this hotel across the street from the Prudential Center is "We mean business," but vacationing families will also find it convenient and comfortable. The guest rooms in the triangular 26-story hotel were renovated in 1993, and many were redecorated in Southwest style. All have either one king-size or two double beds. Soundproofing in the rooms helps keep the level of street noise down.

Dining/Entertainment: Boodles Restaurant is known for grilled steaks and seafood; Boodles Bar offers a huge variety of American microbrews; the Rendezvous Lounge is open for continental breakfast, cocktails, and light meals.

Services: Room service; valet laundry; secretarial services; currency exchange.

Facilities: Pay-per-view movies; heated indoor pool; well-equipped fitness center; sun deck; conference rooms. Rooms for nonsmokers are available.

Boston Marriott Copley Place

110 Huntington Ave., Boston, MA 02116. ☎ **800/228-9290** or 617/236-5800. Fax 617/236-5885. 1,139 rms, 77 suites. A/C TV TEL. $199–$210 double; $250–$1,100 suite. Senior discount available. Children stay free in parents' room. Special packages available. AE, DC, DISC, JCB, MC, V. Valet parking $21; self-parking $17. MBTA: Orange Line to Back Bay or Green Line, E train to Prudential.

Yes, 1,139 rooms. You may not feel that you're asserting your individuality, but at least you'll feel comfortable. This 38-story tower has something for everyone—it's part of upscale Copley Place, with complete business facilities in the heart of Boston's shopping wonderland. Enter from the street or from Copley Place, and you'll find yourself in a giant lobby with a four-story-long chandelier, Italian marble floors, full-size trees, and a waterfall. Between guests, restaurant-goers, and pedestrians, the lobby is almost always so busy that a room anywhere else would be a nice break.

The guest rooms, which were renovated in 1995, are far more than just rooms and echo the finery of the lobby, with Queen Anne–style mahogany furniture, including a desk and table and armchairs or an ottoman. Rooms are equipped with full-length mirrors, hair dryers, ironing boards, and phones with dataports. Ultrasuites feature individual whirlpool baths. One suite even holds a grand piano. Guests in Concierge Level rooms have, yes, their own concierge, and access to a private lounge where complimentary continental breakfast, cocktails, and hors d'oeuvres are served.

Dining/Entertainment: Champions Sports Bar is a fun place to watch sports on TV and eat bar food. Sunday brunch, with entertainment, is served in the Terrace Lounge. There are two Italian restaurants and a sushi bar as well.

Services: Concierge; 24-hour room service; valet laundry; valet parking.

Facilities: Pay-per-view movies; heated indoor pool; well-equipped health club with exercise room, whirlpools, saunas; full-service business center with personal computers; conference rooms; car-rental desk; tour desk. Rooms for nonsmokers and the disabled are available.

✪ Eliot Hotel

370 Commonwealth Ave. (at Massachusetts Ave.), Boston, MA 02215. ☎ **800/44-ELIOT** or 617/267-1607. Fax 617/536-9114. 16 rms, 78 suites. A/C MINIBAR TV TEL. $195–$225 double room; $225–$265 suite for two. Extra person $20. Children under 12 stay free in parents' room. AE, DC, MC, V. Valet parking $18. MBTA: Green Line, B, C, or D train to Hynes/ICA.

This exquisite hotel combines the flavor of Yankee Boston with European-style service and amenities. Built in 1925 as a retirement residence for Harvard alumni (the Harvard Club is next door), the nine-story hotel underwent a complete renovation from 1990–94. The cozy lobby is lit by a 5-foot-wide imported crystal chandelier and decorated with period furnishings and porcelain. Spacious suites are furnished with traditional English-style chintz fabrics, authentic botanical prints, and antique furnishings. French doors separate the living and bedrooms, and modern conveniences, such as Italian marble baths, dual-line telephones with modem capability, and two TVs are standard in suites. Many suites also have a pantry with a microwave.

The hotel is convenient to Boston University and MIT (across the river), and the location on tree-lined Commonwealth Avenue makes for a pleasant contrast with the urban bustle of Newbury Street, a block away.

Dining/Entertainment: Breakfast is served in the Charles Eliot Room.

Services: Concierge; room service and secretarial services available; valet parking.

Facilities: Smoke-free floor; rooms for the disabled; safe-deposit boxes. A health club is scheduled to open in 1997.

The Lenox Hotel

710 Boylston St., Boston MA 02116. ☎ **800/225-7676** or 617/536-5300. Fax 617/267-1237. 214 rms, 3 suites. A/C TV TEL. $190–$250 double. Executive corner room with fireplace $300; suite with fireplace $450. Extra person $20. Children under 18 stay free in parents' room. Cots $20. Cribs free. Corporate and weekend packages available. AE, CB, DC, DISC, JCB, MC, V. Parking $20. MBTA: Green Line to Copley.

From the grandfather clock in the lobby to the wood-burning fireplaces in the corner rooms, the Lenox feels more like an inn than an 11-story hotel. The central location—near the Prudential Center, Copley Place, and Copley Square—is a draw on its own, and a renovation completed in 1995 has left the hotel (built in 1900) in a state of turn-of-the-century splendor. The high-ceilinged rooms have separate sitting areas with Chippendale-style furnishings, and many have in-room fax machines and marble baths. Despite such signs of luxury as hand-carved gilt moldings, this is an affordable hotel with rooms in moderate, superior, and deluxe categories.

Dining/Entertainment: The Upstairs Grille and the Samuel Adams Brewhouse serve meals.

Services: Room service until midnight; valet laundry; newspaper delivery; nightly turndown; secretarial services available; valet parking.

Facilities: Pay-per-view movies; small exercise room; children's TV channel; conference rooms. One hundred rooms for nonsmokers; rooms for the disabled available; wheelchair lift to the lobby.

Sheraton Boston Hotel & Towers

39 Dalton St., Boston, MA 02199. ☎ **800/325-3535** or 617/236-2000. Fax 617/236-1702. 1,208 rms, 85 suites. A/C MINIBAR TV TEL. $210–$255 double; suites from $255. Children under 17 stay free in parents' room. 25% discount for students, faculty, and retired persons with ID, depending on availability. Weekend packages available. AE, CB, DC, DISC, JCB, MC, V. Parking $16. MBTA: Green Line, B, C, or D train to Hynes/ICA or E train to Prudential.

You might get lost once you're actually in this gigantic hotel, but you won't have trouble finding the 29-story towers attached to the Prudential Center. Neither does anyone else, apparently—this hotel is one of the most popular in the city. The location, lavish convention facilities, a range of accommodations, and huge pool make it a favorite with travelers pursuing both business and pleasure. It's connected directly to the Hynes Convention Center and the new Shops at Prudential Center, and by walkways to Copley Place.

Standard rooms are fairly large, with traditional furnishings in mahogany and cherrywood. Many suites have a phone in the bathroom, a wet bar, and a refrigerator. Executive Level guests get free local calls and no access charges on long distance calls, and admission to the Executive Lounge, where complimentary breakfast and hors d'oeuvres are served. In-room amenities on this level include a desk, phone with dataport, morning newspaper, coffeemaker, and iron.

The luxurious Sheraton Towers, located on the 26th floor of the hotel and accessible via private elevator, features private check-in, an elegant atmosphere, some antique furnishings, and a wonderful view from the lounge, where Towers guests are offered complimentary breakfast, afternoon tea, and hors d'oeuvres and beverages. Rooms are outfitted with Egyptian cotton sheets, goose-down comforters, plush bathrobes, electric blankets, shoe trees, and phones in the bathroom (some even have a wall-mounted TV). Guests on this floor have their own butler.

Dining/Entertainment: The Mass. Bay Company and Turning Point Lounge serve light and full meals in clubby surroundings. The casual A Steak in the Neighborhood serves breakfast, lunch, dinner, and more than 70 varieties of beer in a fun, noisy setting that also serves as a sports bar with a dance floor.

Services: Concierge; 24-hour room service; valet laundry; valet parking.

Facilities: Pay-per-view movies; heated indoor/outdoor pool with retractable dome, pavilion, Jacuzzi, and sauna; well-equipped health club; conference rooms. Rooms for nonsmokers and the disabled available.

The Westin Hotel

10 Huntington Ave., Boston, MA 02116. ☎ **800/228-3000** or 617/262-9600. Fax 617/424-7483. 800 rms, 46 suites. A/C MINIBAR TV TEL. $179–$250 double; $285–$1,500 suite. Extra person $20; $30 on Executive Club Level. Weekend packages available. AE, CB, DC, DISC, JCB, MC, V. Valet parking $21. MBTA: Green Line to Copley.

Looming 36 stories in the air above Copley Place, the Westin is popular with convention-goers, sightseers, and dedicated shoppers. Determined consumers don't even have to step outside—the hotel is linked by skybridges to Copley Place and the Prudential Center. Others may want to start exploring at Copley Square, across the street from the pedestrian entrance. The entrance is dominated by two-story-high twin waterfalls on either side of escalators that run to the Grand Lobby, where you'll find a multilingual staff that emphasizes quick check-in.

Upstairs, you might not notice the comfortable oak and mahogany furniture in the spacious guest rooms (at least at first), because you won't be able to take your eyes off the view. The qualms you might have had about choosing a huge chain hotel will fade as you survey downtown Boston, the airport and harbor, or the Charles River and Cambridge. Executive Club Level guests have private check-in and a private lounge where a complimentary continental breakfast and hors d'oeuvres are served.

Dining/Entertainment: The Palm, the newest branch of the famous New York–based chain, serves steak, chops, and jumbo lobsters at lunch and dinner. Turner Fisheries, a seafood restaurant known for its clam chowder, features live jazz nightly. Ten Huntington is a casual bar serving light meals. The Lobby Lounge is a relaxing spot for drinks and conversation that also serves coffee and pastries each morning.

Services: Concierge, 24-hour room service, valet service, in-room safes.

Facilities: Pay-per-view movies; indoor pool, health club with Nautilus equipment, saunas, business center with computer rentals and secretarial services, conference rooms. Forty guest rooms are designed for the disabled; they adjoin standard rooms to accommodate guests traveling with the disabled person.

MODERATE

Copley Square Hotel

47 Huntington Ave., Boston, MA 02116. ☎ **800/225-7062** or 617/536-9000. Fax 617/236-0351. 143 rms, 12 suites. A/C TV TEL. $155–$185 double; $260 suite. Children under 17 stay free in parents' room. Packages and senior discount available. AE, DISC, JCB, MC, V. Parking available in adjacent lot for $16. MBTA: Green Line to Copley.

Although it was built in 1891 and is located in the shadow of the megahotels near Copley Place and the Prudential Center, the seven-story Copley Square Hotel, with attractively decorated rooms, good value, and excellent service, is definitely not overshadowed. Each room has two double beds, a queen-size or king-size bed, and a unique layout. All rooms are equipped with hair dryers, coffeemakers, safes, and phones with modem hookups and guest voice mail. Rooms for nonsmokers are available, and there is a 24-hour currency exchange in the lobby. Guests are treated to afternoon tea and have access to the health club at the nearby Westin Hotel.

This hotel was one of the first in the country to institute an environmental policy, which includes energy and water conservation and waste reduction and recycling. Environmentally sound products are supplied in the guest rooms and are used throughout the hotel.

There are three dining options in the hotel: Pop's Place serves breakfast, and the Original Sports Saloon, a local landmark for its great barbecue, serves lunch and dinner, as does Café Budapest, one of Boston's finest restaurants.

⑤ The MidTown Hotel

220 Huntington Ave., Boston, MA 02115. ☎ **800/343-1177** or 617/262-1000. Fax 617/262-8739. 159 rms. A/C TV TEL. $109–$149 double. Extra person $15. Children under 18 stay free in parents' room. 10% senior discount with AARP card; government employees' discount subject to availability. AE, DC, DISC, MC, V. Free parking. MBTA: Green Line, E train to Prudential.

Even without free parking, this two-story hotel would be a good deal. It's on a busy street within easy walking distance of Symphony Hall, the Museum of Fine Arts, and the Back Bay attractions. The good-sized rooms are bright and attractively outfitted with contemporary furnishings, and some have connecting bedrooms for families. For business travelers, the phones have dataports, and photocopying and fax services are available at the front desk. The heated outdoor pool is open from Memorial Day through Labor Day. Tables of Content, an American cafe, is open from 7am to 10pm.

INEXPENSIVE

Berkeley Residence YWCA

40 Berkeley St., Boston, MA 02116. ☎ **617/482-8850.** Fax 617/482-9692. 200 rms (none with bath). $35 single; $50 double; $60 triple. Long-term stay (4-week minimum) $130 per week, including breakfast and dinner daily. JCB, MC, V. Parking $14 in public lot one block away. MBTA: Green Line to Arlington or Orange Line to Back Bay.

This pleasant, conveniently located hotel/residence for women offers a dining room, patio garden, pianos, a library, and laundry facilities. The rooms are basic, containing little more than a bed, but are clean and comfortable; definitely not luxurious, but not cells either. Passes are available to the pool and exercise room at the nearby YWCA Boston.

Central Branch YMCA

316 Huntington Ave., Boston, MA 02115. ☎ **617/536-7800.** 67–150 rms, depending on season (none with bath). TV. $39 single; $56 double. AE, DISC, MC, V. All rates include breakfast. Parking in nearby lots or on street. MBTA: Green Line, E train to Northeastern.

The Central Branch Y is about 10 minutes from downtown, near Symphony Hall and the Museum of Fine Arts. The gloomy lobby is slated for renovations that should bring it up to the level of the modern (but not air-conditioned) accommodations for men and women 18 years of age and over. Rooms have televisions and maid service, and rates include the use of a pool, gym, weight room, fitness center, and indoor track. There is also a cafeteria on the premises. Luggage and an ID are required for check-in. The Y offers rooms for singles, couples, and families. Call for reservations.

Chandler Inn

26 Chandler St. (at Berkeley St.), Boston, MA 02116. ☎ **800/842-3450** or 617/482-3450. Fax 617/542-3428. 56 rms. A/C TV TEL. Nov–Apr $79 double; May–Oct $99 double. Children under 12 stay free in parents' room. Rates include continental breakfast. AE, CB, DC, DISC, MC, V. Parking available in nearby garages. MBTA: Orange Line to Back Bay.

The Chandler Inn is technically in the South End, near the Boston Center for the Arts, but so convenient to the Back Bay and such a good deal that you won't mind the slightly lower-budget address. The guest rooms were recently redecorated, recarpeted, and, most importantly, air-conditioned. They're still nothing fancy, but if your needs are basic, you'll be fine. And the staff is friendly and helpful. This is a practical choice for bargain-hunters who don't care about a tony address and a lot of extras.

Hostelling International—Boston

12 Hemenway St., Boston, MA 02115. ☎ **617/536-9455.** Fax 617/424-6558. 205 beds. $17 per bed for members; $20 per bed for nonmembers. JCB, MC, V. MBTA: Green Line B, C, or D train to Hynes/ICA.

Located near Symphony Hall, this hostel can accommodate 205 people. There are two dine-in kitchens, 19 bathrooms, and a large common room. The hostel provides a "sheet sleeping sack," or you can bring your own (sleeping bags are not permitted). To get a bed during the summer season you must be a member of Hostelling International—American Youth Hostels. For information and a membership application write to Hostelling International—American Youth Hostels (Dept. 481, 733 15th Street, NW, #840, Washington, DC 20005; ☎ **800/444-6111** or 202/783-6161).

ⓘ Family-Friendly Hotels

The moderately priced chain hotels are probably the ones in the area most accustomed to dealing with young guests, but their higher-end brethren put on a good show.

Boston Park Plaza Hotel & Towers (64 Arlington St., ☎ 617/426-2000) The "Cub Club" can make life a joy for parents. The kids get a coupon book, Red Sox sundaes, environmental gifts, and swan boat rides. They can play in the video-game room or go to a story hour where milk and cookies are served. Picnic lunches/suppers, family movies, and bedtime snacks are also available. And there's a big bag of peanuts for feeding the ducks and swans in the Public Garden. Special family rates with free parking are also available.

Charles Hotel (1 Bennett St., Cambridge, ☎ 617/864-1200) Le Pli Spa, which adjoins the hotel, sets aside time for family swimming. The Harvard Square scavenger hunt is fun, and so is the room service menu, which includes pepperoni pizza. The snack bars are stocked with juice, milk, and cookies. The "Children's Storyline" is a special telephone line that features four bedtime stories for children under 7.

Four Seasons Hotel (200 Boylston St., ☎ 617/338-4400) Kids (and their parents) love the pool and spa and the executive suite, where they can get children's videos for the VCR, milk and cookies delivered by room service, child-size bathrobes, and any needed child accessories. The concierge has food packets for the ducks and squirrels at the Public Garden.

Le Meridien Boston (250 Franklin St., ☎ 617/451-1900) The "Kids Love Boston" weekend program offers parents the chance to book a separate room next to their own for children under 12 for $60 a night (based on availability). Milk and cookies are served when you check in, and meals at the Cafe Fleuri include child-friendly options throughout the weekend.

Ritz-Carlton Hotel (15 Arlington St., ☎ 617/536-5700) This hotel pampers the kids with a video library, games and toys, snacks and beverages, all served up in a "Junior Presidential Suite" for a mere $495 a night. These lucky guests get a stuffed Carlton the Lion, too. The Ritz also has occasional special weekends (a nice way of saying lessons are involved) for young ladies and gentlemen, including "A Weekend of Social Savvy" and "The Junior Chef Debut." At Christmas there's a *Nutcracker* package.

Royal Sonesta Hotel (5 Cambridge Pkwy., Cambridge, ☎ 617/491-3600) Summerfest features supervised programs for children 5 to 12 years old, with complimentary use of bicycles, Polaroid cameras, the health club, and indoor/outdoor pool, boat rides along the Charles River, and unlimited ice cream.

4 Kenmore Square & Environs

Hotels in this area are located near Fenway Park, the hospitals at the Longwood Medical Area, and several colleges and museums. Some are in Boston, some in Brookline, which starts about two blocks beyond Kenmore Square.

EXPENSIVE

Ⓢ Doubletree Guest Suites

400 Soldiers Field Rd., Boston, MA 02134. ☎ **800/222-TREE** or 617/783-0090. Fax 617/783-0897. 310 rms. A/C MINIBAR TV TEL. $169–$229 double. Extra person $20. Children 18 and under stay free in parents' room. Weekend packages from $109 per night. AAA discount available. AE, CB, DC, DISC, JCB, MC, V. Parking $14 Sun–Thurs, $7 Fri–Sat.

This hotel is one of the best deals in town—every unit is a two-room suite with a living room, bedroom, and bath. Business travelers can entertain in their rooms, and families can spread out, making this a good choice for both. Overlooking the Charles River near a Massachusetts Turnpike exit, the hotel isn't in an actual neighborhood, but complimentary van service to and from attractions and business areas in Boston and Cambridge is available.

The suites surround a 15-story sunlit atrium and can be reached via glass elevators. Rooms are large and attractively furnished, and most bedrooms have king-size beds and a writing desk. Living rooms feature full-size sofa beds, a dining table, and a good-sized refrigerator. Each suite has two TVs and three telephones (one in the bathroom).

Dining/Entertainment: Scullers Grille and Scullers Lounge serve meals from 6:30am to 11pm. Scullers Jazz Club has two nightly shows.

Services: Valet service; newspaper delivery; secretarial services; van service.

Facilities: Pay-per-view movies; heated indoor pool; exercise room; whirlpool; sauna; conference rooms; laundry room. Suites for the disabled on each floor.

MODERATE

Best Western Boston/The Inn at Children's Hospital

342 Longwood Ave., Boston, MA 02115. ☎ **800/528-1234** or 617/731-4700. Fax 617/731-6273. TDD 617/731-9088, for the hearing impaired. 152 rms, 14 kitchenette suites. A/C TV TEL. $109–$169 double, $170 suite. Children under 18 stay free in parents' room. Extra person $15. AE, CB, DISC, MC, V. Parking $14 with in/out privileges. MBTA: Green Line, E train to Longwood, or B, C, or D train to Kenmore, then bus to Longwood Ave.

Next to Children's Hospital in the Longwood Medical Area (Beth Israel, Brigham and Women's, and Deaconess hospitals, the Dana-Farber Cancer Institute and the Joslin Diabetes Center are nearby), this six-story hotel is a good base for those with business at the hospitals. It's also near museums, colleges, and Fenway Park, and about 15 minutes from downtown Boston by public transportation.

The guest units are quite large—each has a sitting area—and three-quarters of the rooms are reserved for nonsmokers. Facilities include a restaurant and lounge and meeting rooms, and there's valet laundry service. The hotel is attached to the Longwood Galleria business complex, with a food court, retail stores, and a fitness center available to hotel guests for $12 a day.

Holiday Inn Boston Brookline

1200 Beacon St., Brookline, MA 02146. ☎ **800/HOLIDAY** or 617/277-1200. Fax 617/734-6991. 207 rms. A/C TV TEL. $145–$170 double; $160–$200 suite. Extra person $10. Children under 18 stay free in parents' room. AE, DC, DISC, JCB, MC, V. Free parking. MBTA: Green Line, C train to St. Paul St.

Just 15 minutes from downtown on the subway, this sparkling hotel is built around a colorful atrium with a garden lounge, putting green, sun deck, and a small swimming pool plus whirlpool. Rooms are large and have standard furnishings, and valet laundry service is available. One floor (out of six) is reserved for nonsmokers, and 10 rooms are equipped for disabled guests. The Café on the Green restaurant serves breakfast, lunch, and dinner, and there's a lounge.

Howard Johnson Hotel—Kenmore

575 Commonwealth Ave., Boston, MA 02215. ☎ **800/654-2000** or 617/267-3100. Fax 617/424-1045. 180 rms. A/C TV TEL. $100–$160 double. Children under 18 stay free in parents' room. Extra person $10. Senior and AAA discount available. AE, CB, DC, DISC, JCB, MC, V. Free parking. MBTA: Green Line, B train to Blandford St.

If the location doesn't get you, the pool and free parking might. This eight-story hotel is surrounded by the Boston University campus, with the subway to downtown out front and Kenmore Square and Fenway Park nearby. Rooms are standard-issue Howard Johnson's—comfortable, but nothing fancy—and some are small. The hotel has a glass-enclosed elevator, which goes to the rooftop lounge and provides a good view of the area. The indoor swimming pool and skylit sun deck on the roof are open year-round from 11am to 9pm.

INEXPENSIVE

Anthony's Town House

1085 Beacon St., Brookline, MA 02146. ☎ **617/566-3972**. 12 rms (none with bath). A/C TV. $45–$75 double. Extra person $10. Special weekly rates available. No credit cards. Free on-site parking. MBTA: Green Line, C train to Hawes St. (two stops past Kenmore).

Located one mile from Boston's Kenmore Square, about 10 minutes from downtown by subway, this turn-of-the-century restored four-story brownstone townhouse is listed in the National Register of Historic Places. Each floor has three rooms and a shared bath with enclosed shower. Rooms are decorated with Queen Anne– and Victorian-style furnishings, and the large front rooms have bay windows with comfortable lounge chairs. *Note:* Rates listed above cover all seasons. Rates during most of the year are generally on the higher end, dipping slightly in the dead of winter.

Howard Johnson Lodge Fenway

1271 Boylston St., Boston, MA 02215. ☎ 800/654-2000 or 617/267-8300. Fax 617/267-2763. 94 rms. A/C TV TEL. $85–$123 double. Extra person $10. Senior and AAA discount and special family packages. Children under 18 stay free in parents' room. AE, CB, DC, DISC, JCB, MC, V. Free parking. MBTA: Green Line, B, C, or D train to Kenmore; 10-minute walk.

This is as close to Fenway Park as you can get without buying a ticket. If you're not visiting during baseball season, this motel on a busy street in a commercial-residential neighborhood is convenient to the Back Bay colleges, the Museum of Fine Arts, and the Isabella Stewart Gardner Museum. When the Red Sox are playing, guests contend with crowded sidewalks and raucous baseball fans who flood the area. There's an outdoor pool, open 9am to 7pm in the summer, and an Italian restaurant, Pranzáre Ristorante, that has a popular lounge. Some rooms are outfitted with a microwave oven and a refrigerator.

Longwood Inn

123 Longwood Ave., Brookline, MA 02146. ☎ **617/566-8615**. Fax 617/738-1070. 22 rms (17 with bath). A/C. May 1–Oct 31 $59–$69 double; Nov 1–Apr 30 $54–$64 double. 1-bedroom apt (sleeps four plus) $425 week. No credit cards. Free parking. MBTA: Green Line, D train to Longwood Ave.

Located in a residential area near the Boston-Brookline border three blocks from Boston, this three-story Victorian guesthouse offers comfortable accommodations at modest rates. Guests have the use of a fully equipped kitchen, coin-operated washer and dryer, common dining room, and TV lounge. Telephones are in the lobby. A nearby park offers tennis courts, a running track, and a children's playground. Public transportation is easily accessible, and the Longwood Medical Area is close by.

5   Cambridge

A suburb so close to Boston that they're usually thought of as a unit, Cambridge has its own appeal, its own attractions, its own colleges, and its own excellent hotels. If your trip involves more than just visiting Boston, Cambridge is a good base for day trips, and when you get back to the hotel, you'll still have plenty to do. The MBTA Red Line links Cambridge and Boston, and some hotels provide shuttle service. As in Boston, getting a room during the May–June college graduation season can sometimes be difficult.

VERY EXPENSIVE

✪ The Charles Hotel

1 Bennett St., Cambridge, MA 02138. ☎ **800/882-1818** outside MA or 617/864-1200. Fax 617/864-5715. 252 rms, 45 suites. A/C MINIBAR TV TEL. $239–$259 double; $325–$1,500 suite. Children under 18 stay free in parents' room. Weekend packages available. AE, CB, DC, DISC, JCB, MC, V. Parking $18. MBTA: Red Line to Harvard.

The Charles Hotel is a curious phenomenon—an instant classic. The nine-story brick hotel a block from Harvard Square has been *the* place to stay in Cambridge since it opened in 1985. Much of its fame derives from its excellent restaurants, jazz bar, and day spa, and the service is, if anything, equally exalted.

Antique blue-and-white New England quilts, handcrafted between 1865 and 1885, hang in the lobby's oak staircase and at the entrance to each floor. In the guest rooms, the style is contemporary country, with custom-designed adaptations of early American Shaker furniture and down quilts. Bathrooms are equipped with telephones, TVs, hair dryers, and scales. All rooms have large windows that open, dataports, and state-of-the-art Bose wave radios equipped with powerful speakers for true audiophiles. And it wouldn't be Cambridge if your intellectual needs went unfulfilled—you can order books over the phone, and a Charles staffer will pick them up at the WordsWorth discount bookstore and bill your room.

There are five great weekend packages, including a workout weekend for two with a full day of pampering at the spa for about $500. The $1,000 spa weekend includes spa and salon treatments and gourmet low-calorie meals.

Dining/Entertainment: Rialto, one of the best restaurants in greater Boston, serves Mediterranean cuisine by award-winning chef Jody Adams. Henrietta's Table offers New England country cooking at breakfast, lunch, dinner, and Sunday buffet brunch. The Regattabar features live jazz every night.

Services: Concierge, 24-hour room service, laundry service, turndown service, twice-daily maid service, valet parking.

Facilities: Pay-per-view movies; glass-enclosed pool, Jacuzzi, sun terrace, and exercise room at the Well Bridge Health and Fitness Center. Beauty treatments are available at the European-style Le Pli Day Spa. Facilities for teleconferencing. Seven floors for nonsmokers; 13 rooms for the disabled; rooms with special amenities for women travelers.

EXPENSIVE

Hyatt Regency Cambridge

575 Memorial Dr., Cambridge, MA 02139. ☎ **800/233-1234** or 617/492-1234. Fax 617/491-6906. 469 rms. A/C TV TEL. $154–$239 double. Suites $400–$575. Extra person $25. Children under 18 stay free in parents' room. Weekend packages available. AE, DC, DISC, JCB, MC, V. Valet parking $16; self-parking $14.

Cambridge Accommodations

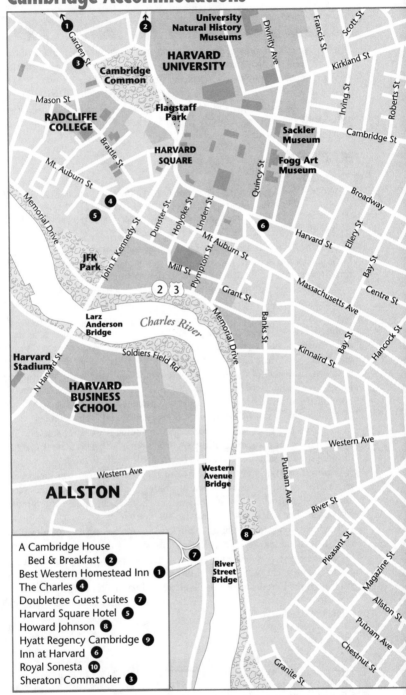

A Cambridge House
  Bed & Breakfast **2**
Best Western Homestead Inn **1**
The Charles **4**
Doubletree Guest Suites **7**
Harvard Square Hotel **5**
Howard Johnson **8**
Hyatt Regency Cambridge **9**
Inn at Harvard **6**
Royal Sonesta **10**
Sheraton Commander **3**

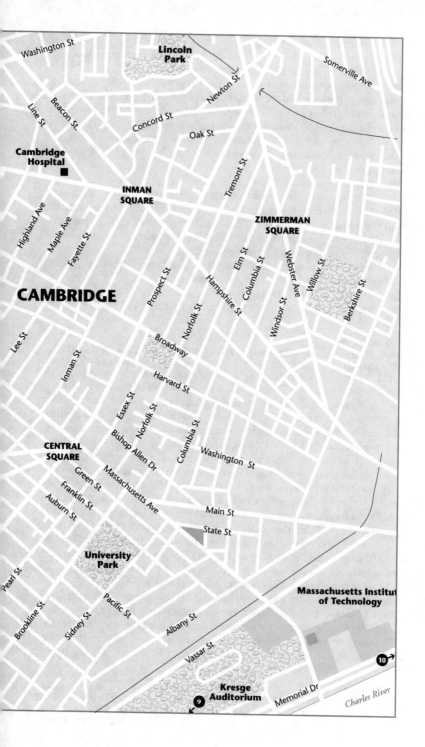

This dramatic hotel, a prominent feature of the Cambridge skyline, is just as eye-catching inside. The terraced red-brick structure across the street from the Charles River encloses a 16-story atrium complete with diamond-shaped glass elevators, fountains, trees, and balconies. Rooms are nicely appointed, and some have breathtaking views of the river and the Boston skyline. Families are especially welcome. There are special reduced room rates for parents whose children sleep in a different room, and adult's and children's bicycles are available for rental.

The Hyatt Regency is about 10 minutes from downtown Boston and especially convenient for those visiting colleges, since it's halfway between Harvard and MIT and across the bridge from Boston University.

Dining/Entertainment: Jonah's Seafood Cafe, open to the atrium on one side and to a view of the river on the other, serves breakfast, lunch, dinner, and Sunday brunch. On the rooftop, the revolving, glass-enclosed Spinnaker restaurant serves dinner and Sunday brunch, and offers drinks and dancing until 12:30am during the week, 1:30am on Friday and Saturday. The Pallysadoe Sports Bar features billiard tables, darts, board games, and pinball machines.

Services: Concierge; shuttle service to points of interest; babysitting; currency exchange; laundry/valet service; room service; car rental service.

Facilities: Pay-per-view movies; junior Olympic-size swimming pool; full health club with steam room, sauna, and whirlpool. Floor for nonsmokers; 23 rooms for the disabled.

The Inn at Harvard

1201 Massachusetts Ave., Cambridge, MA 02138. ☎ **800/458-5886** or 617/491-2222. Fax 617/491-6520. 109 rms, 4 suites. A/C TV TEL. $165–$249 double; $450 presidential suite. Extra person $10. Children 18 and under stay free in parents' room. Senior, AAA, and AARP discount and special packages available. AE, CB, DC, MC, V. Parking $18. MBTA: Red Line to Harvard.

At first glance, the Inn at Harvard looks almost like a dormitory. It's a stone's throw from Harvard Yard at the intersection of Massachusetts Avenue and Quincy Street, and its red brick and Georgian-style architecture would fit nicely on campus. Step inside, though, and there's no mistaking it for anything other than an upscale hotel, popular with business travelers and university visitors. The four-story, skylit atrium opens from the "living room," where you'll find antique tables mixed with contemporary furniture, bookshelves stocked with current periodicals, newspapers, and Harvard University Press publications, and a small, upscale restaurant serving breakfast and dinner. (Guests can use the nearby Faculty Club for lunch.)

Guest rooms have cherry furniture and are elegantly decorated in neutral tones, and each room has a lounge chair or two armchairs around a table, windows that open, and an original painting from the Fogg Art Museum. Some have dormer windows and window seats. There are two phones with voice mail in each room, one of which has computer modem hookups. All rooms have night-lights.

Dining/Entertainment: The atrium restaurant serves seasonal New England fare.

Services: Business services with fax, courier, typing, copying, and package receiving and shipping; complimentary newspaper delivery; free shoeshine; room service.

Facilities: Pay-per-view movies; two floors for nonsmokers; six wheelchair-accessible rooms; safe-deposit boxes; backgammon and chess tables in the atrium library.

Royal Sonesta Hotel

5 Cambridge Pkwy., Cambridge, MA 02142. ☎ **800/SONESTA** or 617/491-3600. Fax 617/661-5956. 400 rms, 28 suites. A/C MINIBAR TV TEL. $185–$235 double; $275–$635 suite. Children under 18 stay free in parents' room. AE, CB, DC, DISC, JCB, MC, V. Parking $15. MBTA: Green Line to Lechmere; 10-minute walk.

This hotel is in a curious location: It's close to only a few things, but it's convenient to everything. Across the street is the CambridgeSide Galleria mall, and the Boston Museum of Science is around the corner on the bridge to Boston (which is closer than Harvard Square). In the other direction, MIT is a 10-minute walk. Original contemporary artwork (including work by Andy Warhol and Frank Stella) is displayed throughout the public spaces, as well as in some guest rooms. Most rooms have a lovely view of the Charles River or the city. Everything is custom designed, with decorative furnishings, living-room and bedroom combinations, and luxurious bathrooms. Each room is equipped with a safe. Business-class rooms have personal computers, fax machines, and multiline phones. The hotel has seasonal promotions, such as free ice cream during the summer, with special rates, giveaways for children, and events for adults.

Dining/Entertainment: Davio's restaurant serves breakfast, lunch, and dinner and has an outdoor patio overlooking the Charles River that's great for warm-weather dining. The Gallery Cafe is casual.

Services: Room service (Sun–Thurs 6am–1am, Fri–Sat 6am–2am); baby-sitting service; secretarial services; courtesy van service to Boston and Cambridge.

Facilities: Heated indoor/outdoor pool with retractable roof; well-equipped health club; conference rooms. Rooms for nonsmokers and the disabled are available.

Sheraton Commander Hotel

16 Garden St., Cambridge, MA 02138. ☎ **800/325-3535** or 617/547-4800. Fax 617/868-8322. 175 rms, 5 suites. A/C MINIBAR TV TEL. $165–$225 double; $225–$375 suite. Extra person $20. Children under 18 stay free in parents' room. AE, CB, DC, DISC, JCB, MC, V. Free parking. MBTA: Red Line to Harvard.

In the heart of the historic district of Cambridge, this six-story hotel opened in 1927, and it's exactly what you'd expect of a traditional hostelry a stone's throw from the Harvard campus. The colonial-style decor begins in the elegant lobby and extends to the guest rooms, which aren't huge but are attractively furnished. Each unique room features electronic locks, in-room coffeemakers, and phones with dataports and voice mail. The Executive Level offers additional amenities and a private lounge. Some rooms have refrigerators and whirlpools.

Dining/Entertainment: The 16 Garden Street Restaurant serves breakfast, lunch, dinner, and Sunday brunch. The 16 Garden Street Cafe serves lighter fare throughout the afternoon and evening.

Services: Concierge; room service until 11pm; valet parking.

Facilities: Pay-per-view movies; small fitness center; sundeck; conference rooms; laundry room.

MODERATE

A Cambridge House Bed & Breakfast Inn

2218 Massachusetts Ave., Cambridge, MA 02140. ☎ **800/232-9989** or 617/491-6300 in U.S. and Canada, 800/96-2079 in the United Kingdom. Fax 617/868-2848. 14 rms (10 with bath). A/C TV TEL. $109–$225 double. Extra person $35. Rates include breakfast. AE, DISC, MC, V. Free parking. MBTA: Red Line to Porter.

A Cambridge House is a beautifully restored 1892 colonial home listed in the National Register of Historic Places. The three-story building is on a busy stretch of Cambridge's main street (Mass. Ave.), set back from the sidewalk by a beautiful lawn. Rooms are warmly decorated with Waverly fabrics and antiques. Most have fireplaces and four-poster canopy beds with down comforters. Complimentary beverages and fresh pastries are served by the fireplace in the library or parlor. And a full breakfast, also complimentary, prepared by a professionally trained chef, is offered every morning. There's something different each day—omelets, crêpes, waffles, or fresh fruit. Every evening complimentary wine and cheese are also offered. Smoking is not allowed at the inn.

Best Western Homestead Inn

220 Alewife Brook Pkwy., Cambridge, MA 02138. ☎ **800/528-1234** or 617/491-8000. Fax 617/491-4932. 69 rms. A/C TV TEL. Mid-Mar–Oct $109–$154 double; Nov–mid-Mar $79–$119 double. Extra person $10. Rates include continental breakfast and may be higher during special events. Children under 12 stay free in parents' room. AE, CB, DC, DISC, JCB, MC, V. Free parking. MBTA: Red Line to Alewife, 10-minute walk.

The gritty commercial neighborhood is nothing to write home about, but this four-story motel is comfortable and convenient for motorists. Guest rooms are spacious, with contemporary or reproduction colonial furnishings, and at least one floor up from the busy street. There's an indoor pool with a Jacuzzi, and a $2^1/_2$-mile jogging trail around Fresh Pond is across the street. Laundry service (weekdays only) and rental-car pickup and dropoff are available. There's a restaurant next door, and a shopping center with a 10-screen movie theater nearby. It's about a fifteen-minute drive or a thirty-minute ride on the "T" to Boston from the Homestead Inn.

Harvard Square Hotel

110 Mount Auburn St., Cambridge, MA 02138. ☎ **800/458-5886** or 617/864-5200. Fax 617/864-2409. 73 rms. A/C TV TEL. $125–$160 single or double. Children 16 and under stay free in parents' room. Corporate, AAA, and AARP rates available. AE, DC, DISC, JCB, MC, V. Parking $15. MBTA: Red Line to Harvard.

Smack in the middle of Harvard Square, this hotel is a great favorite with visiting parents and budget-conscious business travelers. In early 1996 the six-story brick hotel was completely refurbished and renamed (it used to be the Harvard Manor House), and the guest rooms were redecorated. Some rooms overlook Harvard Square, and the atmosphere is comfortable and unpretentious. Fax and copy services and complimentary newspapers (weekdays only) are available at the front desk, and there's same-day laundry service. Guests have dining privileges at the Inn at Harvard—like the Harvard Square Hotel, managed by Doubletree Hotels Corporation—and the Harvard Faculty Club.

Howard Johnson Hotel Cambridge

777 Memorial Dr., Cambridge, MA 02139. ☎ **800/654-2000** or 617/492-7777. Fax 617/492-6038. 205 rms. A/C TV TEL. $85–$155 double. Extra person $10. Free cribs. Children under 18 stay free in parents' room. Senior (with AARP card) and AAA discounts available. AE, CB, DC, DISC, JCB, MC, V. Free parking.

An attractive, modern hotel with a swimming pool and sun deck, this 16-story tower is near the major college campuses and the Massachusetts Turnpike, and just a 10-minute drive from downtown Boston. Each room has a picture window, giving guests who are up high enough a panoramic view of the Boston skyline. Rooms are large, with modern furnishings, and some have a private balcony. Prices vary with the size of the room, the floor, and the view. Valet laundry service and conference rooms are available.

Also at the hotel is the Bisuteki Japanese Steak House, where dinners are prepared at the table in the hibachi style of "firebowl" cooking.

6   At the Airport

Harborside Hyatt Conference Center & Hotel

101 Harborside Dr., Boston, MA 02129. ☎ **800/233-1284** or 617/568-1234. Fax 617/568-6080. 270 rms. A/C TV TEL. $220 double. Children under 12 stay free in parents' room. AE, CB, DC, DISC, JCB, MC, V. Parking $7 maximum for overnight guests. MBTA: Blue Line to Airport, then take shuttle bus. By car, follow signs to Logan Airport and take Harborside Dr. past the car-rental area and tunnel entrance.

This striking 14-story waterfront hotel, which opened in 1993, has unobstructed views of the harbor and city skyline. The turret at one end of the building is a light-house whose light is controlled by the Logan Airport control tower so it doesn't interfere with runway lights. Inside, fiber-optic stars change color in the skydome ceiling in the reception area. Public spaces are accented with nautical memorabilia, and the first-class guest rooms have all the amenities you'd expect from a deluxe hotel, plus such extras as irons and ironing boards in each room, luxury baths, fine wood furnishings, and excellent views.

Dining/Entertainment: The restaurant serves breakfast, lunch, and dinner. Floor-to-ceiling windows allow for spectacular views.

Services: Valet laundry; water taxi to Rowes Wharf from the hotel dock; 24-hour airport shuttle service.

Facilities: Pay-per-view movies; health club with indoor lap pool, whirlpool, and sauna; business center; conference rooms.

7   Highway High Spots

Staying outside of town can save you some money, some aggravation, or both. Here are three suburban options—two in Dorchester off the Southeast Expressway (Exit 12 southbound, Exit 13 northbound), close to the Kennedy Library; one at Exit 27A off Route 128.

⑤ Susse Chalet Boston Inn

900 Morrissey Blvd., Boston, MA 02122. ☎ **800/258-1980** or 617/287-9200. Fax 617/282-2365. 106 rms. A/C TV TEL. $64.70–$81.70 double. Extra person $5. AE, CB, DC, DISC, MC, V. Free parking.

Under the same management as the Susse Chalet Boston Lodge (see below), this attractive inn also has high standards and low prices. It's a four-story building with large guest rooms, including rooms for nonsmokers and the disabled. All double-bedded rooms have a reclining chair, and each room is equipped with a mini-refrigerator. A suite on the second floor has three skylights, two windows, two double beds that can be folded into a wall niche, a sofa bed, and a wet bar. It's a good choice for a large family of up to six people. The current rate is between $100 and $125.

There is a seasonal outdoor swimming pool, and coin-operated washers and dryers are available for guest use. Just across the lot is Boston Bowl, a popular recreational facility with 10 pocket billiard tables, 20 candlepin lanes, 30 tenpin lanes, and a video-game room, open 24 hours. The adjoining Swiss House Restaurant (☎ 617/825-3800) is open for breakfast, lunch, and dinner.

Susse Chalet Boston Lodge

800 Morrissey Blvd., Boston, MA 02122. ☎ **800/258-1980** or 617/287-9100. Fax 617/265-9287. 175 rms. A/C TV TEL. $61.70–$79.70 double. Extra person $5. AE, CB, DC, DISC, MC, V. Free parking.

This chalet-style motor lodge has three floors of rooms. The single-bedded room is the same size as the double, and each room is equipped with a mini-refrigerator. An outdoor swimming pool is open in the warmer months. The facilities in the adjacent Susse Chalet Boston Inn (see above) are also available to Motor Lodge guests.

The Westin Hotel, Waltham

70 3rd Ave., Waltham, MA 02154. ☎ **800/228-3000** or 617/290-5600. Fax 617/290-5626. 346 rms, 33 suites. A/C MINIBAR TV TEL. $129–$215 double. Extra person $20. Children stay free in parents' room. Weekend packages and senior and AAA discounts available. AE, CB, DC, DISC, JCB, MC, V. Free parking.

This dramatic blue-glass structure is on a hilltop overlooking Route 128, centrally located for travelers with business in the surrounding high-tech heartland. The guest rooms in the eight-floor tower are decorated with light-colored fabrics and rich woods. All rooms have two telephones, hair dryers, ironing boards and irons, business-size desks, message retrieval, express checkout service via in-room cable TV, and windows that open. There's an Executive Business Center where secretarial services and business equipment rentals are available; to conduct business on a smaller scale, Guest Office rooms offer amenities such as in-room printer-fax-copiers, office supplies, and free access to toll-free, local, and credit card calls. Hourly shuttle service to Logan Airport ($10 per person), currency exchange, and 24-hour room service are available.

There are four floors for nonsmokers, 18 rooms for the disabled, and a health club with an indoor pool, whirlpool, sauna, and fitness room.

Vacationing guests will find the Westin convenient for driving to Boston (25 minutes), Lexington and Concord (15 minutes), Rockport and Gloucester (40 minutes on Route 128), and Sturbridge Village (one hour on the Massachusetts Turnpike).

The hotel restaurant, the Vineyard Café, serves breakfast, lunch, dinner and Sunday brunch. The Lobby Lounge offers jazz entertainment in the evenings, and Circuits is a pub and nightclub.

8 Nearby Resorts

Complete vacation packages are available at these resort hotels, all within a half-hour drive of the city.

Colonial Hilton and Resort

427 Walnut St., Lynnfield, MA 01940. ☎ **800/HILTONS** or 617/245-9300. Fax 617/245-0842. 280 rms. A/C TV TEL. $129–$169 double. Extra person $10. Children stay free in parents' room. Senior discounts and special packages available. AE, DC, DISC, MC, V. Free parking.

Just off I-95 on the Lynnfield–Wakefield border, this 220-acre luxury resort hotel offers an 18-hole golf course, indoor and outdoor tennis courts, racquetball courts, indoor basketball court, an Olympic-size swimming pool, and health club. The largest and most luxurious rooms are in the 11-story tower. On a hilltop overlooking the golf course is the Colonial at Lynnfield Restaurant, specializing in prime rib and New England fare; there's also another casual restaurant. Rooms for nonsmokers and the disabled are available.

Stouffer Renaissance Bedford Hotel

44 Middlesex Tpke., Bedford, MA 01730. ☎ **800/HOTELS-1** or 617/275-5500. Fax 617/275-3042. 285 rms. A/C MINIBAR TV TEL. Sun–Thurs $170–$200 double; Fri–Sat $125–$155

double. Children 18 and under stay free in parents' room. Senior discounts and weekend packages available. AE, CB, DC, DISC, JCB, MC, V. Free parking. Directions: North of I-95 on the Middlesex Turnpike (exit 32B) for 2.5 miles.

This three-story hotel is convenient to the sights in Lexington and Concord, and there's plenty to do without leaving the grounds. The country lodge–style building on landscaped, wooded grounds has a fitness center, indoor pool, whirlpool, sauna, and indoor and outdoor tennis courts. A restaurant and lounge are in the hotel, which neatly makes the transition from a primarily business destination during the week to a family resort on weekends.

The larger rooms have king-size beds; a few units have twin beds. Rooms for nonsmokers are available, and 11 rooms have special facilities for the disabled. Several suites have sofas and conference tables for meetings, and all rooms have in-room movies. Complimentary morning paper and coffee are brought to your room with your wake-up call; there is also 24-hour room service.

Tara's Ferncroft Conference Resort

50 Ferncroft Rd., Danvers, MA 01923. ☎ **800/THE-TARA** or 508/777-2500. Fax 508/750-7959. 367 rms, 17 suites. A/C TV TEL. $129–$149 double; $175–$550 suite. Extra person $15. Children stay free in parents' room. Weekend packages available. 20% senior discount for AARP members. AE, CB, DC, DISC, MC, V. Free parking.

This is a great spot for a golfing vacation. The 18-hole championship course was designed by Robert Trent Jones, and the rooms located high above Route 1 (at I-95) have a view of either the golf course or the surrounding countryside. The eight-story hotel is 30 minutes from Boston, about 20 minutes from Gloucester and Rockport, and even closer to Salem.

All rooms have a sofa, desk, heat controls, coffeemaker, and either double or king-size beds. A number of rooms at the top of the Tara offer additional amenities, including whirlpools, and are priced slightly higher. There are also floors for nonsmokers and 20 rooms for the disabled.

If golf isn't your game, facilities are available for other sports, including tennis and racquetball. There are an indoor and an outdoor pool, and a health and fitness center with cardiovascular room, Nautilus room, aerobics studio, sauna, and masseuse. Sports enthusiasts might also enjoy cross-country skiing, ice-skating, and sledding.

The Ferncroft Grille features steak and seafood specialties, and Bogey's Restaurant and Pub serves light fare.

6 Dining

When we first tackled the restaurant section of this travel guide, a Bostonian friend laughed and said, "From 1940 to 1970, you could have used the same book every year—now you could probably do a new one every six months or so." The restaurant scene in Boston is one of the most dynamic in the country, with hot spots opening and former hot spots closing almost as often as blockbuster movies, and top chefs and their protégés turning up everywhere.

One ingredient found at all of the city's restaurants—trendy and classic, expensive and cheap, typical American (whatever that is) and ethnic—is seafood. Bostonians have turned to the ocean for sustenance since before there even were Bostonians, and Ipswich and Essex clams, Atlantic lobsters, Wellfleet oysters, mussels, cod, haddock, and flounder are available in every imaginable form. If you consider yourself a chowder fan but have never sampled any in Boston, the New England recipe available here (which employs ultra-fresh clams) will be a revelation.

You'll also find vegetarian offerings on almost every menu. The days when herbivores had to settle for a salad are gone, and places where you have to cobble together a vegetarian meal out of side dishes are vastly outnumbered by restaurants (many of them ethnic) that wouldn't think of skimping on meatless dishes. Another recent trend has seen restaurants focusing on two or more cuisines, side-by-side or in combination. One of them is usually French—classical training is classical training—and the influences of Asian flavors and textures, in particular, can be seen on many menus. For overtly ethnic food, you'll find many little restaurants that serve a variety of cuisines, from Argentine to Russian to Persian to Polynesian.

The guiding thought for this chapter, without regard to price, was: "If this were your only meal in Boston, would you be delighted with it?" All of the restaurants listed fit, in one way or another, under the wide umbrella of "delightful." They're divided by neighborhood and listed alphabetically under the following main-course price ranges: **Very Expensive,** $18 to $35; **Expensive,** $12 to $20; and **Moderate,** $8 to $15. Wine, appetizers, soups, salad, dessert, and coffee can easily make the total bill double, and in the top restaurants, dinner for two may come to more than $125. The **Inexpensive** category includes restaurants charging around $8 for a meal. Note that the price of lobster at market and at most restaurants fluctuates daily.

At restaurants that take reservations, it's always a good idea to make them, particularly for dinner, and for lunch as well at the better restaurants. A quirk of Bostonian restaurant-goers is their apparent reluctance to go out for dinner if it's not Friday or Saturday. If you're flexible about when you indulge in fine cuisine and when you go for pizza and a movie, opt for the low-budget option on weekends and pamper yourself on a weeknight.

1 Best Bets

- **Best Spot for a Romantic Dinner:** The soft lighting, well-spaced tables, and cushy surroundings at **Icarus** (3 Appleton St. ☎ **617/426-1790**) make it the perfect place for trysting. And because it's underground, there's no view to distract you from your beloved.

- **Best Spot for a Business Lunch:** Numerous business deals are finalized at the private clubs in town, but for deal-making out in the open, put on your three-piece suit and head for **Julien** (in Le Meridien Boston, 250 Franklin St. ☎ **617/451-1900**). It's always been a prime business location—the building used to be a bank.

- **Best Spot for a Celebration:** Something about **Cornucopia on the Wharf** (100 Atlantic Ave. ☎ **617/367-0300**) makes people think of proposing a toast—calmly at lunch, raucously at dinner. And if your good news is of a personal nature, you can even arrange to party in private in an upstairs room.

- **Best Decor:** The luxurious banquettes, gorgeous paintings and flowers, and picture windows overlooking the Public Garden make **Aujourd'hui** (in the Four Seasons Hotel, 200 Boylston St. ☎ **617/451-1392**) feel like an extremely elegant treehouse.

- **Best View:** The **Bay Tower** (60 State St. ☎ **617/723-1666**) dining room isn't the highest in Boston, but its view is one of the most impressive. From the palatial 33rd floor, everyone in the room (not just people near the windows) can see what's afoot on the waterfront and watch planes taking off and landing at Logan Airport. A close second is the view from 52 stories up at **Top of the Hub** (800 Boylston St., Prudential Center. ☎ **617/536-1775**), especially at dusk.

- **Best Wine List:** It's nearly impossible to single out just one noteworthy element of the **L'Espalier** (30 Gloucester St. ☎ **617/262-3023**) experience, but here goes. Much like the food, the offerings on the wine list seem to have been chosen just for you.

- **Best Value:** The magical words "half price" make the generous portions of hearty Italian food at lunch every day at **Pagliuca's** (14 Parmenter St. ☎ **617/367-1504**) the best deal in Boston.

- **Best for Kids:** The wood-fired brick ovens of the **Bertucci's** (Faneuil Hall Marketplace, ☎ **617/227-7889** and Harvard Square, 21 Brattle St., Cambridge, ☎ **617/864-4748**) chain are magnets for little eyes, and the pizza that comes out of them is equally enthralling. Picky parents will be happy here, too.

- **Best American Cuisine:** Regular old American food is taken to a new level at the **Grill & Cue** (256 Commercial St. ☎ **617/227-4454**), where skillful grilling is only part of the kitchen's superb repertoire.

- **Best Chinese Cuisine:** It's hard to go wrong at any busy restaurant in Chinatown, and especially hard on Beach Street near Harrison Avenue, where **Chau Chow** (52 Beach St. ☎ **617/426-6666**) and **Grand Chau Chow** (45 Beach St. ☎ **617/292-5166**) face one another. Chau Chow is no-frills; Grand Chau Chow a little more, well, grand—both are excellent.

- **Best Continental Cuisine:** In the same way that clichés become clichés because they're true, Continental cuisine becomes classic because it's delicious. Put this theory to the test at **Café Budapest** (in the Copley Square Hotel, 90 Exeter St. ☎ **617/266-1979**), where the cuisine is Hungarian and delectable.

- **Best French Cuisine:** At **Maison Robert** (45 School St. ☎ **617/227-3370**), the atmosphere is as impressive as the food. You won't find better French cuisine anywhere in the city—in fact, when visiting French chefs come to town, Maison Robert is their first choice.

- **Best Italian Cuisine:** "Cuisine" suggests a certain refinement, and **Mamma Maria** (3 North Sq. ☎ **617/523-0077**) has it. The restaurant offers remarkable Northern Italian fare in a part of town renowned for its Italian food, the red-sauce paradise of the North End.

- **Best Seafood: Legal Sea Foods** (800 Boylston St., in the Prudential Center. ☎ **617/266-6800**) does one thing and does it exceptionally well. It's a chain for a great reason—people can't get enough of the freshest seafood in the area.

- **Best Steakhouse:** The food, service, and atmosphere at **Grill 23 & Bar** (161 Berkeley St. ☎ **617/542-2255**) will turn the head of the most dedicated vegetarian. Whether you eat meat twice a day or twice a year, you'll want to return soon.

- **Best Pizza:** Considering how well pizza travels, it's surprising that the branches of **Pizzeria Regina** throughout the Boston area can't seem to get it quite right. For the real thing, head to the North End original (10$^1/_2$ Thacher St.; ☎ **617/227-0765**) and be patient. It's worth the wait.

- **Best Late-Night Dining:** Maybe that should be *only* late-night dining. If you're starving in the wee hours, the **Tasty Sandwich Shop** (2A John F. Kennedy St., Cambridge; ☎ **617/354-9016**) is always open. Boston's **Blue Diner** (150 Kneeland St.; ☎ **617/338-4639**) keeps round-the-clock hours on weekends, and if you have a car, you'll find an **International House of Pancakes** in Brighton (1850 Soldiers Field Rd.; ☎ **617/787-0533**) that's busier at 3am than it is at 3pm.

- **Best Outdoor Dining:** Good food in a comfortable open-air setting sounds easy but apparently is quite difficult to provide, judging by the number of restaurants that can't manage both. Have no fear: The planets were perfectly aligned when the terrace at **Upstairs at the Pudding** (10 Holyoke St., Cambridge, ☎ **617/864-1933**) opened, for an excellent al fresco dining experience.

- **Best People-Watching:** Take the genteel route and park yourself in the **Lobby Lounge** (10 Huntington Ave., ☎ **617/262-9600**) of the Westin Hotel. Or check out the freak show in and around the Harvard Square **Au Bon Pain** (right near the Harvard Square "T" station).

- **Best Afternoon Tea:** Afternoon tea at the **Ritz-Carlton** (15 Arlington St. ☎ **617/536-5700**) is an elegant and traditional affair. A harpist plays quietly in the background while diners enjoy scones and Devonshire cream (among other treats).

- **Best Brunch:** The insane displays at many of the top hotels are well worth the monetary and caloric compromises, but if you're looking for a delicious meal that won't destroy your budget and waistline, join the throng outside the **S&S Restaurant** (1334 Cambridge St., Inman Sq. ☎ **617/354-0777**).

- **Best for Pre-Theater Dinner:** The whole restaurant is such a trendy scene that it's easy to forget you can eat at the bar at **Biba** (272 Boylston St. ☎ **617/426-7878**) and be on your way before the air-kissing upstairs really gets going.

- **Best Picnic Fare:** On the way to a concert or movie on the Esplanade, stop for food to go at **Figs** (42 Charles St.; ☎ **617/742-3447**), a miniscule pizzeria that's an offshoot of its sister restaurant, Olives. The upscale fare isn't cheap, but you get what you pay for—and you get to eat long, long before the people waiting for a table.

- **Best Barbecue:** The **Original Sports Saloon** (in the Copley Square Hotel, 47 Huntington Ave. ☎ **617/536-9000**) is about the size of a large bus and perilously close to a Hungarian restaurant (Cafe Budapest). Somehow it still cranks out the best barbecue in town, which is also available to go.

- **Best Raw Bar:** After just a few moments of gobbling fresh seafood and being hypnotized by the shuckers at **Ye Olde Union Oyster House** (41 Union St.

☎ 617/227-2750), you might find yourself feeling sorry for the people who wound up with the pearls instead of the oysters.

- **Best Places for a Classic Boston Experience:** There are two classic Boston dining experiences: Blue blood, at **Locke-Ober** (3 and 4 Winter Pl. ☎ **617/542-1340),** and populist, at **Durgin-Park** (340 Faneuil Hall Marketplace. ☎ **617/227-2038**).
- **Best, Period:** If you have only one meal during your visit, have it at **Rialto** (One Bennett St., in the Charles Hotel. ☎ **617/661-5050**) in Cambridge.

2   Restaurants by Cuisine

AFGHAN

The Helmand (Cambridge, *M*)

AMERICAN

Bartley's Burger Cottage
  (Cambridge, *I*)
The Bay Tower (Faneuil Hall
  Marketplace, *VE*)
Bob the Chef's (South End, *I*)
Cornucopia on the Wharf
  (on the Waterfront, *E*)
Durgin-Park Inc. (Faneuil Hall
  Marketplace, *M*)
The Grill & Cue (Waterfront, *E*)
Grill 23 & Bar (Public Garden, *VE*)
The Harvest Restaurant
  (Cambridge, *VE*)
Jacob Wirth Company
  (Theater District, *M*)
L'Espalier (Back Bay, *VE*)
Locke-Ober (Downtown
  Crossing, *VE*)
The Original Sports Saloon
  (Copley Square, *I*)
Rowes Wharf Restaurant
  (on the Waterfront, *VE*)
Salamander (Cambridge, *VE*)
Ye Olde Union Oyster House
  (Faneuil Hall Marketplace, *M*)

BARBECUE

The Original Sports Saloon
  (Copley Square, *I*)

BRAZILIAN

Pampas Churrascaria (Cambridge, *E*)

CAMBODIAN

The Elephant Walk (Brookline, *M*)

CANTONESE

Chau Chow (Chinatown, *M*)
East Ocean City (Chinatown, *M*)
Grand Chau Chow (Chinatown, *M*)

CARIBBEAN

Chez Henri (Cambridge, *E*)
Green Street Grill (Cambridge, *M*)

CHINESE

Buddha's Delight (Chinatown, *I*)

CONTINENTAL

Botolph's on Tremont
  (South End, *M*)
Parker's Restaurant
  (Government Center, *VE*)
Plaza Dining Room
  (Copley Square, *VE*)
Top of the Hub (Back Bay, *E*)
Upstairs at the Pudding
  (Cambridge, *VE*)

DELI

Rubin's (Brookline, *M*)
S&S Restaurant (Cambridge, *M*)

ECLECTIC

Biba Food Hall (Public Garden, *E*)
Hamersley's Bistro (South End, *M*)
Icarus (South End, *M*)
Les Zygomates (Financial District, *M*)
Olives (Charlestown, *E*)
Providence (Brookline, *E*)

FRENCH

Ambrosia on Huntington
  (Back Bay, *VE*)
Chez Henri (Cambridge, *E*)
The Elephant Walk (Brookline, *M*)

Key to abbreviations: *VE* = Very Expensive; *E* = Expensive; *M* = Moderate; *I* = Inexpensive

Julien (Near Faneuil Hall, *VE*)
Maison Robert (Government
   Center, *VE*)
Rialto (Cambridge, *E*)
Ritz-Carlton Dining Room
   (Public Garden, *VE*)

GERMAN

Jacob Wirth Company
   (Theater District, *M*)

HUNGARIAN

Café Budapest (Copley Square, *VE*)

INDIAN

Bombay Club (Cambridge, *M*)

INTERNATIONAL

Aujourd'hui (Public Garden, *VE*)
Café Jaffa (Back Bay, *M*)
House of Blues (Cambridge, *M*)
Salamander (Cambridge, *VE*)
Seasons (Faneuil Hall
   Marketplace, *VE*)

ITALIAN

Botolph's on Tremont
   (South End, *M*)
Daily Catch (on the Waterfront, *M*)
Davio's (Copley Square, *E*)
The European (the North End, *I*)
Galleria Umberto
   (the North End, *I*)
Giacomo's (the North End, *E*)
La Groceria (Cambridge, *M*)
La Piccola Venezia
   (the North End, *I*)
Lo Conte's (the North End, *M*)
Mamma Maria (the North End, *E*)
Pagliuca's (the North End, *I*)
Rialto (Cambridge, *E*)
Ristorante Toscano (Beacon Hill, *E*)
Upstairs at the Pudding
   (Cambridge, *M*)

JAPANESE

Sakura-Bana (Financial District, *M*)
Tatsukichi-Boston (Faneuil Hall
   Marketplace, *M*)

KOSHER

Milk Street Cafe
   (Financial District, *I*)
Rubin's (Brookline, *M*)

MEXICAN

Casa Romero (Back Bay, *E*)
Fajitas & 'Ritas (Downtown
   Crossing, *I*)

MIDDLE EASTERN

Algiers Coffeehouse (Cambridge, *I*)

NEW ENGLAND

Henrietta's Table (Cambridge, *M*)
Portuguese
Casa Portugal (Cambridge, *M*)

SEAFOOD

Anthony's Pier 4 (on the
   Waterfront, *E*)
Daily Catch (on the Waterfront, *M*)
East Coast Grill (Cambridge, *M*)
Jimbo's Fish Shanty (on the
   Waterfront, *I*)
Jimmy's Harborside Restaurant
   (on the Waterfront, *E*)
Legal Sea Foods (Back Bay, *E*)
Rowes Wharf Restaurant (on the
   Waterfront, *VE*)
Turner Fisheries (Back Bay, *M*)
Ye Olde Union Oyster House
   (Faneuil Hall Marketplace, *M*)

SOUTHERN

East Coast Grill (Cambridge, *M*)

SOUTHWESTERN

Border Café (Cambridge, *M*)
Cottonwood Café (Cambridge, *E*)

SPANISH

Dalí (Cambridge, *M*)
Rialto (Cambridge, *E*)

TEX-MEX

Zuma's Tex-Mex Cafe (Faneuil
   Hall Marketplace, *I*)

THAI

Bangkok Cuisine (Back Bay, *M*)

VEGETARIAN

Buddha's Delight (Chinatown, *I*)
Country Life Vegetarian Buffet
   (Financial District, *I*)
Milk Street Cafe (Financial District, *I*)

VIETNAMESE

Buddha's Delight (Chinatown, *I*)
Pho Pasteur (Chinatown, *I*)

3   On the Waterfront

VERY EXPENSIVE

Rowes Wharf Restaurant

In the Boston Harbor Hotel, 70 Rowes Wharf (entrance on Atlantic Ave.). ☎ **617/439-3995.**
Reservations recommended. Main courses $10–$16.75 at lunch, $20–$31 at dinner. Breakfast
$2–$12.75. AE, DC, DISC, MC, V. Mon–Sat 6:30–11am, Sun 7–10am; Mon–Sat 11:30am–
2pm, Sun 10:30am–2pm; Mon–Sat 5:30–10pm, Sun 5:30–9pm. MBTA: Blue Line to
Aquarium. REGIONAL AMERICAN.

Tucked away on the second floor of the Boston Harbor Hotel, the wood-paneled
Rowes Wharf Restaurant feels almost like a private club. The richly upholstered
chairs with arms encourage you to relax, and for service that puts you at ease
and anticipates your every desire, the dining room staff is perfect (the employees at
the door can be a bit chilly—hang in there). And that's not even mentioning the
cuisine, which is among the best in the city, and the gorgeous china with the same
border that's around the hotel's landmark archway.

The enormous picture windows afford a breathtaking harbor view, and the
tables are far enough apart that you won't hear your neighbors admiring it. You
might hear them exclaiming over the food, though. Chef Daniel Bruce uses local
ingredients when possible, prepared in deceptively simple ways that accent natural flavors without overwhelming them. The signature appetizer is luscious Maine
lobster meat seasoned and formed into a sausage, grilled, sliced, and served in a
light cream sauce with lobster claw meat and lemon pasta. Spinach salad comes
topped with oysters that taste of the sea, poached just enough to firm them up.
Entrees range from pan-roasted Nova Scotia salmon to grilled chicken breast with
a maple and chili glaze, to pecan-smoked filet mignon grilled and served with
whiskey sauce. Desserts vary with the inspiration of the chef—there's usually an
excellent sorbet sampler. The lunch menu indicates which items are low in fat,
sodium, and calories.

EXPENSIVE

Anthony's Pier 4

140 Northern Ave. ☎ **617/423-6363.** Reservations recommended. Main courses
$9.95–$24.95 at lunch, $13.95–$29.95 at dinner. AE, CB, DC, MC, V. Mon–Sat 11:30am–
11pm, Sun and holidays 12:30–10:30pm. Closed Christmas Day. MBTA: Red Line to South
Station. SEAFOOD.

Long considered one of New England's outstanding places for special-occasion
dining, and even once referred to as America's most popular restaurant, today's
Anthony's seems to have lost a few feet off its fastball. But it's still in an amazing
location, and if you don't order anything too fancy, you can have an enjoyable meal.
The restaurant is at the end of a pier, with glass walls facing the water that allow
clear views of incoming sea vessels. There's outdoor dining in the summer. To start,
you're served marinated mushrooms and relishes, cheese and crackers, then hot
popovers. If you have room for more appetizers, the clam chowder is good. Stick to
the basic offerings—fresh New England seafood, simply prepared; Dover sole from
the English Channel (flown over especially for Anthony's); roast beef, and lobster.
Ask your server for dessert recommendations, or try the excellent chocolate mint pie
or baked Alaska. It's best to drive to this restaurant; there is free parking on the
wharf. Men are asked to wear jackets at dinner.

Boston Dining

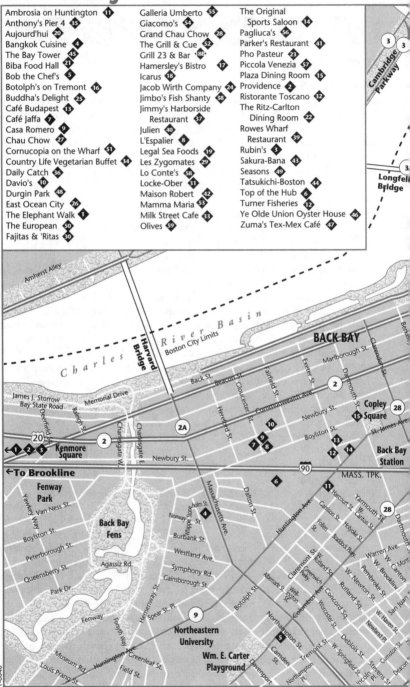

Ambrosia on Huntington **11**
Anthony's Pier 4 **35**
Aujourd'hui **20**
Bangkok Cuisine **4**
The Bay Tower **45**
Biba Food Hall **21**
Bob the Chef's **5**
Botolph's on Tremont **16**
Buddha's Delight **25**
Café Budapest **13**
Café Jaffa **7**
Casa Romero **9**
Chau Chow **27**
Cornucopia on the Wharf **51**
Country Life Vegetarian Buffet **34**
Daily Catch **36**
Davio's **10**
Durgin Park **48**
East Ocean City **26**
The Elephant Walk **1**
The European **50**
Fajitas & 'Ritas **30**

Galleria Umberto **55**
Giacomo's **54**
Grand Chau Chow **28**
The Grill & Cue **52**
Grill 23 & Bar **18**
Hamersley's Bistro **17**
Icarus **18**
Jacob Wirth Company **24**
Jimbo's Fish Shanty **38**
Jimmy's Harborside
    Restaurant **37**
Julien **40**
L'Espalier **8**
Legal Sea Foods **19**
Les Zygomates **29**
Lo Conte's **58**
Locke-Ober **31**
Maison Robert **42**
Mamma Maria **53**
Milk Street Cafe **53**
Olives **59**

The Original
    Sports Saloon **14**
Pagliuca's **56**
Parker's Restaurant **41**
Pho Pasteur **23**
Piccola Venezia **57**
Plaza Dining Room **15**
Providence **2**
Ristorante Toscano **32**
The Ritz-Carlton
    Dining Room **22**
Rowes Wharf
    Restaurant **39**
Rubin's **3**
Sakura-Bana **43**
Seasons **49**
Tatsukichi-Boston **44**
Top of the Hub **6**
Turner Fisheries **12**
Ye Olde Union Oyster House **46**
Zuma's Tex-Mex Café **47**

1-0046

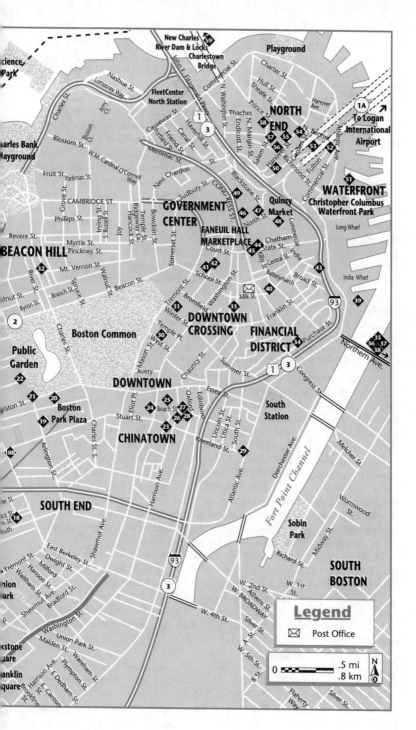

✪ Cornucopia on the Wharf

100 Atlantic Ave. ☎ **617/367-0300.** Reservations recommended at dinner. Main courses $13.50–$23.95. AE, MC, V. Daily 5:30–10:30pm; Apr 15–Oct 15 daily 11:30am–2:30pm. Patio (seasonal) open daily 11:30am–9:30pm. MBTA: Blue Line to Aquarium. AMERICAN REGIONAL.

This festive spot is a great stop if you're visiting the waterfront, and it's worth a trip if you're not. Jutting out into the harbor across a marina from Long Wharf, the dining room feels like the cabin of a ship, with lots of glass windows, polished wood trim, hand-painted columns and a large bar. The popular outdoor patio is shielded from direct exposure to the street by a small park. The menu is short and changes regularly, offering the innovative seafood you might expect in this location as well as meat options. Menu items are accompanied by wine recommendations, a practice that makes many people secretly sigh with relief. Crispy calamari are usually available as an appetizer, ethereally fried and served in a white-paper cone. The seafood pasta specials often available at lunch are outstanding. At dinner, the Thai fish stew with lobster, littlenecks, and mussels in a green curry broth and the baked scrod over roasted garlic mashed potatoes are excellent, but the pan-roasted lobster can be on the scrawny side. Events such as wine tastings are scheduled throughout the year—call to see if something's happening during your visit.

✪ The Grill & Cue

256 Commercial St. ☎ **617/227-4454.** Reservations recommended at dinner. Main courses $6.95–$9.95 at lunch, $12.95–$16.50 at dinner; cafe fare $6.95–$9.95. AE, CB, DC, DISC, MC, V. Mon–Fri noon–2pm; Mon–Wed 5–10pm, Thurs–Fri 5–10:30pm; Sat–Sun 2pm–1am. MBTA: Blue Line to Aquarium. CONTEMPORARY AMERICAN.

The newest restaurant near the harbor is also one of the best in town. Across the street from the former home of the late, lamented Jasper's, the Grill & Cue scooped up many members of the displaced staff of that legendary New England seafood institution when it opened in 1995. One was chef Jon Dabelstein, who has a way with meat and pasta as well as fish. Everything is good here, and there's lots of it, starting with the great bread basket and excellent soups. At lunch, try the most sophisticated tuna melt ever, a focaccia sandwich with grilled tuna steak and onions, topped with fontina cheese. The cafe menu, available at lunch and dinner, offers casual fare such as feathery ricotta cavatelli with roasted plum tomatoes, and a mountain of steak tips with grilled peppers and onions. Dinner entrees are sturdy cuts of meat and fish with phenomenal side dishes—pan-roasted salmon with roasted vegetables, pesto-marinated grilled leg of lamb with artichoke-and-potato pie, or grilled sirloin with mashed potatoes and red onion rings.

The setting, like the food, is familiar yet daring, softly lit, with purple and black enamel accents, a tropical fish tank over the bar, and French doors that open to the street from the front dining room. The second floor is an upscale pool parlor (that's the "Cue" in the name), featuring a half-dozen imported slate tables with purple felt tops that go for as much as $18 an hour. You might prefer to splurge on dessert—anything with chocolate in it is excellent, and the ridiculous-sounding maple-ginger tiramisu is actually quite good.

Jimmy's Harborside Restaurant

242 Northern Ave. ☎ **617/423-1000.** Reservations recommended. Main courses $10.95–$25.95. Children's menu $4.95–$6.95. AE, CB, DC, MC, V. Mon–Sat noon–4pm; nightly 4–9:30pm. MBTA: Red Line to South Station. SEAFOOD.

This Boston landmark—the sign on the front reads "Home of the Chowder King"—offers a fine view of the harbor and Logan Airport from both the main downstairs dining room and the sunny Merchant's Club on the upper level. Try a

---

ⓘ Family-Friendly Restaurants

Like chocolate and Champagne, well-behaved children are welcome just about anywhere, and we've seen children comporting themselves better than many adults at some of the nicest restaurants in town. If your kids aren't willing or able to sign a good-conduct pledge, here are some suggestions.

The **Bertucci's** chain of pizzerias appeals to children and adults equally, with wood-fired brick ovens that are visible from many tables, great rolls made from pizza dough, and pizza and pastas that range from basic to sophisticated. There are convenient branches in Faneuil Hall Marketplace (☎ **617/227-7889**) and Harvard Square (21 Brattle St., Cambridge; ☎ **617/864-4748**).

The **Bristol Lounge,** in the Four Seasons Hotel (200 Boylston St.; ☎ **617/ 351-2053**), has a kids' menu featuring appetizers, plain main courses, desserts, and beverages. High chairs are available, the staff is unflappable and accommodating, and sticker fun books are available.

The **Ground Round** chain of suburban family restaurants has a branch at the Prudential Center (800 Boylston St.; ☎ **617/247-0500**). There's free popcorn on the table, cartoons on a wall screen, video games, and crayons. On special days kids pay a penny a pound for their entree.

Fuddrucker's, another family-oriented chain, serves burgers and other grilled items in the Theater District (137 Stuart St.; ☎ **617/723-3833**), not far from the Common and the Public Garden. Order at the counter, hit the condiment bar, and make as much noise as you want—this is also a rowdy business lunch spot.

TGI Friday's (26 Exeter St., at Newbury St.; ☎ **617/266-9040**) made its reputation by catering to singles, and all that pairing off apparently has led to children, who are courted as well. Available all day, the kids' package includes balloons and surprises wrapped in the chain's signature red and white stripes. Crayons, a coloring book, peanut butter, and crackers are included.

---

shore dinner (a meal consisting of seafood harvested from the New England shore), perhaps broiled scallops à la Jimmy or Atlantic lobster. Dinners include appetizer (order the creamy fish chowder with generous chunks of whitefish), salad, potato, dessert, and beverage. Occasionally there are specialties not listed on the menu that only the regular diners ask for, such as the excellent and moderately priced gray sole—check to see if it is available. The à la carte menu includes prime rib and Jimmy's famous finnan haddie (smoked haddock in cream sauce), a specialty of the house. Special dinners are available for children. While you're waiting to be seated, you can enjoy complimentary hors d'oeuvres in the lounge. It's best to drive to this restaurant; metered and valet parking are available.

MODERATE

Daily Catch

261 Northern Ave. ☎ **617/338-3093**. Reservations not accepted. Main courses $10–$16.50. AE. Sun–Thurs noon–10:30pm, Fri–Sat noon–11pm. MBTA: Red Line to South Station. SOUTHERN ITALIAN/SEAFOOD.

Make sure your fellow travelers accompany you to this Fish Pier institution, because you're going to emanate garlic for at least a day and you might as well have someone to share it with. This is a basic storefront, where the waitstaff sometimes seems overwhelmed and it can take forever to get a table, but the food is terrific. There's

Sicilian-style calamari (squid stuffed with bread crumbs, raisins, pine nuts, parsley, and tons of garlic), freshly shucked clams, mussels in garlic-flavored sauce, broiled and fried fish, and shellfish. Calamari is prepared at least eight ways—even the standard garlic-and-oil pasta sauce has ground-up squid in it. If you've never tasted it before, try the fried version as an excellent appetizer. And if you really want to try something different, order the squid ink pasta Alfredo. All food is prepared to order, and is usually served in the frying pans in which it was cooked.

The other two branches of this mini-chain don't accept credit cards. The original Daily Catch is in the North End, at 323 Hanover St. (☎ **617/523-8567**). Another is in Brookline at 441A Harvard St. (☎ **617/734-5696**). The hours are the same for all three.

INEXPENSIVE

Jimbo's Fish Shanty
245 Northern Ave. ☎ **617/542-5600.** Main courses $6–$14. AE, DC, MC, V. Mon–Thurs 11:30am–9:30pm, Fri–Sat 11:30am–10pm, Sun noon–8pm. MBTA: Red Line to South Station. SEAFOOD.

Bring your sense of humor to this jam-packed restaurant, where model trains run overhead on tracks suspended from the fairly low ceiling, there are road signs everywhere, and the waitress will probably call you "honey." Under the same management as Jimmy's Harborside across the street, Jimbo's serves good, fresh seafood, skewers threaded with fish or beef, and pasta dishes (at dinner only) with varied sauces, including a lobster cream version. The truly decadent desserts generally involve ice cream and chocolate.

4   The North End

Boston's Italian-American enclave has at least three dozen restaurants and at least that many people dedicated to keeping more of them from opening. A lot of the restaurants are tiny and, to keep the tables turning over, don't serve dessert and coffee. In a relatively recent development, most of them do accept credit cards. Hit the caffès (bring cash) for coffee concoctions and fresh pastry in an atmosphere where lingering is encouraged.

VERY EXPENSIVE

Mamma Maria
3 North Sq. ☎ **617/523-0077.** Reservations recommended. Main courses $8–$14 at lunch, $14.50–$26 at dinner. AE, DC, DISC, MC, V. Tues–Sat 11:30am–2pm; nightly 5:30–10pm. MBTA: Green or Orange Line to Haymarket. NORTHERN ITALIAN.

In a townhouse overlooking North Square and the Paul Revere House, this is a traditional setting where you'll find innovative cuisine. The bread, pasta, and desserts are homemade, the service is exceptional, and the cool, whitewashed rooms are among the most popular in town for getting engaged. The menu changes seasonally, but you can usually start with excellent pasta fagioli (bean-and-pasta soup) or the excellent risotto. The entrees are like nothing else in this neighborhood, presented so beautifully that it's hard to dig in. You'll be glad you did—try the roasted chicken with lightly steamed green beans, garlic poached to bring out its sweetness, and a hunk of potato casserole; the goat cheese ravioli with arugula, walnuts, oven-cured tomatoes, and capers; or the grilled salmon with beet-and-basil salad and artichoke pesto. Valet parking is available in the evening.

EXPENSIVE

Giacomo's

355 Hanover St. ☎ **617/523-9026.** Reservations not accepted. Main courses $15–$24. No credit cards. Mon–Thurs 5–10pm, Fri–Sat 5–10:30pm, Sun 4–10pm. MBTA: Green or Orange Line to Haymarket. ITALIAN/SEAFOOD.

Fans of Giacomo's seem to have adopted the Postal Service's motto, and they aren't deterred by snow, sleet, rain, gloom of night, or anything else. The line forms early and stays, especially on weekends. No reservations, no credit cards, a tiny dining room with an open kitchen—what's the secret? Well, the food is terrific. The fried calamari appetizer approaches tempura-level greaselessness, and you can take the chef's advice or put together your own main dish from the list of daily ingredients on a board on the wall. Salmon in pesto cream sauce with fettucine is a keeper, as is any dish with shrimp. Service is incredibly quick, and lingering is definitely not encouraged—but unless you have a heart of stone, you won't want to take up a table when people are standing outside in 90-degree heat or an ice storm (literally) waiting for your seat.

For those who don't consider privation fun, there's a Giacomo's in the South End (431 Columbus Ave.; ☎ **617/536-5723**) that takes reservations and credit cards (AE, MC, V) and offers valet parking. But then you can't say you waited an hour for a luscious meal that took 40 minutes.

MODERATE

❍ Lo Conte's

116 Salem St. ☎ **617/720-3550.** Reservations not accepted. Main courses $9.95–$14.95. AE, DC, DISC, MC, V. Sun–Thurs 11:30am–10pm, Fri–Sat 11:30am–11pm. MBTA: Green or Orange Line to Haymarket. SOUTHERN ITALIAN.

This is a real neighborhood place, with chummy service and large portions of excellent food. On weekend nights the wait can be long, but once your name is on the list, you're part of the gang—you'll be sent across the street to hang around at the Grand Cafe until your table is ready. When it is, you're seated in one of the two glorified-storefront dining rooms, decorated with photos of Italy on the walls and filled with the satisfied chatter of happy diners. Salads and appetizers aren't cheap, but portions are large and quality is high—the house salad dressing is a cheese-infused wonder; broccoli orata is battered and sautéed until it's both tender and crispy; and eggplant rolatini, when it's available as a special, is out of this world. Main dishes are divided into pasta, chicken, veal, and seafood, but you may not get past the specials. The house special chicken, broccoli, and ziti (a dish you'll find on more menus than chicken parmigiana) is the best in town, and the daily specials actually taste as good as they sound. If seafood is involved, go for it.

Pagliuca's

14 Parmenter St. ☎ **617/367-1504.** Reservations not accepted. Main courses $12–$22. AE, MC, V. Sun–Thurs 11am–10:30pm, Fri–Sat 11am–11pm. MBTA: Green or Orange Line to Haymarket. SOUTHERN ITALIAN.

This spot, a sparsely decorated and unadorned little place, doles out southern Italian cooking the way Americans like it—great pastas with lots of garlicky tomato sauce and big chunks of Italian bread to mop it up, plus such specialties as cioppino, or chicken with peppers, onions, and potatoes. The lunch special, good until 4pm, is one of the best in town—everything on the menu is half-price.

Piccola Venezia

263 Hanover St. ☎ **617/523-3888.** Reservations not accepted. Main courses $9.95–$16.95. AE, DISC, MC, V. Daily 11:30am–10pm. MBTA: Green or Orange Line to Haymarket. ITALIAN.

Once upon a time, Piccola Venezia was a hole in the wall on Salem Street. In 1994 it moved to a larger, more inviting space on Hanover Street, and it's hardly had a slow night since. The glass front shows off the exposed-brick dining room, decorated with prints and photos and filled with happy patrons. Portions are large and the food tends to be heavy on red sauce, but more sophisticated specials are available. Some people feel the red sauce has a burned taste—you might want to try it as part of an appetizer (the excellent eggplant, perhaps) to see if it suits you. Then dig into your spaghetti and meatballs, chicken parmigiana, or pasta puttanesca. *Tip:* If you're dining as a pair, you're sometimes permitted to jump ahead of larger parties in line and be seated almost immediately.

INEXPENSIVE

The European

218 Hanover St. ☎ **617/523-5694.** Main courses $7.95–$13. AE, CB, DC, DISC, MC, V. Sun–Thurs 11am–11pm, Fri–Sat 11am–12:30am. MBTA: Green or Orange Line to Haymarket. SOUTHERN ITALIAN.

The menu at this Boston institution includes reasonably priced complete dinners, among many, many other offerings, but the real reason to come here is the pizza. The European claims to be Boston's oldest Italian restaurant, and it'll probably be up and running for another 80 years if it keeps cranking out its thin-crusted, perfectly proportioned pies. Other dishes are fine—though the squid pie sounds as if it might be pizza, it's actually a turnover of pizza crust filled with calamari and served with marinara sauce—and if you're with a group, the European is a good choice because the dining rooms are huge. This is not the place to go for a romantic dinner, as it can get quite noisy, but that's part of the charm. Look for the famous clock above the front door—it's been there since the restaurant opened in 1917.

Galleria Umberto

289 Hanover St. ☎ **617/227-5709.** Reservations not accepted. Pizza 70¢ per slice, calzones $2.10–$2.50, croquettes 80¢. No credit cards. Mon–Sat 11am–2pm. MBTA: Green or Orange Line to Haymarket. ITALIAN.

The long, fast-moving line tips you off to the fact that Galleria Umberto is a real bargain. And the food is good, too. You can fill up on pizza, but if you're feeling adventurous, try the arancini (a rice ball filled with gravy, ground beef, peas, and cheese). The calzones (ham and cheese, spinach, spinach and cheese, and spinach and sausage) are also tasty. Have a quick lunch pit stop and then get on with your sightseeing.

5   Faneuil Hall/Government Center/Financial District

This is expense-account land, where standards, service, and prices are sky-high (as is one of the restaurants). You'll also find excellent places that cater to office workers on a budget.

VERY EXPENSIVE

The Bay Tower

60 State St. ☎ **617/723-1666.** Reservations recommended. Main courses $17–$36. AE, CB, DC, MC, V. Mon–Thurs 5:30–10pm, Fri–Sat 5–11pm. MBTA: Blue or Orange Line to State. CREATIVE AMERICAN.

Let's cut to the chase: Would you pay this much at a restaurant with a view of a brick wall or a street corner? No. But is it worth it? Absolutely. One of the most beautiful dining rooms in Boston, the 33rd-floor Bay Tower has glass walls facing a glorious panorama of Faneuil Hall Marketplace, the harbor, and the airport. The terraced table area is arranged so that the view is visible from every seat, and it's reflected in many shiny (polished, not mirrored) surfaces that lend a casino-like air to the candlelit room.

Chef Raoul Jean-Richard's menu changes seasonally and includes a nice mix of traditional and contemporary preparations. You might start with a smoked-salmon napoleon, butternut squash ravioli, or shrimp cocktail. Entrees include the usual steaks, chops, chicken, and seafood, often with a twist. Baked haddock arrives in a mild horseradish crust on a bed of roasted vegetables with beet juice, and a generous portion of ratatouille is a good option for vegetarians. Special dietary preparations are available on request. As you might expect at a restaurant where many people come just for dessert, drinks, and dancing, desserts are wonderful, with an emphasis on chocolate. A $12 minimum is charged in the lounge after 9:30pm (on Friday and Saturday only, dining room customers are exempt). Validated parking is available in the 60 State Street garage.

Julien

In Le Meridien Boston, 250 Franklin St. ☎ **617/451-1900.** Reservations recommended. Main courses $14.50–$18.75 at lunch, $26–$33 at dinner. Business Lunch $22. AE, CB, DC, MC, V. Mon–Fri noon–2pm; Mon–Thurs 6–10pm, Fri–Sat 6–10:30pm. MBTA: Blue or Orange Line to State, or Red Line to Downtown Crossing. CLASSIC FRENCH.

Julien is in one of the most beautiful rooms in the city, under a vaulted, gilt-edged ceiling and five crystal chandeliers. The setting suits the excellent food and service. The seasonal menus emphasize fresh regional products and are concocted by executive chef Raymond Ost in consultation with visiting French chefs. Specialties to start with include terrine of fresh, homemade foie gras with truffles, and Maine lobster salad on a bed of diced vegetables. The roasted halibut with mashed potatoes, olives, tomatoes, and red pepper sauce is an excellent choice, as is the salmon soufflé, and the lamb loin with spinach mousse, served with olive- and thyme-flavored potatoes, is also delicious. The desserts are among the best in town, especially the aptly named "Chocolate Decadence." The wine list includes selections from the best French, American, German, and Italian wineries priced from about $18 to $200 per bottle. Julien also offers daily specials at lunch, which include one soup, one appetizer, one pasta, one meat dish, and one fish dish. The Business Lunch, a good deal, includes a soup or salad, a choice of entrees, and coffee or tea.

Note: **Café Fleuri,** Le Meridien's atrium-style informal dining room, serves lunch from 11:30am to 2:30pm weekdays and Sunday brunch at 11 and 11:30am and 1 and 1:30pm. Café Fleuri is open from 7am to late evening, serving breakfast, lunch, and dinner.

✪ Maison Robert

45 School St. ☎ **617/227-3370.** Reservations recommended. Main courses $9–$22 at lunch, $17–$30 at dinner. Le Café has a fixed-price menu ($17 or $23) as well as à la carte selections. AE, CB, DC, MC, V. Mon–Fri 11:45am–2:30pm; Mon–Sat 5:30–10pm. MBTA: Green Line to Government Center or Red Line to Park Street. INNOVATIVE FRENCH.

Maison Robert is one of the finest French restaurants anywhere. Like many excellent restaurants, it's family-owned and operated—proprietors Lucien and Ann Robert are the parents of executive chef Andrée Robert, and Lucien's nephew Jacky Robert took over in the kitchen in 1996 after many years as a top chef in San Francisco (including 10 years at Ernie's).

A legend in Boston since it opened in Old City Hall in 1972, Maison Robert has only improved since Jacky Robert returned. The dining room was already spectacular, decorated in a formal style that complements the building's French Second Empire architecture, with majestic crystal chandeliers and tall windows overlooking the Old Granary Burying Ground (a gloomy thought, perhaps, but a peaceful spot in the hubbub of downtown). The food is every bit the equal of the setting, classic but dramatic. You might start with a tender, airy Roquefort souffle, or a giant smoked-duck ravioli, which is indeed giant in both its size and the flavor of the filling and the luscious broth. Entrees include options you would expect and others that come as a pleasant surprise—steak au poivre is a meat-lover's delight, splendid roast rack of lamb is accompanied by an equally delicious potato cake, and the acorn squash of plenty overflows with crisp-tender vegetables and looks so beautiful you'll reach for your camera. Desserts are truly impressive, ranging from excellent souffles to a selection of sorbets with a giant cookie (yes, "giant" again) to a heart-stopping chocolate-cake-and-mixed-berry concoction garnished with a chocolate Eiffel Tower too pretty to eat and too delicious not to.

The upstairs dining room is the formal counterpart of cozy Le Café on the ground floor, which has a more casual atmosphere and less expensive food, but is also thoroughly French in style. In the summer, cafe seating spills onto the lovely terrace next to the statue of Benjamin Franklin that you might have visited on the Freedom Trail. Valet parking is available for both restaurants.

Parker's Restaurant

In the Omni Parker House, 60 School St. ☎ **617/725-1685.** Reservations recommended. Main courses $16–$28; breakfast buffet $11.95. AE, CB, DC, DISC, MC, V. Daily 7–10:30am; Mon–Fri 11:30am–2:15pm. MBTA: Green Line to Government Center or Red Line to Park Street. CONTINENTAL.

In the era of Emerson and Longfellow, the Parker House was *the* literary meeting place in town. Today you're more likely to see a business deal winding up, but this elegant chamber, the hotel's main dining room, is still a bastion of fine dining. The original walnut paneling makes an elegant backdrop for sparkling chandeliers and large paintings. The seasonal weekday luncheon menu features salads, several seafood choices (including tasty clam chowder), and mainstream chicken, pork, and beef dishes. Try the rack of lamb, roasted veal tenderloin with pasta, pesto, and shrimp, or lobster and linguine. All entrees include vegetables, potato and, of course, the famous Parker House rolls. Valet parking is available.

Seasons

In the Bostonian Hotel, 40 North St. ☎ **617/523-4119.** Reservations recommended. Main courses $9–$17 at lunch; two-course dinner $28, three-course dinner $35, four-course dinner $39. AE, CB, DC, JCB, MC, V. Mon–Fri 7–10:30am, noon–2:30pm, Sat 7–11am, Sun 7am–12:30pm; daily 6–10pm. MBTA: Green or Blue Line to Government Center, or Orange Line to Haymarket. INTERNATIONAL.

This rooftop restaurant on the fourth floor of the Bostonian Hotel offers stunning views of Faneuil Hall Marketplace, but once you begin studying the menu, your attention will be riveted on the action indoors. The menu changes (you guessed it) seasonally, and executive chef Peter McCarthy's creativity never fails to impress. You might try an Asian-influenced dish such as tempura-fried prawns with plum sauce, or a slab of wood-grilled Idaho trout or beef tenderloin. Lunch, less expensive and equally enjoyable, might consist of a salmon burger or a salad with enough protein (shrimp, roast chicken, even veal) to be a complete meal. Like the rest of the menu, the dessert list is short but high-quality. The wine list is entirely American and ency-clopedic, with 50 Chardonnays, 65 Cabernet Sauvignons, and some rare selections from top producers.

Whether this is a quibble or a plus depends on your attitude toward an evening out, but there's no dress code, so you might find yourself seated between people dressed for the theater and people dressed for the movie theater. Valet parking is available.

MODERATE

⑤ Durgin-Park

340 Faneuil Hall Marketplace. ☎ **617/227-2038.** Reservations not accepted. Main courses $4.95–$16.95, specials $15.90–$24.95. AE, MC, V. Daily 11:30am–2:30pm; Mon–Sat 2:30–10pm, Sun 2:30–9pm. MBTA: Green or Blue Line to Government Center, or Orange Line to Haymarket. NEW ENGLAND.

For huge portions of fresh, delicious food, a rowdy atmosphere where CEOs share tables with students, and famously cranky waitresses who can't seem to bear the sight of any of it, people have been flocking to Durgin-Park since 1827. It really is everything it's cracked up to be—a tourist magnet that also attracts hordes of local residents, where politicians rub shoulders with blue-haired grandmothers and every-one's disappointed when the waitresses are nice, as they often are. Approximately 2,000 people a day find their way to the end of the line that stretches down a flight of stairs to the first floor of the North Market building of Faneuil Hall Marketplace (look for the giant sign). The queue moves quickly, and you'll probably wind up seated at a long table with other people, although smaller tables are available.

The food is wonderful, and there's plenty of it—prime rib the size of a hubcap, giant lamb chops, piles of fried seafood, and roast turkey that will fill you up till Thanksgiving. All steaks and chops are broiled on an open fire over wood charcoal. Seafood, including salmon, sole, haddock, shrimp, oysters, scallops, and lobster, is received twice daily, and fish dinners are broiled to order. Vegetables are served à la carte, and if you've been waiting to try Boston baked beans, now's the time. Homemade corn bread comes with every meal. For dessert, the strawberry short-cake is justly celebrated, and molasses-lovers (this is not a dish for dabblers) will want to try Indian pudding, a mixture of molasses and cornmeal slow-baked for hours and served with ice cream.

If you're going for "dinner" (otherwise known as lunch; the evening meal is called "supper"), beat the crowd by arriving when the restaurant opens. Or jump the line by starting out at the ground-floor Gaslight Pub, which has a private staircase that leads upstairs.

Les Zygomates

129 South St. ☎ **617/542-5108.** Reservations recommended. Main courses $12–$20. AE, MC, V. Mon–Fri 11:30am–2:30pm; Mon–Thurs 6–10:30pm, Fri–Sat 6–11:30pm. MBTA: Red Line to South Station. FRENCH/ECLECTIC.

Pick your way across the construction wasteland near South Station to this delight-ful bistro and wine bar. It's worth the trouble. Over the bar in the large, brick-walled room is a great selection of wine, available by the bottle, by the glass, and as a two-ounce "taste." The pleasant staff will recommend something or just guide you to a good accompaniment for the delicious food. Salads are excellent, lightly dressed and garden fresh, and main courses are hearty and filling but not heavy. A large piece of sauteed trout is flaky and light, and the roasted chicken breast stuffed with Vermont goat cheese and served with a white wine tomato sauce is simple, but tasty. The sup-ply of baguette slices on every table is constantly replenished. For dessert, try not to fight over the lemon mousse, a cloud of citrus and air. "Zygomates" supposedly are facial muscles, and the motto here is "Zygomates make you smile." True.

Sakura-Bana

57 Broad St. ☎ **617/542-4311.** Reservations recommended at dinner, not accepted at lunch. Main courses $8.75–$29. AE, DC, MC, V. Mon–Fri 11:30am–2:30pm; Sun–Thurs 5–10pm; Fri 5–11pm; Sat 1–11pm. Closed first Sun each month. MBTA: Blue Line to State or Aquarium. JAPANESE.

Sakura-Bana is Japanese for "cherry blossom." It seems incongruous in the Financial District, but you won't care when you join the lively scene in this small, welcoming room. Traditional Japanese food and drink are served to a somewhat frantic lunch crowd and more relaxed dinner patrons. The main attraction is the small but excellent sushi bar, one of the best in town. Or you might want to start with the feather-light shumai (shrimp dumplings) and move on to teriyaki, yakitori, or tempura. Ten don, tempura over rice with a sweetish sauce, is wonderful. Arrive early for lunch to avoid a long wait.

Tatsukichi-Boston

189 State St. ☎ **617/720-2468.** Reservations recommended. Main courses $10–$20. AE, DC, DISC, JCB, MC, V. Restaurant Mon–Fri 11:45am–2:30pm; Sun–Thurs 5–10pm, Fri–Sat 5–11pm; VIP karaoke lounge Tues–Sat 7pm–1am. MBTA: Blue Line to Aquarium. JAPANESE.

A block away from Faneuil Hall Marketplace, this award-winning restaurant is a favorite with the Japanese community and other fans of Japanese cuisine. At half of the tables, patrons sit on chairs; at the rest, they kneel on an elevated platform. There's an excellent sushi bar, and if your taste runs to cooked food, choose from an extensive array of authentic Japanese dishes, including sukiyaki, shabu shabu, teriyaki, and kushiage—meat, seafood, and vegetables arranged on skewers, lightly battered, breaded, and quickly fried, served with special dipping sauces. At lunch, the unagi-don, or grilled eel, is as tasty as it is scary-sounding. There are private tatami rooms and a karaoke lounge (the cover charge is $7.50 for dinner guests, half the usual rate).

Ye Olde Union Oyster House

41 Union St. (between North and Hanover sts.) ☎ **617/227-2750.** Reservations recommended. Main courses $6.50–$13.95 at lunch, $8.95–$18.95 at dinner; lobster $21.95–$34.95. AE, CB, DC, DISC, MC, V. Sun–Thurs 11am–9:30pm, Fri–Sat 11am–10pm. Lunch served until 5pm Sun–Thurs, until 6pm Fri–Sat. Union Bar: 11am–3pm lunch, 3–11pm late-supper fare. Bar open until midnight. MBTA: Green Line to Government Center or Orange Line to Haymarket. NEW ENGLAND/SEAFOOD.

America's oldest restaurant in continuous service, the Union Oyster House opened in 1826, and the booths and oyster bar haven't moved since. At the crescent-shaped bar on the lower level of the cramped, low-ceilinged building, "where Daniel Webster drank many a toddy in his day," try the sampler, a mixed appetizer of about a dozen pieces each of oysters, clams, and scampi. The food is tasty, traditional New England fare. Oyster stew made with fresh milk and country butter makes a good beginning. Follow that with a broiled or grilled dish such as scrod or salmon, or perhaps seafood primavera, fried seafood, or a grilled veal chop. A complete shore dinner with chowder, steamers, broiled lobster, salad, corn, and dessert is an excellent introduction to local favorites. Low-calorie menu selections, introduced in 1994, are popular too. For dessert, try gingerbread with whipped cream. Ask to be seated at John F. Kennedy's favorite booth (number 18), which is marked with a plaque.

INEXPENSIVE

Country Life Vegetarian Buffet
200 High St. ☎ **617/951-2685** or 617/951-2462 (prerecorded menu). Buffet $7 lunch, $5–$8 dinner, $8.50 brunch. AE. Daily 11:30am–3pm; Sun and Tues–Thurs 5–8pm. Sun 10am–3pm (brunch). MBTA: Blue Line to Aquarium. VEGETARIAN.

On a construction-racked corner where the Financial District meets the Waterfront, vegetarians meet carnivores and everyone leaves happy with the great selection of grains, soups, vegetables, fruits, and nuts—no animal products are served. A hot entree, soup and one or two vegetables are featured each day (call the menu line or pick up a monthly schedule to learn the day's specials), along with two tremendous salad bars—one with fresh vegetables, tabbouleh, and tofu, and one with fresh fruits and nuts. Specials include lasagna, "sunburgers" with fries, vegetable pot pie, and "cream" soups that taste as rich as their dairy-laden counterparts. There are always two or three varieties of whole-grain bread, herbal tea, grain coffee, and spring water. Diners can make unlimited trips to the buffet tables, or you can pay for salads by the ounce. Desserts are extra. No alcohol is served. Herbal teas and fruit juice are popular, and soy milk and rice milk are available.

Milk Street Cafe
50 Milk St. ☎ **617/542-2433** or 542-FOOD. Main courses $3–$7. No credit cards. Mon–Fri 7am–3pm. MBTA: Blue Line to State. KOSHER VEGETARIAN.

In the heart of the Financial District, this popular spot offers fresh, homemade vegetarian fare. The restaurant is strictly kosher, but most customers are neither kosher nor vegetarian. They come for the excellent food, which includes two homemade vegetarian soups (one with cream and one dairy-free), salads, a hot entree special, quiche, sandwiches, and salad plates. The veggie melts, Middle Eastern plates, and fruit and cheese platters are very popular. At breakfast there are scones, bagels, muffins, pastries, fruit salad, and fresh-squeezed juices along with herbal teas and coffee.

There is another Milk Street Cafe at Zero Post Office Square (☎ **617/350-7275**), open Monday through Thursday 7am–6pm (8pm in summer) and Friday 7am–3pm. In a copper-roofed, glass-enclosed kiosk in a lovely park, it does a lively takeout business. Within the glass pavilion, the cafe serves only vegetarian kosher food, but outside, during spring, summer, and fall, it maintains four food carts that sell glatt kosher deli, kosher hot dogs, pizza, and ice cream.

Zuma's Tex-Mex Café
7 N. Market St., Faneuil Hall Marketplace. ☎ **617/367-9114.** Main courses $4.97–$13.99. AE, CB, DC, DISC, MC, V. Mon–Thurs 11:30am–11pm, Fri–Sat 11:30am–midnight, Sun noon–10pm. MBTA: Green or Blue Line to Government Center, or Orange Line to Haymarket. TEX-MEX.

Because of its great location on the lower level of the North Market building at Faneuil Hall Marketplace, Zuma's could probably get away with serving so-so food and still draw enormous crowds. Happily, its southwestern cuisine is excellent, with guacamole and salsa cruda made from scratch, and tortilla chips cut and fried throughout the day right in the dining room. This casual, friendly spot is somewhat dark, spotted with neon and small lights in the ceiling. Portions are large, especially considering the low prices. An appetizer of calamari fried in a spicy batter is big enough for three, and the noisy fajitas constantly flying out of the kitchen are substantial and delectable. The firecrackers, or fried jalapeños stuffed with shrimp and cheese, are marked with a skull on the menu and are not for the uninitiated. Tacos are just $1.97 each; the chimichangitas are also a bargain at $1.47. Owner Steve

Immel boasts about the phenomenal key lime pie, the famous margaritas (including a neon version), and the most popular dish, enchiladas verdes. And you can order lunch to go.

6 Downtown Crossing

VERY EXPENSIVE

Locke-Ober
3 and 4 Winter Pl. ☎ **617/542-1340.** Reservations required. Main courses $8–$24.50 at lunch, $17–$40 at dinner. AE, DC, MC, V. Mon–Fri 11:30am–3pm; Fri 3–10pm, Sat 5:30–10:30pm, Sun 5:30–10pm. Closed Sundays in the summer. MBTA: Red or Orange Line to Downtown Crossing. AMERICAN.

"Locke's" is *the* traditional Boston restaurant, a favorite since 1875. Some Bostonians have the same lunch every day at the same table, and probably shudder when they see "lower fat specials" if they happen to look at a menu. In a tiny alley off the Winter Street pedestrian mall, this restaurant feels like a club, with carved paneling, stained-glass windows, crystal chandeliers, and silver buffet covers on the long, mirrored downstairs bar, which dates from 1880. The upstairs dining rooms are dark, elegant, and quiet. The food, once you get over the shock of seeing tofu on the menu in a place that looks like this, is magnificent, as is the service. Start with oysters (raw or Rockefeller) or the famous Jonah crab cakes, then immerse yourself in tradition—steak tartare, grilled salmon with horseradish sauce, Weiner schnitzel à la Holstein, lobster stew, and the most famous dish on the menu, lobster Savannah, for which the meat of a three-pound lobster is diced with pepper and mushrooms, bound with cheese-sherry sauce, stuffed into the shell, and baked. If your heart doesn't stop on the spot, you won't be hungry again for a long time. The dessert menu lists about two dozen items, and as you might expect, the chocolate mousse is a dish for the ages. Valet parking is available at dinner.

INEXPENSIVE

Fajitas & 'Ritas
25 West St. (between Washington and Tremont sts.). ☎ **617/426-1222.** Most dishes $8 and less. AE, DISC, MC, V. Mon–Sat 11:30am–9pm. MBTA: Red or Green Line to Park Street. MEXICAN.

This entertaining storefront restaurant may not be the most authentic in town, but it's one of the most fun. You order by filling out a slip, checking off your choices of fillings and garnishes to go with your tacos, enchiladas, burritos, chimichangas, and, of course, fajitas. There's nothing exotic, just the usual beef, chicken, shrimp, beans, and so forth. A member of the somewhat harried staff relays your order to the kitchen and returns with huge portions of fresh food (this place is too busy for anything to be sitting around for very long). As the name indicates, margaritas, or 'ritas, are a house specialty, but this is closer to a family restaurant than a bar.

7 Chinatown

Chinatown is a small, crowded neighborhood packed with shops, restaurants, and people, especially on weekends. There are a number of good places to dine, but the most entertaining and delicious introduction to the neighborhood is dim sum. Head for Chinatown—between the Southeast Expressway, the downtown shopping district, the Theater District, and the edge of the South End—by way of Washington Street from downtown, on Charles Street from Beacon Hill or the Back Bay (to Stuart Street, which becomes Kneeland Street), or on the MBTA Orange Line to Chinatown or New England Medical Center, or the Green Line to Boylston.

Most Chinese restaurants are open every day, begin serving at midmorning, and stay open till 3am or later. The menus are geared to American palates, but sometimes there's a second menu for Chinese patrons (often written in Chinese). Ask for it, or tell your waiter you want your meal Chinese style.

DIM SUM

Many restaurants in Chinatown offer dim sum, the traditional midday meal featuring a wide variety of appetizer-style dishes, including dumplings filled with meats and vegetables; steamed buns filled with pork or bean paste; shrimp balls; spareribs; stewed chicken wings; and sweets such as coconut gelatin and sesame balls. Waitresses wheel carts laden with tempting snack-sized morsels up to your table, and you order by pointing (unless you know Chinese). Your check is then stamped with the symbol of the dish, adding about $1 to $3 to your tab. Unless you're really ravenous or you decide to include à la carte dishes from the regular menu, the grand total won't be more than about $10 per person.

Dim sum varies from restaurant to restaurant and chef to chef; if something looks familiar, don't be surprised if it's different from what you're used to, but equally good. This is a great group activity, especially on weekends, when you'll see two and three generations of families sharing dishes and calling for more. Even picky children can usually find something they enjoy. If you don't like or can't eat pork and shrimp, be aware that many, but not all, dishes include one or the other.

Excellent choices include the **Golden Palace Restaurant** (14 Tyler St.; ☎ 617/423-4565) and **China Pearl** (9 Tyler St.; ☎ 617/426-4338). Although both specialize in Hong Kong–style food, the real reason to visit is for dim sum. Many people consider Golden Palace's the best dim sum in Boston, but this is an area where strong preferences develop quickly (maybe you'll have some of your own). Two other popular destinations are **Imperial Seafood Restaurant** (70 Beach St.; ☎ 617/426-8439) and **Dynasty Restaurant** (33 Edinboro St.; ☎ 617/350-7777).

MODERATE

Buddha's Delight

5 Beach St. ☎ **617/451-2395.** Main courses $5.25–$10.95. No credit cards. Sun–Thurs 11am–10pm, Fri–Sat until 11pm. MBTA: Orange Line to Chinatown. VEGETARIAN VIETNAMESE/CHINESE.

This restaurant doesn't serve meat, poultry, fish, or dairy (some beverages have condensed milk), but through the wizardry of the chef, tofu and gluten are fried and barbecued to taste like chicken, pork, beef, and even lobster. Cuong Van Tran learned the secrets of vegetarian cooking from Buddhist monks in a temple outside Los Angeles. The results are delicious, healthy, and inexpensive. Try the Vietnamese fried spring rolls and "pizza" (similar to egg foo yong, but without the egg). The house specialties are always good, as are soups and selections from the "Chow Fun" and "Stir Fried Noodles" sections of the menu.

Chau Chow

52 Beach St. ☎ **617/426-6266.** Reservations not accepted. Main courses $4.25–$26.50. No credit cards. Sun–Thurs 11am–2am, Fri–Sat 10am–4am. MBTA: Orange Line to Chinatown. CANTONESE.

It seems a shame even to use the word "decor" in describing Chau Chow, one of the plainest restaurants you'll ever see. The line is out the door because of the food and reasonable prices, not the unyielding red plastic benches. You won't care, anyway, when you're trying to figure out how to get the last of the salt-and-pepper shrimp into your mouth before someone else takes it. Other specialties include jumbo shrimp with ginger, scallions, and onions; shrimp and chicken in cream and tomato sauce (inauthentic but delicious) on a bed of fried rice; and sizzling flounder in black bean sauce with onions and green pepper. The menu is heavy on seafood, but there are also traditional beef, chicken, and pork dishes. Sauces are not overpoweringly spicy, and the food is some of the freshest around.

East Ocean City

27 Beach St. ☎ **617/542-2504.** Reservations accepted only for parties of six or more. Main courses $5–$22. MC, V. Sun–Thurs 11am–3am, Fri–Sat 11am–4am. MBTA: Orange Line to Chinatown. CANTONESE.

Don't get too attached to the inhabitants of the fish tanks at East Ocean City—they may turn up on your plate. The encyclopedic menu offers a huge range of dishes, but as the name indicates, people come here for seafood, which some consider the best in the city. It's fresh, delicious, and carefully prepared. One specialty is clams in black bean sauce, a spicy rendering of a messy, delectable dish. Just about anything that swims can be ordered steamed with ginger and scallions, and if you'd like to branch out a little, make a selection from the chow foon section of the menu.

Grand Chau Chow

45 Beach St. ☎ **617/292-5166.** Reservations accepted only for parties of 10 or more. Main courses $5–$22. AE, DC, DISC, MC, V. Sun–Thurs 10am–3am, Fri–Sat 10am–4am. MBTA: Orange Line to Chinatown. CANTONESE.

Chau Chow's quieter sibling across the street offers niceties the smaller restaurant doesn't, including tablecloths and tuxedoed waiters. There are also large fish tanks here, both salt- and freshwater, where you can watch your dinner swimming around if you have the stomach for it. Clams with black bean sauce is a signature dish, as is grey sole with fried fins and bones. Stick to seafood and you can't go wrong. Lunch specials are a great deal for anything other than chow fun, which quickly turns gelatinous. If you're in town during Chinese New Year celebrations, phone ahead and ask that a banquet be prepared for your group. For about $25 a person, you'll get so many courses that you'll lose track. It's a great way to start any year.

Pho Pasteur

8 Kneeland St. ☎ **617/451-0247,** and 682 Washington St. ☎ 617/482-7467. Menu items $3.75–$9. MC, V. Daily 8am–8pm. MBTA: Orange Line to Chinatown. VIETNAMESE.

The specialty at these holes-in-the-wall is, fittingly, meals-in-a-bowl. The chicken and beef soups include noodle beef, rice noodle chicken, and egg noodle beef and chicken. Other specialties include chicken, shrimp, or beef with lemongrass, and the seafood firepot. Instead of (or in addition to) dessert, try a milkshake.

Pho Pasteur has another, larger location in Allston at 137 Brighton Ave. (☎ **617/783-2340**). The menu there includes lo mein and chow mein; rice with pork, chicken, beef, or shrimp; and noodles with fish balls. There are several special

Sunday Brunch

Many restaurants serve an excellent Sunday brunch, but for true decadence, head to a top hotel for a buffet of monstrous proportions. Do *not* make elaborate dinner plans.

The **Ritz-Carlton, Boston** (15 Arlington St.; ☎ 617/536-5700) serves brunch in the beautiful main dining room. You can choose delicacies such as oysters on the half shell, caviar and blinis, gravlax, seafood mousse, sturgeon, assorted pâtés, soup, roast beef carved to order, crêpes, omelettes to order, quiche, salads, and hot and cold vegetables. There's a dessert table for pastries, fruit tarts, cakes, cheese, and fruit. Reservations are necessary and are taken for 10:45am to 2:30pm. Jackets are requested for men, and jeans and sneakers are not allowed. Adults eat for $46, children for $23.

The Sunday brunch at **Aujourd'hui** in the Four Seasons Hotel (200 Boylston St.; ☎ 617/451-1392) is a bountiful New England buffet served in a lovely dining room with a view of the Public Garden. Serving tables are piled high with pâtés, salads, smoked and steamed fish, roast sirloin, chicken, lobster, egg dishes, waffles, and a fabulous assortment of desserts. It's served from 11:30am to 2:30pm, and reservations are recommended. Adult $39, child $19.50.

Overlooking the waterfront, the **Rowes Wharf Restaurant** at the Boston Harbor Hotel (70 Rowes Wharf, entrance on Atlantic Ave.; ☎ 617/439-3995) offers a traditional American buffet of fresh and smoked seafood, carved prime rib and rack of lamb, seasonal garden salad, soused shrimp, and regional specialty items. Also featured are omelettes made to order, Belgian waffles, freshly baked pastries, and desserts. Brunch is served from 10:30am to 2:30pm. When you make reservations, be sure to ask for a table overlooking the harbor. There is a dress code (no jeans or sneakers). Adult $42, child $21.

The **Café Fleuri** at Le Meridien Boston (250 Franklin St.; ☎ 617/451-1900) is in a magnificent garden court, light and airy, with lots of greenery. The food is just as elegant, with a hot and cold buffet befitting the hotel's French background, and the price includes a sparkling wine cocktail. The desserts are fabulous. Seatings are at 11 and 11:30am and 1 and 1:30pm. Adult $39, child $19.50.

---

dinners at $9. Pho Pasteur in Allston stays open from 11am to 11pm Monday through Saturday and from 11am to 10pm on Sunday.

8 At the Public Garden/Beacon Hill

VERY EXPENSIVE

✪ Aujourd'hui

In the Four Seasons Hotel, 200 Boylston St. ☎ **617/451-1392.** Reservations recommended (imperative on holidays). Main courses $16.50–$19.50 at lunch, $29–$39 at dinner; Sun buffet brunch $39. AE, CB, DC, MC, V. Daily 6:30–10:30am; Mon–Fri 11:30am–2:30pm, Sun 11:30am–2:30pm (brunch); Mon–Sat 5:30–10:30pm, Sun 6–10:30pm. MBTA: Green Line to Arlington. INTERNATIONAL.

On the second floor of the city's premier luxury hotel, the most beautiful restaurant in town has floor-to-ceiling windows overlooking the Public Garden, but even if it were under a pup tent, the incredible service and food would make Aujourd'hui a hit. The executive chef, David Fritchey, uses regional products and the freshest ingredients available, and the wine list is one of the best in the country. The menu changes often. To start, you might try a perfectly balanced squash-and-apple soup or a huge salad of arugula and other greens so fresh they practically crackle. Entrees might include a juniper-roasted venison chop with a sweet potato, and turnip cake and cider-glazed chard; or grilled Atlantic salmon served with minted couscous and chicory salad. In addition, the crab cakes are among the best outside of Maryland. The dessert menu also changes, but might include a wonderful fruit tart or a decadent chocolate creation. A wonderful (to most) menu note asks that cellular phones not be used in the restaurant.

Biba Food Hall

272 Boylston St. ☎ **617/426-7878.** Reservations recommended. Main courses $17–$34 at dinner; bar menu $3.50–$8.50. CB, DC, DISC, MC, V. Mon–Fri 11:30am–2pm, Sun 11:30am–2:30pm; Sun–Thurs 5:30–9:30pm, Fri–Sat 5:30–10:30pm. Bar menu offered until 2am. MBTA: Green Line to Arlington. ECLECTIC.

The mastermind behind Biba is Lydia Shire, a legend in culinary circles not just in Boston but in the United States. The menu here is well past the cutting edge, divided into categories that include "offal" (organ meats) and "legumina" (vegetables) as well as fish and meat. The restaurant, in the posh Heritage on the Garden complex across from the Public Garden, is decorated in bright geometric patterns based on Albanian kilim rug motifs. A grand spiral staircase with shiny, red handrails leads from the bar (where you can have a light meal) to the second-floor dining room, which attracts a chic crowd, especially at dinner.

The food is as dynamic as the decor. Some of it is prepared in the brick wood-burning oven visible from the dining room or the tandoori oven used for roasting and baking. Everything is made on the premises, from bread and sausages to desserts. The menu is à la carte, changes regularly, and always includes the signature lobster pizza and steak au poivre. Sometimes those are the only dishes you'll recognize as they pass by, but exploring is half the fun. Try grey sole with baccala (salt cod) croquettes; beef carpaccio with warm crumbled Roquefort; or yam raviolis with sweetbreads dusted in white truffle flour. Desserts are luxurious; sticky toffee pudding comes with warm toffee sauce, and the white chocolate cake with fresh berries is almost too rich.

Although Biba is hyped as a glamorous international bistro, there is no dress code (you can even come in shorts), and the price range is wide, so there is something on the menu for everyone, especially if you eat at the bar. Valet parking is available.

The Ritz-Carlton Dining Room

15 Arlington St. ☎ **617/536-5700.** Reservations required. Jacket and tie required for men. Main courses $28–$43. Grand buffet (Sun) $46. AE, CB, EU, DC, DISC, JCB, MC, V. Sun–Thurs 5:30–10pm, Fri–Sat 5:30–11pm; Sat noon–2:30pm. Sun 10:45am–2:30pm (brunch). MBTA: Green Line to Arlington. FRENCH.

In proper blue-blooded Boston society, only one place will do when celebrating an occasion or a milestone like a son's graduation from Harvard law school or the successful completion of a profitable corporate takeover: the magnificent second-floor restaurant of the elegant Ritz-Carlton, overlooking the Public Garden. Whether Sunday brunch or dinner under the crystal chandeliers with soft piano music playing in the background, a meal here is a memorable experience.

Less traditional dishes are available, but people come here for the French classics, such as rack of lamb with thyme, broiled sirloin steak in shallot sauce, and lobster "au whiskey," in a cream and bourbon sauce seasoned with tomatoes, thyme, and scallions. More than two dozen superb appetizers range from smoked north Atlantic salmon to lobster bisque with armagnac to beluga caviar with blinis. The wonderful desserts include chocolate and Grand Marnier soufflés and baked Alaska. Valet parking is available.

On Saturdays in the fall, winter, and spring, there's a series of Fashion Luncheons showcasing the designs of local designers and established boutiques.

EXPENSIVE

Ristorante Toscano

41 Charles St. ☎ **617/723-4090.** Reservations recommended at dinner. Main courses $7–$12 at lunch, $16–$28 at dinner. AE. Mon–Sat 11:30am–2:30pm; Mon–Thurs 5:30–9:30pm, Fri–Sat 5:30–10:30pm, Sun 5:30–10pm. MBTA: Red Line to Charles/MGH. NORTHERN ITALIAN.

The owners of this establishment call it a neighborhood restaurant, but it probably wouldn't pass for one anywhere but on Beacon Hill. Luckily, that's where it is. Toscano (named after Tuscany) is a warm, friendly place where the Florentine chef prepares authentic northern Italian cuisine. From the plainest spaghetti with pesto to veal scaloppine to tortellini with ham, cheese, and cream, the food is excellent. In addition to the printed menu, which includes chicken, steak, and seafood dishes, there are daily specials. If you opt for dessert, the tiramisù (a lavish concoction of sponge cake with four kinds of cream, mascarpone cheese, espresso, and cognac) is good. Valet parking is available.

9   Back Bay

THEATER DISTRICT TO COPLEY SQUARE

VERY EXPENSIVE

Grill 23 & Bar

161 Berkeley St. ☎ **617/542-2255.** Reservations recommended. Main courses $19–$30. AE, CB, DC, DISC, MC, V. Mon–Thurs 5:30–10:30pm, Fri–Sat 5:30–11pm, Sun 5:30–10pm. MBTA: Green Line to Arlington. AMERICAN.

In certain areas—delis, theater, late-night activity, sane drivers—Boston pales in comparison to New York. In the steakhouse category, Bostonians can point to Grill 23 and dare New Yorkers to top it. To be fair, Grill 23 is more than just a steakhouse. Slabs of beef and chops with all the trimmings are the stars of the show, but less aggressively carnivorous entrees attract equal attention from the kitchen and the diners. Steak au poivre and lamb chops are excellent examples of grilling done exactly right, crusty and juicy, so tender that your knife glides through the meat. Trout also arrives with a delectable crust of cornmeal and cumin, and the other grilled and roasted fish dishes rival those at any seafood restaurant. Side dishes, served à la carte, include huge plates of creamed spinach, home fries, and out-of-this-world garlic mashed potatoes, and could easily be entrees if your attention could be drawn away from the main dishes. Desserts show as little restraint as the meat offerings—try the deliriously good cappuccino cheesecake or flourless chocolate cake, or, if you insist on moderation, risk being called a wimp and request a dish of berries (not on the menu, but available if you ask).

On what was once the trading floor of the Salada Tea Building, Grill 23 is a wood-paneled, glass-walled, high-ceilinged room with a business-like air. The service is exactly right for the setting, helpful but not familiar. Two caveats: Smoking is not only allowed but encouraged, as evinced by the humidor that makes the rounds of the dining room in the arms of a staff member. The ventilation is good, but you can smell smoke in your clothes and hair later. And the noise level grows louder in tiny increments as the evening progresses—you won't realize you're shouting until you're outside yelling about what a good time you had.

Plaza Dining Room

In the Copley Plaza Hotel, 138 St. James Ave. ☎ **617/267-5300**, ext. 1638. Reservations recommended. Jacket and tie required. Main courses $20–$28. AE, CB, DC, DISC, JCB, MC, V. Tues–Thurs 6–10pm, Fri–Sat 5:30–10pm. MBTA: Orange Line to Back Bay or Green Line to Copley. CONTINENTAL.

This elegant, wood-paneled room, with Waterford crystal chandeliers and ornately sculpted vaulted ceilings, is one of Boston's premier special-occasion destinations. Whatever you're celebrating, the opulent setting and top-notch service will do justice to your good news. The menu changes seasonally and always features classic continental dishes (some with contemporary flair), with recipes based on fresh, seasonal local ingredients. Quality is emphasized over quantity, but choosing just one of the half-dozen appetizers and dozen or so entrees isn't easy. To start, the grilled Brie with sun-dried tomatoes (wrapped in grape leaves and served with baguettes) is a favorite, and more traditional oysters Rockefeller and seafood on the half-shell are excellent. Among the exceptionally presented main courses are duck breast à l'orange, a classic with a twist—it's served with sliced kiwi and papaya and topped with a Grand Marnier-peppercorn sauce. Jazzed-up classics are also good choices here. Try the pan-seared sirloin with Cabernet Sauvignon sauce, or sautéed Gulf shrimp with a sauce of tomato, garlic, and Chardonnay. For dessert, the menu notes that the chef recommends the souffles—he knows what he's doing. The wine list is extensive, featuring about 180 different varieties.

EXPENSIVE

✪ Legal Sea Foods

800 Boylston St., in the Prudential Center. ☎ **617/266-6800**. Reservations recommended at lunch. Main courses $5.95–$12.95 at lunch, $13.95–$23.95 at dinner. AE, CB, DC, DISC, MC, V. Mon–Thurs 11am–10pm, Fri–Sat 11am–11pm. Sun noon–10pm. MBTA: Green Line, B, C, or D train to Hynes/ICA, or E train to Prudential. SEAFOOD.

The food at Legal Sea Foods ("Legal's," in Bostonian parlance) isn't the fanciest or the cheapest or the trendiest. What it is is the freshest, and management's commitment to that policy has produced a thriving chain. The family-owned business began as a small fish market in Cambridge in 1950 and opened its first restaurant in 1968. It has an international reputation for serving only top-quality fish and shellfish—broiled, baked, stir fried, grilled, fried, steamed, and in casserole. The menu includes regular selections—scrod, haddock, bluefish, salmon, shrimp, calamari, and lobster, among others—plus whatever looked good at the market that morning, and it's all splendid. The clam chowder is a winner, and the fish chowder has its own appeal. Or start with creamy, salty smoked bluefish pâté. Entrees run the gamut from plain grilled fish to seafood fra'diavolo on fresh linguine. The seafood casserole—shrimp, scallops, whitefish, and lobster meat in a cream or butter sauce, topped with cheese—is sinfully good, as is salmon baked in parchment with vegetables and white wine.

The Prudential Center branch is suggested because it takes reservations (only at lunch), a deviation from a long tradition. There are also branches at the Boston Park Plaza Hotel & Towers (35 Columbus Ave.; ☎ **617/426-4444**), Copley Place (100 Huntington Ave.; ☎ **617/266-7775**), Kendall Square (5 Cambridge Center; ☎ **617/864-3400**), and eight other locations with the blue-and-white-checked decor and menu—for now. In 1996, legendary New England chef Jasper White came on board as executive chef. White, the person credited with revolutionizing the concept of both the hotel restaurant and the seafood restaurant (he owned and ran Jasper's, on the waterfront, until it closed in 1995), is expected to spruce up the menu and individualize the restaurants.

MODERATE

Jacob Wirth Company

31 Stuart St. ☎ **617/338-8586.** Reservations recommended. Main courses $5.95–$15. AE, DC, DISC, MC, V. Mon–Thurs 11:30am–11pm, Fri–Sat 11:30am–midnight, Sun noon–6pm. MBTA: Green Line to Boylston or Orange Line to New England Medical Center. GERMAN/AMERICAN.

In the heart of the Theater District, "Jake's" has been serving Bostonians for 129 years—since before there were theaters here. The wood-planked floor and brass accents give the room the feeling of a saloon, but a saloon with a view of the Rhine. The hearty German meals are reasonably priced; dinner offerings include Wiener schnitzel, sauerbraten, mixed grills, and bratwurst and knockwurst along with fish and prime rib. There are daily blackboard specials and a large selection of sandwiches. Service at lunchtime is snappy, but if you have theater tickets and want to be on time, the suspense may be greater in the restaurant than at the show. There's a large selection of beers on tap.

Turner Fisheries

In the Westin Hotel, 10 Huntington Ave., Copley Place. ☎ **617/424-7425.** Reservations recommended. Main courses $14–$26.95 at dinner. AE, CB, DC, DISC, MC, V. Mon–Sat 11am–11:30pm; Sun 10:30am–3pm (brunch) and 3–11:30pm. MBTA: Orange Line to Back Bay or Green Line to Copley. SEAFOOD.

This restaurant is best known for winning the Boston Harborfest Chowderfest contest so many times that its clam chowder was elevated to the Chowderfest Hall of Fame (you can also order lobster, fish, and dairy-free "clear" clam chowder). There's more to seafood than just chowder, though, and Turner Fisheries serves some of the freshest fish in town. The menu features each day's special catch; you can request your choice pan-fried, broiled, grilled, baked, or steamed. All are served with vegetables and a potato or rice. If you'd like something fancier, specialties run from paella to bouillabaisse to crabcakes to New England seafood in a wonderful lobster cream sauce. The raw bar here is also a big draw, and at dinner you can order from the understandably short "not seafood" menu. Ask for a booth if you want privacy or a table if you want to enjoy the atrium-like atmosphere.

COPLEY SQUARE TO MASSACHUSETTS AVENUE

VERY EXPENSIVE

✪ Ambrosia on Huntington

116 Huntington Ave. ☎ **617/247-2400.** Reservations recommended at dinner. Main courses $5–$12 at lunch, $16–$29 at dinner. AE, DISC, MC, V. Mon–Fri 11:30am–2:30pm; Mon–Thurs 5:30–10pm, Fri–Sat 5–11pm, Sun 5–9pm. MBTA: Orange Line to Back Bay or Green Line, E train to Prudential. FRENCH/ASIAN.

Felicitously named proprietors Tony and Dorene Ambrose (he's the chef) have turned the vacant ground floor of an office building into a dazzling room, where the dramatic architecture of the restaurant is matched only by the dramatic architecture of . . . the food. Every dish here is a feast for the eyes as well as the mouth and nose, with towering garnishes, accents of vegetables and pastry, and rich, unusual flavors that tie it all together. Starters are divided into exotic appetizers and shellfish, and simple salads. The Peruvian purple potato spring roll in crispy paper with Cabernet truffle oil is a plump pocket of potato infused with winey flavor, and a green salad is served with a Champagne mustard-seed vinaigrette. An entree of Gulf Stream swordfish in sage Provencal broth with potato galette arrives already carved into five huge chunks, separated by upright fans of thinly sliced potato and resting comfortably on a mound of potatoes redolent with chives and garlic. A special pasta of shrimp in a light curry sauce on a bed of noodles is so pretty you just want to stare at it, but when you finally do taste it you'll be glad you did. There's an awful lot to look at inside, with contemporary art on the walls and, of course, the art on the plates, which provides more interesting scenery than the uninspiring view of a corner of the Prudential Center through the floor-to-ceiling windows. Service here, by teams rather than individuals, is excellent, and your water glass will never be empty. Valet parking is available.

Café Budapest

In the Copley Square Hotel, 90 Exeter St. ☎ **617/266-1979.** Reservations recommended. Main courses $8.50–$24 at lunch, $19.50–$33 at dinner. AE, DC, DISC, MC, V. Mon–Sat noon–3pm; Mon–Thurs 5–10:30pm, Fri–Sat 5pm–11:30; Sun 1–10:30pm. MBTA: Green Line to Copley. HUNGARIAN.

In much the same way that a good movie transports you to another time and place, a meal at Café Budapest will leave you standing on the sidewalk, blinking and a bit disoriented. Your brain is pretty sure it's in Hungary, but you're outside the Copley Square Hotel, having spent a couple of hours in the luxurious basement restaurant. For the full romantic effect, ask to be seated in the Pink Room (the Blue Room and the main dining room are nice, too, but not as plush) and prepare for fine Continental cuisine.

This is food from another era, before cholesterol counts and fat grams. Start with the signature chilled cherry soup, flavored with Hungarian burgundy. Hors d' oeuvres include crepes and caviar, chicken liver mousse and smoked salmon. Everything is perfectly prepared and presented, and the service exactly suits the formal atmosphere. Throw caution to the wind and try chicken paprikas as an entree, infused with sour cream and served over homemade noodles. And there's also beef Stroganoff, sauerbraten, and *skekely gulyas*, pork chops and sausage with home-fermented sauerkraut. A pair of hearty eaters can attempt the full-course mixed grill of filet mignon, Wiener schnitzel, pork chops, potato, and vegetable, topped off by a rich pastry and coffee. Be sure to have dessert (you've gone back in time—what calories?). The signature chocolate-raspberry-walnut cake is wonderful, or be traditional and stick with the excellent strudel. Complete lunches, including entrée, soup, salad, dessert, tea or coffee, are a great deal for less than $20.

✪ L'Espalier

30 Gloucester St. ☎ **617/262-3023.** Reservations required. Prix fixe dinner (four courses) $62; vegetable dégustation menu (six courses) $68; dégustation menu (seven courses) $78. AE, DISC, MC, V. Mon–Sat 6–10pm. MBTA: Green Line, B, C, or D train to Hynes/ICA. NEW ENGLAND/FRENCH.

Dinner at L'Espalier is a unique experience, certainly in Boston and perhaps anywhere. It's very much like eating at the home of a dear friend who has only your complete pleasure in mind . . . and happens to have a dozen highly trained helpers in the kitchen. Owners Frank and Catherine McClelland preside over the three dining rooms, on the second floor of an 1876 townhouse. Reached by a spiral mahogany staircase, the space is formal yet inviting, with fireplaces, ornately carved moldings, and bay windows. Service is beyond excellent, in that eerie realm where it seems possible that the waiter just read your mind.

The quality of the food, if anything, exceeds the trappings. Chef Frank McClelland has supervised the evolution of the restaurant from its original *nouvelle cuisine* identity into a regularly changing adventure, an exploration of the freshest and most interesting ingredients available. The breads, sorbets, ice creams, and desserts (many adapted from the family's heirloom cookbooks) are made on the premises. The prix fixe menu includes an *amuse geulle,* first course, main course, and dessert. There are five to seven choices in each category, always including a caviar selection (for an additional charge), hot or cold soup, fish, lamb, veal, beef, or venison. Flavors explode in your mouth. An appetizer of chimney-roasted Maine lobster, garnished with the shell, arrives standing in a pool of lemon grass, carrot juice, and star anise broth, accented with chickpea–sweet garlic puree. The salad offered as a first course sounds almost too trendy, with greens, chanterelles, apples, grilled radicchio, and Hubbardston blue goat cheese, but something this good should be more of a trend-setter. A main course of pan-roasted duck breast in fava bean crust with black quinoa and confit duck jambon and black cherry sauce is strong-flavored and savory; salmon in a sesame crust over noodles in a ginger-and-sesame broth is equally impressive. Desserts are alarmingly good—even if you have one of the superb soufflés, which are ordered with dinner; ask to see the tray.

The dégustation menus, both vegetarian and non, are available to entire tables only. The vintner's tasting of wines selected to go along with each course adds $45 to the cost of the regular dégustation menu. One course that's also available à la carte is the celebrated cheese tray (the Grand Fromage, with two local cheeses). The wine cellar is extensive, and wines can be ordered by the glass or bottle. Valet parking is available.

EXPENSIVE

Casa Romero

30 Gloucester St. ☎ **617/536-4341.** Reservations recommended. Main courses $12–$20; buffet lunch $8.95. DC, DISC, MC, V. Mon–Fri 11:30am–2:30pm. Sun–Thurs 5–10pm, Fri–Sat 5–11pm. MBTA: Green Line, B, C, or D train to Hynes/ICA. MEXICAN.

There's something about restaurants in alleys—they feel like secret clubs or speakeasys, and if they're really worth seeking out, so much the better. Casa Romero is just such a place. It feels authentically Mexican (because it is), with a tiled floor, heavy wood furnishings, dim lighting, clay pots, and many other decorations. The food is wonderful, both authentic and accessible, with generous portions of spicy-hot and milder dishes; the friendly staff will help you negotiate the menu. Señor Romero or one of the waiters will be happy to describe ingredients and preparation. If the soup of the day is garlic, don't miss it. Main-dish specialties include several kinds of enchiladas and fajitas, excellent stuffed deviled squid in tomato and chipotle sauce, chicken breast in *mole poblano* (spicy chocolate) sauce, and terrific pork tenderloin marinated with oranges and smoked peppers. In the summer, reserve a table in the walled garden. In 1996, Casa Romero began serving a weekday buffet lunch, with six standard dishes and daily specials. It's a great value and a good introduction to the cuisine.

Davio's

269 Newbury St. ☎ **617/262-4810**. Reservations recommended. Main courses $9.95–
$24.95. Pizzas $6.95–$8.50. AE, CB, DC, DISC, MC, V. Mon–Sat 11:30am–3pm, Sun 11:30am–
3pm (brunch); Mon–Thurs and Sun 5–10pm, Fri–Sat 5–11pm. MBTA: Green Line to Copley.
CREATIVE NORTHERN ITALIAN.

While it seems the rest of the Boston-area culinary community regularly plays musical chefs, owner-chef Steve DiFillipo has buckled down and turned Davio's into a
local favorite. The restaurant's excellent reputation rests on its top-notch kitchen,
dedicated staff, and pleasing atmosphere. In a Back Bay brownstone, you wouldn't
expect to find typical Italian fare, and you won't. Try the grilled veal chop in port
wine sauce, penne pasta with smoked chicken, or grilled red snapper with crab frit-
ters and a tomato-chili pepper-honey glaze. There are usually three special entrees
daily, plus a house pâté, homemade pasta, and a ravioli creation. There's also a soup
of the day in addition to the superb minestrone. Dessert choices include a white
chocolate torte and a mixed-fruit tart. Davio's has a fine selection of Italian, French,
and California wines, including some rare and expensive old Italian vintages. Half
bottles are also available. The restaurant offers valet parking. Davio's also has an
upstairs cafe with an outside dining terrace in good weather. (Hours at the cafe are
11:30am–3pm and 5–11pm.)

There's a Davio's in Cambridge, at the Royal Sonesta Hotel (5 Cambridge Pkwy.;
☎ 617/661-4810), open the same hours, except that dinner service ends at 10pm
nightly.

Top of the Hub

800 Boylston St., Prudential Center. ☎ **617/536-1775**. Reservations recommended. Jacket
advised for men. Main courses $7–$16 at lunch, $16–$29 at dinner. Menu dégustation $65
per person (two-person minimum). Sun brunch $29 adults, $14 children. AE, DC, DISC,
MC, V. Mon–Fri 11:30am–2pm, Sat noon–3pm, Sun 11am–2:30pm (brunch); Sun–Thurs
5:30–10pm, Fri–Sat 5:30–11pm. MBTA: Green Line, B, C, or D train to Hynes/ICA, or E train
to Prudential. CONTEMPORARY AMERICAN.

For many years, the answer to the question "How's the food at Top of the Hub?"
was, "The view is spectacular." Since a complete overhaul of the space and the menu
in 1995, the cuisine has been improved so dramatically that even if it's not quite a
match for the 52nd-story panorama outside, you probably won't notice. Check the
weather forecast and plan to eat here when it's clear out and you'll be able to see as
much of Boston and the suburbs as is possible through the three glass-walled sides
of the restaurant and lounge. At night the spectacle below is especially lovely.
Consider coming before sunset and lingering over your meal until dark—it's the
best of both worlds.

Executive chef Dean Moore emphasizes seafood and grilling, tastes that meet in
the entree of north Atlantic sea scallops grilled and served with polenta, seasonal
vegetables, and citrus. Lemon and garlic roasted chicken is another good choice at
dinner. Lunch offerings include four pizzas and half a dozen tasty sandwiches served
with sweet potato fries. At either meal, the clam chowder is a standout, light and
tasty, with more broth than cream. Salads are large and varied, but if you don't like
your vegetables drowning in dressing, ask for it on the side.

Reduced parking rates are available in the Prudential Center garage after 4pm
weekdays and all day on Saturday and Sunday. When you make your reservation,
ask for a table by the window.

MODERATE

Bangkok Cuisine

177A Massachusetts Ave. ☎ **617/262-5377.** Reservations not accepted. Main courses $4.75–$6.50 at lunch, $8–$13.50 at dinner. AE, DISC, MC, V. Mon–Sat 11:30am–3pm; Mon–Thurs 5–10:30pm, Fri 5–11pm, Sat 3–11pm, Sun 4–10pm. MBTA: Green Line, B, C, or D train to Hynes/ICA. THAI.

Bangkok Cuisine, opened in 1979, was the first Thai restaurant in Boston. It has set (and maintained) high standards for the many others that followed. The dishes run the gamut from excellent chicken and basil to all sorts of curry offerings, pan-fried or deep-fried whole fish, and hot and sour salads. The green curry in coconut milk and vegetables prepared with strong green Thai chili pepper are the most incendiary. You can order nonspicy food and, of course, pad Thai, the famous noodle dish. A rice plate special is served at lunch. The iced coffee and iced tea served Thai-style with sweetened condensed milk might be all the dessert you need, but there's also excellent homemade ice cream.

The Original Sports Saloon

In the Copley Square Hotel, 47 Huntington Ave. ☎ **617/536-9000.** Main courses $6.50–$17.95. AE, DC, DISC, MC, V. Daily 11:30am–1:30am. Full menu served until 10pm, appetizers until closing. MBTA: Green Line to Copley. AMERICAN/BARBECUE.

This tiny saloon serves award-winning barbecue in a pleasant, if loud, room with 11 large-screen TVs, photographs of sports figures, and cartoons by the *Boston Globe*'s Paul Szep. The specialty is barbecued baby back ribs, which take more than 30 hours to prepare. The ribs are slow-cooked, using an authentic Memphis smoker, over a secret blend of hickory, ash, cherry, and apple woods. Other menu items include a Bloomin' Saloon'ion (an addictive battered, deep-fried whole onion) and the Larry Bird sandwich (marinated chicken breast served on a whole wheat bun with bacon, melted Swiss cheese, and honey mustard).

INEXPENSIVE

⑤ Café Jaffa

48 Gloucester St. ☎ **617/536-0230.** Reservations not accepted. Main courses $3–$8.75. AE, MC, V. Mon–Thurs 11am–10:30pm, Fri–Sat 11am–11pm, Sun 1–10pm. MBTA: Green Line, B, C, or D train to Hynes/ICA. MIDDLE EASTERN.

A long, narrow brick room with a glass front, Café Jaffa looks more like a snazzy pizza place than the wonderful Middle Eastern restaurant it is. Young people flock here, drawn by the low prices, excellent quality, and large portions of food, which includes burgers and steak tips as well as traditional Middle Eastern offerings such as falafel, baba ghanoush, and hummus. Lamb, beef, and chicken kebabs come with Greek salad and pita bread. If the desserts are fresh, try the baklava. There is a short list of beer and wine and (somewhat incongruously) many fancy coffee offerings.

10 Cambridge

The dining scene in Cambridge, as in Boston, offers something for everyone, from penny-pinching students to the tycoons many of them hope to become. The MBTA Red Line runs from downtown Boston to the heart of Harvard Square. Many of the restaurants listed here can be reached on foot from there. If inexpensive ethnic food is more your speed, head for Central and Inman squares, each a virtual United Nations of budget cuisine.

Cambridge Dining

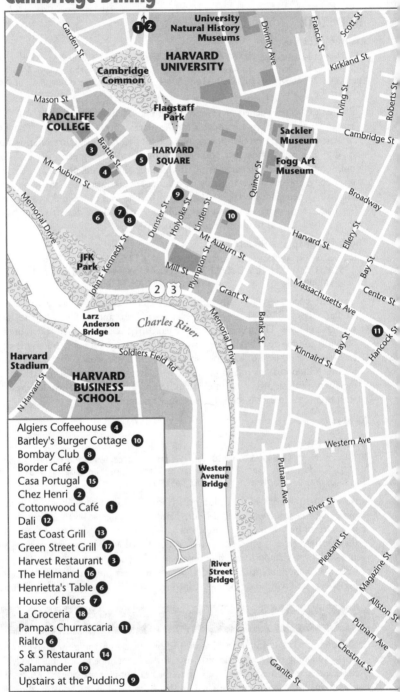

Algiers Coffeehouse ④
Bartley's Burger Cottage ⑩
Bombay Club ⑧
Border Café ⑤
Casa Portugal ⑮
Chez Henri ②
Cottonwood Café ①
Dali ⑫
East Coast Grill ⑬
Green Street Grill ⑰
Harvest Restaurant ③
The Helmand ⑯
Henrietta's Table ⑥
House of Blues ⑦
La Groceria ⑱
Pampas Churrascaria ⑪
Rialto ⑥
S & S Restaurant ⑭
Salamander ⑲
Upstairs at the Pudding ⑨

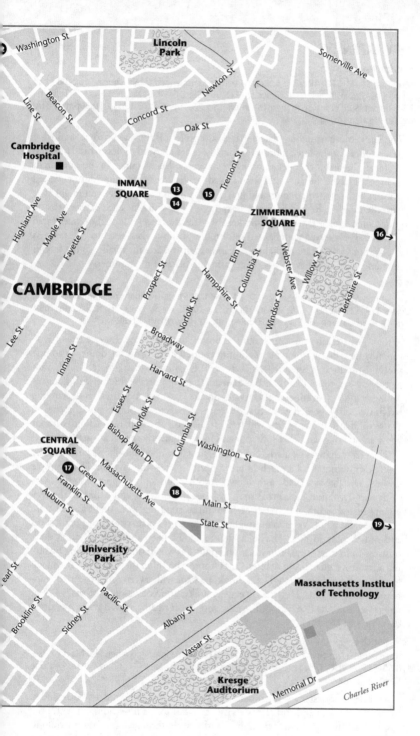

VERY EXPENSIVE

Harvest Restaurant

44 Brattle St. ☎ 617/492-1115. Reservations recommended. Main courses $6.50–$11 at lunch, $16–$26 at dinner. Cafe dinner $8–$18. AE, CB, DC, DISC, MC, V. Mon–Fri 11:30am–2:30pm; Sat–Sun 11am–3pm (brunch). Mon–Thurs 6–10pm, Fri–Sat 5:30–10:30pm. MBTA: Red Line to Harvard. AMERICAN.

The Harvest is a gathering place for Harvard professors, business people, and what passes for celebrities in Cambridge (generally, other Harvard professors and business people). The menu changes about every six weeks. Main courses in the cafe might include a Harvest burger with potato salad, grilled vegetable canneloni or roasted chicken with mashed potatoes and gravy. In the main dining room you might start with the excellent herbed liver pâté or spinach salad with blue cheese, walnuts, and grilled onion, then try grilled lamb kebabs with couscous (at lunch) or sage-seared pheasant breast served with braised mushrooms, risotto cakes, and broccoli rabe. As a rule, meals in the cafe are lighter and less expensive, and the quality of the food is the same. The courtyard is a popular gathering place in the summer.

✪ Rialto

One Bennett St., in the Charles Hotel. ☎ 617/661-5050. Reservations recommended. Main courses $19–$29. AE, DC, MC, V. Sun–Thurs 5:30–10pm, Fri–Sat 5:30–11pm. Bar Sun–Thurs 5pm–1am, Fri–Sat 5pm–1:30am. MBTA: Red Line to Harvard. MEDITERRANEAN.

If Rialto isn't the best restaurant in the Boston area, it's close. Every element is so carefully thought out that you might find yourself pausing during dinner to admire the end product as an intellectual as well as culinary masterpiece. You'll want to pause a lot, to look around the dramatic but comfortable room, with floor-to-ceiling windows overlooking Harvard Square, cushy banquettes, and standing lamps that cast a golden glow. Rialto attracts a chic crowd, but it's not a "scene" in the sense that out-of-towners will feel left behind. The staff is solicitous without being smothering, and chef Jody Adams's food eloquently speaks for itself.

The menu changes regularly, but you might start with a blue-cheese tart in a flaky crust with walnuts and a patch of green on the plate—the excellent "local simple greens," available as a salad on their own. Another outstanding appetizer is the *soupe de poisson* (Provençal fisherman's soup with rouille, Gruyère, and basil oil), the very essence of seafood. Main courses each sound so good that you might as well close your eyes and point. Vegetarians might come up with a plate of creamy potato slices and mushrooms so thick and juicy they're almost like eating meat. Seared duck breast with foie gras, squash raviolis, and quince is wonderful, and anything involving salmon is a guaranteed winner—even those who think they don't like it will fall for the perfectly flaky, orange-pink hunk, perhaps with sweet potatoes, dried cranberries, and pine nuts. Desserts are equally funky; a trio of seasonal sorbets is a great choice, as is *cassata* (Sicilian sponge cake with sweet ricotta, shaved chocolate, dried cherries, and Marsala).

Salamander

1 Athenaeum St. (at First St.). ☎ 617/225-2121. Reservations recommended. Main courses $18.50–$35. AE, DC, DISC, MC, V. Mon–Thurs 6–10pm, Fri–Sat 6–10:30pm. MBTA: Red Line to Kendall; 10-minute walk. AMERICAN/ASIAN.

Cambridge's hottest new restaurant, in every sense of the word, is Salamander. Chef-owner Stan Frankenthaler is a visionary, and this is his vision. You enter the Carter Ink Building, a block from the Charles River, through a four-story atrium to find Salamander humming on the ground floor, a foodie haven in a dimly lit room in the center of which is a grill over a wood fire. Seating spills into the courtyard, where it's brighter and less warm and smoky (from the fire), but also less cozy.

The first sure indication that this won't be a typical experience is the menu, two heavy slabs of copper bound with leather. The descriptions within are as long as menu entries can be without growing into actual paragraphs, and they still don't do justice to the flights of fancy that land in front of you. "Wood oven baked potato stuffed nan, shallot jam and a mizuna salad; with cumin-saffron oil" nearly spills off the plate in a frenzy of Indian bread (*nan*) and heaps of salad; "fresh spring rolls, wrapped in rice paper, with torn herbs and many condiments" is practically an Asian smorgasbord. And those are just the appetizers; there are eight or nine on the regularly changing menu and as many entrees, at least one vegetarian and each more interesting than the last. The simplest (a relative term), almost always available, is lightly fried lobster with chiles, lemongrass, and Thai basil; you might also find black tea–flavored rotisserie-cooked chicken breast, in gingery broth with hand-rolled dumplings and shiitake mushrooms, or "one wood fire grilled double thick lamb chop over a pan seared braised lamb and eggplant 'pattie' surrounded by fragrant cardamom scented rich shank sauce." The enthusiasm in the descriptions alone is contagious, although service could be a bit more attentive while the necessarily lengthy preparation process is going on. After all this, a complicated dessert seems like overkill; if apple pie is on the menu, it makes an excellent contrasting finish.

Salamander is noted for its selection of beers and wine by the glass (and the half-glass, or tasting portion). Validated parking is available in the building.

Upstairs at the Pudding

10 Holyoke St. ☎ **617/864-1933.** Reservations recommended. Main courses $8–$12 at lunch, $16–$27 at dinner, $9–$12 at brunch; tasting menu (dinner) $45. AE, DC, MC, V. Mon–Fri 11:30am–2:30pm; Sun 11:30am–2pm (brunch); nightly 6–10pm. MBTA: Red Line to Harvard. CONTINENTAL/NORTHERN ITALIAN.

An oasis of calm above the tumult of Harvard Square, Upstairs at the Pudding is a special-occasion spot with food so good you'll want to make up a reason to go there. At the top of the Hasty Pudding Club's creaky stairs is a high-ceilinged room with green walls and soft, indirect lighting that make it feel almost cozy. There is a lovely terrace and herb garden off the dining room for seasonal al fresco dining. The knowledgeable, friendly staff reinforces the sense that you've made a nice discovery.

Noodle fans will want to try the hand-rolled pasta, which you'll see in main dishes and side dishes. The menu changes daily. To start, you might try venison-filled ravioli with port and lingonberry sauce, or pizza with four cheeses and white truffle oil. Tossed and composed salads, on the menu after the entrees, can also be ordered before the main course. There you'll find at least one pasta dish and a small but choice selection of meat and fish. If you like garlic mashed potatoes, you can't go wrong by ordering the main course (any main course) that comes with them, perhaps peppered beef tenderloin with blue cheese and charred tomato coulis. Atlantic salmon might be offered with sautéed spinach over polenta (properly gummy), and grilled veal chops with maple demi-glaze, grilled leeks, and wild-mushroom risotto. Portions are large, but try to save room for dessert. Pot de creme (flavors change regularly) is a good choice, as is anything with chocolate.

EXPENSIVE

Chez Henri

1 Shepard St. ☎ **617/354-8980.** Reservations recommended. Main courses $14.95–$18.95; three-course prix fixe menu $28; bar food $4.95–$7.95. AE, MC, V. Mon–Thurs 6–10pm,

Fri–Sat 6–11pm, Sun 11am–2pm (brunch) and 6–9pm. Bar food Mon–Sat until midnight, Sun until 10pm. MBTA: Red Line to Harvard. FRENCH/CUBAN.

In a dark, elegant space off Massachusetts Avenue near Harvard Law School, Chez Henri is an example of how good fusion cuisine can be. Under the same ownership as Providence in Brookline, Chez Henri has a more focused menu that concentrates on French bistro-style food with Cuban accents. The menu changes regularly; it might include appetizers of frog legs (the version with tamarind cream is silky and delicious) and pan-crisped sweetbreads served with warm arugula salad and strawberries *au poivre,* a tantalizing assemblage of flavors and textures. Entrees include generous portions of meat and fish—perhaps a juicy chicken breast served with black bean sauce, avocado slaw, and two spicy *empanadas* (turnovers) filled with potato and cheese; or halibut with plantains, roasted potatoes, mango coulis, and kiwi slices. The prix fixe menu, a good deal, includes one of two appetizers and one of two entrees as well as dessert, of which the crème brûlée is a terrific choice. The food at the bar is Cuban, as are the sweet specialty drinks.

Cottonwood Café

In the Porter Exchange Building, 1815 Massachusetts Ave. ☎ 617/661-7440. Reservations recommended. Main courses $9–$16 at lunch, $13–$26 at dinner. MC, V. Sun–Fri 11:30am–3pm; Sun–Thurs 5:30–10pm, Fri–Sat 5:30–11pm. MBTA: Red Line to Porter. SOUTHWESTERN.

An attractive, trendy restaurant decorated in southwestern style with cacti and pottery, the Cottonwood serves "modern Southwest cuisine," a blend of Native American, Mexican, Spanish, and European styles. This would be news to a lot of people who come here only for the excellent margaritas, but the food is quite good. Among the specials you might find are Rocky Mountain lamb, four excellent little chops arranged on red raspberry-chipotle sauce and green cilantro pesto; salmon Colorado, a grilled fillet with smoked tomato sauce and cilantro-garlic cream; and an unusual preparation of chicken coated with pulverized popcorn, then sautéed and served with roasted red pepper sauce and a cilantro mousse. Try the Milagro black-bean soup sprinkled with cilantro, a house specialty, or the six-chile chili, made with all meat. A great dessert is the caramel custard flan.

The Cottonwood Restaurant & Café (☎ **617/247-2225**), in the Back Bay at 222 Berkeley St., near St. James Ave., keeps the same hours and serves a lighter cafe menu Thursday through Saturday until midnight.

Dalí

415 Washington St., Somerville. ☎ **617/661-3254.** Reservations not accepted. Tapas $2.50–$7.50, main courses $14–$19. AE, DC, MC, V. Nightly 5:30–10:30pm. MBTA: Red Line to Harvard; follow Kirkland St. to intersection of Washington and Beacon sts. SPANISH.

Dalí casts an irresistible spell—it's noisy and crowded, it's on a grim corner not all that close to Harvard Square (though it's a short cab ride), it doesn't take reservations, and it still fills up with people cheerfully waiting more than an hour to get a table on weekends. The bar offers plenty to look at while you wait, including colorful paintings, dried flowers, sleeves of garlic, and a clothesline festooned with lingerie. The crowds come for the authentic Spanish food, especially the tapas, little plates of hot or cold creations that burst with flavor, perfect for sampling and sharing. There are about a dozen entrees (including excellent paella), but most people come in a group and cut a swath through the tapas offerings, 32 dishes on the regular menu and eight specials that change monthly. The *patatas ali-oli* (garlic potatoes) look like dull potato salad and taste so good you'll want to order more immediately. But hold off while you try the crunchy-tender *gambas con gabardina* (saffron-battered fried shrimp), the addictive *setas al ajillo* (sauteed mushrooms), and the rich but light *queso de cabra montañes* (goat cheese baked with tomato and basil). The waiters, in brightly embroidered vests, seem a bit overwhelmed but never fail to make sure there's enough bread for sopping up juices and sangria for washing it all down. If you want to experiment and order food in several stages, that's fine, too. Finish up with flan for a traditional ending, or try the *tarta de chocolates*. Order your own if you like chocolate—it's so good the spirit of sharing will evaporate and you'll suddenly become territorial.

Go early for a leisurely meal since the restaurant gets very crowded late in the evening. The owners of Dalí also run **Tapèo** (☎ **617/267-4799**) at 266 Newbury St. between Fairfield and Dartmouth sts. in the Back Bay, which offers the same menu and similarly wacky decor.

East Coast Grill

1271 Cambridge St. ☎ **617/491-6568.** Reservations accepted only for parties of five or more. Main courses $12.50–$22. AE, DISC, MC, V. Fri–Sat 11:30am–2:30pm, Sun 11:30am–2:30pm (brunch); Sun–Thurs 5:30–10pm, Fri–Sat 5:30–10:30pm. MBTA: Red Line to Harvard; from there take no. 69 bus toward Lechmere. SEAFOOD/INTERNATIONAL/BARBECUE.

By the time you read this, the madly popular East Coast Grill will have doubled in size and absorbed its corporate sibling, Jake & Earl's Dixie Barbecue. A complete overhaul in mid-1996 was expected to make chef-owner Chris Schlesinger's creations available to a larger audience, so the notorious lines outside probably will have shrunk somewhat. Things that were not expected to change were the friendly service, country and rock music, and dizzying menu. Specialties are seafood, hearty soups, and southern barbecue in three forms: Texas beef, Missouri spareribs, and North Carolina pork. Barbecue platters come with baked beans, corn bread, and a slice of watermelon. Appetizers include buttermilk fried chicken and the scorching "pasta from Hell," which appears on the menu alongside the wholly inadequate word "warning." If you choose to ignore it, beware; it's *hot*.

⑤ Pampas Churrascaria

928 Massachusetts Ave. ☎ **617/661-6613.** Reservations accepted only for parties of six or more. *Rodizio* $16.95, salad bar $7.99. AE, DC, MC, V. Mon–Fri 5:30–10:30pm, Sat 5–10:30pm, Sun 1–10:30pm. MBTA: Red Line to Harvard or Central. BRAZILIAN.

If you love meat, Pampas is a dream come true. Even if you don't eat meat at all, this rowdy spot between Harvard and Central squares still has a lot to offer in the form of a salad bar that nearly bows beneath the piles of pasta and potato salads, olives, bread, marinated vegetables, and other tasty morsels. The real reason to come here, though, is the *rodizio*. Meats of every description are marinated and threaded onto swords, then roasted in the giant fireplace (don't lean on anything brick here—it's hot). Waiters then shuttle back and forth with the giant skewers, stopping to offer each diner chicken, beef, pork, goat, ribs, and even, somewhat disconcertingly, chicken hearts. Then they come back again, and again. Soon you'll understand the true meaning of "all you can eat." If you can still move, you're doing something wrong. The location, a solid 20 minutes from the nearest subway stops, might seem inconvenient at first, but when you finish, you'll want to walk for at least that long just to make sure you still can.

MODERATE

Bombay Club

57 John F. Kennedy St., in the Galleria Mall. ☎ **617/661-8100.** Main courses $4.95–$8.95 at lunch, $8.95–$15.95 at dinner. Lunch buffet $6.95 Mon–Fri, $8.95 Sat–Sun. AE, DC, MC, V. Daily 11:30am–11pm. MBTA: Red Line to Harvard. INDIAN.

Under the same ownership as the more traditional Kebab-'N'-Kurry (30 Massachusetts Ave., Boston; ☎ **617/536-9835**), this third-floor restaurant overlooking Harvard Square is noted for not looking like a typical Indian restaurant and serving food that's a step up from what you'd find at one. True fame has come to this contemporary-looking spot through its lunch buffet, a generous assortment of some of the best items on the menu at a price that can't be beat. The chicken, lamb, seafood, and rice specialties are the best in town. From the tandoori ovens come dishes baked to perfection in the traditional charcoal-fired clay oven. The flavorful Indian breads *tandoori roti* and *tandoori nan* are also baked there. The house specials include *barra kebab*, lamb marinated in a spicy sauce for three days and then baked on skewers, and "royal platters" combining several items.

Border Café

32 Church St. ☎ **617/864-6100.** Reservations not accepted. Main courses $6–$12. AE, MC, V. Mon–Thurs 11am–1am, Fri–Sat 11am–2am, Sun noon–11pm. MBTA: Red Line to Harvard. SOUTHWESTERN.

When you first catch sight of this thoroughly southwestern restaurant your thoughts may turn to, of all people, Yogi Berra. The baseball Hall of Famer supposedly said, "No one goes there anymore—it's too crowded;" Yogi was talking about a popular New York club, but it's something people have been saying about this Harvard Square hangout for 10 years. The festival atmosphere is only enhanced by the fact that people hang around the bar for hours waiting to be seated for the generous portions of tasty, if not completely authentic, food. The menu features Cajun, Tex-Mex, and some Caribbean specialties. The beleaguered wait staff keeps the chips and salsa coming, and if your order can be heard over the deafening roar of the crowd, try the excellent seafood enchiladas, any kind of tacos, Caribbean shrimp (dipped in coconut and spices before frying), or popcorn shrimp. The fajitas, served in the traditional way—good and loud—sizzling in a large iron frying pan, are also a popular choice. Set aside a couple of hours, be in a party mood, and ask to be seated downstairs if you want to be able to hear your companions. But beware: your clothes will smell like the restaurant (smoky, greasy, and spicy) for hours after you leave; small price to pay for one of the best deals in the area.

Casa Portugal

1200 Cambridge St. ☎ **617/491-8880.** Reservations recommended on weekends. Main courses $7.95–$13.95. AE, DISC, MC, V. Daily 4:30–10pm. MBTA: Red Line to Harvard; from there take the Lechmere bus (no. 69) to Inman Sq./Cambridge St. PORTUGUESE.

To evaluate this restaurant we enlisted a friend of Portuguese descent, who kept glancing around and saying, "It looks like my grandmother's house." She apparently favored stucco, colorful decorations, and a low-ceilinged, cozy atmosphere, but we had to guess—after the food arrived the conversation ran to "Wow, this is good," and "Are you going to finish that?" Generous portions of hearty, inexpensive Portuguese fare draw the locals to this comfortable spot, where a soup of the day, rice, and traditional fried potatoes come with all entrees. Try a dish that includes the flavorful Portuguese sausages, linguiça and chouriço. The tureens, which combine several types of shellfish, are excellent, as is the *bacalhau assado a cuca* (reconstituted salt cod, garlic, peppers, and potatoes baked with lots of olive oil).

Green Street Grill

280 Green St. ☎ **617/876-1655.** Reservations not accepted. Main courses $12.95–$17.95. AE, MC, V. Nightly 6–10pm. MBTA: Red Line to Central Square. CARIBBEAN.

This is a bar (and not a very promising-looking one, either) that serves Caribbean food that's among the tastiest and the hottest in town. If you have a taste for fiery dishes and can take the heat, you'll be in heaven; if not, you'll feel like a cartoon character with flames licking out of your head by the time the Green Street Grill is through with you. Chef Steve Cobble uses five kinds of peppers in preparing some dishes. The goat stew has jalapeños, Anaheims, chipotles, serranos, and Scotch bonnets. Seafood pepper pot—a combination of mussels, lobster, Caribbean pumpkin, and eggplant in a white wine sauce—is nearly as incendiary. Grilled seafood is also done well here.

○ The Helmand

143 First St. ☎ **617/492-4646.** Reservations recommended. Main courses $8.95–$14.95. AE, MC, V. Sun–Thurs 5–10pm, Fri–Sat 5–11pm. MBTA: Green Line to Lechmere. AFGHAN.

Even in cosmopolitan Cambridge, Afghan food is something novel, and if any competitors are setting their sights on the Helmand, they're contemplating a daunting task. The elegant setting belies the reasonable prices at this airy, spacious spot near the CambridgeSide Galleria mall. Knowing that this is probably all new to many diners, the courteous staff patiently answers questions about the food, which is distinctly Middle Eastern with Indian and Pakistani influences. Many vegetarian dishes are offered, and when meat appears it's often used as one element of a dish rather than the centerpiece. Every meal is accompanied by delectable bread made in the wood-fired brick oven in the dining room. To start, you might try the baked pumpkin topped with a spicy ground meat sauce, a good contrast of flavors and textures. Entrees include several versions of what Americans would call stew, including *deygee kabob,* an excellent melange of lamb, yellow split peas, onion and red peppers. Or try the *aushak,* pasta pockets filled with leeks and buried under a sauce of split peas and carrots.

Henrietta's Table

One Bennett St., in the Charles Hotel. ☎ **617/661-5005.** Reservations recommended. Main courses $2.25–$9.50 at breakfast; $7.50–$11.50 at lunch; $8–$12.50 at dinner. AE, MC, V. Mon–Fri 6:30–11am, Sat 7–11:30am, Sun 7–10:30am; Mon–Sat noon–3pm, Sun 11:30am–3pm (brunch); Sun–Thurs 5:30–10pm, Fri–Sat 5:30–11pm. Market Mon–Fri 6:30am–10pm, Sat–Sun 7am–10pm. MTBA: Red Line to Harvard. NEW ENGLAND.

The country-kitchen atmosphere here reflects the straightforward cooking style, which depends on the excellent quality of the produce for the daily menus. It's right there on the menu: "Fresh & Honest." You can see how fresh by pausing at the entrance to look around the little farmstand market filled with fruits, vegetables, breads, and condiments. The adjoining dining room, with its plain wood floor and white walls, green-and-white color scheme, and homey wooden tables and chairs, is a perfect match for the food—it looks like Grandma's house, but more sophisticated. The menu changes daily. You might start with a grilled portabella mushroom, topped with Vermont brie, and served over greens dressed with walnut vinaigrette. Maine rock crab and corn chowder is often available, the sprightly flavors contrasting nicely with the bacon in the soup. Entrees are limited in number but not in execution: roast chicken is flavorful and juicy, a grilled pork chop is smoked and served with chunky applesauce, and wood-smoked Maine salmon meshes perfectly with beach-plum vinaigrette. You can wash it all down with a New England microbrew from a long list. The incredibly fresh vegetables are served only à la carte, which can make the tab a bit higher than you might have expected. Even people who think they don't like bread pudding love the chocolate version here. The lunch menu features sandwiches, Yankee pot roast, and baked scrod, among other items. And at breakfast you can get hotcakes, waffles, farm-fresh eggs, and fresh-squeezed juice.

The restaurant's namesake, a 1,000-pound pig who belongs to the hotel owner and lives on Martha's Vineyard, is pictured in a photograph near the front desk, but (we couldn't resist asking) is not on the menu in any way, shape, or form.

⑤ La Groceria

853 Main St. ☎ **617/876-4162** or 617/547-9258. Reservations recommended at dinner. Main courses $5.95–$8.95 at lunch, $9.95–$17.95 at dinner. Pizzas $5.95–$8.95. Children's menu $4.95–$5.95. AE, DC, DISC, MC, V. Mon–Fri 11:30am–4pm; Mon–Thurs 4–10pm, Fri–Sat 4–11pm. Sun 1–10pm. MBTA: Red Line to Central Square. ITALIAN.

On a drab street just outside Central Square, this colorful, family-run restaurant has dished up large portions of delicious Italian food since 1972. At lunch you'll see business meetings, at dinner, family outings, and at all times, students. Cheery voices bounce off the stucco walls and tile floors, but it seldom gets terribly noisy, probably because everyone's mouth is full. Start with the house garlic bread, which overflows with chopped tomato, red onion, fennel seed, and olive oil. The antipasto platter is crowded with meats, cheeses, roasted vegetables, and whatever else the chef feels moved to include. Main dishes might include homemade pasta from the machine you see as you enter. Lasagna (a vegetarian version) is an excellent choice, as is the chicken marsala. Chicken is also available roasted, and the brick-oven pizzas are available in individual and large sizes.

House of Blues

96 Winthrop St. ☎ **617/491-2583.** Reservations not accepted. Main courses $4.95–$14.95. AE, MC, V. Sun–Wed 11:30am–1am, Thurs–Sat 11:30am–2am. MBTA: Red Line to Harvard. CAJUN/PIZZA/INTERNATIONAL.

This is the original House of Blues, in a blue clapboard house near Harvard Square. Everything is blue here, and the walls and ceilings are dotted with whimsical pieces of folk art by various artists. On the ceiling near the bar area are plaster bas-reliefs of great blues musicians, and actual musicians play every night at 10 and on Saturday afternoon. The menu is essentially bar food, with enough variety to keep the legions of tourists who flock here contented. Try the buffalo legs (much bigger and meatier than buffalo wings), followed by jambalaya, a burger, or a pulled-pork sandwich. There's a wide selection of pizzas (try the one topped with feta cheese and garlic) that are baked in a wood-fired oven. The Sunday Gospel brunch requires reservations at least two weeks in advance.

S&S Restaurant

1334 Cambridge St., Inman Sq. ☎ **617/354-0777.** Main courses $2.95–$10.95. No credit cards. Mon–Sat 7am–midnight, Sun 8am–midnight. Sat–Sun brunch 8am–4pm. MBTA: Red Line to Harvard; then bus no. 69 (toward Lechmere). DELI.

"Es" is Yiddish for "eat," and this Cambridge classic is as straightforward as its name ("eat and eat"). Founded in 1919 by the great-grandmother of the current owners, this wildly popular weekend brunch spot is northeast of Harvard Square, west of MIT, and worth a visit during the week, too. The menu includes such traditional deli items as corned beef, pastrami, tongue, and Reuben sandwiches; potato pancakes, blintzes, knockwurst, lox, and whitefish. The S&S is also a full-service restaurant with entrées of beef, chicken, and fish, plus quiche and croissants, and serves breakfast anytime during restaurant hours. Be early for brunch, or plan to spend a good chunk of your Saturday or Sunday standing in line people-watching and getting hungry.

INEXPENSIVE

Algiers Coffeehouse

40 Brattle St. ☎ **617/492-1557.** Main courses $2.25–$7.95. AE, MC, V. Mon–Thurs 8am–midnight, Fri–Sat 8am–1am. MBTA: Red Line to Harvard. MIDDLE EASTERN.

This is an excellent place to take a break from rushing around Harvard Square and have a snack or a drink (try the special Algiers mint coffee), but you might find yourself lingering. That's the nature of coffeehouses, after all, and this is a particularly nice one. Long known as a dark, smoke-filled literary hangout, the new Algiers (which came about in the late 1980s as a result of a fire) is upstairs in Brattle Hall, and is still a favorite with Cambridge intellectuals and would-be intellectuals. Smoking is allowed on the upper level. This a good spot to eavesdrop while you eat, and the soups, sandwiches, homemade sausages, falafel, and hummus are terrific. Or just order from the extensive beverage menu.

✪ Bartley's Burger Cottage

1246 Massachusetts Ave. ☎ **617/354-6559.** Most items under $8. No credit cards. Mon–Sat 11am–10pm. MBTA: Red Line to Harvard. AMERICAN.

A cross-section of Cambridge, from Harvard students to regular folks, makes this perennial favorite a regular stop for great burgers and the best onion rings anywhere. Burgers bear the names of local and national celebrities; the names change, but the ingredients stay the same. Anything you can think of to put on ground beef is available here, from American cheese to béarnaise sauce. There are also some good dishes that don't involve meat, notably the creamy, garlicky hummus. Bartley's is one of the only places in the area where you can still get a real raspberry lime rickey— raspberry syrup, lime juice, lime wedges, and club soda, the taste of summer even in the winter.

11 Charlestown

✪ Olives

10 City Sq., Charlestown. ☎ **617/242-1999.** Reservations accepted only for parties of six or more. Main courses $15.95–$30. AE, DC, MC, V. Tues–Fri 5:30–10pm, Sat 5–10:30pm. MBTA: Orange or Green Line to North Station; 10-minute walk. ECLECTIC.

This small, informal bistro near the Charlestown Navy Yard is one of the hottest spots in town. Patrons line up shortly after 5pm to get a table—you might be better off just making five friends and calling for a reservation. If you don't get there by 5:45, expect to wait at least an hour (at the bar if there's room) until a table opens. Once you're seated, you'll find many of the tables small and crowded, the service uneven, the ravenous customers festive, and the noise level high. The open kitchen in the rear of the restaurant, with a rotisserie and a huge brick oven, adds to the din.

Happily, the food is worth the aggravation. Todd English, chef and co-owner with his wife, Olivia, is a culinary genius. The menu changes regularly and always includes "Olives Classics," one of which is a meltingly delicious tart of olives, caramelized onions, and anchovies. Ginger spinach salad dressed with tahini arrives surrounded by shredded carrots with orange and cumin vinaigrette, a complex combination that works perfectly. Another Olives Classic, spit-roasted chicken flavored with herbs and garlic, oozes succulent juices into the old-fashioned mashed potatoes. Braised lamb shank with a sherry-and-olive sauce is so tender it falls off the bone, and the sweet lady celebrating her birthday at the next table (in other words,

Afternoon Tea

This is Boston, the only city that has a whole tea party named after it. Although coffee was considered the patriotic beverage at the time of the original tea party (1773), and coffee shops and bars have done a remarkable job of colonizing modern Boston, the tradition of afternoon tea at a plush hotel is alive and well. Pots of tea and individual food items are available á la carte, but for the full effect, order light or full tea with all the trimmings.

The **Ritz-Carlton, Boston** (15 Arlington St.; ☎ **617/536-5700**) serves the city's most celebrated tea in the Ritz Lounge every day from 3 to 5:30pm. You'll feel compelled to sit up and act like a lady or gentleman in this elegant room, where harp music plays as you're served a light tea ($12.50) of pastries and breads, including delectable scones, or full tea ($16), including finger sandwiches and pastries.

Around the corner, the **Bristol Lounge** at the Four Seasons Hotel (200 Boylston St.; ☎ **617/351-2053**) offers a great view of the Public Garden every day from 3 to 4:30pm as you snack on scones ($9.50) or stuff yourself with sandwiches, scones, and nut bread ($16).

The Boston Harbor Hotel, across the Northern Avenue Bridge from the site of the original tea party, serves tea in the **Harborview Lounge** (70 Rowes Wharf, entrance on Atlantic Ave.; ☎ **617/439-7000**) on weekdays from 2 to 4:30pm. It makes an excellent late lunch, with a choice of cream tea ($7) with scones; light tea ($11), which adds strawberries; and complete tea ($15), with sandwiches and pastries as well.

Tea service at the **Copley Plaza Hotel** (138 St. James Ave.; ☎ **617/267-5300**) is in the dining room, a shamelessly opulent chamber where pastries, scones, and cookies make up the light tea ($10.50). Complete tea ($15) also includes sandwiches. Tea is available every day from 2:30 to 5pm.

practically sitting with us) spoke highly of the Cuban steak. For dessert, when you order your entree you'll be asked if you want falling chocolate cake with raspberry sauce and vanilla ice cream. Say yes.

12   The South End

The South End, an area known for its old brownstones and young professionals, has made its mark on Boston maps by virtue of the excellent dining offered at several highly acclaimed bistros.

MODERATE

Botolph's on Tremont

569 Tremont St. ☎ **617/424-8577.** Reservations accepted only for parties of eight or more. Main courses $7.75–$13.25, sandwiches $6.50–$8.50, grilled pizzas $5.95–$11.95. AE, MC, DC, DISC, V. Daily 11:30am–11:30pm. MBTA: Orange Line to Back Bay. CONTINENTAL.

This spinoff of the now-closed St. Botolph Restaurant in the Back Bay is a friendly neighborhood place that serves sandwiches, salads, grilled pizzas, pasta, and risotto. Pizzas range from five-cheese with tomato sauce to barbecued pork and onion with cilantro and sour cream. Caesar salad is available plain or with chicken, shrimp, or smoked salmon, and pastas come with seafood, vegetables, sausage, or chicken. The soups, which include Botolph's clam chowder, are hearty and delicious. It's a small storefront restaurant, long and narrow, decorated with paintings by local artists (which change monthly).

Hamersley's Bistro

553 Tremont St. ☎ **617/423-2700.** Reservations recommended. Main courses $18.50–$27. Menu dégustation varies. AE, DISC, MC, V. Mon–Fri 6–10pm, Sat 5:30–10pm, Sun 5:30–9:30pm. MBTA: Orange Line to Back Bay. ECLECTIC.

This is the place that made the South End a compass point on Boston's culinary map. The husband-and-wife team of Gordon and Fiona Hamersley presides over a long, narrow dining room decorated in cool yellow with lots of soft surfaces that absorb sound, so you can see but not hear what's going on at the tables around you. That means you'll have to quiz your server about the delicious-looking dish that just passed by—perhaps a marvelous appetizer of potato galette, smoked salmon, créme fraîche, and three caviars, or a celery root, apple, and beet salad with walnuts and mustard sauce. The menu changes seasonally and offers about a dozen carefully considered entrees (always including vegetarian dishes) noted for their emphasis on taste and texture. The signature roast chicken is flavored with garlic, lemon, and parsley and served with roast potato, roast onions, and whole cloves of sweet baked garlic. Oriental salmon roulade stuffed with jasmine rice and baby bok choy is wonderful, and grilled filet of beef is served with garlic mashed potatoes and a delectable red wine sauce. The wine list is excellent. There is valet parking.

✪ Icarus

3 Appleton St. ☎ **617/426-1790.** Reservations recommended. Main courses $19–$28. Sun brunch main courses $5–$12.50. AE, CB, DC, MC, V. Sun–Thurs 6–10pm, Fri 6–11pm, Sat 5:30–11pm. Sun 11am–3pm (brunch). MBTA: Green Line to Arlington or Orange Line to Back Bay. ECLECTIC.

Every element that goes into a great dining experience is present at this subterranean restaurant, which manages to be both spacious and cozy. The upper level of the dining room overlooks the main floor, and the marble accents and dark wood trim lend an elegant air. Chef Chris Douglass, also an owner, prepares choice local seafoods, poultry, meats, and produce in a combination of styles to create imaginative menus that seem more like alchemy than cooking. The menu changes regularly—you might start with a salad of baked goat cheese, beets, endive, and lemon vinaigrette, or the daily "pasta whim." Move on to cod encased in a shredded potato cake and floating in grass-green herbal broth, or lamb shank served with lamb tenderloin and roast garlic whipped potatoes so good you'll want to ask for a plate of them. Don't—save room for one of the unbelievable desserts. Chocolate coconut cake with toasted coconut ice cream and cherry rum sauce was pronounced a favorite and instantly dethroned (in the estimation of an unregenerate chocoholic) by a trio of fruit sorbets. Valet parking is available.

INEXPENSIVE

⑤ Bob the Chef's

604 Columbus Ave. ☎ **617/536-6204.** Breakfast $2.50–$7.50; dinners $7.50–$10.50; sandwiches $3–$6.50. AE, DC, MC, V. Mon–Thurs 11am–10pm, Fri–Sat 8am–11pm, Sun 8am– 10pm. MBTA: Orange Line to Massachusetts Ave. SOUTHERN.

Where the South End meets Roxbury, Bostonians of every color meet for gargantuan portions of authentic soul food at this diner-style eatery. Perch at the Formica counter or take a booth or table and dig into "glorifried" chicken, alone or with barbecued ribs; pork chops; liver and onions; or "soul fish" (two whole pan-fried porgies). Dinners come with a tasty corn muffin and your choice of two delectable side dishes—black-eyed peas, macaroni and cheese, collard greens, rice with gravy or butter, and sweet potatoes—that could easily be a meal in themselves. If you're having trouble deciding, the warm-spirited staff will make a suggestion (and maybe call you "honey"). The vegetable plate is your choice of three vegetables and a corn muffin, and most of the main dishes are available in sandwich form. Whether it's a case of every little bit helps or closing the barn door after the horse is out, the frying medium has been changed from lard to vegetable oil, and everywhere you'd expect bacon for flavoring, as in collard greens and black-eyed peas, smoked turkey is used instead. Take a break and a deep breath and order dessert. The sweet-potato pie will ruin pumpkin pie for you from the moment you taste it.

This neighborhood is a parking nightmare, and after dark it can get a little scary. Come in a group, in a cab, or both, and make sure you're ravenous.

13 Brookline & Environs

Smoking is not allowed in bars and restaurants in Brookline. Coincidence or not, that 1994 law went into effect just before a batch of good restaurants opened.

EXPENSIVE

✪ Providence

1223 Beacon St. ☎ **617/232-0300.** Reservations recommended. Main courses $10.95–$24.95. AE, DC, MC, V. Tues–Thurs 5:30–10pm, Fri–Sat 5:30—11pm, Sun 5–9:30pm. MBTA: Green Line, C train to St. Paul St. ECLECTIC.

Providence is not the city in Rhode Island, although the name can touch off a nice "who's on first"–type discussion. A glance around seems to reveal a typical American restaurant, until you look a little closer. There's a wood-paneled bar, but the light fixtures over it look like metal spaghetti. You're in a formal room, with columns and intricate moldings, but the warm tones of the paint on everything lend a casual air. Turning to the food, there are a lot of grilled meats and fish, but also a lot of vegetarian offerings. The courteous, helpful staff can help you navigate the list of specials, which is almost as long as the menu. It might include an appetizer of fresh fried Ipswich clams—standard stuff, until you taste the garlic-and-chipotle mayonnaise dribbled on top. The flatbread with eggplant puree and olives could be from any menu with Middle Eastern influences, but the flatbread is made of chick peas, the eggplant exudes cardamom, and there's goat cheese on the plate. A main dish of tagliatelle pasta with prosciutto looks ordinary, but it's tossed with radicchio, smoked Maine shrimp, balsamic vinegar, and butter. There's even pastrami on the menu . . . veal pastrami, cured and smoked at the restaurant and served with sweet potato dumplings. And desserts are spectacular—for the signature warm chocolate fondant cake, it might even be worth going to Rhode Island. Chef Paul O'Connell is a wizard with flavors, combining ingredients in such a way that everything brings out the best in everything else, including the stuffed, contented diners.

MODERATE

The Elephant Walk

900 Beacon St., Boston. ☎ **617/247-1500.** Reservations recommended at dinner Sun–Thurs, not accepted Fri–Sat. Main courses $5.95–$18.50 at lunch, $9.50–$18.50 at dinner. AE, DISC, MC, V. Mon–Sat 11:30am–2:30pm; Mon–Thurs 5–10pm, Fri 5–11pm, Sat 4:30–11pm, Sun 4:30–10pm. MBTA: Green Line, C train to St. Mary's St. FRENCH/CAMBODIAN.

France meets Cambodia on the menu at the Elephant Walk, located four blocks from Kenmore Square on the Boston-Brookline border and decorated with lots of little pachyderms. This madly popular spot has a two-part menu (French on one side, Cambodian on the other), but the boundary seems quite porous. Many of the Cambodian dishes have part-French names, such as poulet phochani (chicken and green beans in a flavorful coconut milk–galangal sauce) and curry de crevettes (shrimp curry with picture-perfect vegetables). The Asian influence is evident on the French side, where you'll find pan-seared duck breast and leg confit served with scallion raviolis, and pan-seared tuna served over red and green chile cream sauces. There's a "challenging flavors" section on the Cambodian menu if you're feeling bold, and many dishes are available with tofu substituted for animal protein. Members of the pleasant wait staff will help out if you need guidance. Ask to be seated in the plant-filled front room, which is less noisy than the main dining room and has a view of the street.

The original Elephant Walk is at 70 Union Sq., Somerville (☎ **617/623-9939**). It keeps the same hours but is harder to get to than the Boston location, even from most places in Cambridge.

Rubin's

500 Harvard St., Brookline. ☎ 617/731-8787. Reservations not accepted. Main courses $8–$17.95. No credit cards. Mon–Thurs 10am–8pm, Fri 9am–midafternoon, Sun 9am–8pm. MBTA: Green Line, B train to Harvard St. KOSHER DELI.

The knock on this restaurant is that it's not a New York deli, and you shouldn't come expecting one. For what it is, though, it's excellent. Rubin's bills itself as the only full-service kosher deli and restaurant in greater Boston, and it's outlasted lots of competition in its nearly 70 years here. It maintains the highest standards of kashrut, and no dairy is served. You'll find omelettes, deli platters, and sandwiches in large and "overstuffed" sizes. The chopped liver is excellent, and the "Traditionals" section of the extensive menu includes tasty potato pancakes (a better choice than the potato knish). Entrées include roast brisket of beef, barbecued chicken, and broiled salmon, halibut, and schrod. The noodle pudding makes a good dessert in the unlikely event that you have room.

7

What to See & Do in Boston

Take a day, take a week, take a month—Boston offers something for everyone, and plenty of it. Throw out your preconceptions about the city being some sort of open-air history museum (although that's certainly one of the guises it can assume), and allow your own interests to dictate where you go. It's possible to visit most of the major attractions in two or three days if you don't linger anywhere for too long, but you may prefer to schedule fewer activities and spend more time on them.

In an effort to boost attendance at the sites along the Freedom Trail, in 1996 the city announced plans to spend $45 million sprucing up the buildings and updating the exhibits. A massive refurbishment was already under way at the Old South Meeting House; it's scheduled to reopen in August 1997 with multimedia installations that will make the events leading up to the Revolution as compelling as they were 220 years ago. And in an attempt to attract families, admission to the Museum of Fine Arts has been free to those under 18 since mid-1996.

SUGGESTED ITINERARIES

If You Have One Day

Sample some experiences that are unique to Boston—you won't have time to immerse yourself, but you can touch on several singular attractions. Follow part of the Freedom Trail on your own from Boston Common to Faneuil Hall Marketplace (see Chapter 8, "Boston Strolls") or take a 90-minute tour led by a National Park Service ranger from the Visitor Center (15 State St.; ☎ 617/242-5642). Pick up carry-out food at Faneuil Hall Marketplace or in the North End and head toward the water for a picnic lunch in Christopher Columbus Park, across Atlantic Ave. from the marketplace, or on Long Wharf (pass the Marriott and keep going to the end of the wharf). If the weather keeps you indoors, stay at the marketplace and have lunch at Durgin-Park (see Chapter 6, "Dining," for a description). In the afternoon, complete your independent Freedom Trail foray in the North End or take a sightseeing cruise from the waterfront (Long Wharf or Rowes Wharf). If you have time, pop into the New England Aquarium or head over to Museum Wharf and visit the Computer Museum. Or skip the sightseeing altogether (you packed a lot into the morning) and head back to Downtown Crossing for a pilgrimage to Filene's Basement. Splurge on dinner in a fine restaurant in Boston or Cambridge (see

Impressions

I have just returned from Boston. It is the only thing to do if you find yourself up there.

—Fred Allen, letter to Groucho Marx (1953)

I guess God made Boston on a wet Sunday.

—Raymond Chandler, letter (1949)

Never go to Boston. Boston is a singularly horrific city, full of surly weirdos with scraggly beards and terrible manners.

—Cynthia Heimel, *Sex Tips for Girls* (1983)

Chapter 6 for suggestions), then enjoy a panoramic view of Boston by night from the John Hancock Observatory or the Prudential Center Skywalk.

If You Have Two Days

On the first day, follow the suggestions for one day or pick and choose—you can spend a little more time along the Freedom Trail, on a longer harbor cruise, or perhaps at Filene's Basement (get there early if possible). On the second day, branch out a little, again letting your personal preferences be your guide. Spend the morning at the Museum of Fine Arts and have lunch there or at the Isabella Stewart Gardner Museum. Start the afternoon at the Gardner Museum or, if it's a Friday during the season, at the Boston Symphony Orchestra (see Chapter 10, "Boston After Dark"). If art isn't your passion, the Boston Museum of Science might be a better choice, followed by lunch at the Prudential Center and a Duck Tour. Then enjoy a leisurely trek around the Back Bay (see Chapter 8, "Boston Strolls") or a high-intensity shopping trip to Newbury Street On weekdays, Boston By Foot (☎ 617/367-2345) conducts a tour of Beacon Hill that starts at the State House at 5:30. Decompress with dinner in the North End, then coffee and perhaps dessert at a caffè. The Comedy Connection at Faneuil Hall is nearby if you want to cap off the day with some laughs. Or dress up for dinner and enjoy dessert and dancing at the Custom House Lounge at the Bay Tower, or a drink and a turn around the dance floor in the lounge at the Top of the Hub restaurant on the 52nd floor of the Prudential Center.

If You Have Three Days

The options seem to expand to fill the time you have. The suggestions for the first two days can easily be spread out to fill another day, but you'll probably want to explore farther afield, and a visit to Cambridge is the logical next step. Ride the MBTA Red Line to Harvard and take in some of the sights (see Chapter 8, "Boston Strolls"), squeeze in a round of shopping, or head straight to one of the museum complexes. Have lunch in Harvard Square and continue exploring, or ride the bus to Mount Auburn Cemetery. Motorists have even more options—you might start in Cambridge, have lunch in Lexington or Concord, and spend the afternoon learning about the historical or literary legacy of the area, or communing with nature at Walden Pond (see Chapter 11, "Side Trips from Boston"). Without wheels, you can use public transportation to reach Lexington or Concord, but not to travel between them—forced to choose, history buffs will opt for Lexington, literary types for Concord. Have dinner in Cambridge (or back in Boston if that wasn't part of your itinerary on the first day), and enjoy some live music at the Hatch Shell, a jazz or rock club, or the House of Blues.

If You Have Five Days or More

Now you're cooking. Having scratched the surface in the first three days, you'll have a better sense of what interests you want to indulge more extensively. Check out other Boston attractions that catch your fancy, perhaps including one or more of the historic house museums, and plan a full day trip—to Plymouth, to Lexington and Concord, to Salem and Marblehead, or to Gloucester and Rockport. If you didn't have time for the Computer Museum at first, visit Museum Wharf, where you'll also find the Children's Museum and the Boston Tea Party Ship & Museum. If you haven't taken a sightseeing cruise, try one that goes to Charlestown, where you can explore the USS *Constitution* and Bunker Hill. Take in a show at the Mugar Omni Theatre at the Museum of Science, and do some field work to see whether Boston's reputation as a great sports town is deserved by attending a pro or college event. And if you're just plain sick of sightseeing, don't worry, you're not alone (just the only one brave enough to say so). An excellent antidote is a day-long cruise to Provincetown, at the tip of Cape Cod. A boat leaves from Commonwealth Pier in Boston at 9:30am, gives you three hours for world-class people-watching, strolling around the novelty shops, dining on seafood, admiring the scenery, and—dare we say it—sightseeing in P-Town. It gets back to Boston at 6:30pm. Have dinner on or near the waterfront and start planning your next trip.

1   The Top Attractions

The number one people-magnet in Boston is the Quincy Market and Faneuil Hall Marketplace complex, which attracts 14 million visitors a year. The Freedom Trail (see Chapter 8, "Boston Strolls") is second, with about 5 million visitors a year, a number the city is trying to increase with renovations and improvements of the sites along the trail. Next come the Museum of Fine Arts, the Boston Museum of Science, and the USS *Constitution,* which each attract about 1 million people a year. But regardless of which attractions are most popular, sightseeing in Boston, a city with something for everyone, is primarily a personal quest in search of sights that are personally interesting and entertaining.

✪ Faneuil Hall Marketplace

Between North, Congress, and State sts. and I-93. ☎ **617/338-2323.** Marketplace Mon–Sat 10am–9pm, Sun noon–6pm; Colonnade food court opens earlier; some restaurants open early for Sun brunch and remain open until 2am daily. MBTA: Orange Line or Blue Line to State Street, Orange Line or Green Line to Haymarket, or Green Line to Government Center.

It's impossible to overestimate the effect of Faneuil Hall Marketplace on Boston's economy and reputation. A daring idea when it opened in 1976, the festival market has been widely imitated, but to good effect since each new complex of shops, food stands, restaurants, bars, and public spaces in urban centers around the country tends to reflect the city in which it is situated. Faneuil Hall Marketplace, brimming with Boston flavor and regional goods and souvenirs, is no exception. The marketplace includes five buildings—the central three-building complex is listed in the National Register of Historic Places—set on brick and stone plazas that teem with crowds shopping, eating, performing, watching performers, and just people-watching. Quincy Market itself (you'll hear the whole complex called by that name as well) is a three-level Greek revival-style building reopened after renovations turned it into a festival market on August 26, 1976, 150 years of hard use after Mayor Josiah Quincy opened the original market. The South Market Building opened on August 26, 1977, and the North Market Building in 1978 on, yes, August 26.

The central corridor of Quincy Market, known as the Colonnade, is the food court, where you can find anything from a bagel to a full Greek dinner, a fruit smoothie to a hunk of fudge. On either side, under the glass canopies, are pushcarts bearing the full range of crafts created by New England artisans and hokey souvenirs hawked by enterprising merchants. In the plaza between the South Canopy and the South Market Building is a visitor information kiosk, and throughout the complex, including the ground floor of Faneuil Hall, you'll find an enticing mix of chain stores and unique shops (see Chapter 9, "Shopping"). On summer evenings the tables that spill outdoors from the bars fill with people unwinding, listening to or performing karaoke, or just enjoying the passing scene. One constant since the year after the market opened—after the *original* market opened, that is—is Durgin-Park, a traditional New England restaurant with traditionally crabby waitresses (see Chapter 6, "Dining," for details).

Faneuil Hall itself sometimes gets overlooked, but it's well worth a visit. Known as the "Cradle of Liberty" for its role as a center of inspirational (some might say inflammatory) speeches in the years leading to the Revolutionary War, the building opened in 1742 and was expanded using a Charles Bulfinch design in 1805. National Park Service rangers give free 20-minute talks every half-hour from 9am to 5pm in the second-floor auditorium, which, after a recent refurbishment, is now in mint condition.

⊙ Museum of Fine Arts, Boston

465 Huntington Ave. ☎ **617/267-9300.** Adults $10 when the entire museum is open, $8 when only the West Wing is open. Students and senior citizens $8 when the entire museum is open, $6 when only the West Wing is open. Children under 18 free. Free admission for all, Wed 4–9:45pm. No admission fee for those visiting only the Museum Shop, restaurants, library, or auditoria. Entire museum, Tues, Thurs–Fri, Mon holidays, Mon from Memorial Day through Labor Day 10am–4:45pm; Wed 10am–9:45pm; Sat–Sun 10am–5:45pm; West Wing only, Thurs–Fri 5–9:45pm. Closed Mon mid-Sept–late May and major holidays. MBTA: Green Line, E train, to Museum of Fine Arts.

Not content with the MFA's reputation as the second-best museum in the country (after the Metropolitan Museum of Art in New York), the museum's management team works nonstop to make the collections more accessible and interesting. Under new director Malcolm Rogers, in recent years the task of raising the museum's profile even higher has run the gamut from apparently little things, such as opening the Huntington Ave. entrance, to mounting even more top-notch exhibitions, expanding educational programs, and making admission free to children under 18.

The 121-year-old museum's not-so-secret weapon in its quest is a powerful one: its magnificent collections. Your visit is guided by the best sort of curatorial attitude, the kind that makes even those who go in with a sense of obligation leave with a sense of discovery and wonder. The MFA is especially noted for its Asian and Old Kingdom Egyptian collections, classical art, its Buddhist temple and medieval sculpture and tapestries, but the works you may find more familiar are American and European paintings and sculpture, notably the Impressionists. Some particular favorites: John Singleton Copley's 1768 portrait of Paul Revere, Gilbert Stuart's 1796 portrait of George Washington, Winslow Homer's *Long Branch, New Jersey*, a bronze casting of Edgar Degas's sculpture *Little Dancer*, Paul Gauguin's *Where Do We Come From? What Are We? Where Are We Going?*, Fitz Hugh Lane's *Owl's Head*,

Boston Attractions

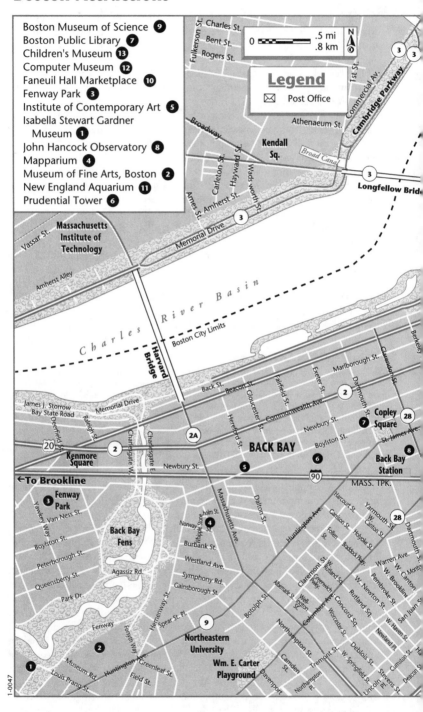

Boston Museum of Science **9**
Boston Public Library **7**
Children's Museum **13**
Computer Museum **12**
Faneuil Hall Marketplace **10**
Fenway Park **3**
Institute of Contemporary Art **5**
Isabella Stewart Gardner
  Museum **1**
John Hancock Observatory **8**
Mapparium **4**
Museum of Fine Arts, Boston **2**
New England Aquarium **11**
Prudential Tower **6**

Legend
⊠ Post Office

0 —— .5 mi
  —— .8 km
N

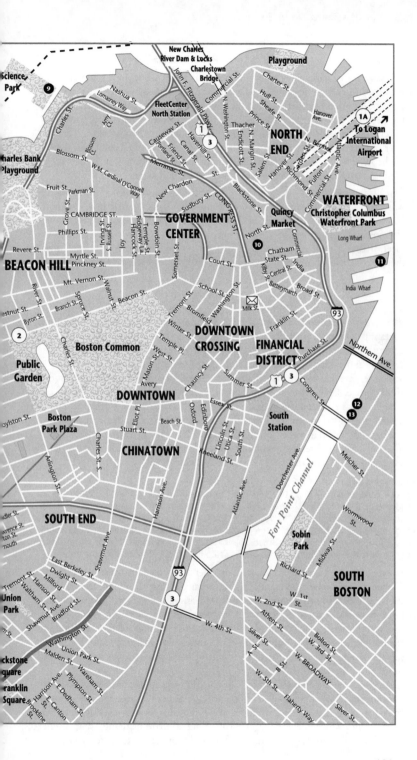

Touring Local Art Galleries

Everyone has to start somewhere, and the artists whose work you'll find in the big museums years from now may be showing at galleries today. You'll find the greatest concentration of galleries along Newbury Street (see Chapter 9, "Shopping," for details). The elegant Back Bay shopping strip has, if anything, grown in importance recently because the other main area, around South Street, is a prisoner of the Central Artery/Third Harbor Tunnel project. You'll still find galleries in the neighborhood, between South Station and Chinatown (sometimes called the Leather District), but you're more likely to see bulldozers.

One way to see artists at work is to check the listings in the *Globe* and *Herald* when you arrive for information about open studio days in a particular neighborhood. The artists' communities in the South End, the Fort Point Channel area and Somerville stage weekend events once or twice a year that allow visitors to meet artists in their work spaces (which are often their homes) and see what they're concocting. You may be asked to make a contribution to charity in exchange for a map of the studios.

Penobscot Bay, Maine, and all 43 Monets. There are also magnificent print and photography collections, and that's not even touching on the furnishings and decorative arts, including the finest collection of Paul Revere silver in the world.

I.M. Pei designed the West Wing (1981), the latest addition to the original 1909 structure. It contains the main entrance, climate-controlled galleries, an auditorium, the excellent Museum Shop, and an atrium with a tree-lined "sidewalk" cafe. The Fine Arts Restaurant is on the second floor, and there's also a cafeteria. Pick up a floor plan at the information desk or take one of the free guided tours.

For a taste of what you'll see, the museum has a web site (http://www.mfa.org). The museum is located between Huntington Avenue and the Fenway. If you're driving, you can park in the garage or lot off Museum Road.

✪ Boston Museum of Science

Science Park. ☎ **617/723-2500.** Admission to the exhibit halls $8 adults, $6 seniors and children age 3–14, free for children under 3. To the Mugar Omni Theater, the Hayden Planetarium, or the laser theater, $7.50 adults, $5.50 seniors and children age 3–14, free for children under 3. Tickets to two or three parts of the complex available at discounted prices. Daily 9am–5pm, Fri until 9pm. Closed Thanksgiving Day, Christmas. MBTA: Green Line to Science Park; the North Station commuter rail stop is a 10-minute walk from the museum.

For the ultimate pain-free educational experience, head to the Museum of Science. The demonstrations, experiments, and interactive displays introduce facts and concepts so effortlessly that everyone winds up learning something. Take a couple of hours or a whole day to explore the permanent and temporary exhibits. Some visitors who think they object to being here may prefer to pretend they're waiting for the rest of the group, but watch out—when they realize that they're mesmerized by, say, the visible inner workings of the escalator you just rode, they'll want to learn more.

Among the more than 450 exhibits, you might meet an iguana or a dinosaur, find out how much you'd weigh on the moon, or climb into a space module. If you've cooled your heels in traffic downtown, you'll probably want to check out the "Big Dig" exhibit, which allows you to try your hand at urban planning using an interactive computer display about the Central Artery project. And there's a Discovery

Center especially for preschoolers. The newest permanent exhibit is an activity center called "Investigate!" The goal is to help visitors learn to think like scientists, formulating questions, finding evidence, and drawing conclusion through activities such as strapping on a skin sensor to measure reactions to stimuli or sifting through an archaeological dig. You can also visit the theater of electricity to see lightning manufactured indoors.

The separate-admission theaters are worth planning for. If you're making a day or a half-day of it (or even if you're skipping the exhibits), try to see a show. Buy all your tickets at once, not only because it's cheaper but because they sometimes sell out. Tickets for daytime shows must be purchased in person. Evening show tickets can be ordered over the phone using a credit card, but there's a service charge for doing so.

The **Mugar Omni Theater,** one of only 17 in the country, is an intense experience. You're bombarded with images on a four-story domed screen and sounds from a 12-channel sound system with 84 speakers. Even though you know you're not moving, the engulfing sensations and steep pitch of the seating area will have you hanging on for dear life, whether you're watching a film on Yellowstone, hurricanes and tornadoes, or the *Titanic.* The films change every four to six months.

The **Charles Hayden Planetarium** takes you deep into space with daily star shows and shows on special topics that change several times a year. On weekends, rock 'n' roll laser shows take over the planetarium—Pink Floyd fans, this is the place for you.

The museum has a web site (http://www.mos.org), a terrific gift shop where the toys and games promote learning without lecturing, and three restaurants. If you're driving, there's a garage on the premises.

✪ Isabella Stewart Gardner Museum
280 The Fenway. ☎ **617/566-1401.** Admission $7 adults, $5 seniors and college students with valid ID, $3 youths ages 12–17 and college students on Wed, free for children under 12. Tues–Sun 11am–5pm and some Mon holidays. Closed Mon. MBTA: Green Line, E train, to Museum of Fine Arts.

Isabella Stewart Gardner (1840–1924) was an incorrigible individualist long before such behavior was acceptable for a woman in polite Boston society, and her 19th century eccentricity has proven a great boon to art lovers in contemporary Boston. "Mrs. Jack" designed her home in the style of a 15th-century Venetian palace and filled it with European, American, and Asian painting and sculpture, much chosen with the help of her friend and protégé Bernard Berenson. You'll see works by Titian, Botticelli, Raphael, Rembrandt, Matisse, and Mrs. Gardner's friends James McNeill Whistler and John Singer Sargent. The building, which was opened to the public after Mrs. Gardner's death, features furniture and architectural details imported from European churches and palaces. The *pièce de résistance* is a magnificent interior skylit courtyard filled year-round with fresh flowers (lilies at Easter, chrysanthemums in the fall, poinsettias at Christmas), stained-glass windows; and exquisite antique furnishings. A new special exhibition gallery, which opened in September 1992, features two or three changing exhibitions a year.

The Tapestry Room fills with music on weekends from September through April for the **concert series** (☎ **617/734-1359** for recorded information), which showcases soloists, chamber groups, and local students. The tiled floor and gorgeous wall hangings make a lovely setting for classical music. Concerts begin at 1:30pm on Saturday and Sunday. Tickets, which include museum admission, are $15 for adults, $9 for seniors and college students with valid ID, and $7 for youths ages 12–17.

Lunch and desserts are served in the museum cafe, and unique items are available at the gift shop.

New England Aquarium

Central Wharf. ☎ **617/973-5200.** Admission $8.75 adults, $4.75 children 3–11, $7.75 senior citizens. Children under 3 free. $1 off all fees Thurs 4–7:30pm. July 1–Labor Day Mon–Tues and Fri 9am–6pm, Wed–Thurs 9am–8pm, Sat–Sun and holidays 9am–7pm. Early Sept–June Mon–Wed and Fri 9am–5pm, Thurs 9am–8pm, Sat–Sun and holidays 9am–6pm. Closed Thanksgiving, Christmas, and until noon New Year's Day. MBTA: Blue Line to Aquarium.

Frolicking seals greet you from outdoor enclosures as you approach the Aquarium, the perfect welcome to an entertaining complex that's home to more than 7,000 fish and aquatic mammals. You might be tempted to settle in near the outdoor (and free) seal display, especially at feeding time. When you head inside, buy an exhibit guide and plan your route as you commune with the penguin colony. The focal point of the main building is the aptly named Giant Ocean Tank. You'll climb four stories on a spiral ramp that encircles the cylindrical glass tank, which contains 187,000 gallons of saltwater, a replica of a Caribbean coral reef, and a conglomeration of sea creatures who seem to coexist amazingly well. Part of the reason for the prevailing calm may be that the sharks are fed five times a day by scuba divers who bring the food right to them. Other exhibits show off freshwater specimens, denizens of the Amazon, and jellyfish, and at the "Edge of the Sea" exhibit, you're encouraged to touch the starfish, sea urchins, and horseshoe crabs in the tide pool. A new installation, "Ponds: The Earth's Eyes," introduces you to the ecosystems and their resident reptiles, fish, and turtles. Be sure to leave time for a show at the floating marine mammal pavilion, "Discovery," where sea lions perform every 90 minutes throughout the day.

Note: The aquarium sponsors whale-watching expeditions (☎ **617/973-5281**) daily from May through mid-October and on weekends in April and late October. You'll travel several miles out to sea to Stellwagen Bank, feeding ground for the whales as they migrate from Newfoundland to Provincetown. Tickets (cash only) are $24 for adults, $19 for senior citizens and college students, $17.50 for children age 12–18, and $16.50 for children age 3–11. Children must be 3 years old and at least 30 inches tall. Reservations are recommended and can be held with a MasterCard or Visa.

The Computer Museum

300 Congress St. (Museum Wharf). ☎ **617/426-2800** or 617/423-6758 for the "Talking Computer." Admission $7 adults, $5 students and senior citizens, free for children under 5. Tickets are half-price on Sun 3–5pm. Fall, winter, and spring Tues–Sun and Mon during Boston school holidays and vacations 10am–5pm; summer daily 10am–6pm. MBTA: Red Line to South Station. Walk north on Atlantic Ave. one block past the Federal Reserve Bank, and turn right onto Congress Street.

As computer technology develops, the world's premier computer museum changes and grows with it. The exhibits at the Computer Museum tell the story of computers from their origins in the 1940s to the latest in PCs and virtual reality. The signature exhibit is the Walk-Through Computer 2000™, a networked multimedia machine 50 times larger than the real thing. When the computer's the size of a two-story house, the mouse is the size of a car, the CD-ROM drive is 8 feet long, the monitor is 12 feet high, and humans enjoying the 30 hands-on activities are the equivalent of crayon-size. The exhibit is so cutting-edge that it even has a 7-foot-square Pentium processor, installed in 1995 during a million-dollar upgrade.

Computers don't exist in a vacuum, of course, and a permanent exhibit called "The Networked Planet" allows visitors to explore the information superhighway and its offshoots by logging on to real and simulated networks and learning about medicine, financial markets, and air-traffic control. There are also exhibits on robots, the history of the computer, and the practical and recreational uses of the PC—you might compose music, forecast the weather, or "drive" a race car. In all, you'll find more than 160 hands-on exhibits, three theaters, and countless ideas to try out on your home computer. For starters, you can check out the museum's web site (http://www.tcm.org).

Special activities, including Internet lessons, are offered on weekends. Call the Talking Computer for information about special programs and events. And before you leave, you can pick up some chocolate floppy disks or microchip jewelry at the Museum Store.

Mapparium

World Headquarters of the First Church of Christ, Scientist, 250 Massachusetts Ave. (at Huntington Avenue) ☎ **617/450-3790**. Free admission. Mon–Sat 10am–4pm. Mother Church Sun 11:15am–2pm, Mon–Sat 10am–4pm. Bible exhibit Sun 11:15am–2pm, Wed–Sat 10am–4pm. Closed major holidays. MBTA: Green Line, E train, to Symphony, or Orange Line to Massachusetts Avenue.

For a real insider's view of the world, step . . . inside. This unique hollow globe 30 feet across is a work of both art and history. The 608 stained-glass panels are connected by a bronze framework and surrounded by electric lights, and because sound bounces off the nonporous surfaces, the acoustics are as unusual as the aesthetics. As you cross the glass bridge just south of the equator, you'll see the political divisions of the world from 1932–35, when the globe was constructed.

Also in the 14-acre Christian Science complex are the Mother Church and the Bible exhibit "A Light Unto My Path." The Romanesque church, opened in 1894, is notable for its stained glass windows; the domed Mother Church Extension, opened in 1906, is in Renaissance-Byzantine style and has one of the largest pipe organs in the world. Call for information on tours. The Bible exhibit includes a 30-minute film and slide program (shows every hour on the hour), an audiovisual time line, and a sculptured map where 12 journeys of figures from the Bible are illustrated and narrated.

Boston Public Library

666 Boylston St., at Copley Sq. ☎ **617/536-5400**. Free admission. Mon–Thurs 9am–9pm, Fri–Sat 9am–5pm. Sun (Oct–May only) 1pm–5pm. Closed Sun June–Sept and legal holidays. MBTA: Green Line to Copley.

The central branch of the city's library system is an architectural as well as intellectual monument. The original 1895 building, a registered National Historic Landmark designed by Charles F. McKim, is an Italian Renaissance–style masterpiece that fairly drips with art. The front doors are the work of Daniel Chester French (who also designed the *Minute Man* statue in Concord); the murals are by John Singer Sargent and Pierre Puvis de Chavannes, among others; and you'll see notable frescoes, sculptures, and paintings. Visit the lovely courtyard or peek at it from a window on the stairs. The adjoining addition, of the same height and material (pink granite), was designed by Philip Johnson and opened in 1972. It's a utilitarian building with a dramatic skylit atrium. Visitors are welcome to wander throughout both buildings—the lobby of the McKim building alone could take half an hour—but you must have a library card (available to Massachusetts residents) to check out materials. The library has more than 6 million books and more than 11 million other items, such as prints, photographs, films, and sound recordings. It also has a web site (http://www.bpl.org).

On Top of the World

Two of the city's top attractions are literally *top* attractions. From hundreds of feet in the air, you'll get an entirely different perspective on Boston.

The **John Hancock Observatory** (200 Clarendon St.; ☎ **617/572-6429**) would be a good introduction to Boston even if it didn't have a sensational 60th-floor view. The multimedia exhibits include a multimedia show that chronicles the events leading to the Revolutionary War and demonstrates how Boston's land mass has changed. You'll see paintings, drawings, and photos and hear narration in a round room with a relief map of the Boston area on the floor. There's an illustrated time line, an interactive computer quiz about the city, and a display that allows you to ask for travel directions (by foot, car, and public transportation) to various points of interest. Telescopes and binoculars allow a close-up look at the faraway ground. Admission is $4.25 for adults and $3.25 for seniors and children ages 5 to 15. Hours are 9am to 11pm Monday through Saturday, 10am to 11pm on Sunday (May to October), and noon to 11pm on Sunday from November to April. The ticket office closes at 10pm. The nearest "T" stops are Copley on the Green Line (B, C, and D trains) and Back Bay on the Orange Line and the Commuter Rail.

The **Prudential Center Skywalk,** on the 50th floor of the Prudential Tower (800 Boylston St.; ☎ **617/236-3318**), offers the only 360° view of Boston and beyond. From the enclosed observation deck you can see for miles, even (when it's clear) as far as the mountaintops of southern New Hampshire in the north or the beaches of Cape Cod to the south. Hours are 10am to 10pm daily. Admission is $4 for adults and $3 for seniors and children ages 5 to 15. On the 52nd floor the view can be enjoyed with food and drink at the Top of the Hub restaurant and lounge (see Chapter 6, "Dining"). The nearest "T" stops are Copley on the Green Line and Back Bay on the Orange Line and the commuter rail.

Art & Architecture Tours are conducted Monday at 2:30pm, Tuesday and Wednesday at 6:30pm, Thursday and Saturday at 11am, and Sunday at 2pm, with additional tours scheduled for the weekend before the Boston Marathon, in mid-April.

2 More Museums

Boston Tea Party Ship & Museum

Congress Street Bridge. ☎ **617/338-1773.** Admission $6.50 adults, $5.20 students, $3.25 children 6–12, free for children under 6. Ship and museum, Mar 1–Nov 30 daily 9am–dusk (about 6pm in summer, 5pm in winter). Closed Dec 1–Feb 28 and Thanksgiving. MBTA: Red Line to South Station. Walk north on Atlantic Avenue one block past the Federal Reserve Bank, and turn right onto Congress Street. The ship is docked at the Congress Street Bridge.

On December 16, 1773, a public meeting of independent-minded Bostonians led to the symbolic act of resistance that's commemorated here. The brig *Beaver II*, a full-size replica of one of the three merchant ships emptied by colonists poorly disguised as Indians on the night of the raid, is alongside a museum with exhibits on the "tea party." You can dump your own bale of tea into Boston Harbor (it will be retrieved by the museum staff), drink some complimentary tea (served iced in summer, hot in winter), and buy some tea to take home at the museum store.

Institute of Contemporary Art

955 Boylston St. ☎ **617/266-5152.** Admission $5.25 adults, $3.25 students, $2.25 seniors and children under 16; free to all Thurs 5–9pm. Thurs noon–9pm, Wed, Fri–Sun noon–5pm. Closed major holidays. MBTA: Green Line, B, C, or D train to Hynes/ICA.

Across from the Hynes Convention Center, the ICA showcases rotating exhibits of 20th-century art, including painting, sculpture, photography, and video and performance art. The institute also offers films, lectures, music, video, poetry, and an educational program for children and adults.

✪ John F. Kennedy Presidential Library and Museum

Columbia Point, Dorchester. ☎ **617/929-4523.** Admission $6 adults, $4 seniors and students with ID, $2 children age 6–16, free for children under 6. Daily 9am–5pm (last film begins at 3:50). Closed Thanksgiving, Christmas, and New Year's Day. MBTA: Red Line to JFK/UMass, then take the free shuttle bus, which runs every 20 minutes. By car, take the Southeast Expressway (I-93/Route 3) south to Exit 15 (Morrissey Boulevard/JFK Library), and follow signs to parking lot.

The Kennedy era springs to life at this dramatic library, museum, and educational research complex overlooking Dorchester Bay, where the 35th president's accomplishments and legacy are illustrated with sound and video recordings and fascinating displays of memorabilia and photos.

Your visit begins with a 17-minute film narrated by John F. Kennedy himself—a detail that seems eerie for a moment, then perfectly natural. Through skillfully edited audio clips, he discusses his childhood, education, war experiences, and early political career. Then you're turned loose to spend as much or as little time as you like on each museum exhibit. Starting with the 1960 presidential campaign, you're immersed in the period. In a series of connected galleries, you'll see three-cent newspapers and campaign souvenirs, film of Kennedy debating Richard Nixon and being sworn in, gifts from foreign dignitaries, letters, and political cartoons. There's a film about the Cuban Missile Crisis, and displays on the civil rights movement, the Peace Corps, the space program, the First Lady, and the Kennedy family. Replicas of the Oval Office and the office of Attorney General Robert F. Kennedy, the president's brother, and a darkened chamber where news reports of John Kennedy's assassination and funeral play in a continuous loop leads to a room simply called "Legacy." Here you'll find books, archival documents, and interactive computers that explain the programs the president initiated and how they affect the world today.

From the final room, the soaring glass-enclosed pavilion that is the heart of the I.M. Pei–designed building, you have a glorious view of the water. Outside, JFK's boyhood sailboat, *Victura,* is on a strip of dune grass between the library and the harbor. Behind is the Archives Tower, nine stories of papers, books, films, and oral histories of John and Robert Kennedy. The material is available free to scholars and researchers.

Museum of Transportation

15 Newton St. (in Larz Anderson Park), Brookline. ☎ **617/522-6547.** Admission $5 adults, $3 seniors, students with valid ID, and children ages 4–17. March–Dec, Wed–Sun 10am–5pm. Hours may vary when installations are changing; call for information. Closed Thanksgiving and Christmas. MBTA: Green Line (D train) to Reservoir, then take bus 51 (Forest Hills); the museum is five blocks from the intersection of Newton and Clyde streets.

Automobile buffs will want to park themselves at this museum, in a carriage house modeled after a French chateau. In a span of 50 years around the turn of the century, Larz and Isabel Anderson collected the antique cars that form the core of the museum's collection. The cars boast what was then the very latest equipment, from a two-cylinder engine (in a race car—a 1901 Winton) to a full lavatory (in the 1906 CGV). Various Anderson cars are usually shown with other vehicles rather than as an entire collection; the themed exhibits change regularly. Cars are shown on the lawn on summer weekends, with a different theme each time, such as Corvettes, Cadillacs, Edsels, German cars, or Italian imports. Call to find out the focus during your visit.

If you're driving (in your own car), the museum is off Route 1 south, which you can reach from Storrow Drive. Follow Route 1 past Jamaica Pond to the first rotary (traffic circle); at the light, turn right onto Pond Street. Follow Pond Street one-half mile; the museum is on the right. Call for directions if you're not coming from downtown.

The Sports Museum of New England
CambridgeSide Galleria, 100 CambridgeSide Place, Cambridge. ☎ **617/57-SPORT.** Admission $6 adults, $4.50 seniors and children 4–11, children under 4 free. Mon–Sat 10am–9:30pm, Sun 11–7pm. The museum occasionally closes early for private functions. MBTA: Green Line to Lechmere, then walk two blocks; Red Line to Kendall, then take shuttle bus.

The Sports Museum of New England's collection highlights local sports history at every level of competition. Little Leaguers, professionals, Olympians, Special Olympians, and college stars are represented in displays of uniforms, equipment, newspaper clippings, and photographs. There are life-size statues of Larry Bird, Bobby Orr, Carl Yastrzemski, and Harry Agganis, small theaters modeled after Fenway Park, Boston Garden, and Harvard Stadium, and many interactive exhibits, including "Catching Clemens" (in which you find out what it's like to catch a Roger Clemens fastball—ouch), "In the Net" (in which you see what it's like to be hockey goalie), "Treadwall" (in which you try your hand at rock climbing), and "Stump Haggerty" (an interactive trivia contest). There's also a wall where you can see how you measure up against life-size photos of sports stars and an exhibit that spotlights memorabilia from a different New England town each month.

3 More Sights of Historical Interest

HISTORIC HOUSES
The most historic home in Boston is the **Paul Revere House** (19 North Sq.; ☎ **617/523-2338**), and not just because it's the oldest in the city, built around 1680. Many people know no more about Revere than the first few lines of Henry Wadsworth Longfellow's poem "Paul Revere's Ride"—many people don't even know that—but the tour brings the legendary revolutionary to life. It's self-guided, allowing you to linger on the artifacts that hold your interest, and particularly thought-provoking. Revere had 16 children with two wives, supported them with his thriving silversmith's trade—and put the whole operation in jeopardy with his role in the events that led to the Revolutionary War.

The house is open daily April 15 through October from 9:30am to 5:15pm, and from November through April 14 from 9:30am to 4:15pm. It's closed Mondays from January through March and on Thanksgiving, Christmas, and New Year's Day. Admission is $2.50 for adults, $2 for seniors and students, and $1 for children 5–17. Special programs and events are scheduled to coincide with Patriots' Day, Fourth of July, and Christmas; call for details.

The adjacent **Pierce/Hichborn House,** a Georgian structure built around 1711 and occupied by Revere's cousins, is shown by guided tour only. Call the Paul Revere House for current schedules.

Houses that are as interesting for their architecture as for their occupants can be found on Beacon Hill. The south slope, facing Boston Common, has been a fashionable address since the 1620s; excellent tours of two houses (one on the north slope) focus on the late 18th and early 19th century. The homes were designed by Charles Bulfinch, who was also the architect of the nearby Massachusetts State House.

The **Harrison Gray Otis House** (141 Cambridge St.; ☎ **617/227-3956**), a property owned by the Society for the Preservation of New England Antiquities, was designed in 1796 for an up-and-coming young lawyer who later became mayor of Boston. The restoration was one of the first in the country to use computer analysis of paint, and the result was revolutionary—it revealed that the colors on the walls were drab because the paint was faded, not because they started out dingy. Furnished in the style to which a wealthy family in the young United States would have been accustomed, the restored Federal-style mansion is a colorful, elegant treasure. It is at the foot of Beacon Hill, near the Government Center and Charles "T" stops. Tours, which also touch on the history of the neighborhood, are given on the hour Tuesday through Friday from noon to 4pm and Saturday 10am to 4pm. Admission is $4 for adults, $3.50 for seniors, $2 for children 12 and under.

The Society for the Preservation of New England Antiquities is headquartered at the Otis House, which is just the tip of the iceberg. SPNEA owns and operates 33 historic properties throughout New England, and the results of its radical restoration techniques can be seen at museums all over the area. Write or call the society at 141 Cambridge St., Boston, MA 02114 (☎ **617/227-3956**), for brochures, visiting hours, and admission fees.

The **Nichols House Museum** (55 Mount Vernon St.; ☎ **617/227-6993**) is an 1804 Beacon Hill home with beautiful antique furnishings collected by several generations of the Nichols family. From May through October, it's open Tuesday through Saturday; February through April and November and December, it's open Monday, Wednesday, and Saturday (open days may vary, so call ahead). Tours start at 12:15pm and continue every half-hour on the quarter-hour through 4:15pm. Admission is $4.

In the Back Bay, the **Gibson House Museum** (137 Beacon St.; ☎ **617/267-6338**) is an 1859 brownstone that embodies the word "Victorian." You'll see dozens of family photos, petrified-wood hat racks, a sequined pink-velvet pagoda for the cat, a Victrola, and all manner of decorations. The museum is open for tours at 1, 2, and 3pm Wednesday through Sunday from May to October, and weekends only from November to April. It's closed on major holidays. Admission is $4.

John F. Kennedy National Historic Site

83 Beals St., Brookline. ☎ **617/566-7937.** Guided tours $2 adults, free for children under 16. Mid-May–Oct Wed–Sun 10am–4:30pm. Closed Nov–mid-May. MBTA: Take the Green Line C train to Coolidge Corner, then walk four blocks north on Harvard Street.

The 35th president's birthplace is restored to its appearance in 1917, affording a fascinating look at domestic life of the period and the roots of the Kennedy family. A unit of the National Park Service, the house is shown only by guided ranger tour, at 10:45 and 11:45am and 1, 2, 3, and 4pm. *Tip:* If the Henry Wadsworth Longfellow House is also on your itinerary, ask about purchasing a $10 Park Pass, which admits the holder and immediate family to both sites for one year.

FOR TRAVELERS INTERESTED IN AFRICAN-AMERICAN HISTORY

Before you leave home, contact the **Greater Boston Convention & Visitors Bureau** (P.O. Box 990468, Prudential Tower, Suite 400, Boston, MA 02199; ☎ **800/888-5515** outside MA or 617/536-4100; Fax 617/424-7664) and ask for a copy of the 22-page "Boston African American Discovery Guide," which is packed with information about cultural and historical activities and events.

The **Black Heritage Trail** covers sites on Beacon Hill that are part of the history of 19th-century black Boston. You can take one of the two-hour guided tours given by the rangers at the National Park Service's **Boston African American National Historic Site,** which start at the Visitor Center (46 Joy St.; ☎ 617/742-5415), or you can go on your own, using a brochure that includes a map and descriptions of the buildings. They include stations of the Underground Railroad, homes of famous citizens, and the first integrated public school.

One of the most interesting sites on the Black Heritage Trail is the 191-year-old **African Meeting House** (8 Smith Ct., Beacon Hill), the oldest standing black church in the United States. It was there that William Lloyd Garrison founded the New England Anti-Slavery Society and Frederick Douglass made some of his great abolitionist speeches. Following extensive restoration work, the building once known as the "Black Faneuil Hall" offers an informative audiovisual presentation, lectures, concerts, and church meetings. Another must-see for travelers interested in black history is the **Museum of Afro American History** (46 Joy St.; ☎ 617/742-1854). The museum has the most comprehensive information on the history and contributions of blacks in Boston and Massachusetts, and is open Monday through Friday from 10am to 4pm. Admission is free.

The **Museum of the National Center of Afro-American Artists** (300 Walnut Ave., Roxbury, MA 02119; ☎ 617/442-8614) in Roxbury is dedicated to the cultural and visual arts heritage of African-Americans and others of African descent from all over the world. Admission is $4 for adults, $3 for children and seniors. The museum is open Tuesday to Sunday from 1 to 5pm. To get there, take the MBTA Orange Line or commuter rail to Ruggles, then bus 22 or 29 to Walnut Avenue and Seaver Street.

FOR TRAVELERS INTERESTED IN WOMEN'S HISTORY

The **Boston Women's Heritage Trail** is a relatively new walking trail with stops at the homes, churches, and social and political institutions where 20 dedicated women lived, made great contributions to society, or both. Subjects include Julia Ward Howe, Dorothea Dix, and other famous Bostonians, as well as the lesser known, such as Phyllis Wheatley, a slave who became the first African-American published poet, and Lucy Stone, a feminist and abolitionist. Guides can be purchased at the National Park Service Visitor Center on State Street, at local bookstores, and at historic sites, such as the Paul Revere House. For more detailed information, call **617/522-2872.**

Massachusetts Archives

220 Morrissey Blvd., Columbia Point. ☎ **617/727-2816.** Free admission. Mon–Fri 9am–5pm, Sat 9am–3:30pm. Closed legal holidays. MBTA: Red Line to JFK/UMass.

The history of one of Boston's most famous families is explored at the nearby Kennedy Library; the history of your family may be documented here. The state archives contain passenger lists for ships that arrived in Boston between 1848 and 1891, state census schedules that date to 1790, and documents, maps, and military and court records starting with the Massachusetts Bay Company (1628–29). Knowledgeable staff members are on hand to answer researchers' questions in person, by mail or phone.

In the same building, you'll find the **Commonwealth Museum** (☎ 617/ 727-9150), which has videos, slide shows, and other interactive exhibits on the people, places, and politics of Massachusetts. Exhibits change frequently; recently covered topics include war photography, the state's geological history, and the Quabbin Reservoir.

4 Beacon Hill & Chinatown

BEACON HILL

The original Boston settlers, clustered around what are now the Old State House and the North End, considered Beacon Hill outlandishly far away. Today the distance is a matter of atmosphere; climbing "the Hill" is like traveling back in time. Lace up your walking shoes (the brick sidewalks will gnaw at anything fancier, and driving is next to impossible), wander the narrow streets, and admire the brick and brownstone architecture.

At Beacon and Park streets is a figurative high point (literally it's *the* high point): the Bulfinch-designed State House. The 60-foot monument at the rear (away from the Common) illustrates the hill's original height before the top was shorn off to use in the landfill projects of the 19th century. Beacon and Mount Vernon streets run downhill to commercially dense Charles Street, but if ever there was an area where there's no need to head in a straight line, it's this one. Your travels might take you past where Louisa May Alcott lived at 10 Louisburg Sq., Henry Kissinger at 1 Chestnut St., Julia Ward Howe at 13 Chestnut St., Edwin Booth at 29A Chestnut St., and Robert Frost at 88 Mount Vernon St. One of the oldest black churches in the country, the African Meeting House, is at 8 Smith Ct.

Louisa May Alcott probably wouldn't even be able to afford the rent for a home on Louisburg (say "Lewis-burg") Square today. The lovely private park is surrounded by 22 homes where a struggling writer would be more likely to be an employee than a resident. The iron-railed square is open only to residents with keys.

Your wandering will probably land you on Charles Street sooner or later, and after you've had your fill of the shops and restaurants, you might want to investigate the architecture of the "flats," between Charles Street and the Charles River. Built on landfill, the buildings are younger than those higher up, but often just as eye-catching.

CHINATOWN

This close-knit residential and commercial community is constantly pushing its borders, expanding into the nearly defunct "Combat Zone" (red-light district) on Washington Street and crossing the Massachusetts Turnpike extension into the South End. It's also expanding to include more Vietnamese and Cambodian residents. The heart of Chinatown is bordered by the expressway, the downtown shopping district, the Theater District, and the Tufts University medical complex. You'll know you're there when the phone booths suddenly sprout pagoda tops.

Start your visit at the arch at Beach Street and the Surface Artery. There aren't many street signs, but you can't miss the three-story Chinatown Gateway. The gate with its four marble lions was a bicentennial gift from the government of Taiwan.

Beach Street is the closest thing Chinatown has to a main drag, and the streets that cross it and run parallel are nearly as congested and equally interesting. You'll see fish tanks full of entrees-to-be, fresh produce stands, gift shops, and markets. After wandering around for a while and working up an appetite, stop for dim sum—dumplings and other small dishes that circulate through the restaurant on carts. You order by pointing and nodding (unless you know Chinese); each dish corresponds to a stamp on your check, which won't be terribly large unless you really go wild. Two excellent spots for dim sum are the Golden Palace Restaurant (14 Tyler St.; ☎ **617/423-4565**) and China Pearl (9 Tyler St.; ☎ **617/426-4338**). Dishes are both savory and sweet; if you still have room for dessert, stop at a bakery—perhaps Ho Yuen Bakery (54 Beach St.; ☎ **617/426-8320**)—for giant walnut cookies, pastries in the shape of animals, or moon cakes. The wares in the gift shops run the gamut from classic to cartoonish, and prices tend to be quite reasonable.

During the celebration of Chinese New Year (January or February, depending on the moon), masses of people turn out even in the harshest weather to watch the parade. Dragons dance in the streets, and firecrackers punctuate the musical accompaniment. In August, try to see the Festival of the August Moon, a local street fair. Call the Chinese Merchants Association, 20 Hudson St. (☎ **617/482-3972**), for information on special events. The building's bronze bas-reliefs represent the eight immortals of Taoism, and there are mirrored plaques along Oxford Alley to ward off evil spirits.

Before you leave, stop in a food store for supplies to take home. One of the largest in size and selection, the 88 Supermarket (50 Herald St., at Washington St.; ☎ **617/423-1688**), is across the Pike extension. It's not just Chinese—every ingredient that you can imagine including in Asian cuisine seems to be on the shelves somewhere, and the fresh produce ranges from lemons to lemongrass. In Chinatown proper, See Sun Co. (25 Harrison Ave.; ☎ **617/426-0954**) isn't as large, but the selection and prices are good.

To get to Chinatown, follow Washington Street to Beach Street, or Kneeland Street (which starts as Stuart Street in the Theater District) to Tyler Street; take the MBTA Orange Line to the Chinatown stop; or take the Green Line to Boylston and walk one block to Stuart Street If you must drive, take the Surface Artery, turn right onto Kneeland Street before the entrance to the Expressway, and take the third left onto Washington Street for the garage at Tufts-New England Medical Center.

5   Parks & Gardens

Green space is an important part of Boston's appeal, and the public parks are hard to miss. The latest development on this front can be viewed at City Hall Plaza, where flowers, trees, and plants are welcome invaders on the vast expanse of brick. It's not a park yet, but it's getting there.

The best-known park, for good reason, is the spectacular **Public Garden**, bordered by Arlington, Boylston, Charles, and Beacon streets Something lovely is blooming at least six months out of the year, but the spring flowers are particularly impressive, especially if your visit should happen to coincide with the first really warm day of the year. It's hard not to enjoy yourself when everyone around you seems ecstatic just sitting in the sun. For many people, the official return of spring coincides with the return of **the swan boats** (☎ **617/522-1966** or 617/451-8558). The pedal-powered vessels plunge into the lagoon on the Saturday before Patriots' Day (the third Monday of April), and although they don't move fast, they'll transport you. They operate from 10am to 6pm in summer, 10am to 4pm in spring and fall. The cost is $1.50 for adults, 95¢ for children.

❓ Did You Know?

- Martin Luther King, Jr., studied at Boston University and left it many of his important papers.

- The Boston subway system, which opened in 1897, was the first in the Western Hemisphere.

- Susan B. Anthony (now immortalized on the dollar coin) was arrested in Boston in 1872 for trying to vote in the presidential election.

- Kahlil Gibran, the Lebanese-American poet who wrote *The Prophet,* grew up in Boston's South End.

- The French Protestants known as Huguenots were a small but important group in colonial Boston. Two Huguenot names you'll see today: Faneuil and Revere.

- The toothpick was first used in the United States at the Union Oyster House. The owner hired Harvard students to dine there and ask for toothpicks as a way to promote his new business.

- The first school in America, attended by John Hancock and Benjamin Franklin, among others, was located on School Street in Boston.

Across Charles Street is **Boston Common**, the country's first public park. The property was purchased in 1634 and officially set aside as public land in 1640, so if it seems a bit run-down (especially compared to the Public Garden), it's no wonder. A massive overhaul of the Frog Pond should be complete by the time you visit, allowing visitors to splash around in the summer and ice skate in the winter. There's also a bandstand where you might take in a free concert, and many beautiful shady trees, neatly identified with little plaques near the roots.

The most spectacular garden of all is the **Arnold Arboretum** (125 Arborway, Jamaica Plain; ☎ **617/524-1718**). One of the oldest parks in the United States, it opened in 1872 and is open daily from sunrise to sunset. A National Historical Landmark, it is administered by Harvard University in cooperation with the Boston Department of Parks and Recreation. You can have a great time here wandering through some 265 acres containing more than 15,000 ornamental trees, shrubs, and vines from all over the world. In the spring, the air is perfumed with the scent of dogwood, azaleas, rhododendrons, and hundreds of varieties of lilacs, for which the arboretum is especially famous. Lilac Sunday is in May, and it's the only time picnicking is allowed in the arboretum. This is definitely a place to take a camera. There is no admission charge. To get there, take the MBTA Orange Line to the Forest Hills stop and follow the signs to the entrance. The Visitor Center is open from 9am to 4pm weekdays and from noon to 4pm weekends. Call for information about educational programs.

6 Cambridge

Cambridge is so closely associated with Boston that many people believe they're the same city—a notion both cities' residents and politicians would be happy to dispel.

Cambridge Attractions

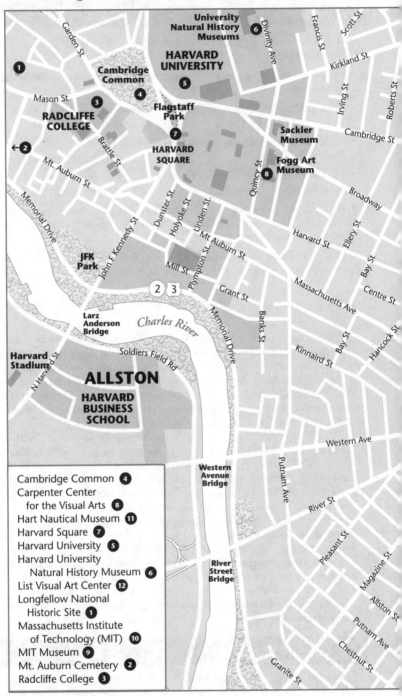

University Natural History Museums

HARVARD UNIVERSITY

Garden St

Scott St

Francis St

Divinity Ave

Kirkland St

Mason St

Cambridge Common

RADCLIFFE COLLEGE

Irving St

Roberts St

Brattle St

Flagstaff Park

Cambridge St

HARVARD SQUARE

Sackler Museum

Mt. Auburn St

Quincy St

Fogg Art Museum

Broadway

Memorial Drive

Dunster St.

Holyoke St.

Linden St.

Mt Auburn St

Ellery St

Harvard St

John F Kennedy St

JFK Park

Mill St

Plympton St.

Grant St

Massachusetts Ave

Bay St

Centre St

Larz Anderson Bridge

Charles River

Memorial Drive

Banks St

Bay St

Hancock St

Harvard Stadium

N Harvard St

Soldiers Field Rd

Kinnaird St

ALLSTON

HARVARD BUSINESS SCHOOL

Western Ave

Western Avenue Bridge

Putnam Ave

River St

Pleasant St

Magazine St

Cambridge Common ❹
Carpenter Center
  for the Visual Arts ❽
Hart Nautical Museum ⑪
Harvard Square ❼
Harvard University ❺
Harvard University
  Natural History Museum ❻
List Visual Art Center ⑫
Longfellow National
  Historic Site ❶
Massachusetts Institute
  of Technology (MIT) ❿
MIT Museum ❾
Mt. Auburn Cemetery ❷
Radcliffe College ❸

River Street Bridge

Allston St

Putnam Ave

Chestnut St

Granite St

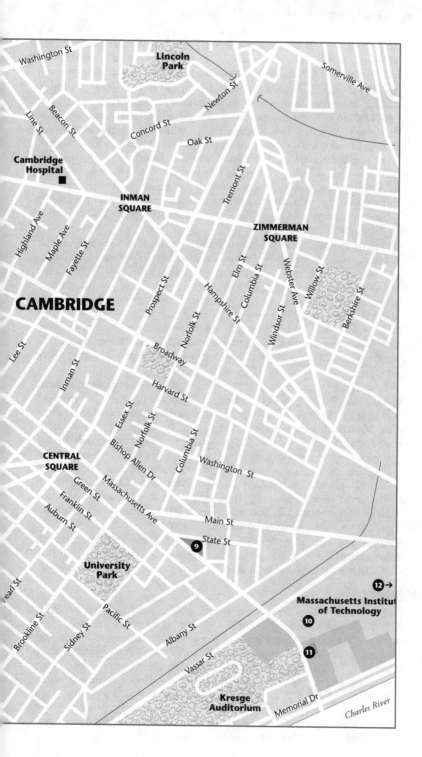

Cantabrigians are often considered more liberal and better educated than Bostonians, which is another idea that's sure to get you involved in a heated discussion. Take the MBTA Red Line to Harvard (or Kendall/MIT) and see for yourself.

For a good overview, begin at the main Harvard "T" entrance. The information booth run by Cambridge Discovery, Inc. (P.O. Box 1987, Cambridge, MA 02238; ☎ 617/497-1630) is in the middle of Harvard Square at the intersection of Massachusetts Avenue, John F. Kennedy Street, and Brattle Street. Trained volunteers dispense maps and brochures and answer questions Monday to Saturday from 9am to 5pm and Sunday 1 to 5pm. From mid-June through Labor Day there are guided tours that include the entire old Cambridge area. Check at the booth for rates, meeting places, and times, or call ahead. If you prefer to sightsee on your own, you can purchase an old Cambridge or East Cambridge walking guide prepared by the Cambridge Historical Commission for $1. Or see Chapter 8, "Boston Strolls," for one possible route.

Whatever you do, spend some time in Harvard Square. It's a hodgepodge of college and high school students, instructors, commuters, street performers, and sightseers. Near the information booth are two well-stocked newsstands, Nini's Corner and Out of Town News (which, with its extensive collection of papers and magazines from all over the world, is where you can find out what's happening at home), and the Harvard Coop. There are restaurants and stores along all three streets that spread out from the center of the square and the streets that intersect them. If you follow Brattle Street to the residential area just outside the square, you'll come to a part of town once known as "Tory Row" because the residents were loyal to King George.

The ravishing yellow mansion at 105 Brattle St. is the **Longfellow National Historic Site** (☎ 617/876-4491), where the books and furniture have remained intact since the poet Henry Wadsworth Longfellow died there in 1882. Now a unit of the National Park Service, during the seige of Boston in 1775–76 the house served as the headquarters of Gen. George Washington, with whom Longfellow was fascinated. The house is open from mid-May through mid-October, Wednesday to Sunday from 10am to 4:30pm; tours (the only way to see the house) are offered at 10:45am, 11:45am, 1pm, 2pm, 3pm, and 4pm. Admission is $2 for adults, free for children under 16 and seniors. *Tip:* If the John F. Kennedy National Historic Site is also on your itinerary, ask about purchasing a $10 Park Pass, which admits the holder and immediate family to both sites for one year.

Farther west, near where Brattle Street, and Mount Auburn Street intersect, is Mount Auburn Cemetery. It's a pleasant but long walk and you may prefer to drive or take the bus. Or, of course, you can return to the square and investigate Harvard.

HARVARD

Free, student-led tours leave from the Holyoke Center Information Office (1350 Massachusetts Ave.; ☎ 617/495-1573) during the school year twice a day during the week and once on Saturday, except during vacations; and during the summer four times a day Monday through Saturday and twice on Sunday. Call for exact times; reservations aren't necessary. And you're also free to wander on your own (see Chapter 8, "Boston Strolls"). The Information Center has maps, illustrated booklets, and self-guided walking-tour directions, as well as a bulletin board where campus activities are publicized. Note that Harvard buildings are integrated into the community as well as set apart from it—structures in use by the school typically have plaques or other identifying features on the front.

The best-known part of the university is Harvard Yard, actually two large quadrangles. The statue of John Harvard, one of the school's original benefactors, is in the Old Yard, which dates to the college's founding in 1636. Most first-year students live in the dormitories here—even in the school's oldest building, Massachusetts Hall (1720), where the university president's office takes up the first floor. The other side of the Yard (sometimes called Tercentenary Theater because the college's 300th-anniversary celebration was held there) is home to the imposing Widener Library, named after a Harvard graduate who perished on the *Titanic*. Visitors are allowed to view the dioramas of Cambridge on the main level and can browse in the large reading room upstairs, but you must have a university ID to enter the rest of the building.

The architectural consistency at the center of the Yard frays at the edges and breaks up completely on the outside of the brick walls, often to good effect. On Quincy Street you'll find the curvilinear Carpenter Center for Visual Arts, the only building in North America designed by the famous Swiss-French architect Le Corbusier. At the corner of Quincy and Cambridge streets is Memorial Hall, which, depending on your perspective, is either a monstrosity or a fitting monument to the Union soldiers who died in the Civil War. Next door, somewhat incongruously, is the Science Center, which, if you face it with your back to the Yard and use your imagination, resembles a Polaroid camera in honor of benefactor Edwin H. Land, the founder of Polaroid. Behind the Science Center is the campus of Harvard Law School; on the far side of the Yard from the Law School, between Mass. Ave. and the river, are residential houses where many upperclassmen live (other dorms, formerly Radcliffe College residences, are northwest of the Yard).

Also on campus are two engaging museum complexes.

The **Harvard University Museum of Cultural and Natural History** (26 Oxford St.; ☎ **617/495-3045**) is actually four fascinating institutions: the Botanical Museum, the Museum of Comparative Zoology, the Mineralogical & Geological Museum, and the Peabody Museum of Archaeology & Ethnology. Under new director Cherrie Corey, a push began in 1995 to make the world-famous scholarly resource center even more accessible to the public, an initiative that should be bearing fruit by the time you visit. Even if you're not interested in new interdisciplinary programs and exhibitions that tie in elements of all four collections, you'll find something interesting here, be it a dinosaur skeleton, a hunk of meteorite, a Native American artifact, or the world-famous Glass Flowers. Hours are Monday to Saturday from 9am to 5pm, Sunday from 1 to 5pm; the museums are closed New Year's Day, July 4th, Thanksgiving Day, and Christmas. Admission is free on Saturday from 9am to noon. At other times the admission charge is $5 for adults, $4 for students and seniors, $3 for children 3–13, children under 3 free. One charge covers admission to all the buildings.

The best-known of the four is the Botanical Museum, and the best-known display there is the Glass Flowers, 3,000 models of more than 840 plant species devised between 1887 and 1936 by the German father-and-son team of Leopold and Rudolph Blaschka. You may have heard about them, and you may be skeptical, but it's true: They actually look real. Children love the Museum of Comparative Zoology, where the dinosaurs share space with preserved and stuffed insects and animals that range in size from butterflies to giraffes. Young visitors also enjoy the dollhouse-like "Worlds in Miniature" display at the Peabody Museum of Archaeology & Ethnology, which capture people from all over the world in scaled-down homes. The Peabody also boasts the Hall of the North American Indian, where 500 Native American artifacts representing 10 cultures are on display.

The complex has a web site (http://fas-www.harvard.edu/~peabody/museum_cult.html).

The **Harvard University Art Museums** (☎ 617/495-9400) house a total of about 150,000 works of art in three collections, at the Fogg Art Museum, the Busch-Reisinger Museum, and the Arthur M. Sackler Museum. These exhibit spaces, which also serve as teaching and research facilities, are across the street from Harvard Yard. Hours are Monday through Saturday from 10am to 5pm and Sunday from 1 to 5pm; closed major holidays. Admission to all three is $5 for adults, $4 for senior citizens, $3 for students, and free for children under 18. Admission is free to all on Saturday mornings. One-hour guided tours are available every weekday.

The **Fogg Art Museum** (32 Quincy St., near Broadway) centers around an impressive 16th-century Italian stone courtyard, with two floors of galleries opening off it. You'll see something different in each of the 19 rooms—17th-century Dutch and Flemish landscapes, 19th-century British and American paintings and drawings, French paintings and drawings from the 18th century through the Impressionist period, contemporary sculpture, and changing exhibits. In the morning, you might also see bleary-eyed students heading to the lecture hall in the basement.

The **Busch-Reisinger Museum** in Werner Otto Hall (enter through the Fogg at 32 Quincy St.) opened in 1991 and is the only museum in North America devoted to the painting, sculpture, and decorative art of northern and central Europe—specifically Germany. Its encyclopedic collection also includes prints and illustrated books, and is particularly noted for its early 20th-century collections, including works by Klee, Feininger, Kandinsky, and artists and designers associated with the Bauhaus.

The **Arthur M. Sackler Museum** (485 Broadway, at Quincy St.) houses the university's Asian, ancient, and Islamic art. Included are a collection of Chinese jades and cave reliefs that's considered the best in the world, as well as Korean ceramics, Roman sculpture, Greek vases, and Persian miniature paintings and calligraphy.

MASSACHUSETTS INSTITUTE OF TECHNOLOGY (MIT)

The public is also welcome at the Massachusetts Institute of Technology campus, a mile or so down Mass. Ave. from Harvard Square, across the Charles River from Beacon Hill and the Back Bay. Visit the Information Center (77 Mass. Ave.; ☎ 617/253-4795) to take a free guided tour (weekdays, 10am and 2pm) or pick up a copy of the "Walk Around MIT" map and brochure. At the same address, the Hart Nautical Galleries contain ship and engine models that trace the development of marine engineering. The school has an excellent outdoor sculpture collection, which includes works by Picasso and Alexander Calder, and notable modern architecture by Eero Saarinen and I.M. Pei. Even more modern are the holography displays at the MIT Museum (265 Mass. Ave.; ☎ 617/253-4444), where you'll also find works in more conventional media.

To get to MIT, take the MBTA Red Line to Kendall/MIT. Pause on the platform before exiting to pull on the handles that work the kinetic sculptures between the tracks. One shakes a sheet of metal, approximating the sound of thunder; the other sets a hammer in motion that strikes another piece of metal and makes a melodious sound. By car from Boston, cross the river at the Museum of Science, Cambridge St., or Mass. Ave. and follow signs to Memorial Drive, where you'll usually be able to find parking during the day.

Mount Auburn Cemetery

580 Mount Auburn St., Cambridge; ☎ **617/547-7105.**

In addition to being the final resting place of many well-known people, Mount Auburn Cemetery is famous simply for existing. Dedicated in 1831, it was the first of America's rural, or garden, cemeteries. The establishment of burying places removed from city and town centers reflected practical and philosophical concerns. Development was encroaching on urban graveyards, and the ideas associated with the Greek revival ("sleeping place") and Transcendentalism dictated that communing with nature take precedence over organized religion. Since the day it opened, Mount Auburn has been a popular place to retreat and reflect—in the 19th century, it was often the first place visitors from out of town were taken, and the first place they wanted to go.

A modern visitor will find history and horticulture coexisting with celebrity. The graves of Henry Wadsworth Longfellow, Oliver Wendell Holmes, Julia Ward Howe, and Mary Baker Eddy are here, as are those of Charles Bulfinch, James Russell Lowell, Transcendentalist leader Margaret Fuller, and abolitionist Charles Sumner. In season, you'll see gorgeous flowering trees and shrubs (the Massachusetts Horticultural Society had a hand in the design). Stop at the office or front gate to pick up brochures and a map or to rent the 60-minute audiotaped tour ($5; a $12 deposit is required), which you can listen to in your car or on a portable tape player. The Friends of Mount Auburn Cemetery (☎ **617/864-9646**) conduct workshops and coordinate walking tours. Call for topics, schedules, and fees.

The cemetery is open daily from 8am to dusk. Admission is free. Animals and recreational activities such as jogging and picnicking are not allowed. MBTA bus routes 71 and 73 start at Harvard station and stop near the cemetery gates; they run frequently on weekdays, less often on weekends. By car, take Mount Auburn Street or Brattle Street west from Harvard Square; just after they intersect, the gate is on the left.

7 Especially for Kids

If you're a parent travelling with your kids, you're asking, "What can children do in Boston?" A better question might be "What can't children do in Boston?" The answer: Not much. Just about every major destination in the city either is specifically designed to appeal to youngsters or can be easily adapted to do so. They're covered extensively elsewhere in this chapter; here's the boiled-down version for busy parents.

Hands-on exhibits are a big draw at several institutions: The **New England Aquarium** (☎ 617/973-5200), the **Computer Museum** (☎ 617/426-2800 or 617/423-6758), the **Boston Tea Party Ship & Museum** (☎ 617/338-1773), and the **Sports Museum of New England** (☎ 617/57-SPORT). Hard-core sports fans will enjoy a visit to a **Red Sox game** (see "Spectator Sports," below).

The **Boston Museum of Science** (☎ 617/723-2500) is not only a hands-on paradise but is also home to the **Hayden Planetarium** and the **Mugar Omni Theatre.**

For those in the mood to let other people do the work, take in the shows by the street performers at **Faneuil Hall Marketplace** (☎ 617/338-2323).

Under a new policy, admission is free for those under 18 at the **Museum of Fine Arts** (☎ 617/267-9300), which has special Sunday and after-school programs.

The allure of seeing people the size of ants draws young visitors to the **John Hancock Observatory** (☎ 617/572-6429) and the **Prudential Center Skywalk**

(☎ 617/236-3318). And they can see actual ants—though they might prefer dinosaurs—at the Museum of Comparative Zoology, part of the **Harvard University Museum of Cultural and Natural History** (☎ 617/495-3045).

Older children who have studied modern American history will enjoy a visit to the **John F. Kennedy Presidential Library and Museum** (☎ 617/929-4523). And kids interested in cars will like the **Museum of Transportation** (☎ 617/522-6547).

Young visitors who have read Robert McCloskey's children's classic *Make Way for Ducklings* will relish a visit to the **Public Garden,** as will fans of E.B. White's *The Trumpet of the Swan,* who certainly will want to ride on the **swan boats** (☎ 617/522-1966 or 617/451-8558). Considerably less tame and much longer are **whale watches** (see "Organized Tours," below).

The walking-tour company **Boston By Foot** (77 N. Washington St.; ☎ 617/367-2345 or 617/367-3766 for recorded information) has a special program, **Boston By Little Feet,** geared to children 6 to 12 years old. The 60-minute walk gives a child's-eye view of the architecture along the Freedom Trail and of Boston's role in the American Revolution. Children must be accompanied by an adult, and a map is provided. Tours run from May through October and meet at the statue of Samuel Adams on the Congress Street side of Faneuil Hall, Saturday at 10am, Sunday at 2pm, and Monday at 10am, rain or shine. The cost is $5 per person.

The **Historic Neighborhoods Foundation** (99 Bedford St.; ☎ 617/426-1885) offers a 75-minute "Make Way for Ducklings" tour ($5 per person aged 5 or older). It's popular with children and adults, follows the path of the Mallard family described in Robert McCloskey's famous book, and ends at the Public Garden. Every year on Mother's Day, the HNF organizes the Ducklings Day Parade.

✪ Children's Museum

300 Congress St. (Museum Wharf). ☎ **617/426-8855.** Admission $7 adults, $6 children age 2–15 and seniors, $2 toddlers age 1, free for infants under age 1. Fri 5–9pm, $1 for all. Sept–June Tues–Sun 10am–5pm, Fri until 9pm; June–Aug daily 10am–5pm, Fri until 9pm. Closed Mon during school year, except Boston school vacations and holidays; Thanksgiving, Christmas, and New Year's Day. MBTA: Red Line to South Station. Walk north on Atlantic Avenue. one block past the Federal Reserve Bank, and turn right onto Congress Street. Call for information about discounted parking.

As you approach the Children's Museum, don't be surprised to see adults suddenly being dragged by the hand as their young companions realize how close they are and start running. You know the museum is near when you see the 40-foot-high red-and-white milk bottle out front. It makes both children and adults look small in comparison—which is probably part of the point. No matter how old, everyone behaves like a little kid at this delightful museum.

Not only is touching encouraged, it's practically a necessity if you're going to enjoy the exhibits. Children can stick with their parents or wander on their own, learning, doing, and role-playing. Some favorites: "Under the Dock," an environmental exhibit that teaches young people about the Boston waterfront and allows them to dress up in a crab suit; the "Kids' Bridge," where interactive videos allow a virtual visit to Boston's ethnic neighborhoods to learn about cultural differences and ways to combat racism; and the "Dress-Up Shop," a souped-up version of playing in Grandma's closet.

You'll also see "El Mercado," a marketplace that immerses children in Hispanic culture, surrounding them with Spanish newspapers, ethnic food products, and salsa music. The "Climbing Sculpture" is a giant maze designed especially for children (adults may get stuck). Another oversize display is a desk with a phone so big it doubles as a slide. "We're Still Here" concentrates on Northeast Native Americans and offers the chance to play in a wigwam. You can also explore a Japanese house from Kyoto (Boston's sister city) and learn about young adults in "Teen Tokyo." "Playspace" is a special room for children under 4 and their caregivers.

For bargain-priced craft supplies and materials for toys and games, check out the bags of industrial leftovers on sale at the RECYCLE Resource Center that can be used in many ways. Admission is free.

Note: When the kids get hungry, try the ice cream and tasty sandwiches at the stand in the giant milk bottle, or go to the McDonald's adjoining the museum gift shop.

Franklin Park Zoo

Northeast section of Franklin Park, Dorchester. ☎ **617/442-2002.** Admission $5.50 adults and children 12 and up; $4 seniors, military personnel, and students with ID; $3 children 4–11; free for children under 4. Mon–Fri 9am–4pm, Sat–Sun and holidays 10am–5pm. MBTA: Orange Line to Forest Hills, then bus number 16 to the main entrance.

The Franklin Park Zoo's claim to fame (and main point of interest) is the African Tropical Forest exhibit, a sprawling complex where you'll see more than 50 species of animals, including western lowland gorillas, who appear to be roaming free in an approximation of their natural habitat. Moats, glass, and other unobtrusive barriers—not bars and cages—separate visitors from the animals and from New England's largest collection of tropical plants. If you're traveling with animal-mad youngsters, the Children's Zoo is both entertaining and educational. *Note:* It's a fairly long walk from the main gate and the parking area to the zoo itself, so leave plenty of time, especially for those with little legs.

The Commonwealth Zoological Corporation also administers the **Stone Zoo** (☎ 617/438-5100), about 30 minutes north of Boston in Stoneham. The Stone Zoo is smaller and more manageable than the Franklin Park Zoo, with about 75 species of animals (including bison, llamas, otters, and Major the polar bear), an eight-story tropical aviary with 50 kinds of birds, and a learning center with inter-active computer stations. The zoo is off exit 34 from I-93 north. It's open daily 10am to 4pm (closed nonholiday Mondays from December through March).

Blue Hills Trailside Museum Visitor Center

1904 Canton Ave., Milton. ☎ **617/333-0690.** Admission $3 adults, $1.50 children age 3–15, free for children under 3 and Massachusetts Audubon Society members with a valid member-ship card. Wed–Sun and Mon holidays 10am–5pm. Closed New Year's Day, Thanksgiving Day, and Christmas.

An outdoor spot children will love is the Blue Hills Trailside Museum, at the 7,500-acre Blue Hills Reservation, just a short drive south of Boston on Route 138. There's room to hike, climb hills, and study replicas of the natural habitats of the Blue Hills. Visitors can climb the lookout tower, crawl through logs, experience a Native American wigwam and see a variety of native animals, including owls, hon-eybees, deer, otters, foxes, bobcats, snakes, and turtles. The big animals are in pens outside, the little ones are inside. Children can feed the ducks and deer. A wall of glass overlooks an outdoor pond. Weekend activities for children of all ages include story time (11am) and educational/instructional programs run by staff naturalists: a live "mystery animal" presentation (12:30pm), family hour (2pm), and the Naturalist's Choice (3:30pm). Special events change with the seasons and include maple sugaring in early spring, honey harvest in the fall, and owl prowls in January and February.

Puppet Showplace Theatre

32 Station St., Brookline. ☎ **617/731-6400.** Tickets $6.

Puppet Showplace stages programs of favorite fables, ethnic legends, and folk and fairy tales from around the world. They are produced for children, year-round, by professional puppeteers in a lovely theater that seats about 120. Historic puppets and puppet posters are on display, and toy puppets are for sale. Call for the current schedule and reservations.

8 Organized Tours

ORIENTATION TOURS

GUIDED WALKING TOURS

If you prefer not to explore on your own, **Boston By Foot** (77 N. Washington St.; ☎ 617/367-2345 or 617/367-3766 for recorded information) provides excellent tours. From May through October, Boston By Foot conducts historical and architectural tours that focus on particular neighborhoods or themes. The rigorously trained guides are volunteers (Boston By Foot is a nonprofit educational corporation), and questions are encouraged. The 90-minute tours take place rain or shine.

The newest Boston By Foot tour is "Boston Underground," which looks at subterranean technology, including crypts, the subway, and the depression of the Central Artery. The tour starts at Faneuil Hall Sunday at 2pm. The "Heart of the Freedom Trail" tour starts at Faneuil Hall, Tuesday through Saturday at 10am. Tours of Beacon Hill begin at the foot of the State House steps on Beacon Street Monday through Friday at 5:30pm, Saturday at 10am, and Sunday at 2pm. Other tours and meeting places are: Copley Square Tour, Trinity Church at 10am on Friday and noon on Saturday; the Waterfront Tour, Faneuil Hall, Friday at 5:30pm and Sunday at 10am; and the North End Tour, Faneuil Hall, Saturday at 2pm and Sunday at noon.

Tours that begin at Faneuil Hall meet at the statue of Samuel Adams on Congress Street. Rates for all tours are $7 for adults and $5 for children; reservations are not required. Tickets may be purchased from the guide.

Special theme tours may be arranged if there are enough requests. Included in the request tours are "Great Women of Boston," "Literary Landmarks," and a Chinatown tour.

The **Society for the Preservation of New England Antiquities** (☎ 617/ 227-3956) offers a fascinating tour that describes and illustrates life in the mansions and garrets of Beacon Hill in 1800. "Magnificent and Modest," a two-hour program, costs $10 and starts at the Harrison Gray Otis House, 141 Cambridge St., on Saturdays at 10am May through October, and Saturdays at 3pm from June through October. Reservations are recommended.

The **Historic Neighborhoods Foundation** (99 Bedford St.; ☎ 617/426-1885) offers several walking tours that focus on neighborhood landmarks, including Beacon Hill, the North End, Chinatown, the Waterfront, and the Financial District. Schedules change with the season, and the programs are based on themes, such as social history and topographical development. Write or call the Historic Neighborhoods Foundation for current schedules, fees, and meeting places.

The **Boston Park Rangers** (☎ 617/635-7383) offer free guided walking tours of the Emerald Necklace, a loop of green spaces designed by the first landscape architect, Frederick Law Olmstead. You'll see and hear about the city's major parks and gardens, including Boston Common, the Public Garden, the Commonwealth Avenue Mall, the Muddy River in the Fenway, Olmstead Park, Jamaica Pond, the

Arnold Arboretum, and Franklin Park. The full six-hour walk includes a one-hour tour of any of the sites. Call for schedules.

TROLLEY TOURS

You might want to take a narrated trolley tour for an overview of the sights before focusing on specific attractions, or you might want to use your all-day pass as a way to hit as many places as possible in eight hours or so. Whatever your approach, you'll have plenty of company. The business is competitive, with various companies offering different stops in an effort to distinguish themselves from the rest. All cover the major attractions and offer informative narratives and anecdotes in their 90- to 120-minute tours, as well as free reboarding if you want to visit the sites. Rates are between $16 and $18. Boarding spots are at hotels, historic sites, and tourist information centers.

Trolley companies are identified by the colors of their cars. **Old Town Trolley** (329 W. Second St.; ☎ 617/269-7010) has orange-and-green cars; **Boston Trolley Tours** (☎ 617/TROLLEY) uses blue cars; **Red Beantown Trolleys** (☎ 617/ 236-2148) are red; and the **Discover Boston Multilingual Trolley Tours** (73 Tremont St.; ☎ 617/742-1440) vehicle is white. Boston Trolley Tours has ramps to make it handicapped-accessible, and the Red Beantown Trolleys are the only ones that stop at the Museum of Fine Arts and the Hard Rock Cafe. Only Old Town and the Red Beantown Trolleys stop at the Boston Tea Party Ship & Museum. Only Old Town offers a tour of Cambridge.

SIGHTSEEING CRUISES

Take to the water for a taste of Boston's rich maritime history or a day-long break from walking and driving. You can cruise around the harbor or go all the way to Provincetown or Gloucester. If you're traveling in a large group, call ahead for information about reservations and discounted tickets.

Boston Harbor Cruises (1 Long Wharf; ☎ **617/227-4321**) offers narrated trips around the harbor. From the white ticket center, you set out on either the 90-minute historic sightseeing cruise of the Inner and Outer Harbor, which departs every two hours beginning at 11am, or the 45-minute *Constitution* cruise, which takes you around the Inner Harbor and docks at Charlestown Navy Yard so you can go ashore and visit the USS *Constitution*. These tours leave every hour on the half hour from Long Wharf, and on the hour from the navy yard. During the summer, the John F. Kennedy Library cruise leaves every two hours beginning at 10am. The cruise departs from the library at 10:45am, 12:45pm, 2:45pm, and 4:45pm. The 90-minute historic sightseeing and JFK Library cruises cost $8 for adults, $6 for seniors, and $4 for children. The *Constitution* cruise is $5 for adults, $4 for seniors, and $3 for children. And every evening at 7pm there's a sunset cruise, a wonderful way to unwind. It takes 90 minutes and features the lowering of the flag and a cannon blast at sunset. The fare is $8 for adults, $6 for seniors, and $4 for children.

Also on Long Wharf, at the red ticket office, **Bay State Cruise Company, Inc.** (☎ **617/723-7800**) offers inner and outer harbor cruises. Ninety-minute cruises to the Outer Harbor with an optional stop at George's Island State Park depart several times a day; the price is $7 for adults, $6 for seniors, and $5 for children under 12. A 55-minute tour of the Inner Harbor is also available, with the option of going ashore at the Charlestown Navy Yard to see the *Constitution*; adult fare is $5, seniors $4, and children $3. In addition, cruises to Provincetown are available. Call for exact dates and schedules.

Duck, Duck, Loose

The newest and perhaps best way to see Boston is with **Boston Duck Tours** (☎ 617/723-DUCK). Sightseers board a "duck," a reconditioned Second World War amphibious landing craft, behind the Prudential Center at 101 Huntington Ave. The 80-minute narrated tour hits the high points, including Trinity Church, the Boston Public Library, the North End, Faneuil Hall, and the Old State House. The real high point comes when the duck lumbers down a ramp and splashes into the Charles River for a spin around the basin. Tickets are $18 for adults, $15 for seniors and students, and $9 for children 12 and under. Children 3 and under are free but need a ticket. Tours leave every hour or so starting at 9am and ending one hour before sunset. There are no tours from December through March; call for schedules.

Massachusetts Bay Lines (☎ 617/542-8000) offers 45-minute harbor tours from Memorial Day through Labor Day. Cruises leave from Rowes Wharf on the hour from 10am to 4pm, and at 5 and 6pm weekends and holidays; the price is $7.50 for adults, $5 for children 5–12 and seniors. The same company offers three-hour live-music cruises (blues, Wednesday at 7pm; rock, Thursday at 8pm) for $10. You must be at least 21 and have a photo ID.

The **Charles River Boat Company** (☎ 617/621-3001), offers 55-minute narrated cruises around the lower Charles River basin. Boats depart from the CambridgeSide Galleria on the hour from noon to 5pm; price is $7 for adults, $6 for seniors, $5 for children.

For almost a full day at sea, Bay State Cruises' *MV Provincetown II* (☎ 617/723-7800) sails from Commonwealth Pier daily from mid-June to Labor Day, and on weekends in May and September. Be at the pier by 9:30am (the water shuttle from Long Wharf leaves at 8:30 and costs $1) for the three-hour trip to Provincetown, at the tip of Cape Cod. The return trip leaves at 3:30pm giving you a few hours for shopping and sightseeing. Same-day round trip fares are $29 for adults, $22 for senior citizens, and $20 for children. Bringing a bike cost $5 extra each way.

Another day trip is offered by **A.C. Cruise Line** (☎ 800/422-8419 or 617/261-6633). The *Virginia C II* sails to Gloucester from Pier 7 (290 Northern Ave.) daily from late June through Labor Day at 10:30am and returns at 5pm. You'll have about 2¹/₂ hours to explore Gloucester. The round-trip charge is $18 for adults, $14 for senior citizens. A.C. Cruise Line also offers a three-hour country-western dance cruise ($12) with live entertainment Thursdays at 8pm.

The *Spirit of Boston*, a sleek 192-foot harbor-cruise ship operated by Bay State Cruises (☎ 617/457-1499), offers a New England lobster clambake luncheon cruise (daily, noon to 2:30pm) and a dinner dance cruise (nightly, 7 to 10pm). It sails from 60 Rowes Wharf near the Boston Harbor Hotel. Call for reservations.

WHALE WATCHING

The New England Aquarium (see listing above) runs its own whale watches.

Boston Harbor Whale Watch (☎ 617/345-9866) sends the 100-foot *Majestic* out to sea at speeds topping 20 knots and promises more time watching whales than trying to find them. Tours depart from Rowes Wharf beginning in mid-June and operate Friday, Saturday, and Sunday only through June. From July through early

September there's daily service. Departure times are Monday through Friday at 10am, Saturday and Sunday at 9am and 2pm. Expect to spend about 4¹/₂ hours at sea. Tickets are $18 for adults, $15 for seniors and children under 13. Reservations are suggested, and discounted parking is available.

A.C. Cruise Line (☎ 800/422-8419 or 617/261-6633) offers a whale watch cruise Tuesday through Sunday, leaving at 10:30am and returning at 5pm. The fare is $19 for adults, $15 for seniors, $10 for children. Call for reservations and more information.

SPECIALTY TOURS

FOR KENNEDY BUFFS

The newest offering from Old Town Trolley (☎ 617/269-7150) is "JFK's Boston," a three-hour tour that stops at John F. Kennedy's birthplace in Brookline and the presidential library in Dorchester (a co-presenter of the tour). The 3¹/₂-hour excursion starts at Atlantic Avenue and State Street and passes through the North End and Beacon Hill. Tickets are $22 for adults, $17 for seniors, and $12 for children, and include admission to the John F. Kennedy National Historic Site and the Kennedy Library. Tours start at 9:30am on Friday, Saturday, and Sunday from Memorial Day through Labor Day.

FOR BEER NUTS

In addition to the brewery tours described below, Old Town Trolley stages a tour of three brew pub/restaurants twice a month. The three-hour journey includes stops at the Commonwealth Brewing Co. and Brew Moon Restaurant and Microbrewery in Boston, and John Harvard's Brew House in Cambridge. Food is served along with two 10-ounce beer samples at each location. Tickets are $38 and must be purchased in advance when you call **617/269-7150** for reservations.

Mass. Bay Brewing Co.

306 Northern Ave. ☎ **617/574-9551.** Free admission. Tours Fri–Sat, 1pm. MBTA: Red Line to South Station or Blue Line to Aquarium. Follow Atlantic Avenue to the Northern Avenue Bridge, cross over, and take Northern Avenue past the World Trade Center and the Fish Pier; the brewery is on the left.

This company brews and bottles Harpoon Ale and other Harpoon products in small batches without preservatives. Visitors can sample the wares and see the stages of processing from an enclosed platform above the brewery floor. Parking is available; leave time if you take the "T," because the closest stations are about a mile away.

Boston Beer Company

30 Germania St., Jamaica Plain. ☎ **617/522-9080.** $1 requested for guided tour; proceeds go to charity. Tours Thurs–Fri at 2pm, Sat at noon, 1pm, and 2pm. MBTA: Orange Line to Stony Brook; go left onto Boylston Street At the first traffic light, turn right onto Amory Street, then take the first left onto Porter Street At the end of Porter Street, turn right into the parking lot.

The Boston Beer Company produces Samuel Adams beer, widely considered (especially by Boston-area beer snobs) the best in the country. The brew is named after the same Samuel Adams whose statue is next to Faneuil Hall, the patriot, revolutionary—and brewer. Samuel Adams Boston Lager has been served at the White House and was the first American beer allowed to be sold in Germany. The company also brews Samuel Adams Scotch Ale, Cream Stout, Honey Porter, and Lightship, and six seasonal brews. During the 30-minute guided tour, you'll learn about the history and process of brewing and have a chance to sample the results. There's also a souvenir shop. If you plan to drive, call the tour hotline for the lengthy directions.

9 Outdoor Activities

BEACHES

The beaches in Boston proper (discussed below) are decent places to catch a cool breeze and splash around, but for real ocean surf, you'll need to head out of town.

NORTH SHORE BEACHES

North of Boston are sandy beaches that complement the rocky coastline. Two caveats: it's not Florida, so don't expect 70-degree water (the operative word is "refreshing"), and parking can be scarce (especially on weekends) and pricey—as much as $15 per car. If you can't set out early, wait till midafternoon and hope that the people who beat you to the beach in the morning have had enough. During the summer, lifeguards are on duty 9am–5pm at larger public beaches. Surfing is generally permitted outside of those hours.

Probably the best-known North Shore beach is **Singing Beach,** off Masconomo Street in Manchester-by-the-Sea, named for the sound the sand makes under your feet. The legions of people walking six-tenths of a mile on Beach Street from the commuter rail station (Singing Beach is the only relatively distant beach accessible by public transport) attest to both the beach's reputation and the difficulty (and expense) of parking. Save some cash and aggravation by taking the MBTA (☎ 617/222-3200) from Boston's North Station.

Nearly as famous and equally popular is **Crane Beach,** off Argilla Road in Ipswich, part of a 1,400-acre barrier beach reservation. Expanses of white sand and fragile dunes lead down to Ipswich Bay, and the surf is calmer than that at less sheltered Singing Beach, but still quite chilly. Also on Ipswich Bay is Gloucester's **Wingaersheek Beach,** on Atlantic Street off Route 133. It has its own exit (number 13) off Route 128, about 15 minutes away. When you finally arrive you'll find beautiful white sand, a glorious view, and more dunes.

Across the bay in Newburyport (follow signs from Route 1A or I-95) is **Plum Island,** part of the Parker River National Wildlife Refuge (☎ 508/465-5753). The beach is *not* open all summer—it closes April 1 for piping plover nesting season. The areas not being used for nesting reopen July 1, and the rest of the beach opens in August when the birds are through with it. The currents are strong and can be dangerous, and there are no lifeguards—you may prefer to stick to surf fishing and exploring the trails that crisscross the gorgeous marshes and dunes and allow you to view the incredible variety of birds and wildlife.

Whether you're swimming or not, watch out for the greenhead flies at Wingaersheek, Plum Island, and Crane beaches in late July and early August. They don't sting—they actually take little bites of flesh. Plan to bring or buy insect repellent.

Other nice beaches in Gloucester are **Good Harbor Beach,** off Route 127A at Thatcher Road in East Gloucester, and **Half Moon Beach** and **Cressy's Beach,** at Stage Fort Park, off Route 127 near the intersection with Route 133. The park also contains a visitor information office (only open in summer), playgrounds, picnic and cookout areas, and the ruins of a Revolutionary War fortress.

Closer to Boston are **Nahant Beach** (follow the signs from the intersection of Routes 1A and 129, near the Lynn-Swampscott border), which is large and extremely popular, and **Revere Beach.** Revere Beach is better known for its pick-up scene than its narrow strip of sand, but the cruising crowds are friendly and parking on the boulevard is free. The MBTA Blue Line has a Revere Beach stop; if you're driving, head north for smaller crowds at **Point of Pines**, which has its own exit off Route 1A. Across the street from the water is **Kelly's Roast Beef** (410 Revere Beach Blvd.; ☎ **617/284-9129**), a local legend for its onion rings, fried clams, and, yes, roast beef sandwiches.

SOUTH SHORE BEACHES

The southern suburbs are riddled with private beaches, but there are a couple of pleasant public options. In Hull (take Route 3 or 3A to Route 228), **Nantasket Beach** (☎ 617/925-4905) is right in town. It's popular with families for its fairly shallow water and the historic wooden carousel in a building across the street from the main parking lot. Nine-mile-long **Duxbury Beach** (take Route 3A to Route 139 north and go right on Canal Street) makes an enjoyable stop on the way to Plymouth, if that's in your plans. **Plymouth Beach,** off Route 3A south of Plymouth at Warren Avenue, is smaller, with mild surf.

BOSTON BEACHES

The condition of Boston Harbor has improved considerably since its pollution was an issue in the 1988 presidential campaign, and the Metropolitan District Commission (☎ 617/727-9547) is working to restore the run-down beaches under its purview, but the MDC sometimes still has to fly red flags when swimming is not recommended (blue flags mean the water's fine). Be aware that these are very much neighborhood hangouts. In Dorchester, off Morrissey Boulevard, **Malibu Beach** and **Savin Hill Beach** are within walking distance of the Savin Hill stop on the MBTA Red Line. South Boston beaches are off Day Boulevard and accessible by taking the Red Line to Broadway or Green Line to Copley, then a bus marked "City Point" (routes 9, 10, and 11). Among them are **Castle Island, L Street,** and **Pleasure Bay.**

BIKING

Expert cyclists who feel comfortable with the layout of the city shouldn't have too much trouble navigating in traffic. If you don't fit that description, you're better off sticking to the many bike paths in the area and not tempting the bloodthirsty drivers. State law requires that children under 12 wear helmets. Bicycles are forbidden on MBTA buses and the Green Line at all times and during rush hour on the other parts of the system. You must have a permit (☎ **617/222-5799**) to bring your bike on the Blue, Orange, and Red lines and commuter rail during non-rush hours.

Shops that rent require you to show a driver's license or passport and leave a deposit using a major credit card. They include **Earth Bikes** (35 Huntington Ave., near Copley Sq.; ☎ 617/267-4733), where rentals start at $12 for four hours; **Back Bay Bikes** (333 Newbury St., near Mass. Ave.; ☎ 617/247-2336), which charges $20 per day; and **Community Bicycle Supply** (496 Tremont St., near E. Berkeley St.; ☎ 617/542-8623), where rentals are $5 an hour or $20 a day. At the Bedford end of the Minuteman Bikeway, **Pro Motion** (1 Minuteman Bikeway, 111 South Rd., Bedford; ☎ 617/275-2223) charges $5 per hour, with a two-hour minimum.

The **Dr. Paul Dudley White Charles River Bike Path** is a 17.7-mile circuit that begins at Science Park (near the Museum of Science) and loops along both sides of the river to Watertown and back. You can enter and exit at many points along the way. Bikers share the path with lots of pedestrians, joggers, and in-line skaters, expecially in Boston near the Esplanade and in Cambridge near Harvard Square. The path is maintained by the Metropolitan District Commission, or MDC (☎ 617/727-9547), as is the five-mile **Pierre Lallement Bike Path,** in Southwest Corridor Park. It starts behind Copley Place and runs for five miles through the South End and Roxbury along the route of the MBTA Orange Line to Franklin Park. The 10¹/₂-mile **Minuteman Bikeway** (☎ 617/641-4891) starts at Alewife station at the end of the Red Line in Cambridge and runs through Arlington and Lexington to Bedford along an old railroad bed. It's a wonderful way to head out to the historic sites in Lexington, and popular with commuters and families. And on summer Sundays from 11am to 7pm, a 1¹/₂-mile stretch of **Memorial Drive** in Cambridge from Western Avenue to the Eliot Bridge (Central Square to west Cambridge) is closed to traffic. It's flat, not especially long, and can get quite crowded.

For additional information, call the **Bicycle Coalition of Massachusetts** (☎ 617/491-7433) or the **Charles River Wheelmen** (☎ 617/332-8546).

BOATING

Technically, riding a swan boat is boating. It's not exactly a transatlantic crossing, but it has been a classic Boston experience since 1877. The lagoon at the Public Garden (see "Parks & Gardens," above) turns into a fiberglass swan habitat every spring and summer and offers an excellent break in the midst of a busy day.

The pedal-powered swan boats (☎ 617/522-1966 or 617/451-8558) operate from the Saturday before Patriots' Day (the third Monday in April) through September, 10am to 6pm in summer, 10am to 4pm spring and fall. The cost is $1.50 for adults, 95¢ for children.

There are also plenty of less tame options (see "Sailing," below). The **Charles River Canoe and Kayak Center** (☎ 617/965-5110) has two locations, on Soldiers Field Road in Allston and at 2401 Commonwealth Ave. in Newton. Both centers rent canoes and kayaks (the Newton location also rents sculls), and lessons are available. From April through October, they open at 10am on weekdays and 9am on weekends and holidays, and close at dusk.

Non-inflatable water craft are allowed on the Charles River and in the Inner Harbor. If you plan to bring your own boat, call the **Metropolitan District Commission** Harbor Master (☎ 617/727-0537) for information about launches.

ICE-SKATING

The lagoons at the **Public Garden** and the **Frog Pond** on Boston Common (see "Parks & Gardens," above) freeze to smooth surfaces if the weather is exactly right, which happens only sporadically. The ongoing renovation of the Frog Pond is expected to help optimize conditions there, but for surfaces that are guaranteed to be frozen, you'll want to head indoors.

The **Skating Club of Boston** (1240 Soldiers Field Rd., Brighton; ☎ 617/782-5900) is a training center for many competitive skaters and was 1992 Olympic silver medalist Paul Wylie's headquarters when he was a Harvard undergrad. The well-maintained surface is open to the public at least twice a week, and skate sharpening and rentals are available all year ($6 adults, $4 children).

Grooming is less consistent at the rinks maintained by the Metropolitan District Commission, which are popular with recreational hockey leagues and don't all have services and concessions. If you've brought along your own sharpened skates, try **Steriti Memorial Rink** (☎ 617/727-4708), on Commercial Street in the North

End, the only MDC rink convenient to downtown. It's open seasonally, and admission is $3 for public sessions; call for days and times.

SAILING

You don't have to get wet to enjoy the glorious sight of sailboats filling up the Charles River basin or the Inner Harbor. If you want to take part, you have several options.

Community Boating, Inc. (21 Embankment Rd., on the Esplanade; ☎ 617/523-1038) offers sailing lessons and boating programs for children and adults from April to November. It runs on a co-op system; a 30-day adult membership is $65. The **Courageous Sailing Center** (Charlestown Navy Yard; ☎ 617/242-3821) offers youth program lessons year-round. A five-lesson program (one in the classroom, four on the water) is $125. The **Boston Sailing Center** (54 Lewis Wharf; ☎ 617/227-4198) offers lessons for sailors of all ability levels. The center is open all year (even for "frostbite" racing in the winter). Ten classes (five indoors, five outdoors) and a 35-day membership will run you $475. And the **Boston Harbor Sailing Club** (200 High St., at Rowes Wharf; ☎ 617/345-9202) offers rentals and instruction. A package of four classes, 16 hours of on-water instruction, and a 30-day membership is $414. Private lessons (three-hour minimum) are $20 an hour plus the rental of the boat (from $25 an hour) plus tax.

SKIING

Generally. speaking, "skiing" means Vermont or New Hampshire, but that doesn't rule out cross-country action in Boston. About 30 minutes from downtown, Charles River Recreation operates the **Weston Ski Track** (200 Park Rd., on the Leo J. Martin Golf Course, Weston; ☎ 617/891-6575) from mid-December to mid-March. Included in the 15 kilometers of groomed trails is a lighted three-kilometer track, and rentals and instruction are available. The track is open Monday to Saturday 9am to 10pm, and Sunday 9am to 6pm.

Should you happen to have your cross-country skis with you after a monster snowstorm, head for Commonwealth Avenue in the Back Bay early in the morning and join the crowd.

Finally, if you insist on downhill skiing, be aware that Boston's official elevation is 20 feet. The closest downhill facility isn't pulling any punches—it has "hills" in its name. The **Blue Hills Ski Area** (4001 Washington St., Canton; ☎ 617/828-5090) is operated by the Metropolitan District Commission and has a 350-foot vertical drop. Night skiing, rentals, and lessons are available. Lift tickets are $20 on weekends, $15 on weekdays. Canton is about 40 miles south of Boston.

HARBOR ISLAND EXPLORATION

The **Boston Harbor Islands** were right under your nose if you arrived by plane, but their accessibility isn't widely known. There are 30 islands in the Outer Harbor, some open for exploring, camping, or swimming. Plan a day trip or even an overnight stay. The most popular is **George's Island,** home of Fort Warren (1834), where Confederate prisoners were kept during the Civil War. Tours are offered periodically. The island has a visitor center, refreshment area, fishing pier, place for picnics, and a wonderful view of Boston's skyline. From there, free water taxis run to **Lovells, Gallops, Peddocks, Bumpkin,** and **Grape islands,** which have picnic areas and campsites. For permits and reservations, call the Department of Environmental Management (☎ 617/740-1605), which administers Bumpkin,

Calf, Gallops, Grape, and Great Brewster islands; or the Metropolitan District Commission (☎ **617/727-5290**), which manages George's, Lovells, and Peddocks islands. Lovells Island also has the remains of a fort (Fort Standish), as well as a sandy beach; it's the only harbor island with supervised swimming. Boats to George's Island leave from Long Wharf and Rowes Wharf. The islands are part of the Boston Harbor Islands State Park. For more information, contact the Friends of the Boston Harbor Islands (☎ **617/740-4290**).

FISHING

Freshwater fishing is permitted at **Turtle Pond** in the Stony Brook Reservation in Hyde Park, at **Jamaica Pond** in Jamaica Plain, and on the banks of the **Charles River** (eating your catch is not recommended.) For offshore saltwater fishing, the **Harbor Islands** are a good choice. You might also try fishing from the pier at **City Point** and the **John J. McCorkle Fishing Pier,** off Day Boulevard in South Boston.

For information on locations and regulations, call the Sport Fishing Information Line (☎ **800/ASK-FISH**). Information is also available from the state Division of Fisheries and Wildlife (100 Cambridge St., Boston, MA 02202; ☎ **617/ 727-3151**), and in the fishing columns in the *Globe* and *Herald* on Fridays in the spring, summer, and fall.

GOLF

You won't get far in the suburbs without seeing a golf course, and with the recent explosion in the sport's popularity, you won't be the only one looking. Given a choice, opt for the lower prices and smaller crowds you'll find on weekdays.

At **Newton Commonwealth Golf Course** (212 Kenrick St., Newton; ☎ 617/ 630-1971), an excellent 18-hole layout, greens fees are $20 on weekdays and $25 on weekends. At nine-hole **Fresh Pond Golf Course** (691 Huron Ave., Cambridge; ☎ 617/349-6282), it's $14, or $20 to go around twice, on weekdays, and $17 and $25 on weekends. Within the city limits there are two 18-hole courses: **Franklin Park Golf Course** (Dorchester; ☎ 617/265-4084), where greens fees are $17 on weekdays and $20 on weekends; and **George Wright Golf Course** (420 West St., Hyde Park; ☎ 617/361-8313), where fees are $21 on weekdays and $24 on weekends.

The **Massachusetts Golf Association** (175 Highland Ave., Needham, MA 02192; ☎ 617/449-3000) represents more than 270 golf courses around the state and will send you a list of courses on request. In addition, **Tee Times** (199 Wells Ave., Suite 9, Newton, MA 02159; ☎ 617/969-0638) organizes golf outings.

HIKING

The **Metropolitan District Commission,** or MDC (☎ **617/727-0460**) maintains hiking trails at several reservation parks throughout the state, some of which are within short driving distance of the city. They include the **Blue Hills Reservation** in Milton, **Beaverbrook Reservation** in Belmont, **Breakheart Reservation** in Saugus, **Hemlock Gorge** in Newton Upper Falls, the **Middlesex Fells Reservation** in five communities north of Boston, and **Belle Isle Marsh Reservation** in East Boston.

The **Boston Harbor Islands** also offer great hiking (it takes a half-day's hike to circle the largest islands, George's and Peddocks.) Contact **Boston Harbor Island State Park** (349 Lincoln St., Building 45, Hingham, MA 02043; ☎ **617/740-1605**).

IN-LINE SKATING

As with biking, unless you're very confident of your ability and your knowledge of Boston traffic, staying off the streets is a good idea.

A favorite spot for in-line skaters is the **Esplanade,** between the Back Bay and the Charles River. It continues onto the bike path that runs to Watertown and back, but be aware that once you leave the Esplanade the pavement isn't totally smooth, which can lead to mishaps. Your best bet is to wait for a Sunday in the summer, when **Memorial Drive** in Cambridge is closed to traffic. It's a perfect surface.

If you didn't bring your skates, you have several options for renting. A former Olympic cyclist runs **Eric Flaim's Motion Sports** (349 Newbury St.; ☎ **617/ 247-3284**). Or try the **Beacon Hill Skate Shop** (135 Charles St. South; ☎ 617/482-7400), **Earth Bikes** (35 Huntington Ave.; ☎ 617/267-4733) or **Ski Market** (860 Commonwealth Ave.; ☎ 617/731-6100).

The **InLine Club of Boston** recently brought out a book, *InLine Skating in Greater Boston,* that's available at skate and sporting goods shops and some bookstores for $8. The club has a web site (http://www.sk8net.com/icb) with up-to-date event and safety information and its extremely clever logo.

JOGGING

Check with the concierge or desk staff at your hotel for a map with suggested routes. The bridges across the Charles River allow for circuits of various lengths. Other sources of information include the Metropolitan District Commission, or MDC (☎ **617/727-1300**) and the Bill Rodgers Running Center in Faneuil Hall Marketplace (☎ **617/723-5612**). As in any large city, you're advised to stay out of park areas (including the Esplanade) at night.

TENNIS

Public courts are available throughout the city at no charge. They are maintained by the Metropolitan District Commission (☎ **617/727-1300**). To find the one nearest you, call the MDC or ask the concierge or desk staff at your hotel. Well-maintained courts near downtown that seldom get busy until after-work hours are available at several spots on the Southwest Corridor Park in the South End (there's a nice one near W. Newton Street) and off Commercial Street near the N. Washington Street bridge in the North End. The courts in Charlesbank Park, overlooking the river next to the State Police barracks on the bridge to the Museum of Science, are more crowded during the day.

10 Spectator Sports

Boston's well-deserved reputation as a great sports town derives in part from the days when at least one of the professional teams was one of the world's best. None of them has done much lately, but passions still run deep—insult the local teams and be ready to defend yourself. This applies to some extent to college sports as well, particularly in hockey, where the Division I schools are evenly matched.

The biggest Boston sports story of the last few years was not about a team but an arena. In September 1995, the **FleetCenter** opened behind 67-year-old Boston Garden and the "Gah-den" was shut down (at press time, it's still standing as various corporate entities wrangle over who will pay for the demolition). The narrow, cramped seats and obstructed views in the incredibly steep Garden were replaced by cushy chairs in a wide-open bowl-shaped arena, and the feeling of being right on top of the action was replaced by the feeling of watching at a distance. One constant is the basketball floor, a collection of wood parquet tiles that made the trip to the new building.

The FleetCenter and the Garden History Center (☎ **617/624-1518**) are open for tours Monday thorugh Saturday on the hour from 10am to 4pm, Sunday from 11am to 3pm, except during events. Tickets are $6 for adults, $5 for seniors and students, and $4.50 for children under 12.

BASEBALL

No experience in sports matches watching the **Boston Red Sox** play at **Fenway Park,** which they do from early April to early October, and later if they make the playoffs. The quirkiness of the oldest park in the major leagues (1912) and the fact that the team last won the World Series in 1918 only add to the mystique. A hand-operated scoreboard is built into the Green Monster, or left-field wall (watch carefully during a pitching change—the left fielder from either team may suddenly disappear into the darkness to cool off), and the wall itself is such a celebrity that it's often called simply The Wall. It's 37 feet tall, a mere 298 feet from home plate, and irresistibly tempting to batters who ought to know better. On two vertical white lines on the scoreboard you'll see Morse code for the initials of legendary owners Thomas A. and Jean R. Yawkey, now dead.

The crowds can be as interesting as the architecture. You'll see Cub Scouts on a field trip, positive that they're going to catch their first foul ball, and season-ticket-holders in their eighties, positive that this is finally the year. Fans are jammed together in narrow, uncomfortable seats close to the field, striking up conversations with total strangers, reminiscing, and making bold predictions. A recent fan-relations campaign called "Friendly Fenway" has produced better-mannered employees, a greater variety of concession items (but not lower prices), and expanded family-seating sections, but for the most part that's window dressing. You're in an intensely green place that's older than your grandparents, inhaling a Fenway Frank and wishing for a home run—what could be better?

Practical concerns: Compared to its modern brethren, Fenway is tiny. Tickets go on sale in early December for the following season, and the earlier you order, the better chance you'll have of landing seats during your visit. Forced to choose between tickets for a low-numbered grandstand section (say, 10 or below) and less expensive bleacher seats, go for the bleachers. They can get rowdy during night games, but the view is better from there than from the deep right-field corner. If you plan to be in town around the same time as the Marathon, your chances of landing tickets for Patriots' Day are poor (the game starts at 11am so that fans can, theoretically, be in Kenmore Square to watch the leading runners pass by), but don't despair. The next two or three games traditionally are scheduled for weekday afternoons, and they almost never sell out. Throughout the season, a limited number of standing room tickets go on sale the day of the game, and there's always the possibility that tickets will be returned. It can't hurt to check, especially if the team isn't playing well. The fans are incredibly loyal, but they're not all obsessed.

The Fenway Park ticket office is at 24 Yawkey Way, near the corner of Brookline Avenue. Call 617/267-8661 for information, 617/267-1700 for tickets. Tickets for the disabled and in no-alcohol sections are available. Smoking is not allowed in the park. Games usually begin at 7:05pm on weeknights and 1pm on weekends. Take the MBTA Green Line (B, C, or D train) to Kenmore.

BASKETBALL

The **Boston Celtics** have fallen on hard times in recent years, but their glorious history is illustrated by the 16 National Basketball Association championship banners hanging from the ceiling of the new FleetCenter (150 Causeway St.). They play from early October to April or May, and unless a top contender is visiting, you should have no trouble buying tickets. For information, call the FleetCenter at 617/624-1000; for tickets, call Ticketmaster at 617/931-2000. To reach the FleetCenter, take the MBTA Green or Orange Line or commuter rail to North Station.

Other than being the site of the sport's creation (it was invented in Springfield, MA around the turn of the century), New England is not noted for its basketball history; but the local teams have all enjoyed a measure of success in recent years. Schools with teams include **Boston College** (Conte Forum, Chestnut Hill; ☎ 617/552-3000), **Boston University** (Walter Brown Arena, 285 Babcock St.; ☎ 617/353-3838), **Harvard University** (Lavietes Pavilion, N. Harvard St., Allston; ☎ 617/495-2211), and **Northeastern University** (Matthews Arena, St. Botolph St.; ☎ 617/373-4700).

DOG RACING

Greyhounds race at **Wonderland Park,** off Route 1A in Revere (☎ **617/284-1300**), which also can be reached by taking the MBTA Blue Line to the last stop (Wonderland).

FOOTBALL

The **New England Patriots** (☎ **800/543-1776**) play football from August through December (or maybe January if they make the playoffs) at Foxboro Stadium on Route 1 in Foxboro, about a half-hour drive south of the city. You can drive or catch a bus from the entrance of South Station, the Riverside "T" station, or Shopper's World in Framingham (west of the city). The team's fortunes have slowly improved over the last several years, and tickets ($23–$50) often sell out. Plan as far in advance as you can.

College football is played by **Boston College** (Alumni Stadium, Chestnut Hill; ☎ 617/552-3000), **Boston University** (Nickerson Field, Commonwealth Ave.; ☎ 617/353-3838), **Harvard University** (Harvard Stadium, N. Harvard St., Allston; ☎ 617/495-2211), **Northeastern University** (Parsons Field, Kent St., Brookline; ☎ 617/373-4700).

GOLF TOURNAMENTS

The three major tours get within about an hour of downtown Boston. The PGA Tour stop is the **CVS Charity Classic** at Pleasant Valley Country Club in Sutton (☎ 508/865-4441) in July. The **Ping Welch's Championship,** an LPGA Tour event, is at Blue Hill Country Club in Canton (☎ 617/828-2000) in August. The **Bank of Boston Senior Classic** (☎ 508/371-0116), a Senior PGA Tour event, takes place at Nashawtuc Country Club in Concord in August. Amateur events for fun and charity are numerous and listed regularly in the *Globe* and *Herald.*

HOCKEY

Boston Bruins games are always exciting, especially if you happen to be in town at the same time as the archrival Montreal Canadiens. Tickets for many Bruins games (held at the FleetCenter, 150 Causeway St.) sell out early despite being among the most expensive in the league. For tickets ($43–$70), call 617/624-1000 or call

Ticketmaster at 617/931-2000. To reach the FleetCenter, take the MBTA Green or Orange Line or commuter rail to North Station.

Economical hockey fans who don't have their hearts set on seeing a pro game will be pleasantly surprised by the quality of play at the college level in Boston. Even for sold-out games, standing room tickets are usually available the night of the game. Colleges with teams include **Boston College** (Conte Forum, Chestnut Hill; ☎ 617/552-3000), **Boston University** (Walter Brown Arena, 285 Babcock St.; ☎ 617/353-3838), **Harvard University** (Bright Hockey Center, N. Harvard St., Allston; ☎ 617/495-2211), and **Northeastern University** (Matthews Arena, St. Botolph St.; ☎ 617/373-4700). These four are the Beanpot schools, who play a tradition-steeped tournament on the first two Mondays of February at the FleetCenter. The games generally sell out, but you can try to order early or wait till the day of the game and check for returned tickets.

HORSE RACING

Suffolk Downs (111 Waldemar Ave., E. Boston; ☎ **617/567-3900**) reopened under new management in 1992 after being closed for several years and ghastly for years before that. Today it's one of the best-run smaller tracks in the country, an excellent family destination (really), sparklingly clean, and the home of the Massachusetts Handicap, run in early June. Horse of the Year Cigar won the MassCap in 1995 and '96, conferring instant cachet on the event and the facility. There are extensive simulcasting options during and after the live racing season (the schedule may change dramatically in 1997; call for exact dates).

MARATHON

Every year on Patriots' Day (the third Monday in April), the **Boston Marathon** is run from Hopkinton to Copley Square in Boston. Cheering fans line the entire route. An especially nice place to watch is tree-shaded Comm. Ave. between Kenmore Square and Mass. Ave., but you'll be in a crowd wherever you stand, particularly near the finish line in front of the Boston Public Library. The centennial event in 1996 drew about 40,000 competitors, four times larger than a normal field, and there may be a residual effect for the 1997 race. For information about qualifying, contact the Boston Athletic Association (☎ **617/236-1652**).

ROWING

In late October, the **Head of the Charles Regatta** attracts more rowers than any other crew event in the country to Boston and Cambridge. Some 4,000 oarsmen and oarswomen race against the clock for four miles from the Charles River basin to the Eliot Bridge in west Cambridge. Tens of thousands of spectators socialize and occasionally even watch the action.

Spring crew racing is far more exciting than the "head" format; the course is 2,000 meters and races last just five to seven minutes. Men's and women's collegiate events take place on Saturday mornings in April and early May in the Charles River basin. You'll have a perfect view of the finish line from Memorial Drive between the MIT boathouse and the Hyatt Regency. To find out who's racing, check the Friday *Globe* sports section.

SOCCER

Boston's Major League Soccer team, the **New England Revolution** (☎ 508/543-0350), plays at Foxboro Stadium on Route 1 in Foxboro from April through July. Tickets are available through Ticketmaster (☎ **617/931-2000**), which charges

Curses, Foiled Again

The most famous of all the famous numbers associated with Boston sports history—more famous than 16 (National Basketball Association championships won by the Celtics), 4 (legendary Bruins defenseman Bobby Orr's jersey), 46-10 (the score of the Super Bowl in 1986, when the Chicago Bears demolished the New England Patriots), or even .406 (Red Sox outfielder Ted Williams's batting average in 1941)—is 1918. In 1918, the Boston Red Sox won the World Series for the fifth time in the 15-year history of the event. They have yet to win another.

Fatalistic Red Sox fans attribute the team's disastrous luck to a transaction executed after the 1919 season. Team owner Harry Frazee, a theatrical producer who needed money to mount a production of the musical *No, No, Nannette,* accepted $100,000 from the New York Yankees in exchange for a promising young pitcher and outfielder—Babe Ruth. The "Curse of the Bambino" is believed to have prevailed ever since, leading to an exorcism, a book, and an uncanny number of postseason catastrophes.

Not that the Red Sox haven't come close. They lost one-game playoffs for the right to go to the World Series in 1948 and 1978. They actually went to the World Series in 1946, 1967, 1975, and 1986—and lost in the seventh and final game each time. The most agonizing loss (or at least the one most people remember best) was in 1986. The Red Sox led the New York Mets, 5-4, in the bottom of the tenth inning of the sixth game. They were one strike away from victory and the champagne was already uncorked when a ground ball skipped through first baseman Bill Buckner's legs. The winning run scored, the demoralized Red Sox went on to lose the seventh game, and the curse lived on.

a service fee. Unless the team or its opponent is doing incredibly well, buying tickets the day of the match shouldn't be too difficult. Be sure to leave extra time to negotiate the congested roads near the stadium.

TENNIS TOURNAMENT

The **U.S. Tennis Championship at Longwood** is held in July at the Longwood Cricket Club (564 Hammond St., Brookline; ☎ **617/731-4500**). Call for tickets and information about the week-long event. The finals often sell out early, but demand isn't as high for preliminary matches.

8

Boston Strolls

Boston is very pedestrian-friendly and actually makes good on the promise of its popular nickname, "America's Walking City." The narrow, twisting streets that make driving here such a headache are a treat for pedestrians, who are never far from something worth seeing. The central city is compact—walking east to west quickly from one end to the other takes about an hour—and dotted with historically and architecturally interesting buildings and neighborhoods.

In this chapter you'll find four tours of Boston and one of Harvard Square in Cambridge. Remember to wear comfortable walking shoes, and if you're not inclined to pay designer prices for designer water, bring your own water bottle and fill it with ice at the hotel. By the time you're ready for it, it will be ready for you.

WALKING TOUR 1
Downtown Boston and Beacon Hill

Start: Boston Common (MBTA Green or Red line, Park Street station).
Finish: Faneuil Hall (Congress and North streets).
Time: At least two hours, and possibly three, depending on how long you spend at the attractions.
Best Times: Early morning to mid-afternoon.
Worst Times: Mid-afternoon, when you will be rushed to see the sights before closing time.

Faced with flat attendance and competition from attractions that offer more innovative exhibits, in 1996 the city of Boston announced a massive overhaul of the Freedom Trail. The trail, which links 16 historical sights with a three-mile red line on the sidewalk first painted in 1958, may be starting to change by the time you visit, but the actual attractions aren't going anywhere. They're divided here into two different tours with some detours.

From Park Street station, exit at the corner of Park and Tremont streets, the easternmost corner of:

1. **Boston Common.** In 1634, when their settlement was just four years old, the town fathers paid the Rev. William Blackstone 30 pounds for this property. In 1640 it was set aside as common land, and in the years since, the 50 or so acres of the country's oldest public park have fed cows, housed soldiers, and witnessed hangings and visits by dignitaries. Today it's a bit run-down, especially compared with the adjacent Public Garden, and it buzzes with activity all day. You might see a demonstration or a musical performance, a picnic lunch or a game of tag, but (except during the Boston Dairy Festival

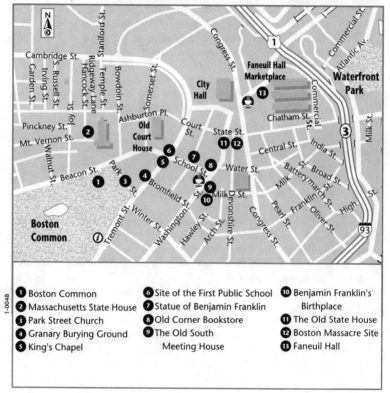

1 Boston Common
2 Massachusetts State House
3 Park Street Church
4 Granary Burying Ground
5 King's Chapel
6 Site of the First Public School
7 Statue of Benjamin Franklin
8 Old Corner Bookstore
9 The Old South
    Meeting House
10 Benjamin Franklin's
    Birthplace
11 The Old State House
12 Boston Massacre Site
13 Faneuil Hall

1-0048

in early June) you won't see a cow. Cows have been banned since 1830, which seems to be one of the only events related to the Common that isn't commemorated with a plaque. One of the loveliest markers is on our route; head up the hill from the train station inside the fence, not on the sidewalk. At Beacon St. is a memorial designed by Augustus Saint-Gaudens to celebrate the deeds (indeed, the very existence) of Col. Robert Gould Shaw and the Union Army's 54th Massachusetts Colored Regiment, who fought in the Civil War. You may remember the story of the first all-black (except for Shaw) American army unit from the movie *Glory.*

Across Beacon Street is the:

2. Massachusetts State House (☎ **617/727-3676**). Boston is one of the only American cities where a building whose cornerstone was laid in 1795 (by Gov. Samuel Adams) would be called the "new" anything. Nevertheless, this is the new State House, to distinguish it from the Old State House, which we'll see shortly. The great Federal-era architect Charles Bulfinch designed the central building of the state capitol, and the original copper sheathing on the golden dome (now covered in gold leaf) was manufactured by Paul Revere. During the blackouts of the Second World War, the dome was painted black to conceal it from enemy bombers. The state legislature, formally named the Massachusetts General Court, meets here. The House of Representatives congregates under a wooden fish, the Sacred Cod. John Rowe, known as "Merchant" Rowe (Rowes Wharf bears his name), donated the carving in 1784 as a reminder of the importance of fishing to the local economy. Tours (free, both guided and self-guided) leave from the second floor. Whether or not you decide to go inside, be sure to study some of the many statues outside the building. Subjects range from Mary Dyer, a Quaker hanged on the Common in 1660 for refusing to abandon her religious beliefs, to President John F. Kennedy.

Leaving the State House, walk down Park Street—laid out by Bulfinch in 1804—and look back at the second-floor balcony, where the governor sometimes steps outside for a breath of air. At the foot of the hill at Tremont Street is:

3. Park Street Church. Henry James described this 1809 structure as "the most interesting mass of bricks and mortar in America." Under its 217-foot steeple, the church has accumulated an impressive number of firsts: The first missionaries to Hawaii left from here in 1819; William Lloyd Garrison gave his first antislavery speech here on July 4, 1829; "America (My Country 'Tis of Thee)" was first sung here on July 4, 1831. You're standing on "Brimstone Corner," named for either the passion of the Congregational ministers who have declaimed from the pulpit, or for the fact that during the War of 1812, gunpowder (made from brimstone) was stored in the basement. One indisputable fact is that this was part of the site of a huge granary that became a public building after the Revolutionary War, when it was no longer needed for the storage of grain. In the 1790s the sails for the USS *Constitution* were manufactured in this very building.

From late June to August, the church is open from 9:30am to 4pm Tuesday through Saturday. Services are on Sunday at 9 and 10:45am and 6:30pm.

Walk away from the Common on Tremont Street. On your left is the:

4. Old Granary Burying Ground. This cemetery, established in 1660, was once part of Boston Common. You'll see the graves of patriots Samuel Adams, Paul Revere, John Hancock, and James Otis, merchant Peter Faneuil (spelled "Funal"), Benjamin Franklin's parents, the victims of the Boston Massacre (five colonists shot during a skirmish with British troops on March 5, 1770), and the wife of Isaac Vergoose, otherwise known as "Mother Goose" from the nursery rhymes of the same name. Note that gravestone rubbing, however tempting, is illegal in Boston's historic cemeteries. Open daily from 8am to 4pm.

Turn left as you leave the cemetery and continue a block and a half on Tremont Street, crossing it at some point. At the corner of School Street is:

5. King's Chapel. Architect Peter Harrison sent the plans for this building from Newport, R.I., in 1749. Instead of replacing the existing wooden chapel, the granite edifice was constructed around it. Completed in 1754, it was the first Anglican church in Boston. George III sent gifts, as did Queen Anne and William and Mary, who presented the communion table and chancel tablets (still in use today) before the church was even built. The Puritan colonists had little use for the royal religion; after the Revolution this became the first Unitarian church in America. Unitarian Universalist services are now conducted here, using the Anglican *Book of Common Prayer*. The chapel is open Tuesday through Saturday from 10am to 2pm. The graveyard on Tremont Street is the oldest in the city; it dates to 1630. Among the scary colonial headstones (winged skulls are a popular decoration) are the graves of John Winthrop, the first governor of the Massachusetts Bay Colony; William Dawes, who rode with Paul Revere; Elizabeth Pain, the model for Hester Prynne in Nathaniel

Hawthorne's novel *The Scarlet Letter;* and Mary Chilton, the first female colonist to step ashore on Plymouth Rock.

Now follow the red-brick line along School Street next to King's Chapel. On the sidewalk is a colorful folk-art mosaic marking the:

6. Site of the First Public School, where Samuel Adams, Benjamin Franklin, John Hancock, and Cotton Mather were students. It was founded in 1634, two years before Harvard College. The original building (1645) was demolished to make way for the expansion of King's Chapel, and the school was moved across the street. Now called Boston Latin School, the institution survives and is located in the Fenway.

The fence to your left encloses a courtyard where you'll see the:

7. Statue of Benjamin Franklin, the first portrait statue erected in Boston, in 1856. Franklin was born in Boston in 1706 and apprenticed to his half-brother James, a printer, but they got along so poorly that in 1723 Benjamin ran away to Philadelphia. It was a productive move for everyone but James. The lovely granite building behind the statue is Old City Hall, designed in Second Empire style by Arthur Gilman (who laid out the Back Bay) and opened in 1865. The administration moved to Government Center in 1969, and the building now houses offices and an excellent French restaurant, Maison Robert (see Chapter 6, "Dining," for details).

🕐 **TAKE A BREAK** At the corner of School and Washington Street, stop into the second-floor cafe at **Borders Books & Music** (☎ **617/557-7188**) for a snack or light meal and a cup of coffee. Order tea if you're feeling rebellious— you may soon be reminded by a disapproving cafe patron that in Boston, drinking tea was once considered an unpatriotic vice. The store and cafe are open Monday through Saturday 7am to 8pm, Sunday 10am to 8pm.

School Street ends at Washington Street On the left, at 3 School Street, is the building that housed the:

8. Old Corner Bookstore and the publishing house of Ticknor & Fields. Built in 1712, it's on a plot of land that was once home to the religious reformer Anne Hutchinson, who was excommunicated and expelled from Boston in 1638 for heresy. In the middle of the 19th century, the little brick building was the literary center of America. Publisher James Fields, known as "Jamie," counted among his friends such literary lights as Henry Wadsworth Longfellow, James Russell Lowell, Henry David Thoreau, Ralph Waldo Emerson, Nathaniel Hawthorne, and Harriet Beecher Stowe. It is now the Globe Corner Bookstore, specializing in travel and adventure books as well as maps.

Across Washington Street near this intersection is what appears to be an alleyway but is actually one of the first streets in Boston, Spring Lane. For the first two centuries of the settlement, it was home to a real spring.

Facing Spring Lane, turn right and walk one block. On your left at the corner of Milk Street is the:

9. Old South Meeting House (310 Washington St.; ☎ **617/482-6439**). Originally built in 1670 and replaced by the current structure in 1729, at press time the building was closed for extensive renovations, but was slated to reopen in August of 1997.

The Old South, as it's known, was a religious and political gathering place, and is best known today as the site of one of the celebrated events leading to the Revolution. On December 16, 1773, a crowd of several thousand, too big to fit into Faneuil Hall, gathered here for word from the governor about whether the three ships full of tea in the harbor would be sent back to England. They were not, and the tea, priced to undercut the cost of smuggled tea and force the colonists to trade with merchants approved by the Crown, was cast into the harbor by revolutionaries poorly disguised as Mohawks. That uprising, the Boston Tea Party, is commemorated here. In 1872 the monstrous fire that destroyed most of downtown stopped at the Old South, a phenomenon considered to be a testament to the building's power. The renovation, which started in 1995, is expected to make the building's storied history even more accessible to visitors through interactive multimedia exhibits. One artifact that will certainly be on display is a vial of tea from the tea party. Call for hours and fees.

Walk down Washington and turn left on Milk Street to see:

10. Benjamin Franklin's Birthplace. In a little house at 17 Milk St., Franklin was born in 1706, the 15th child of Josiah Franklin. The house is long gone, but step to the edge of the curb or even across the street, and look at the second floor of the office building that's in its place. When the building went up after the fire of 1872, the architect guaranteed that the Founding Father wouldn't be forgotten: a bust and the words "Franklin's Birthplace" are worked into the facade.

Backtrack on Washington Street past the Globe Center Bookstore for two blocks and you'll come to the:

11. Old State House (206 Washington Street; ☎ 617/720-3290). It was built in 1713 and served as the seat of colonial government of Massachusetts before the Revolution and the state's capitol until 1797. From its balcony the Declaration of Independence was first read to Bostonians on July 18, 1776. In 1789 President George Washington reviewed a parade from the building. The exterior decorations are particularly interesting—the clock was installed in place of a sundial, and the gilded lion and unicorn are replacements of the symbols of British rule that were ripped from the facade the day the Declaration of Independence was read. Inside you'll find the Bostonian Society's museum of the city's history. There's an introductory video on the history of the building. The Old State House is open daily from 9:30am to 5pm. Admission is $3 for adults, $2 for seniors and students, $1 for children 6–18, and free for children under 6. Discounted combination tickets are available if you plan to visit the USS *Constitution* Museum on the same day.

On a traffic island in State Street, across from the "T" exit under the Old State House, a ring of cobblestones marks the:

12. Boston Massacre Site. This skirmish on March 5, 1770, helped consolidate the spirit of rebellion in the colonies. Colonists, angered at the presence of British troops in Boston, threw snowballs, garbage, rocks, and other debris at a group of redcoats, who panicked and fired into the crowd, killing five men.

Continue on the trail by turning left onto Congress Street, or detour from past to present by walking to the Washington Street side of the Old State House and crossing State Street to Washington Mall. Follow it one block (its entire length) to **Boston City Hall.** The eight-acre red-brick plaza that curves around to the left is in the process of being improved with renovations and the addition of plants and flowers, but it still winds quite a bit. That doesn't stop people from congregating here for celebrations, protests, and farmer's markets. The building itself is an architectural masterpiece or a civic disgrace, depending on whether you're talking to an architect or a citizen who actually has to use it. Free guided tours are given weekdays from 10am to 4pm. The building is open weekdays from 9am to 5pm.

If you detoured, backtrack to Washington Mall and take the steps down to Congress Street. Near the corner of Congress and North streets is:

13. Faneuil Hall, at Dock Square. Built in 1742 (and enlarged using a Charles Bulfinch design in 1805), it was given to the city of Boston by the merchant Peter Faneuil. The "Cradle of Liberty" rang with speeches by orators such as Samuel Adams—whose statue is on the Congress Street side—in the years leading to the Revolution, and with speeches by abolitionists, temperance advocates, and women's suffragists in the years after. The upstairs is still used as a public meeting (and sometimes concert) hall and

the downstairs area is still a market, all according to Faneuil's will. The grasshopper weathervane, the sole remaining detail from the original building, is modeled after the weathervane on London's Royal Exchange.

A recent renovation restored the entire building and upgraded the wiring in the second-floor auditorium so that it's suitable for television production; it's sometimes used for televised debates and other political events. National Park Service rangers give free 20-minute talks every half-hour from 9am to 5pm in the second-floor auditorium and operate a visitor center on the first floor. On the top floor is a small free museum that houses the weapons collection and historical exhibits of the Ancient and Honorable Artillery Company of Massachusetts.

🙂 **TAKE A BREAK**   Faneuil Hall Marketplace spreads out before you (see Chapter 7, "What to See & Do in Boston"), and the Quincy Market Colonnade overflows with carry-away foodstuffs. If you prefer a sit-down restaurant, Durgin-Park is here and Ye Olde Union Oyster House is a block away (see Chapter 6, "Dining").

WALKING TOUR 2
The North End and Charlestown

Start: Faneuil Hall Marketplace (MBTA Green Line to Government Center or Orange Line to State Street).

Finish: Bunker Hill Monument, Charlestown.

Time: Two to three hours.

Best Time: Morning and early afternoon. Aim for Friday or Saturday if you want to see Haymarket.

Worst Time: Late afternoon, when you'll be in the midst of rush-hour gridlock.

Facing the statue of Samuel Adams on the Congress Street side of Faneuil Hall, turn left and cross North Street. Walk up Union Street past the two statues of James Michael Curley. Looming in the sky above are the six glass columns that make up:

1. **The New England Holocaust Memorial.** Erected in 1995, this monument was placed in the midst of attractions that celebrate freedom, with the intention of reminding visitors of the consequences of a world without freedom. The pattern on the glass that appears to be merely decorative is actually 6 million random numbers, one for each Jew who died during the Holocaust. Whether you find it incongruous or moving, you won't soon forget it.

   On a more practical plane, across the street is:

2. **Ye Olde Union Oyster House** (41 Union St.; ☎ **617/227-2750**). First opened in 1826, the Union Oyster House is the oldest restaurant in Boston that's still in operation.

   Continue walking north, then turn right onto Hanover Street. If it's Friday or Saturday you'll be right in the midst of:

3. **Haymarket.** This open-air market consists of stalls piled high with fruit, vegetables, and seafood, but shoppers aren't allowed to touch anything they haven't bought. It's a great scene, and a favorite of photographers. Two blocks up, you can turn right onto Blackstone Street and explore the merchandise further (the market runs to North Street), or cross Blackstone Street and take the pedestrian passage beneath the Central Artery (Fitzgerald Expressway). You'll probably walk near, over, or around indications that the Central Artery project is in the works; if construction appears to block your way, look for signs pointing to the North End.

Walking Tour 2—The North End & Charlestown

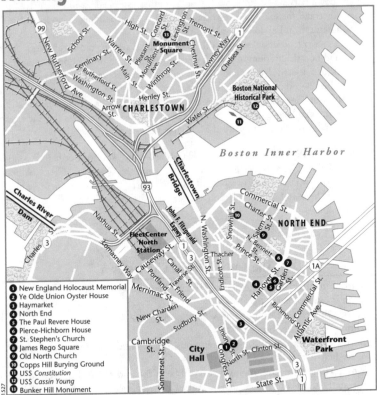

1. New England Holocaust Memorial
2. Ye Olde Union Oyster House
3. Haymarket
4. North End
5. The Paul Revere House
6. Pierce-Hichborn House
7. St. Stephen's Church
8. James Rego Square
9. Old North Church
10. Copps Hill Burying Ground
11. USS Constitution
12. USS Cassin Young
13. Bunker Hill Monument

You'll emerge at Cross and Salem streets, one of several gateways to:

4. **The North End.** This is Boston's Little Italy (although it's never called that), home to natives of Italy and their assimilated children, numerous Italian restaurants and private social clubs, and many historically significant sights. One of the oldest neighborhoods in the city, in the 17th century it was home to the Mather family of Puritan ministers, who certainly would be shocked to see the merry goings-on at the festivals, or street fairs, that take over a different section of the North End each weekend in July and August.

The Italians (and their yuppie neighbors who have made inroads since the 1980s) are only the latest immigrant group to dominate the North End. In the mid-19th century, this was an eastern European Jewish enclave, and later an Irish stronghold. In 1894 Rose Fitzgerald, mother of President John F. Kennedy, was born on Garden Court St. and baptized at St. Stephen's Church.

Turn right onto Cross Street and walk one block to Hanover Street, where you must turn left. At the first traffic light, turn right onto Richmond Street, following the Freedom Trail. Walk one block and turn left onto North Street. Wharves ran up almost this far in colonial days; in the 19th century, this was a notorious red-light district. Half a block up on the left is:

5. **The Paul Revere House** (19 North Sq.; ☎ **617/523-2338**). One of the most pleasant stops on the Freedom Trail, it presents history on a human scale. Revere set out

for Lexington from here on the evening of April 18, 1775, a feat immortalized in Henry Wadsworth Longfellow's poem "Paul Revere's Ride" (*Listen my children and you shall hear / Of the midnight ride of Paul Revere . . .*). The house was built around 1680 (it's the oldest in downtown Boston), purchased by Revere in 1770, and put to a number of uses before being turned into a museum in the early 20th century. The 2½-story brown wood structure is filled with 17th- and 18th-century furnishings and artifacts, neatly arranged and identified. Many of them are the famous Revere silver, considered some of the finest anywhere. You can rush through the self-guided tour or linger over the objects that particularly interest you.

The Paul Revere House is open from November through April 14 9:30am to 4:15pm, and from April 15 through October 9:30am to 5:15pm; it's closed Mondays in January, February, and March, as well as Thanksgiving Day, Christmas, and New Year's Day. Admission is $2.50 for adults, $2 for seniors and students, and $1 for children 5 to 17.

Across the cobblestone courtyard from Revere's house is the home of his Hichborn cousins, the:

6. Pierce-Hichborn House. This 1711 Georgian-style home is a rare example of 18th-century middle-class architecture. It's suitably furnished and shown only by guided tour. Call the Paul Revere House for schedules.

Before you leave North Square, look across the cobblestone plaza at Sacred Heart Church. It was established in 1833 as the Seamen's Bethel, a church devoted to the needs of the mariners who frequented the area. Today it's Roman Catholic and has a large, active Italian-American congregation; one Mass every Sunday is said in Italian.

Turn left as you exit the Paul Revere House and walk up to Prince Street. Here you can turn left and walk one block to Hanover Street, or take a few steps onto Garden Court Street and look for number 4, on the right. The private residence was the birthplace of Rose Fitzgerald (later Kennedy). Pause when you get to the corner of Prince and Hanover streets.

TAKE A BREAK You're in the heart of North End caffè country, the perfect place to have a cup of coffee or a soft drink and feast on sweets. Across the street is **Mike's Pastry** (300 Hanover St.; ☎ **617/742-3050**), which does a frantic takeout business and also has a few tables where you can sit down and order after you check out the confections on display in the cases. Mike's claim to fame is President Clinton's devotion to its cannoli (tubes of crisp-fried pastry filled with sweetened ricotta cheese). You can sit and relax at **Caffè dello Sport** and **Caffè Vittoria,** on either side of Mike's, and across the street at **Caffè Graffiti.**

Back at Prince and Hanover sts., with North Square behind you, turn right and walk two blocks to Clark Street. At the corner is:

7. St. Stephen's Church, the only Charles Bulfinch-designed church still standing in Boston. The church was Unitarian when it was dedicated in 1804, and the next year the congregation purchased a bell from Paul Revere's foundry for $800. Architecture buffs will get a huge kick out of the design, a paragon of Federal-style symmetry. St. Stephen's became Roman Catholic in 1862 and was moved back when Hanover Street was widened in 1870. During refurbishment in 1965 it was restored to its original appearance, with clear glass windows, red carpets, white walls, and gilded organ pipes. It's one of the plainest Catholic churches you'll ever see.

Cross Hanover Street to reach:

8. James Rego Square (Paul Revere Mall), a pleasant little park known as the Prado, with an equestrian statue of Paul Revere.

Walk into the park, past the fountain, and emerge at the side of the:

9. **Old North Church** (193 Salem St.; ☎ **617/523-6676**). Formally known as Christ Church, this is the oldest church in Boston standing on its original site, where it has been since 1723. The building itself is in the style of Sir Christopher Wren, and the original steeple was the one where sexton Robert Newman hung two lanterns on the night of April 18, 1775, to indicate to Paul Revere that British troops were setting out for Lexington and Concord in boats across the Charles River, not on foot ("One if by land, two if by sea"). The impressive 175-foot "new" steeple (16 feet shorter than the original) was designed by the ubiquitous Charles Bulfinch after the original fell in a hurricane in 1804. The spire, long a reference point for sailors, appears on navigational charts to this day. The Revere family attended this church (their plaque is on Pew 54); famous visitors have included Presidents James Monroe, Theodore Roosevelt, Franklin D. Roosevelt, and Gerald R. Ford, and Her Majesty Queen Elizabeth II. There are markers and plaques throughout; note the bust of George Washington, the first memorial to the first president. The gardens on the north side of the church (dotted with more plaques) are open to the public. The Old North Church is open daily 9am to 5pm; Sunday services (Episcopal) are at 9 and 11am and 4pm. The quirky gift shop, in a former chapel, is open daily from 9am to 5pm, and proceeds go to support the church. Donations are appreciated.

As you leave the church, bear left and cross Salem Street onto Hull Street. Turn right and walk uphill past number 44, the narrowest house in Boston (it's 10 feet wide). Across the street is the entrance to:

10. **Copp's Hill Burying Ground**, the second-oldest cemetery (1659) in the city. Again, no gravestone rubbing is allowed. This is the burial place of Cotton Mather and his family, Robert Newman, and Prince Hall. Hall, a prominent member of the free black community that occupied the north slope of the hill in colonial times, fought at Bunker Hill and established the first black Masonic lodge. The highest point in the North End, Copp's Hill was the site of a windmill and of the British batteries that destroyed the village of Charlestown during the Battle of Bunker Hill, June 17, 1775. Charlestown is still clearly visible (look for the masts of the USS *Constitution*) across the Inner Harbor. The burying ground is open daily from 9am to 5pm.

From the burying ground, it's about a mile to Charlestown. Continue on Hull Street and follow it down the hill to Commercial Street. Turn left and walk two blocks to North Washington Street, cross Commercial Street and walk across the bridge. At the end, turn right and follow the signs and the Freedom Trail to the Charlestown Navy Yard, home of the:

11. **USS *Constitution*.** "Old Ironsides," one of the U.S. Navy's six original frigates, never lost a battle. She was constructed in the North End from 1794–97 at a cost of $302,718 using bolts, spikes, and other fittings from Paul Revere's foundry. As the new nation made its naval and military reputation, the *Constitution* played a key role, battling French privateers and Barbary pirates, repelling the British fleet during the War of 1812, participating in 40 engagements and capturing 20 vessels. She earned her nickname during an engagement on August 19, 1812, with the French warship HMS *Guerriere,* whose shots bounced off her thick oak hull as if it were iron. Retired from combat in 1815, she was rescued from destruction when Oliver Wendell Holmes' poem "Old Ironsides" launched a preservation movement in 1830.

She was completely overhauled in 1995–96 in preparation for her bicentennial. The *Constitution* is towed into the harbor by tugs every Fourth of July and turned around to ensure that she weathers evenly. In honor of her 200th birthday in 1997, she is expected to be under sail for the first time since 1881 for the annual turnaround cruise.

Free tours (☎ **617/242-5670**) are given by active-duty sailors in 1812 uniforms daily from 9:30am to 3:50pm.

The **USS *Constitution* Museum** (☎ **617/426-1812**), just inland from the vessel, has several participatory exhibits that allow visitors to hoist a flag, fire a cannon, and learn more about the ship. The museum is open daily, June 1 to Labor Day 9am to 6pm; March to May and the day after Labor Day through November 10am to 5pm; December to February 10am to 3pm, and closed Thanksgiving, Christmas, and New Year's Day. Admission is $4 for adults, $3 for seniors, $2 for children 6–16, and free for children 5 and under. Discounted combination tickets are available if you plan to visit the Old State House on the same day.

Turn left as you leave the museum (or right as you leave the ship) and follow the Big Band music to the:

12. **USS *Cassin Young*** (☎ **617/242-5601**), a World War II destroyer that has been refurbished and is open to the public. Forty-five-minute tours by National Park Service rangers are offered, and visitors can also look around on the deck. Admission is free. Call for tour times.

Many people, especially those traveling with fidgety children, opt to skip the next part of the tour. If your party's not too close to the breaking point, it's an interesting excursion. Leave the Navy Yard, cross Chelsea Street, and climb the hill, following the Freedom Trail along Tremont Street. Your guidepost is also your destination, the:

13. **Bunker Hill Monument** (☎ **617/242-5644**), a 221-foot granite obelisk built in honor of the men who died in the Battle of Bunker Hill on June 17, 1775. The colonists lost the battle, but nearly half of the British troops were killed or wounded, a circumstance that contributed to the decision to abandon Boston nine months later. The Marquis de Lafayette, the celebrated hero of the both the American and French revolutions, helped lay the monument's cornerstone in 1825. The top is at the end of a flight of 295 stairs—a long climb for a decent view that prominently features I-93.

In the lodge at the base of the monument there are dioramas and exhibits. It's staffed by National Park Service rangers and open from 9am to 5pm. The monument is open daily from 9am to 4:30pm. Admission is free.

If you don't feel like retracing your steps, you have two public transportation options. At the foot of the hill on Main St., take bus 92 or 93 to Haymarket (where you can catch the "T"'s Green and Orange lines). Or return to the Navy Yard for the MBTA water shuttle to Long Wharf. The 10-minute trip costs $1 and leaves every hour on the quarter hour from 6:45am to 7:45pm on weekdays and from 10:15am to 6:15pm on weekends. A shuttle bus from the USS *Constitution* will take you to the pier.

WALKING TOUR 3
The Waterfront

Start: Old State House (MBTA Orange or Blue line to State Street).
Finish: Boston Tea Party Ship and Museum.
Time: Approximately two hours to walk without long stops; around five hours if museum stops are included.
Best Times: Morning.
Worst Times: Evening rush hour, especially on Friday.

Boston's waterfront is currently under the spell of the massive Central Artery/Third Harbor Tunnel project. The trip from downtown to the harbor can seem a bit harrowing, but everything is clearly marked (making this the only area of the city where that's true), and the result is worth the trouble.

Walking Tour 3—The Waterfront

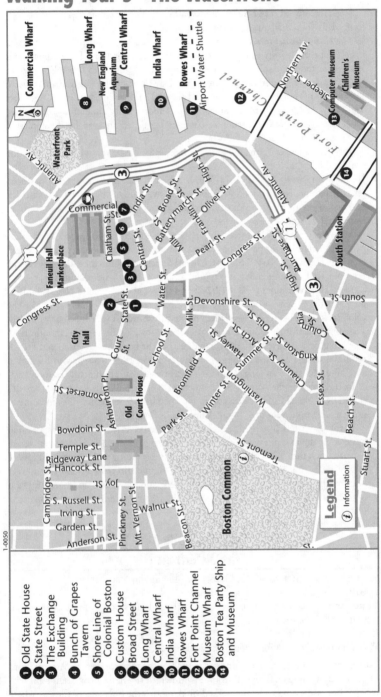

1-0050

Legend
ⓘ Information

① Old State House
② State Street
③ The Exchange Building
④ Bunch of Grapes Tavern
⑤ Shore Line of Colonial Boston
⑥ Custom House
⑦ Broad Street
⑧ Long Wharf
⑨ Central Wharf
⑩ India Wharf
⑪ Rowes Wharf
⑫ Fort Point Channel
⑬ Museum Wharf
⑭ Boston Tea Party Ship and Museum

176

Begin at the:

1. **Old State House** (206 Washington St.; ☎ **617/720-3290**). Traditionally the head of Long Wharf, this is stop number 11 on the first walking tour. Remind yourself that when the bustling waterfront was nearby, this was considered a tall building.

From the Old State House walk past the **Boston Massacre Site** (stop 12 on the first walking tour) and follow:

2. **State Street** toward the waterfront. This was King Street until 1784 (fairly late considering the antiroyal sentiment that inspired the change), and it ran right out into the harbor. As you pass Congress Street, look down the hill to the left at Faneuil Hall. It was situated right on the water before the harbor began to fill with silt and garbage. The filling-in was completed (using earth) and new streets laid out as part of the Quincy Market project of 1826. Now make sure you're on the right-hand side of State Street.

The block of State Street between Congress and Kilby streets became the center of finance in the 19th century. There sea captains and businessmen invested in textile and railroad industries and created the financial institutions for which Boston and modern State Street are known nationally. One landmark you'll see is the:

3. **Exchange Building** (53 State St.). Built in 1887, it was at one time home to a signal tower, part of a system of towers that used flags to signal the arrival of ships in Boston Harbor. This enabled merchants to learn that their ships—and fortunes—had arrived. Since a tower was added in 1984, this has also been known as Exchange Place.

Near the corner of Kilby Street, look up at the plaque honoring the:

4. **Bunch of Grapes Tavern,** at the corner of State and Kilby Streets; this was a gathering place in the 18th century for Bostonians opposed to British taxes. After the British symbols (including the lion and unicorn from the Old State House) were removed from most of the public buildings in town in July 1776, they were made into a bonfire here.

On State Street, where Merchants Row and Kilby Street meet, is the:

5. **Shoreline of Colonial Boston.** The construction of Long Wharf began here in 1709. At its greatest, Boston's main wharf was 1,743 feet long and 104 feet wide, extending so far into the harbor that the water at the end was 17 feet deep.

Proceed along State Street and cross:

6. **Broad Street,** developed in 1805–7 as part of the plan to improve Boston's waterfront. Charles Bulfinch helped design 60 of the brick warehouses that stood here, some of which survive today.

At the corner of State and India streets, probably surrounded with construction equipment, is the:

7. **Custom House,** built from 1837–47. The foundation alone took three years to construct. Arriving ship captains made their first stop at this landmark building to pay duty on their cargoes. The tower, added in 1911–15, was for many years the tallest structure in town, and it had a public observation deck open to the public. The entire structure is being renovated by the Marriott Corporation, with plans to create corporate time-share apartments. When the colorful clock faces on all four sides of the tower are illuminated, the building looks like a gem against the skyline.

There are three equally busy places to cross Atlantic Avenue, the curb-to-curb construction site at the foot of State Street: Cross at State Street to get to Long Wharf, or cut across Faneuil Hall Marketplace and use Commercial Street (near the Warner Bros. Studio Store) to reach Christopher Columbus Park on Atlantic Avenue at Cross Street. Before you brave the Boston traffic, you might want to fortify yourself for the journey.

🔾 **TAKE A BREAK** Faneuil Hall Marketplace is across State Street from the Custom House. Head to Quincy Market for takeout—sandwiches, pizza, ice cream, or just coffee and a bagel—and bring it along. If you cross Atlantic Avenue at State Street, head down Long Wharf. You can eat at the Marriott or continue past it to the brick plaza at the very end of the wharf, where you'll have a great view of the harbor and the airport. Or stay at Christopher Columbus Park, watch the action at the marina, and play in the playground.

Two excellent restaurants are nearby. Next to the park, **Cornucopia on the Wharf** (100 Atlantic Ave.; ☎ 617/367-0300) has an outdoor plaza; two blocks farther, at Fleet Street across from Lewis Wharf, the **Grill & Cue** (256 Commercial St.; ☎ 617/227-4454) has floor-to-ceiling windows that open onto the sidewalk. See Chapter 6, "Dining," for details.

Find your way back to the MBTA Blue Line Aquarium station at Atlantic Avenue and State Street and resume exploring. Past the Marriott is:

8. **Long Wharf,** Boston's principal wharf since 1710. When it was built, the town mandated that the public have access to it. This is the embarkation point for many sightseeing cruises, as well as the MBTA ferry to Charlestown. Near the end of the wharf is a granite building, dating from 1846, that was used by Customs appraisers. Now it houses offices and residences. At the very end of the wharf is the small plaza where you might have had lunch. The view is worth the trip even if you're not dining.

From the Marriott, with the lobby at your back, walk one block on East India Row. To your left you'll see Susumu Shingu's red sculpture *Echoes of the Waves.* This is:

9. **Central Wharf,** home of the New England Aquarium. A walk around the aquarium provides a fine view of East Boston and the harbor. Planned expansion may have turned this into another construction site by the time you visit, but there are no plans to move the seals who cavort out front. The aquarium is a popular attraction (see Chapter 7, "What to See & Do in Boston").

Back on East India Row, walk another block to:

10. **India Wharf.** The two apartment towers (1971) were designed by I.M. Pei. The location hardly looks like a wharf at all, but in the 19th century it ran inland and was packed with stores and warehouses.

Continue past the aluminum sculpture overlooking the water to the boardwalk and:

11. **Rowes Wharf.** Here again we see the legacy of John Rowe (known as "Merchant" Rowe), who donated the Sacred Cod that hangs in the State House. The wharf (which has public docks) was constructed after a fire in 1760 and has long been used as a ferry terminal. It's probably better known today for the dramatic arch in the center of the Boston Harbor Hotel (1985), designed by the Chicago architecture firm Skidmore, Owings, and Merrill. The Airport Water Shuttle leaves from here. Walk past the gangway to the short flight of stairs that leads up to the Northern Avenue Bridge, where there's another construction site (are you starting to detect a pattern here?). The bridge spans:

12. **Fort Point Channel.** You will pass the First District Headquarters of the U.S. Coast Guard. The *Massachusetts,* the first commissioned revenue cutter, was based here. (Revenue cutters were the forerunners of the U.S. Coast Guard.) John Foster Williams, a local naval hero of the Revolutionary War, was its captain. The little white building nearby is the National Oceanographic Tide Gauge Station, where tide levels are continuously recorded.

The ongoing construction of a replacement for the Northern Avenue Bridge, an iron-turntable bridge (which opens to allow ships to pass by moving around on a pivot rather than lifting up like a drawbridge) built in 1908, nicely complements the disorder on either side. Away from the water is the omnipresent Central Artery project; ahead to your left will be the new federal courthouse at Fan Pier, which was taking shape at press time. Carefully cross Northern Ave., turn right onto Sleeper St., and walk one block. The next wharf is:

13. **Museum Wharf**, which takes its name from the two major museums located there: the **Children's Museum** and the **Computer Museum** (see Chapter 7, "What to See & Do in Boston"). The wharf was once the site of a wool warehouse that supplied the once-prosperous New England textile industry.

   At the end of Museum Wharf, turn right at the giant milk bottle onto the Congress Street Bridge. On the bridge is the:

14. **Boston Tea Party Ship & Museum.** Climb aboard the brig *Beaver II,* a full-scale replica of one of the three ships involved in the tea party in 1773. Visit the adjoining floating museum in which the story of the uprising is told through various exhibits and multimedia presentations. And if you really want to get into the spirit of the rebellion, costumed guides can help you throw chests of tea into Boston Harbor (later retrieved by rope harnesses). There is also a gift shop where you can buy tea to bring home. The Tea Party Ship is open from 9am to 5pm in the spring and fall, and 9am to 6pm in the summer. It is closed between December 1 and March 1. Admission is $6 for adults, $4.80 for seniors and students, $3 for children 5 to 12, and free for children under age 5. Reduced rates are available to those on the Old Town Trolley tour.

   You may be ready to collapse at this point, or raring to go. At nearby South Station (follow Congress St. one block, turn left onto Atlantic Ave., and walk one block) you can take the MBTA Red Line. For a seafood meal, backtrack to Northern Ave., turn right, and walk about half a mile to Anthony's Pier 4, Jimmy's Harborside, Jimbo's Fish Shanty, and the Daily Catch (see Chapter 6, "Dining," for details). Or work your way back to Christopher Columbus Park and head up Richmond St. to the caffés and restaurants of the North End.

WALKING TOUR 4
The Back Bay

Start: The Public Garden (MBTA Green Line to Arlington).

Finish: Copley Square.

Time: Two hours if you make good time, three if you detour to the Esplanade, and longer if you take your time while shopping.

Best Time: Any time before late afternoon.

Worst Time: Late afternoon, when the streets are packed with people and cars. And don't attempt the detour on the Fourth of July. This is mostly an outdoor walk, so if the weather is bad you may find yourself in lots of shops, which could wind up costing you some money. Decide for yourself if that makes an overcast day a "best" or "worst" time.

The Back Bay is the youngest neighborhood in Boston, the product of a massive landfill project that took place from 1835–82. It's flat, symmetrical, logically designed—the names of the cross streets go in alphabetical order—and altogether anomalous in Boston's crazy-quilt geography.

   Begin your walk in the:

1. **Public Garden,** which is bounded by Arlington, Beacon, Charles, and Boylston sts. Before the Back Bay was filled in, the Charles River flowed right up to Charles St., which separates the Public Garden from Boston Common. On the night of April 18, 1775, the British troops bound for Lexington and Concord boarded boats to

Walking Tour 4—The Back Bay

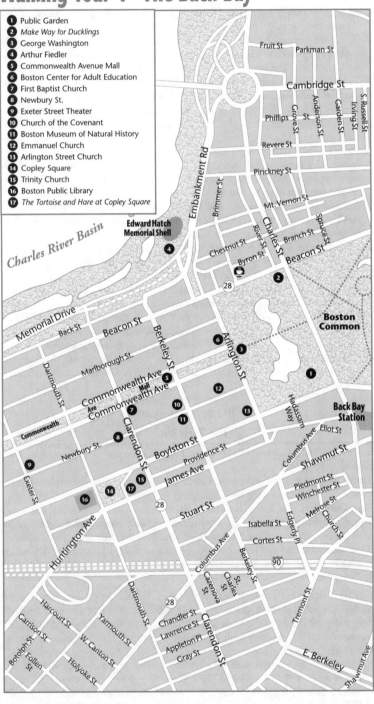

1. Public Garden
2. *Make Way for Ducklings*
3. George Washington
4. Arthur Fiedler
5. Commonwealth Avenue Mall
6. Boston Center for Adult Education
7. First Baptist Church
8. Newbury St.
9. Exeter Street Theater
10. Church of the Covenant
11. Boston Museum of Natural History
12. Emmanuel Church
13. Arlington Street Church
14. Copley Square
15. Trinity Church
16. Boston Public Library
17. *The Tortoise and Hare at Copley Square*

Cambridge ("two if by sea") at the foot of the Common and set off across what's now the Public Garden.

Explore the lagoon, the trees and other flora, and the statuary. Take a ride on the swan boats, if you like, and then make your way toward the corner of Charles and Beacon streets. A short distance away, within the confines of the Public Garden (listen for the squeals of delighted children), you'll see a 35-foot strip of cobblestones topped with the bronze figures that immortalize Robert McCloskey's book:

2. *Make Way for Ducklings.* Installed in 1987 and wildly popular since the moment they were unveiled, Nancy Schön's renderings of Mrs. Mallard and her eight babies are irresistible. Mrs. Mallard is 38 inches tall, making her back just a shade higher than the seat on a tricycle, but that doesn't keep people of all ages from climbing on. If you don't know the whole story of the Mallards' perilous trip across town to meet Mr. Mallard at the lagoon, ask one of the parents or children you'll certainly find here.

The city purchased the site of the Public Garden (it was starting to fill in and getting marshy) in 1824. Planting began in 1837, but it wasn't until the late 1850s that Arlington St. was built and the land permanently set aside. George F. Meacham executed the design.

Cross the lagoon using the little suspension bridge and look for the statue of:

3. **George Washington.** Unveiled in 1875, this was Boston's first equestrian statue. It stands 38 feet tall and is considered an excellent likeness of the first president of the United States, an outstanding horseman. The artist, Thomas Ball, was a Charlestown native who worked in Italy and numbered among his students noted sculptor and artist Daniel Chester French. Pass through the gate onto Arlington Street. Before we begin exploring in earnest, this is a good place to detour and:

⚫ **TAKE A BREAK** Turn right and walk up Arlington Street, passing Marlborough Street, to Beacon Street. Across the busy intersection is the **Bull & Finch Pub** (84 Beacon St.; ☎ **617/227-9605**), the "Cheers" bar. The food is actually quite tasty, but two points must be made—not that anything's going to keep you from visiting if you have your heart set on it—the bar looks nothing like the set of the TV show, and the patrons generally consist of people from everywhere in the world except Boston.

If you'd rather stay outdoors, turn right on Beacon and walk one block to the corner of Charles Street. Diagonally across the intersection, order something to go at **Starbucks** (1 Charles St.; ☎ **617/742-2664**), or, if you want to really run off the beaten track and wander down Charles Street looking for a snack you can't get at home, well, nobody's stopping you. In any case, when you've found something to eat, backtrack along Beacon Street just past Arlington Street to Embankment Road. Take the Arthur Fiedler Footbridge across Storrow Drive to the Esplanade park and unpack your food near the giant head of:

4. **Arthur Fiedler.** Installed in 1985, this sculpture by Ralph Helmick is made up of sheets of aluminum that eerily capture the countenance of the legendary conductor of the Boston Pops, who died in 1979. The amphitheater off to the right is the Hatch Shell, where the Pops perform free during the week leading up to and including the Fourth of July.

When you're ready, retrace your steps to the corner of Arlington Street and Commonwealth Avenue. We are now at the east end of the:

5. **Commonwealth Avenue Mall.** This graceful public promenade is the centerpiece of architect Arthur Gilman's design of the Back Bay. The mall is 100 feet wide (the entire street is 240) and stretches to Kenmore Square, at which point it's known by the more familiar name "Comm. Ave." The elegant Victorian mansions on either side—almost

all divided into apartments or in commercial or educational use—are generally considered a great asset, but the attitude toward the apparently random collection of statues along the mall is hardly unanimous. Judge for yourself as you inspect them, starting with Alexander Hamilton across Arlington Street from George Washington. First, though, stop at the:

6. **Boston Center for Adult Education** (5 Commonwealth Ave.; ☎ 617/267-4430). Constructed in 1904 as a private residence, the building gained a huge ballroom in 1912. If it's not being used for a class or a function (it's extremely popular for weddings), you're welcome to have a look at the ballroom. The Boston Center was established in 1933 and is the oldest continuing-education institution in the country.

Back on the mall, you could easily spend all day pondering the monuments and wondering what in the world William Lloyd Garrison, Boston Mayor Patrick Andrew Collins, Revolutionary War Gen. John Glover, and Leif Eriksson have in common. Perhaps (to sound almost unbearably flip) the only thing they share is that they're all captured here.

Two blocks from the Public Garden at the corner of Clarendon Street is the:

7. **First Baptist Church** (110 Commonwealth Ave.). Built in 1870–72 of Roxbury puddingstone, it originally housed the congregation of the Brattle Street Church (Unitarian), which was downtown, near Faneuil Hall. The design is mainly notable because its creators went on to work on much more famous projects. The architect, H.H. Richardson, is best known for nearby Trinity Church, which we'll see shortly. The artist who created the frieze, which represents the sacraments, was Frederic Auguste Bartholdi, who designed the Statue of Liberty.

At Clarendon Street or Dartmouth Street, turn left and walk one block to:

8. **Newbury Street.** As Commonwealth Avenue is the architectural heart of the Back Bay, Newbury Street is the commercial center. Take some time to roam around here (see Chapter 9, "Shopping," for pointers), browsing in the galleries, window-shopping at the expensive clothing stores, and watching the chicly attired shoppers, artist-types and trendy yuppies who frequent this strip. On Exeter Street you'll see the building that was once the:

9. **Exeter Street Theater,** at 26 Exeter Street Designed in 1884 as the First Spiritualist Temple, it was a movie house from 1914–84. Once known for the crowds flocking to the *Rocky Horror Picture Show*, it's now the home of Waterstone's Booksellers and a Friday's chain restaurant.

When you're ready to continue your stroll or when your credit cards start crying for mercy (whichever comes first), head for Berkeley Street (back towards the Public Garden) and seek out three of Newbury street's oldest buildings, starting with the:

10. **Church of the Covenant** (67 Newbury St.), a Gothic revival edifice built in 1866–67 and designed by Richard Upjohn. The stained-glass windows are the work of Louis Comfort Tiffany.

Across the street, set back from the sidewalk at 234 Berkeley St., is an opulent store in an equally opulent setting. Louis, Boston (see Chapter 9 for details on this famous clothing store) is housed in the original home of the:

11. **Boston Museum of Natural History,** a forerunner of the Museum of Science. Built in 1861–64 using William Preston's French Academic design, it was originally only two stories but still has the original roof, preserved when the third floor was added.

Cross Newbury Street again and continue walking toward the Public Garden. On your left is:

12. **Emmanuel Church** (15 Newbury St.; ☎ 617/536-3355), the first building completed on Newbury Street The Episcopal church ministers through the arts, so there may be a concert (classical to jazz, solo to orchestral) going on during your visit.

Now you're almost back at the Public Garden. On your left is the original (1927) Ritz-Carlton, the pride and joy of the chain. Turn right onto Arlington Street and walk one block to Boylston Street. On your right is the:

13. Arlington Street Church (351 Boylston St.), the oldest church in the Back Bay, completed in 1861. An interesting blend of Georgian and Italianate details, it's the work of architect Arthur Gilman, who laid out the Back Bay. Here you'll see more Tiffany stained glass. Step inside to see the pulpit that was in use in 1788, when the congregation worshipped downtown on Federal Street, in a church that also served as an additional meeting place for Massachusetts delegates to the constitutional convention when the Old State House was full.

Follow Boylston Street away from the Public Garden. You'll pass the famous FAO Schwarz toy store, with the huge bronze bear out front at the corner of Berkeley Street. At the end of the block is:

14. Copley Square. Freshen up near the fountain, visit the farmer's market (Tuesday and Friday from July through November), but whatever you do, don't miss:

15. Trinity Church (to your left), H.H. Richardson's Romanesque masterpiece completed in 1877. It's built on 4,502 pilings driven into the mud that was once the Back Bay. Should you happen to visit on a Friday at lunchtime, organ recitals are given at 12:15. Otherwise, brochures and guides are available to help you find your way around a building considered one of the finest examples of church architecture in the country. It's open daily 8am–6pm.

Across Dartmouth Street is the:

16. Boston Public Library. The work of architect Charles Follen McKim and many, many others, the Boston Public Library was completed in 1895 after 10 years of construction. Its design reflects the significant influence of the Bibliotheque Nationale in Paris. Climb the steps and wander inside if you'd like to check out the building's impressive architecture (See Chapter 7, "What to See & Do in Boston," for more details).

Leave the library through the Daniel Chester French–designed doors facing Dartmouth Street and head across the street into the little Copley Square park. In a sense, we've come full circle; as in the Public Garden, once again you'll be greeted by a playful and compelling sculpture:

17. *The Tortoise and Hare at Copley Square,* also by Nancy Schön. Designed to signify the finish of the Boston Marathon (the finish line is on Boylston Street between Exeter and Dartmouth streets), it was unveiled for the 100th anniversary of the event in 1996 and immediately became another shutterbug magnet.

From here you're in a good position to set out for any other part of town, or just walk a little way in any direction and continue exploring. Copley Place and the Shops at Prudential Center are nearby, Newbury Street is one block over, and there's an MBTA Green Line station on Dartmouth Street. Or just hang around Copley Square, imagine yourself sitting in this spot 150 or so years ago, and be glad there's such a thing as landfill.

WALKING TOUR 5
Cambridge

Start: Harvard Square (MBTA Red Line to Harvard).
Finish: John F. Kennedy Park.
Time: Two to four hours, depending on how much time you spend in shops and museums.

Walking Tour 5—Cambridge

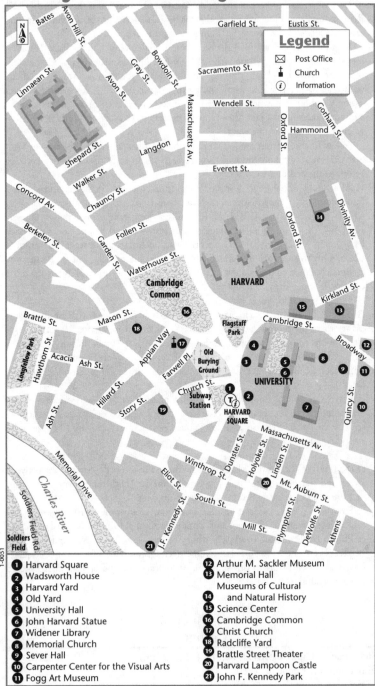

Legend
- ⊠ Post Office
- ⊥ Church
- ⓘ Information

Bates
Avon Hill St.
Linnaean St.
Gray St.
Bowdoin St.
Avon St.
Sacramento St.
Garfield St.
Eustis St.
Wendell St.
Massachusetts Av.
Oxford St.
Hammond
Gorham St.
Shepard St.
Langdon
Walker St.
Chauncy St.
Concord Av.
Follen St.
Everett St.
Divinity Av.
Berkeley St.
Garden St.
Waterhouse St.
Cambridge Common
HARVARD
Oxford St.
14
Kirkland St.
13
15
Brattle St.
Mason St.
18
Appian Way
17
Old Burying Ground
Flagstaff Park
Cambridge St.
Broadway
12
Longfellow Park
Hawthorn St.
Acacia
Ash St.
Hilliard St.
Story St.
Church St.
Subway Station
HARVARD SQUARE
4
3
5
6
UNIVERSITY
8
9
11
Ash St.
19
1
2
7
10
Quincy St.
Memorial Drive
Charles River
Soldiers Field Rd.
Soldiers Field
Eliot St.
Winthrop St.
Dunster St.
Holyoke St.
Linden St.
20
Mt. Auburn St.
J.F. Kennedy St.
South St.
Mill St.
Plympton St.
DeWolfe St.
Athens
21

1-0051

1. Harvard Square
2. Wadsworth House
3. Harvard Yard
4. Old Yard
5. University Hall
6. John Harvard Statue
7. Widener Library
8. Memorial Church
9. Sever Hall
10. Carpenter Center for the Visual Arts
11. Fogg Art Museum
12. Arthur M. Sackler Museum
13. Memorial Hall
14. Museums of Cultural and Natural History
15. Science Center
16. Cambridge Common
17. Christ Church
18. Radcliffe Yard
19. Brattle Street Theater
20. Harvard Lampoon Castle
21. John F. Kennedy Park

Best Time: Almost any time (see below); the Harvard museums are free on Saturday mornings.

Worst Time: The first full week of June. You may have trouble gaining admission to Harvard Yard during commencement festivities. The actual ceremony is Thursday.

Popular impressions to the contrary, Cambridge is not exclusively Harvard. In fact, Harvard Square isn't even exclusively Harvard, and during a walk around the Harvard Square area, you'll see historic buildings and sights, interesting museums, and notable architecture, on and off the university's main campus.

Ride the Red Line to Harvard. Leave the station by the main entrance (take the ramp to the turnstiles and the escalators to the outside) and emerge in the heart of:

1. Harvard Square. Town and gown meet at this lively intersection, where you'll get a taste of the improbable mix of people drawn to the crossroads of Cambridge. To your right is the landmark **Out of Town News** kiosk, which stocks newspapers and magazines from all over the world. **Cambridge Discovery, Inc.** runs the information booth in front of you, where information about the area is available. Step close to it so that you're out of the flow of pedestrian traffic, and look around.

The department store across Massachusetts Avenue is the **Harvard Coop** (see Chapter 9, "Shopping" for details). The name rhymes with "hoop"—say "co-op" and risk being taken for a Yale student. On the far side of the intersection at the corner of John F. Kennedy Street and Brattle Street, look up at the third floor of the brick building and find the sign for "Dewey Cheetham & Howe" (say it out loud). National Public Radio's hilarious show "Car Talk" originates here.

Turn around so that the Coop is at your back and walk half a block, crossing Dunster Street. Across Massachusetts Avenue you'll see:

2. Wadsworth House (1341 Massachusetts Ave.). Most of the people waiting for the bus in front of this yellow wood building probably don't know it was built in 1726 as a residence for Harvard's fourth president (but neither do most Harvard students). Now the headquarters of the alumni association, its biggest claim to fame is a classic: "George Washington slept here."

Cross the street and go left. Follow the red-brick wall past one gate until you see another "T" exit. Turn right and use Johnston Gate to enter:

3. Harvard Yard. This is the oldest part of "the Yard," which was just a patch of grass with animals grazing on it when Harvard College was established in 1636 to train young men for the ministry. It wasn't much more when the Continental Army spent the winter here in 1775–76. Harvard is the oldest college in the U.S., with the most competitive admissions process, and if you suggest aloud that it's not the best, you may run up against the snobby attitude that inspired the saying "You can always tell a Harvard man, but you can't tell him much."

Harvard, a private institution in 1865, includes the college and 10 graduate and professional schools located in more than 400 buildings around Boston and Cambridge. Some of the most interesting are around the perimeter of this quadrangle, the classroom and administration buildings and dormitories for first-year students that make up the:

4. Old Yard. To your right is **Massachusetts Hall.** Built in 1720, this is the university's oldest surviving building and is listed as a National Historic Landmark. Freshmen, who live upstairs, share the building with the first-floor office of the university president (or perhaps it's the other way around), who is traditionally invited upstairs for tea once a year. To your left, across from Massachusetts Hall, is **Harvard Hall,** a classroom building constructed in 1765. Turn left and walk down the side of Harvard

Hall. The matching side-by-side buildings here are **Hollis** and **Stoughton halls.** Hollis dates to 1763 (Stoughton "only" to 1805) and has been home to many students who went on to great fame, among them Ralph Waldo Emerson, Henry David Thoreau, and Charles Bulfinch. Almost hidden across the tiny lawn between these two buildings is **Holden Chapel,** a Georgian-style gem built in 1745. It has been an anatomy lab, a classroom building, and, of course, a chapel, and is now home to the Harvard Glee Club.

Cross the Yard to the building opposite the gate where you entered. This is:

5. **University Hall.** Constructed in 1812–13 of granite quarried in nearby Chelmsford, it's the college's main administration building. In 1969 it was occupied by students protesting the Vietnam War, but it's best known as the backdrop of the:

6. **John Harvard Statue,** one of the most photographed objects in the Boston area. Designed by Daniel Chester French in 1884, it's known as the "Statue of Three Lies" because the inscription reads "John Harvard—Founder—1638." In fact, the college was founded in 1636; Harvard (one of many involved in its establishment) didn't really found the university, instead he donated money and his library; and this isn't John Harvard, anyway. No portraits of him survive, so the model was, according to various accounts, either his nephew or a student. This benevolent-looking bronze gentleman is occasionally doused with paint in the school color of a rival football team during the week before a big game, and almost instantaneously cleaned up. Luckily for him, Harvard's football team hasn't been very good recently, and the heated rivalries have cooled somewhat.

Walk around University Hall into the adjoining quadrangle. This is still the Yard, but it's the "New Yard," sometimes called Tercentenary Theater because the college's 300th-anniversary celebration was held here. This is where commencement and other university-wide ceremonies (most recently the 350th-birthday party in 1986) are held. On your right is:

7. **Widener Library.** The centerpiece of the world's largest university library system was built in 1913 as a memorial to Harry Elkins Widener, a 1907 Harvard graduate. Legend has it that he died when the *Titanic* sank in 1912 because he was unable to swim 50 yards to a lifeboat, and his mother donated $2 million for the library on the condition that every undergraduate prove his ability to swim 50 yards or take swimming lessons. Today the library holds more than 3 million volumes, including 3,500 rare volumes collected by Harry Elkins Widener. It was designed by Horace Trumbauer of Philadelphia, whose primary design assistant was Julian Francis Abele, a student of architecture at the University of Pennsylvania and the first black graduate of L'Ecole des Beaux Arts in Paris. Climb the steps to enter and see the dioramas of Cambridge on the main level and the locked-up memorial room with Widener's collection behind the glass door overlooking the lobby (you need a Harvard ID to get to the reading room and stacks). Or stop before entering and enjoy the view. Facing the library is:

8. **Memorial Church,** built in 1931 and topped with a tower and weathervane 197 feet tall. You're welcome to look around this Georgian Revival–style edifice unless services are going on—or to attend them if they are. Morning prayers are said daily from 8:45 to 9, and the Sunday service is at 11am. The building is also used for private weddings and funerals. The entrance is on the left. On the south wall, toward the Yard, the names of the Harvard graduates who died in the world wars, Korea, and Vietnam are listed, including that of Joseph P. Kennedy, Jr., the president's brother, class of 1938.

With Memorial Church behind you, turn left toward:

9. Sever Hall, a classroom building designed by H. H. Richardson (the architect of Trinity Church) and built from 1878–80. Notice the gorgeous brickwork that includes roll moldings around the doors, and the fluted brick chimneys. The front door is set back in the "whispering gallery." Stand on one side of the entrance arch, station a friend or willing passer-by on the opposite side, and speak softly into the facade. Someone standing next to you can't hear what you say, but the person at the other side of the arch can.

Facing Sever Hall, turn right and go around to the back. The building to the right is Emerson Hall, which appeared in the movie *Love Story* as Barrett Hall, named after the family of the film's main character, Oliver Barrett (Ryan O'Neal). Cross this quadrangle, go through the gate and step onto Quincy Street. On your right on the other side of the street is the:

10. Carpenter Center for the Visual Arts, a concrete and glass structure at 24 Quincy St. There are art exhibitions in the lobby, movies from the extensive Harvard Film Archives are shown in the basement (you can pick up a schedule on the main floor), and the building itself is a work of art. It was constructed from 1961–63 and designed by the Swiss-French architect Le Corbusier, along with the team of Sert, Jackson, and Gourley. It's the only building in North America designed by Le Corbusier. Facing the gate where you emerged from the Yard is the:

11. Fogg Art Museum, founded in 1895 but only located at 32 Quincy St. since the building was completed in 1927. The Fogg's excellent collection of painting, sculpture, and decorative art runs from the Middle Ages to the present. See Chapter 7, "What to See & Do in Boston," for a complete description of the Fogg, the adjacent Busch-Reisinger Museum, and the next stop on our walk, the:

12. Arthur M. Sackler Museum, at 485 Broadway, to the left as you face the Fogg. The university's spectacular collection of Asian art is housed here.

Continue on Quincy Street with the Fogg behind you and cross Broadway, then cross Cambridge Street, watching out for the confused drivers emerging from the underpass to your left. The block between Cambridge Street and Kirkland Street is occupied by:

13. Memorial Hall, a Victorian structure built from 1870–74. The entrance on Cambridge Street puts you in the actual hall of memorials, a transept where you can read the names of the Harvard men who died fighting for the Union during the Civil War—the names of Harvard men who died for the Confederacy are absent. To the right is **Sanders Theater,** prized as both a performance space and a lecture hall for its excellent acoustics and clear views. To the left is **Annenberg Hall,** originally Alumni Hall, which underwent a massive renovation in 1995 and was turned into a dining hall after 70 years as an open space used for class registration, blood drives, and final exams by the thousands. It has gorgeous stained-glass windows that you might be able to get a look at if it's not mealtime. Harvard graduates William Ware and Henry Van Brunt won a design competition for Memorial Hall, which was constructed for a total cost of $390,000 (most of it donated by alumni). If it seems that the building should be taller, that might be because it once was. In 1956 a huge fire tore through the tower, and it was never rebuilt.

Facing in the same direction you were when you entered, walk through the transept and exit onto Kirkland Street. Turn left and take the first right, onto Oxford Street. One block up on the right you'll see an entrance to the:

14. Museum of Cultural and Natural History, at 26 Oxford St. This complex consists of the Botanical Museum, the Museum of Comparative Zoology, the Mineralogical & Geological Museum, and the Peabody Museum of Archaeology & Ethnology. Best known for the Glass Flowers on display at the Botanical Museum, the entire institution is becoming more interdisciplinary and accessible. See Chapter 7, "What to See & Do in Boston," for a full description.

Leave through the back door at 11 Divinity Ave. and look around. Across the street at 6 Divinity Ave. is the **Semitic Museum** (☎ **617/495-4631**), where the second- and third-floor galleries hold displays of archaeological artifacts and photographs from the Near and Middle East. You might want to detour here. The building next door, **Two Divinity Ave.,** was designed by Horace Trumbauer, the architect of Widener Library, and is the home of the Harvard-Yenching Institute, which promotes East Asian studies and facilitates scholar exchange programs. For every person who can tell you that, there are several thousand who only know this building for the pair of Chinese stone lions flanking the front door.

Turn right and return to Kirkland Street. At the intersection of Kirkland and Oxford streets is the university's:

15. Science Center (Zero Oxford St.). A 10-story monolith said to resemble a Polaroid camera (Edwin H. Land, founder of the Cambridge-based Polaroid Corporation, was one of its main benefactors), the Science Center was designed by the Spanish architect Josep Luis Sert and built from 1970–72. Sert, the dean of the university's Graduate School of Design from 1953–69, was a disciple of Le Corbusier, whose Carpenter Center for the Visual Arts we've already seen. On the plaza between the Science Center and the Yard is the **Tanner Rock Fountain,** a group of 159 New England field boulders artfully arranged around a small fountain. Since 1985 this has been a favorite spot for students to relax and watch unsuspecting passers-by get wet; the fountain sprays a fine mist, which begins slowly and gradually intensifies.

☕ **TAKE A BREAK**   The main level of the Science Center is open to the public and has several places to stop for a drink and a snack (including fried chicken and gourmet coffee), but you'll probably want to save room for the delicacies at our next break. Even if you're already full, for a truly authentic Harvard experience, find the **Green House Cafe** on the right beyond the library and have a freshly baked chocolate chip cookie.

Exit near the fountain and turn right. Keeping the underpass on your left, follow the walkway for the equivalent of a block and a half as it curves around to the right. The Harvard Law School campus is on your right. You're back at Massachusetts Ave., which, when you saw it last, took a right at the Coop and turned north. Cross carefully to:

16. Cambridge Common. This well-used plot of greenery and bare earth is dotted with memorials and plaques. Turn left and follow the sidewalk along Massachusetts Avenue and after a block or so you'll walk near or over horseshoes embedded in the concrete. This is the path William Dawes, Paul Revere's fellow alarm-sounder, took from Boston to Lexington on April 18, 1775. Turn right onto Garden Street and continue following the Common for one block. On your right you'll see a monument marking the place where Gen. George Washington took control of the Continental Army on July 3, 1775. The elm under which he assumed command is no longer standing.

Cross Garden Street and backtrack to:

17. Christ Church at Zero Garden St. The oldest church in Cambridge, it was designed by Peter Harrison of Newport, R.I. (who was also the architect of King's Chapel in Boston), and opened in 1761. Note the square wooden tower. Inside the vestibule you can still see bullet holes made by British muskets. At one time the church was used as the barracks for Connecticut troops. During their stay, they melted down the organ pipes to make bullets.

Facing the church, turn right and proceed on Garden Street to the first intersection. This is Appian Way. Turn left and take the first right into:

18. Radcliffe Yard. Radcliffe College was founded in 1879 as the "Harvard Annex" and named for Ann Radcliffe, Lady Mowlson, Harvard's first female benefactor. Undergraduate classes were merged with Harvard's in 1943, Harvard degrees were given to Radcliffe graduates in 1963, and in 1977 responsibility for educating undergraduate women was officially turned over to Harvard. Today, Radcliffe remains an independent corporation within the university and has its own president, though its degrees, classes, and facilities are shared with Harvard. After you've strolled around, return to Appian Way and turn right. You'll emerge on Brattle Street. Turn right to take an interesting detour (and add about an hour to your walk) by visiting the Longfellow National Historic Site, at 105 Brattle St. It's open from mid-May through mid-October (see Chapter 7, "What to See & Do in Boston," for complete information). Otherwise, cross Brattle Street, turn left, and walk half a block.

🙂 **TAKE A BREAK** **The Blacksmith House Bakery & Cafe** (56 Brattle St.; ☎ **617/876-2725**), on your right, is the perfect place to stop for a cup of coffee and some excellent pastry. If the weather is good, you can sit outside and enjoy the passing scene. You can also have lunch (and dinner in the summer), but if you get a look at the dessert tray first, you may not care about lunch.

Continue walking along Brattle Street (there are excellent shops on both sides of the street). Two blocks up on the right is the:

19. Brattle Street Theater, 40 Brattle St. Opened in 1890 as Brattle Hall, it was founded by the Cambridge Social Union and was used as a venue for cultural entertainment. In 1953, it was converted to a movie house and quickly became known as Cambridge's center for art films. The whole building was renovated in the late '80s. The Brattle Street Theater is one of the oldest independent movie houses in the country.

You're now in the Brattle Square part of Harvard Square. You may see street musicians or performers, a protest, a speech, or just more stores to explore. Cross Brattle Street at WordsWorth bookstore, turn right, and follow the curve of the building around the corner to Mount Auburn Street. Stay on the right-hand side of the street as you cross John F. Kennedy Street, Dunster Street, Holyoke Street, and Linden Street. On your left between Dunster and Holyoke streets is Holyoke Center, an administration building designed by Josep Luis Sert with commercial space on the ground floor. The corner of Mount Auburn and Linden streets is a good vantage point for viewing the:

20. Harvard Lampoon Castle, designed by Wheelwright & Haven in 1909. Listed on the National Register of Historic Places, this is the home of Harvard's undergraduate humor magazine, the *Lampoon.* The main tower looks like a face, with windows as the eyes, nose, and mouth, topped by what looks like a miner's hat. The *Lampoon* and the daily student newspaper, the *Crimson,* share a long history of reciprocal pranks and harmless vandalism. Elaborate security measures notwithstanding, *Crimson* editors occasionally make off with the bird atop the castle (it looks like a crane but is actually an ibis), and *Lampoon* staffers have absconded with the huge wooden president's chair from the *Crimson.*

You'll pass the *Crimson* building on your right if you decide to detour for a visit to the Harvard Book Store. Turn left onto Plympton Street and follow it back to

Massachusetts Ave.; the store is at the corner. Otherwise, follow Mount Auburn Street back to John F. Kennedy Street. (Alternatively, cross Mount Auburn Street and walk away from Holyoke Center on Holyoke Street or Dunster Street to get a sense of part of the rest of the campus. Turn right on Winthrop Street or South Street and proceed to John F. Kennedy Street.)

Turn left onto John F. Kennedy Street, cross it at some point, and follow it toward the Charles River, almost to Memorial Drive. On your right is:

21. **John F. Kennedy Park.** This lovely parcel of land was an empty plot near the MBTA train yard in the 1970s (at that time the Red Line ended at Harvard), when the search was on for a site for the Kennedy Library. Traffic concerns led to the library's being built in Dorchester, but the Graduate School of Government and this adjacent park bear the president's name. Walk away from the street to enjoy the fountain, which is engraved with excerpts from the president's speeches. This is an excellent place to take a break and plan the rest of your day.

Shopping 9

Like many other elements of Boston, the shopping scene is a harmonious blend of classic and contemporary. You'll find intimate boutiques and sprawling malls, esoteric bookstores and national chain stores, classy galleries and snazzy secondhand-clothing outlets, and the most famous discount store in the country, if not the world—Filene's Basement. It embodies a quality that has been important to Bostonians throughout the ages: Yankee thrift.

1 The Shopping Scene

The other major shopping areas in Boston and Cambridge have been overshadowed recently by the Back Bay, which seems only fitting—the Prudential Center casts a long shadow over the neighborhood, and the Shops at Prudential Center are the hottest new retail destination in town. You could easily spend a day browsing the stores that the Back Bay has to offer, at the "Pru," upscale Copley Place (linked by a weatherproof walkway across Huntington Avenue), Neiman Marcus, Lord & Taylor, Saks Fifth Avenue, and the dozens of galleries, shops and boutiques along Newbury Street.

Another popular destination is Faneuil Hall Marketplace, the busiest attraction in Boston, not only because of its smorgasbord of food outlets, but also because of its shops, boutiques, and pushcarts filled with everything from rubber stamps to costume jewelry.

If the prospect of the hubbub at Faneuil Hall is too much for you, stroll over to Charles Street, at the foot of Beacon Hill. It's a short but commercially dense (and picturesque) street noted for its antique and gift shops.

One of Boston's oldest shopping areas is Downtown Crossing. Now a traffic-free pedestrian mall along Washington, Winter, and Summer streets near Boston Common, it's home to two major department stores—Filene's and Macy's—tons of smaller clothing and shoe stores, food and merchandise pushcarts, Woolworth's, and outlets of two major bookstore chains (Barnes & Noble and Borders). Next to Macy's on Washington Street is Lafayette Place, the forlorn shell of a mall that closed in the early '90s. In 1996 the city announced a project aimed at refurbishing Washington St. from Downtown Crossing to Chinatown, an undertaking that should be bearing fruit by the time you visit. Most stores are open weeknights and Saturday until 7pm, and Sunday until 5 or 6pm.

Harvard Square in Cambridge, with its bookstores, boutiques, and T-shirt shops, is about 15 minutes from Boston by the Red Line subway. An aggressive neighborhood association has kept the area from being swallowed up by chain stores, and although the bohemian days of "the Square" are long gone, you'll find a mix of national and regional outlets as well as independent retailers. A walk along Massachusetts Avenue in either direction to the next "T" stop (Porter to the north, Central to the southeast) will take an hour or so, which is time well-spent for dedicated shoppers—Mass Ave. is lined with numerous shops carrying various wares.

Note: Massachusetts has no sales tax on clothing (priced below $175) and food. All other items are taxed at 5%. Restaurant meals and food prepared for takeout are also taxed at 5%.

With the erosion of Sunday "blue laws," Massachusetts law no longer prohibits stores from opening before noon on Sunday, but many still wait until noon or don't open at all—call ahead before setting out.

2 Shopping A to Z

ANTIQUES

Boston Antique Center
54 Canal St. ☎ **617/742-1400.**

A stone's throw from North Station and Faneuil Hall, you'll find about 50 dealers spread out over three floors, including one floor with a focus on British goods.

۞ Boston Antique Cooperative I & II
119 Charles St. ☎ **617/227-9810** and 617/227-9811.

These two cooperatives are filled with merchandise from Europe, Asia, and the United States. They specialize in furniture, vintage clothing and photographs, jewelry, and porcelain, but you might come across just about anything. The traffic is heavy and the turnover rapid, so if you see something you like, buy it immediately or risk losing out.

Bromfield Pen Shop
5 Bromfield St. ☎ **617/482-9053.**

The Bromfield Pen Shop has a collection of antique pens that will thrill any collector. The shop also sells new pens, including Mont Blanc, Pelikan, Waterman, and Omas.

Danish Country Antique Furniture
138 Charles St. ☎ **617/227-1804.**

Owner James Kilroy specializes in Scandinavian antique furnishings dating from the 1700s onward. You'll also see folk art, crafts, and Royal Copenhagen porcelain.

۞ Shreve, Crump & Low
330 Boylston St. ☎ **617/267-9100.**

This Boston institution, founded in 1800, is best known for new jewelry, china, silver, crystal, and watches. But Shreve's (as it's widely known) also has an antiques department that specializes in 18th- and 19th-century American and English furnishings, British and American silver, and Chinese porcelain.

ART

If you're passionate or just curious about art, try to set aside a couple of hours for strolling along Newbury Street. You'll find an infinite variety of styles and media in the dozens of galleries at street level and on the higher floors (remember to look up). Twice a year, in late May and late September, the street is closed from the Public Garden to Massachusetts Avenue and more than 30 galleries are open for **Art Newbury Street,** a celebration of the area's galleries displaying work by regional and international artists with special exhibits and outdoor entertainment. Contact the Newbury Street League (158 Newbury St.; ☎ **617/267-7961**) or check the web site (http://www.newbury-st.tne.com).

Alpha Gallery
14 Newbury St. ☎ **617/536-4465.**

Directed by Joanna E. Fink, daughter of founder Alan Fink, the Alpha Gallery specializes in contemporary American paintings, sculpture, and works on paper.

Artsmart
272 Congress St. ☎ **617/695-0151.**

Artsmart encourages touching—of the home accessories, jewelry, and sculpture on display, that is. Contemporary designers and craftspeople, many of them from New England, are represented at the gallery, which has drawn national attention for its funky sophistication. Artsmart also has locations at 34 Charles St. (☎ 723-8111) and 1352 Massachusetts Ave., Cambridge (☎ 497-9472).

Barbara Krakow Gallery
10 Newbury St. ☎ **617/262-4490.**

This prestigious gallery, established more than 30 years ago, specializes in paintings, sculpture, drawings, and prints created after 1945. It's located on the fifth floor.

Copley Society of Boston
158 Newbury St. ☎ **617/536-5049.**

America's oldest art association (founded in 1879), the Copley Society counted James MacNeil Whistler and John Singer Sargent among its members. Today most members come from the New England area, and shows are held regularly.

Gallery NAGA
67 Newbury St. ☎ **617/267-9060.**

Located in the neo-Gothic Church of the Covenant, Gallery NAGA exhibits contemporary paintings, sculpture, prints, furniture, and works in glass.

✪ Gargoyles, Grotesques & Chimeras
262 Newbury St. ☎ **617/536-2362.**

This intentionally gloomy space is decorated with gargoyles of all sizes and plaster reproductions of the details on the facades of famous cathedrals and other buildings. You'll also see non-gargoyle home decorations and haunting photographs that set the Gothic mood.

Haley & Steele
91 Newbury St. ☎ **617/536-6339.**

If you prefer more traditional prints to contemporary art, this is the place for you. You'll find maritime, military, botanical, and historical prints, as well as many 19th-century British sporting prints.

Robert Klein Gallery
38 Newbury St. ☎ **617/267-7997.**

For 19th- and 20th-century photography, head to Robert Klein Gallery. Among the artists represented are Diane Arbus, Robert Mapplethorpe, Man Ray, and Ansel Adams. The gallery is located on the fourth floor.

✪ Nielsen Gallery

179 Newbury St. ☎ **617/266-4835.**

Owner Nina Nielsen personally selects the artists who exhibit in her gallery (which has been here for more than 30 years), and she has great taste. You might come across the work of a young, newly discovered talent or of a more established artist.

Pucker Gallery

171 Newbury St. ☎ **617/267-9473.**

Like many other neighborhood galleries, Pucker Gallery shows contemporary art, some by local artists, but the specialty is Israeli art. The gallery is on the third floor.

Treasured Legacy

100 Huntington Ave. ☎ **617/424-8717.**

Located across Dartmouth Street from Back Bay Station, on the ground level of Copley Place, Treasured Legacy specializes in African-American art, African sculpture and textiles, and books about these and related topics.

Vose Galleries of Boston

238 Newbury St. ☎ **617/536-6176.**

It seems fitting that one of Vose Galleries' specialties is paintings of the Hudson River School—the business and the mid-19th century movement are about the same age. Vose Galleries, the oldest continuously operating gallery in the United States, opened in 1841 and is still run by the Vose family (now in its fifth generation). You'll see works of the Boston School and American Impressionists among the 18th-, 19th-, and early 20th-century American paintings.

BOOKS

Harvard Square is to books what Newbury Street is to art. Bibliophiles will relish wandering around the Square's used and new bookstores (as on Newbury Street, don't forget to look above street level). Though Harvard Square is probably the best source for books, we've also included listings for good bookstores elsewhere. Boston, of course, has outlets for many of the major national bookstore chains—**Barnes & Noble Booksellers** (395 Washington St., ☎ 617/426-5502), **Borders Books & Music** (10–24 School St., ☎ 617/557-7188), and **Walden Books** (2 Center Plaza, ☎ 617/523-3044)—but we have chosen to highlight Boston's specialty stores and outstanding booksellers found only in the area.

Avenue Victor Hugo Bookshop

339 Newbury St. ☎ **617/266-7746.**

This two-story shop buys, sells, and trades new and used books and estate libraries. The stock of more than 100,000 titles is quite comprehensive; the primary specialty is science fiction. You'll also find periodicals, with back issues of magazines that date to 1850, and a stock of general fiction titles that's billed as the largest north of New York City.

Brattle Book Store

9 West St. ☎ **800/447-9595** or 617/542-0210.

This store near Downtown Crossing buys and sells used, rare, and out-of-print titles, and owner Kenneth Gloss does free appraisals. Be sure to check out the carts out front (in all but the nastiest weather) for good deals on books of all ages.

⑤ Harvard Book Store
1256 Massachusetts Ave., Cambridge. ☎ **800/542-READ** (outside 617) or 617/661-1515.

The excellent scholarly selection and discounted best-sellers here attract shoppers to the main level, but the basement is the draw for those in the know. Prices on remainders are good, and used paperbacks (many bought for classes and hardly even opened) are 50% off.

Schoenhof's Foreign Books
76A Mt. Auburn St., Cambridge. ☎ **617/547-8855.**

Schoenhof's stocks adult literature and children's books in more than a dozen languages, as well as dictionaries and language-learning materials for more than 275 languages and dialects.

Waterstone's Booksellers
26 Exeter St. ☎ **617/859-7300.**

Located in the old Exeter Street Theater near the corner of Newbury Street, Waterstone's is a British import with three spacious floors that hold more than 160,000 titles. It's a great place to browse and has good remainders and children's books. There are weekly author readings. A second location, at Faneuil Hall Marketplace on the Upper Rotunda level of Quincy Market (☎ 617/589-0930), has extensive periodicals and travel sections.

✪ WordsWorth
30 Brattle St., Cambridge. ☎ **800/899-2202** or 617/354-5201.

In the heart of Harvard Square, WordsWorth stocks more than 100,000 volumes, all (except textbooks) sold at discount prices. The children's section is particularly good. If they're not too busy, the staff at the information desk will brainstorm with you until the database generates the title you want. WordsWorth has an on-line service (at http://www.wordsworth.com), which will search for books by title and author.

CHINA, SILVER & GLASS

La Ruche
168 Newbury St. ☎ **617/536-6366.**

The scent of Agraria potpourri greets you as you enter La Ruche (which translates as "beehive"). The store features unusual home and garden accessories, hand-painted furnishings, European and American glassware and pottery (including the complete line of Mackenzie-Childs majolica ware), decoupage plates and lamps, and architectural birdhouses.

Stoddard's
50 Temple Pl. ☎ **617/426-4187.**

The oldest cutlery shop in the country, dating from 1800, Stoddard's is full of items you don't know you need until you see them. You'll find sewing scissors, nail scissors (as well as scissors for any other use you can think of), knives of all descriptions (including a spectacular selection of Swiss army knives), shaving brushes, binoculars, fishing tackle, and fly rods. There's also another branch of the store at Copley Place (☎ 617/536-8688).

Villeroy & Boch
288 Boylston St. ☎ **617/542-7442.**

The completely shameless among us have been known to flip over the plates at upscale restaurants to see who made them. Often the answer is Villeroy & Boch, which sells fine European china and crystal. At this shop you'll also find gifts, artwork, and home furnishings.

CRAFTS

The Artful Hand Gallery
Copley Place, 100 Huntington Ave. ☎ **617/262-9601.**

The Artful Hand specializes, as you might guess, in handcrafted items. It shows and sells wonderful jewelry, ceramics, blown glass, wooden boxes, and sculpture exclusively by American artisans.

Society of Arts and Crafts
175 Newbury St. ☎ **617/266-1810.**

Contemporary American crafts, many created by New Englanders, are the focus here. You'll find jewelry and furniture as well as glass and ceramics that range from the practical to the purely decorative. The Downtown Crossing branch, open only on weekdays, is on the second floor of 101 Arch St. (☎ 617/345-0033).

DEPARTMENT STORES

The Coop
1400 Massachusetts Ave., Cambridge. ☎ **617/499-2000.**

The Coop (rhymes with "hoop"), or Harvard Cooperative Society, is in the process of transforming itself from a complete department store to a more student-oriented emporium. It's still no run-of-the-mill college bookstore. You'll find a huge selection of Harvard insignia merchandise, stationery, fine-art prints and posters, computers and electronics, clothes, cosmetics, music, and books—including the required texts for Harvard classes, a good department for browsing in September and February if you're interested. As at Boston University, Barnes & Noble recently assumed responsibility for the book operation. The store is in the center of Harvard Square.

Filene's
426 Washington St. ☎ **617/357-2100.**

Now that Jordan Marsh has become Macy's, Downtown Crossing's remaining fine old New England name is Filene's, pronounced "Fie-leen's," or sometimes "Fleen's." Whatever you call it, you'll find a full-service department store with all the usual amenities, including a good cosmetics department. Filene's is no longer affiliated with Filene's Basement, which is, yes, in the basement.

Macy's
450 Washington St. ☎ **617/357-3000.**

Across Summer Street from Filene's is New England's largest store. Its name was changed from Jordan Marsh when that operation was subsumed by Macy's in 1996, and it bears the hallmarks of the New York-based chain, including excellent selections of housewares, china, and silver.

DISCOUNT SHOPPING

Eddie Bauer Outlet
2 Devonshire Pl. ☎ **617/227-4840.**

For reduced (albeit not spectacular) prices on sportswear, outerwear, camping equipment, and luggage, follow Washington Street toward City Hall. Devonshire Place is between Water and State streets.

✪ Filene's Basement
426 Washington St. ☎ **617/542-2011.**

Follow the crowds to this Downtown Crossing institution, which has spoiled New England shoppers with retail discounts since 1908. Far from passing off their finds as pricey indulgences, true devotees boast about their bargains. Here's how it works: After two weeks on the selling floor, merchandise is automatically marked down 25% from its already discounted price. Check the boards hanging from the ceiling for the crucial dates; the original sale date is on the back of every price tag. Prices fall until, after 35 days, anything that hasn't sold (for 75% off) is donated to charity. Filene's Basement is no longer associated with Filene's, the department store upstairs from which it leases space. The independent chain, founded in 1978, has 47 branches in the Northeast and Midwest that offer great bargains, but the automatic markdown policy is in force only at the original store, which attracts 15,000 to 20,000 shoppers a day.

The crowds swell for the special sales, which come about when a store is going out of business or a classy designer, retailer, or catalogue house (say, Neiman Marcus, Barneys, Saks Fifth Avenue, Tweeds) finds itself overstocked. You'll see the unpredictable particulars, sometimes including an early opening time, advertised in the newspapers. Four times a year, the legendary $199 wedding dress sale sparks a truly alarming display of bridal hysteria usually documented by amused news camera crews; days are also set aside for dresses, men's and women's suits, raincoats, dress shirts, children's clothing, evening gowns, lingerie, cosmetics, leather goods, designer shoes, and anything else that looks promising to the store's eagle-eyed buyers. Two weeks later, leftovers wind up on the automatic-markdown racks, and the real hunting begins. Try to beat the lunchtime crowds, but if you can't, don't despair—just be patient. *Tip:* If you're not wild about trying on clothes in the open dressing rooms, slip them on over what you're wearing, an acceptable throwback to the days before there were dressing rooms. Or make like the natives and return what doesn't suit you, in person or even by mail.

If this is the sort of activity that gets your juices flowing, you haven't lived until you've clipped the original $225 price tag off a dress and responded to the first person who offers a compliment by saying, "Oh, do you like it? It was $17."

FASHION

CHILDREN'S

Saturday's Child
1762 Massachusetts Ave., Cambridge. ☎ 617/661-6402.

Though this store takes its name from a nursery rhyme, the verse in question seems hardly applicable: "Saturday's child works hard for a living," my foot. You won't want your little angel lifting a finger in these precious (in both senses of the word) outfits. Look for preteen fashions in the Zephyr annex.

MEN'S

Brooks Brothers
46 Newbury St. ☎ **617/267-2600.**

Blue blazers, gray flannels, and seersucker suits are widely available, but only at Brooks Brothers will you find the business and casual styles that mark you as a "proper Bostonian." Brooks is also the only place for exactly the right preppy shade of pink button-down oxford shirts. They also stock women's clothes and sportswear. There's another store branch at 75 State St. (☎ 617/261-9990).

Joseph Abboud
37 Newbury St. ☎ **617/266-4200**.

It may have taken a "Seinfeld" episode about a designer blazer with a crest to bring Joseph Abboud to national attention, but locals have been watching the skyrocketing career of their fellow Bostonian for years. Drop in for elegant suits, sweaters, and sportswear (J.O.E. at Joseph Abboud is at the same address), as well as women's clothing.

Louis, Boston
234 Berkeley St. ☎ **800/225-5135** or 617/262-6100.

This ultraprestigious store, housed in a building that was once the Museum of Natural History, sells designer men's suits that can be coordinated with handmade shirts, silk ties, and Italian shoes. Louis, Woman, at the same address caters to an elegant female clientele. Also on the premises are a full-service hair salon and Café Louis, which serves lunch and dinner.

WOMEN'S

Giorgio Armani Boutique
22 Newbury St. ☎ **617/267-3200**.

Perhaps better known for men's fashions, Armani also designs the sleek, sophisticated women's clothing available here at true Armani prices.

CP Shades
115 Newbury St. ☎ **617/421-0846**.

No, not sunglasses, but knits of every description that can be comfortably worn for babysitting, board meetings, or both.

Looks
1607 Massachusetts Ave., Cambridge. ☎ **617/491-4251**.

The elusive combination of chic and comfortable is embodied by the fashions at Looks, four blocks north of Harvard Square, where you'll find mostly natural fibers, funky accessories, and wonderful hats.

FOOD

Cardullo's Gourmet Shoppe
6 Brattle St., Cambridge. ☎ **617/491-8888**.

A veritable United Nations of fancy food, Cardullo's carries specialties (including candy) from just about everywhere. If you can't afford the big-ticket items, order a tasty sandwich to go.

✪ Le Saucier
Quincy Market, North Canopy. ☎ **617/227-9649**.

The sauces collected in this little space may bring tears to your eyes. The variety verges on infinite, and the hot sauces (check the front counter for free samples) are concocted from positively diabolical ingredients.

Paul W. Marks Cheese Shop
Quincy Market Colonnade. ☎ **617/227-0905**.

This place has an amazing selection of imported and domestic cheeses, as well as pâté and caviar.

Savenor's Supermarket
160 Charles St. ☎ **617/723-6328.**

Long a Cambridge institution, Savenor's moved to Beacon Hill after a fire in 1993 but kept its reputation as *the* local purveyor of exotic meats. It's also an upscale grocery store, perfect for loading up on cheese and crackers on the way to a concert or movie on the nearby Esplanade. If you crave buffalo or rattlesnake meat, this is the place to go.

GIFTS/SOUVENIRS

Boston has dozens of shops and pushcarts that sell typical tourist T-shirts, hats, and other assorted Boston gear. But the stores listed below are good places to look for a gift that says Boston without actually having the word emblazoned on it. The shops at all of the major museums in particular offer unique items, including crafts and games, that will serve as reminders of your trip.

Angel Dog
131 Charles St. ☎ **617/742-6435.**

If it can be on a dog or a dog can be on it, you'll find it here.

Museum of Fine Arts Gift Shop
Copley Place. ☎ **617/536-8818.**

Faneuil Hall Marketplace, South Market Building. ☎ **617/720-1266.**

For those who don't have the time or the inclination to visit the museum, these delightful branches are packed with prints, cards, books, educational toys, and reproductions of jewelry contained in the museum's collections. You may even be inspired to make the trip to the real thing.

Peabody Museum Gift Shop
11 Divinity Ave., Cambridge. ☎ **617/495-2248.**

A short distance from Harvard Square, this shop sells folk art and handmade crafts from all over the world, from African sculpture to Chinese porcelain to Native American art and jewelry, all at excellent prices.

The Shop at the Union
356 Boylston St. ☎ **617/536-5651.**

Proceeds from the sale of this shop's home, garden, and personal accessories, antiques, needlework, handmade children's clothes, toys, and confections benefit the Women's Educational and Industrial Union, a nonprofit educational and social-service organization founded in 1877. Look for the golden swan over the door.

INSIGNIA MERCHANDISE

Boston University Bookstore
660 Beacon St. ☎ **617/267-8484.**

The BU crest, mascot (a terrier), or name appears somewhere on at least a floor's worth of clothing and just about any other item with room for a logo.

✪ The Harvard Shop
52 John F. Kennedy St., Cambridge. ☎ **617/864-3000.**

Kids in shopping malls from Jacksonville to Juneau are wearing Harvard shirts in every color of the rainbow and every outlandish pattern under the sun. Visit the Harvard Shop for authentic Harvard paraphernalia a few blocks from the school itself.

JEWELRY & WATCHES

John Lewis, Inc.
97 Newbury St. ☎ **617/266-6665.**

The imaginative women's and men's jewelry at this museum-like shop suits both traditional and trendy tastes. The pieces that mark you as a savvy Bostonian are the earrings, necklaces, and bracelets made of hammered silver (or gold) circles.

Swatch Store
57 John F. Kennedy St. (in the Galleria Mall). ☎ **617/864-1227.**

Swatch watch fiends will find mecca in Harvard Square at the largest Swatch store in the world, also the home of the Swatch Museum (a collection of every design since 1983). There's also a Swatch kiosk at the Shops at Prudential Center.

LOBSTER

If you were most moved by the fresh seafood in Boston and want to share some with a friend, all three of the businesses listed below will pack up a top-quality live lobster, ship it overnight, and make someone at home very happy.

Bay State Lobster
379-395 Commercial St. ☎ **617/523-7960.**

James Hook & Co.
15 Northern Ave. (at Atlantic Ave.). ☎ **617/423-5500.**

Legal Seafoods Fresh by Mail
Logan Airport Terminal C. ☎ **800/477-5342** or 617/569-4622.

MALLS/SHOPPING CENTERS

CambridgeSide Galleria
100 CambridgeSide Pl., Cambridge. ☎ **617/621-8666.**

This three-level mall has three large department stores—**Filene's** (☎ 617/621-3800), **Lechmere** (☎ 617/491-2000), and **Sears** (☎ 617/252-3500)—and more than 100 specialty stores. In addition to the usual suspects, you'll find **Abercrombie & Fitch's** traditional sportswear (☎ 617/494-1338), **Gloria Jean's Coffee Beans** (☎ 617/577-1424), and **J. Crew** (khakis, sweaters and other casual clothing, ☎ 617/225-2739). There are also three restaurants, a food court, and the **Sports Museum of New England** (see Chapter 7, "What to See & Do in Boston," for more information). The mall's business center provides office services such as fax machines and typing. Strollers and complimentary wheelchairs are available.

To get to the Galleria, take the Green Line to Lechmere and walk two blocks, or take the Red Line to Kendall Square, then the free shuttle bus, which runs every 10 minutes Monday to Saturday from 10am to 9:30pm and Sunday from 11am to 7pm. There's plenty of parking in the garage beneath the mall.

✪ Copley Place
100 Huntington Ave. ☎ **617/375-4400.**

Since it opened in 1985, Copley Place has set the standard for upscale shopping in Boston, and its convenient location near the Westin and Marriott hotels and the "Pru" makes it a crossroads for office workers, film fans, out-of-towners, and enthusiastic consumers. You can while away a couple of hours or a whole day shopping and dining here and at the adjacent Shops at Prudential Center (see below) without ever going outdoors.

Some of Copley Place's 100-plus shops will be familiar from the mall at home, but this is emphatically not a suburban shopping complex that happens to be in the city. The real draw are the famous designer stores that don't have another branch elsewhere in Boston: **Caswell-Massey** (☎ 617/437-9292), **Gucci** (☎ 617/247-3000), **Joan & David** (☎ 617/536-0600), **Liz Claiborne** (☎ 617/859-3787), **Louis Vuitton** (☎ 617/437-6519), **Polo Ralph Lauren** (☎ 617/266-4121), **Tiffany** (☎ 617/353-0222), and a suitably classy "anchor" department store, **Neiman Marcus** (☎ 617/536-3660).

Even if you plan to head straight to the 11-screen movie theater, leave time to walk around and examine the design. The six-block, $500 million complex is situated on the border between the Back Bay and the South End neighborhoods. There's pink marble everywhere, incorporated into the exterior and paving the floors, and a skylit atrium is graced with a 60-foot-high waterfall sculpture.

Copley Place is open Monday through Saturday from 10am to 7pm, and Sunday noon to 6pm. Some stores have extended hours, and the theaters and some restaurants are open through late evening. Public transportation is your best bet: Take the Green Line to Copley Square and walk two blocks, or use the tunnel that runs underground from the Orange Line, commuter rail, and Amtrak stops at Back Bay station. By car, the Massachusetts Turnpike eastbound has a Copley exit. Park in the Copley Place garage (☎ **617/375-4488**), off Huntington Avenue at Exeter Street. To pay a reduced rate, have your ticket validated when you make a purchase. Time limits may apply during the day.

Faneuil Hall Marketplace
Between North, Congress, and State sts. and I-93. ☎ **617/338-2323.**

The original festival market didn't become wildly popular and widely imitated by accident, and as Faneuil Hall Marketplace moves into its third decade, the complex changes constantly to appeal to visitors as well as natives wary of its touristy reputation. Faneuil Hall itself has been refurbished, and the lower floors harken back to its retail roots. The Quincy Market Colonnade, in the central building, houses a gargantuan selection of food and confections. The bars and restaurants always seem to be crowded, and the shopping is terrific.

In and around the five buildings surrounded by brick and stone plazas, the mixture of shops is one you'll see all over—"only in Boston" combined with "only at every mall in the country." Marketplace Center and the ground floors of the North Market and South Market buildings have lots of chain outlets, which are a magnet for many, a distraction to some. Most of the unique offerings are under Quincy Market's canopies on the pushcarts piled high with crafts and gifts, and in the market buildings, often upstairs or downstairs. The only way to find what suits you is to explore. Just a few of the shops you'll find are the **Boston Pewter Company** (☎ 617/523-1776), **Celtic Weavers** (☎ 617/720-0750), **Kites of Boston** (☎ 617/742-1455), **Political Americana** (☎ 617/523-3377), and **Whippoorwill Crafts** (☎ 617/523-5149). Not unique except in scale is the **Limited** (☎ 617/742-6837), a separate building seven stories tall.

Shop hours are Monday to Saturday 10am to 9pm and Sunday noon to 6pm. The Colonnade opens earlier, and most bars and restaurants close later. Take the Blue Line to Government Center or the Orange Line to Haymarket, and just follow the crowds. If you must drive, there's parking in the Government Center garage off Congress Street and the marketplace's own crowded garage off Atlantic Avenue.

The Garage
36 John F. Kennedy St., Cambridge. No phone.

Wander up the corkscrew ramp to the boutiques and shops (a record store, a bookstore, a jewelry store, and two stores carrying assorted sci-fi paraphernalia) on the upper levels of this little mall, or stay on the main floor and have a light or filling meal at **Formaggio's Deli** (☎ 617/547-4795) or the **Coffee Connection** (☎ 617/492-4881).

The Shops at Prudential Center
800 Boylston St. ☎ **800/SHOP-PRU** or 617/267-1002.

In the early '90s, the poorly lit, windswept plaza level of the "Pru" was completely renovated, enclosed, and reopened as the Shops at Prudential Center, an instant hit. In addition to **Lord & Taylor** (☎ 617/262-6000) and **Saks Fifth Avenue** (☎ 617/262-8500), there's a food court, a "fashion court," a post office, more than 40 shops and boutiques and five restaurants. Alongside the most famous of the restaurants, Legal Sea Foods, is **Legal Sea Foods Marketplace** (☎ 617/267-5566). The arcades are dotted with vendors selling gifts, souvenirs, and novelty items off pushcarts. There's outdoor space front and back if you need some fresh air, and if you're planning a picnic, at ground level on Boylston Street is a **Star Market** supermarket (☎ 617/267-9721). Complimentary strollers and wheelchairs are available.

The Shops at Prudential Center are open Monday through Saturday 10am to 8pm, and Sunday 11am to 6pm. The restaurants and food court stay open later.

MARKETS

Farmers' Markets
City Hall Plaza, Monday and Wednesday
Copley Square, Tuesday and Friday

Massachusetts farmers and growers under the auspices of the state Department of Food and Agriculture (☎ 617/227-3018) dispatch trucks filled with whatever's in season to the heart of the city from July through November. Depending on the time of year, you'll have your pick of berries, herbs, tomatoes, squash, pumpkins, and corn, just to name a few.

Haymarket
Blackstone St. between North and Hanover sts. No phone.

Adjacent to Faneuil Hall Marketplace and the North End, Haymarket is a produce market, open Friday and Saturday only, where prices are great but shoppers are forbidden to touch the merchandise. Trust your eyes—a stall with beautiful peppers may have tired-looking bok choy, and vice versa—or skip shopping altogether and just watch the boisterous scene as vendors hawk their wares and elderly women slug it out with weekend chefs for the freshest items. In addition to produce from the stalls, you'll find meats and cheeses at the shops on Blackstone Street.

MEMORABILIA

✪ Boston City Store
Faneuil Hall, lower level. ☎ **617/635-2911.**

A great, wacky idea, the Boston City Store sells the equivalent of the contents of the municipal attic and basement, from old street signs (look for your name) to used office equipment and furniture. The selection changes regularly according to what's outlived its usefulness or been declared surplus, but you'll always find lucky horseshoes from the mounted police for $5 apiece. Closed Sunday and Monday.

✪ **Nostalgia Factory**

336 Newbury St. ☎ **800/479-8754** or 617/236-8754.

This is a don't-miss stop if you decide to hit Newbury Street, and maybe even a reason to go there. The Nostalgia Factory has gained national attention for its million-piece collection of old advertising, all for sale and arranged in monthly exhibits according to themes (breakfast foods, cleaning products, cars, and so on). You'll also find an enormous collection of original movie posters of all ages, as well as old-fashioned sheet music.

MUSIC

Briggs & Briggs

1270 Massachusetts Ave., Cambridge. ☎ **617/547-2007.**

Briggs & Briggs has been known for its huge selection of sheet music since 1889.

HMV

1 Brattle Sq., Cambridge. ☎ **617/868-9696.**

On the second floor of an imposing building overlooking Harvard Square, HMV allows you to listen to your selections before making your purchase. They're experts on special orders, too. HMV has a Downtown Crossing store at 24 Winter St. (☎ 617/357-8444).

Tower Records

360 Newbury St. (at Massachusetts Ave.). ☎ **617/247-5900.**

One of the largest record stores in the country, Tower boasts three floors of records, tapes, compact discs, videos, periodicals, and books. The Harvard Square branch, at 95 Mount Auburn St. (☎ 617/876-3377), is smaller but still quite impressive.

PERFUME

✪ **Colonial Drug**

49 Brattle St., Cambridge. ☎ **617/864-2222.**

The perfume counter at Colonial Drug is a perfect example of what happens when a store decides to do one thing exactly right. You can choose from more than 900 fragrances with the help of the gracious staff members, who remain unflappable even during Harvard Square's equivalent of rush hour, Saturday afternoons in the fall.

SECONDHAND CLOTHING

Boomerangs

60 Canal St. ☎ **617/723-2666.**

It's not all used, and it's not all clothing, but the designer duds donated to benefit the AIDS Action Committee and the store's minimalist design are so classy, you'll forget you're in a warehouse building near North Station.

Chic Repeats

117 Newbury St. ☎ **617/526-8580.**

The snob appeal is off the charts at these consignment boutiques (for women's and children's clothing) sponsored by the Junior League of Boston. The carry fancy clothing at down-to-earth prices.

SHOES

Helen's Leather Shop

110 Charles St. ☎ **617/742-2077.**

Native Texans have been known to visit Helen's just to gaze upon the boots. Many are handmade from exotic leathers, including ostrich, buffalo, and snakeskin (of many varieties). Name brands such as Tony Lama and Dan Post are also available, along with a large selection of other leather goods.

Jasmine/Sola

37A Brattle St., Cambridge. ☎ **617/354-6043.**

You'll have an unobstructed view of the cutting edge at this ultrachic Harvard Square boutique, where the men's and women's fashions are as trendy as the spectacular shoe collections.

TOYS

FAO Schwarz

440 Boylston St. ☎ **617/262-5900.**

The giant teddy bear at the corner of Berkeley St. is the first indication that you're in for a rollicking good time, and a teddy bear wouldn't steer you wrong. A branch of the legendary New York emporium, FAO Schwarz stocks top-quality toys, dolls, stuffed animals, games, books, and vehicles (motorized and not). Children can happily spend hours here, and should you happen to find yourself out shopping without a child, go in anyway—the store is on the first floor of an office building, and nobody has to know you're buying that Barbie for yourself.

✪ Joie de Vivre

1792 Massachusetts Ave., Cambridge. ☎ **617/864-8188.**

Joie de Vivre's selection of toys for adults (and sophisticated children) is beyond compare. The kaleidoscope collection alone is worth the trip to this little shop outside Porter Square, and you'll also find salt-and-pepper shakers, jewelry, note cards, puzzles, and games that take you back to your childhood (if your parents shopped at upscale toy stores like this one).

Learningsmith

25 Brattle St., Cambridge. ☎ **617/661-6008.**

Children and parents alike will be delighted with Learningsmith. It offers an excellent selection of toys, games, and other activities that are fun and (shh!) educational.

VINTAGE CLOTHING

Keezer's

140 River St., Cambridge. ☎ **617/547-2455.**

Generations of local college students have been outfitted with their first (and often only) tuxedo at this second-hand clothing institution just south of Central Square. The terrific prices also extend to excellent non-formal designer wear and a decent women's section.

Oona's
1210 Massachusetts Ave. ☎ **617/491-2654.**

From accessories and costume jewelry to dresses nice enough to get married in, Oona's, just outside Harvard Square, has an extensive selection of vintage clothing and good prices.

10 Boston After Dark

Countless musicians, actors, and comedians went to college or otherwise got their start in Boston, and it's a good place to check out rising stars and promising unknowns. You may get the first look at the next Tracy Chapman, Jack Lemmon, Billy Joel or Rosie O'Donnell. And you'll certainly be able enjoy the work of established artists. They perform with one of the world's best symphony orchestras, with a prestigious ballet company, at top-of-the-line jazz and rock clubs, in shows bound for Broadway or out on tour, at a new outdoor venue that overlooks the harbor, and at a spanking-new arena that has introduced rock fans to something revolutionary: air-conditioning. The FleetCenter, which opened in September 1995 behind ancient Boston Garden, has a ventilation system that makes visitors forget the days when acts touring in the summer skipped Boston for health reasons.

For up-to-date entertainment listings, consult the "Calendar" section of the Thursday *Boston Globe,* the "Scene" section of the Friday *Boston Herald,* and the Sunday arts sections of both papers. The weekly *Boston Phoenix* (published on Thursday and available on newsstands all week) has especially good club listings, and the twice-monthly *Improper Bostonian* has extensive live music listings.

GETTING TICKETS Two major ticket agencies serve Boston. Ticketmaster (☎ **617/931-2000**) and Next Ticketing (☎ **617/426-NEXT**) both levy service charges that are calculated per ticket (not per order). To avoid the service charge, visit the venue in person. If you wait until the day before or the day of a performance, you'll sometimes have access to tickets that were held back for one reason or another and have just gone on sale.

DISCOUNT TICKETS Yankee thrift is artistically expressed at the BosTix booths at Faneuil Hall Marketplace and in Copley Square, where same-day tickets to musical and theatrical performances (subject to availability) are on sale for half price. Credit cards are not accepted, and there are no refunds or exchanges. Check the board for the day's offerings. BosTix (☎ **617/723-5181**) also offers full-price advance ticket sales, discounts on more than 100 theater, music, and dance events, as well as tickets to museums, historical sites, and attractions in and around Boston. Both locations are open Tuesday through Saturday from 10am to 6pm (half-price tickets go on sale at 11am), and on Sunday from 11am to 4pm. The Copley Square booth is also open Monday from 10am to 6pm.

Impressions

The Bostonians take their learning too sadly: culture with them is an accomplishment rather than an atmosphere; their "Hub," as they call it, is the paradise of prigs.
—Oscar Wilde, "The American Invasion" (1887)

Their hotels are bad. Their pumpkin pies are delicious. Their poetry is not so good.
—Edgar Allan Poe, *Broadway Journal* (1845)

Tonight I appear for the first time before a Boston audience—4,000 critics.
—Mark Twain, letter (1869)

1   The Performing Arts

Year-round, you'll be able to find a performance that fits your taste and your budget, be it a touring theater company or a children's chorus. The biggest names in classical music, dance, theater, jazz, and world music often appear as part of the **Bank of Boston Celebrity Series** (20 Park Plaza, Boston, MA 02116; ☎ 617/482-2595, or 617/482-6661 for Celebrity Charge). It's a subscription series that also offers tickets to individual events that take place at Symphony Hall, Jordan Hall, the Wang Center, and the DeCordova Museum. Call or write for a brochure.

The **Hatch Shell** on the Esplanade (☎ 617/727-1300, ext. 555) is an amphitheater best known as the home of the Boston Pops' Fourth of July concerts. Almost every other night in the summer, free music and dance performances and films take over the Hatch Shell stage to the delight of the crowds on the lawn.

MAJOR CONCERT HALLS & AUDITORIUMS

Berklee Performance Center
136 Massachusetts Ave. ☎ **617/266-7455** (concert line) or 617/266-1400, ext. 261.

The Berklee College of Music's theater features the work of faculty members, students, and professional recording artists. Offerings are heavy on jazz and folk, but the Center does offer plenty of other options.

Boston Center for the Arts
539 Tremont St. ☎ **617/426-7700** (events line) or 617/426-0320 (box office).

Five performance spaces make the BCA the place to go in the South End for contemporary theater, music, and dance.

Jordan Hall
30 Gainsborough St. ☎ **617/262-1120**, ext. 700 (concert line) or 617/536-2412.

The New England Conservatory of Music's auditorium was completely renovated in 1995, sparking a lively debate about whether the excellent acoustics were ruined, enhanced, or unchanged. Because the refurbishment greatly improved the condition of the hall, even those who were appalled at first are coming around.

Sanders Theatre
45 Quincy St. (corner of Cambridge St.), Cambridge. ☎ **617/496-2222**. Closed June–July.

In Memorial Hall on the Harvard campus, 111-year-old Sanders Theatre was a multipurpose facility before there was such a thing—it's a lecture hall as well as a performance space that features professional big names in classical and world music as well as cultural variety shows.

Symphony Hall

301 Massachusetts Ave. (at Huntington Ave.). ☎ **617/266-1492,** 617/CON-CERT for program information, or 617/266-1200 for Symphony Charge.

Symphony Hall, home to one of the world's best orchestras, is, appropriately, a world-class performance venue. And when the Boston Symphony Orchestra and the Boston Pops are away, the visitors (touring groups from around the country) play classical and chamber music.

Wang Center for the Performing Arts

270 Tremont St. ☎ **617/482-9393** or 617/931-2000 (Ticketmaster).

The Wang Center, the Theater District's art deco palace, is home to the Boston Ballet and numerous touring dramatic, dance, and music companies. On some Monday evenings in the winter, the Wang Center reverts to its roots as a movie theater and shows classic films on its enormous screen.

CLASSICAL MUSIC

✪ Boston Pops

Performing at Symphony Hall, 301 Huntington Ave. (at Massachusetts Ave.). ☎ **617/266-1492,** 617/CON-CERT for program information, or 617/266-1200 for Symphony Charge. Tickets $32–$43 for tables, $12–$27 for balcony seats.

From early May until early July, members of the Boston Symphony Orchestra lighten up, performing a repertoire that ranges from light classical to show tunes to popular music (hence the name), sometimes with celebrity guest stars. The floor seats at Symphony Hall are replaced with tables and chairs, and waitresses serve drinks and light refreshments. New conductor Keith Lockhart hit town in 1995 (he made his official debut in 1996) and quickly became so popular that he is now as much of a draw as the "Pops" themselves. Performances are Tuesday through Sunday evenings, and a week of free outdoor concerts is given at the Hatch Shell on the Charles River Esplanade in early July, including the traditional Fourth of July concert, which features fireworks.

✪ Boston Symphony Orchestra

Performing at Symphony Hall, 301 Huntington Ave. (at Massachusetts Ave.). ☎ **617/266-1492,** 617/CON-CERT for program information, 617/266-1200 for Symphony Charge. Tickets $22–$67. Rush tickets $10 (on sale 9am Fri; 5pm Tues, Thurs). Rehearsal tickets $12.

The Boston Symphony Orchestra, one of the world's greatest, was founded in 1881 and has performed at acoustically perfect Symphony Hall since 1900. Music director Seiji Ozawa is the latest in a line of distinguished conductors presiding over an institution known for contemporary as well as classical music—the 1996 Pulitzer Prize in music was awarded to *Lilacs,* composed for voice and orchestra by George Walker and commissioned by the BSO.

The season runs from October through April. The orchestra performs most Tuesday, Thursday, and Saturday evenings, Friday afternoons, and some Friday evenings. A limited number of rush tickets (one per person) are available on the day of the performance for Tuesday and Thursday evening and Friday afternoon programs. Wednesday evening and Thursday morning rehearsals are sometimes open to the public.

Handel & Haydn Society

300 Massachusetts Ave. ☎ **617/266-3605.**

The Handel & Haydn Society, established in 1815, uses period instruments and techniques in its orchestral and choral performances, and still manages to be as cutting-edge as any ensemble in town. Under the direction of Christopher Hogwood, the society prides itself on its creative programming of "historically informed" concerts. The season runs year-round with performances at Symphony Hall, Jordan Hall, and Sanders Theatre.

ADDITIONAL OFFERINGS

Students and faculty members at two prestigious institutions perform frequently during the academic year; admission is usually free. For information, contact the **New England Conservatory of Music** (290 Huntington Ave.; ☎ **617/262-1120,** ext. 700) or Cambridge's **Longy School of Music** (1 Follen St.; ☎ **617/876-0956**).

DANCE

Boston Ballet

19 Clarendon St. ☎ **617/695-6950,** or 617/931-ARTS (Ticketmaster). Performing at the Wang Center; tickets can be purchased at the box office at 270 Tremont St., Mon–Sat 10am–6pm. Tickets $21–$65. Student rush tickets $12 (one hour before curtain).

Boston Ballet's reputation seems to jump up a notch every time someone says, "Oh, so it's not just *The Nutcracker.*" The country's fourth-largest dance company is a holiday staple, but during the rest of the season (October through May), it builds on 33 years of top-notch productions and a wide-ranging repertoire that includes classic story ballets as well as contemporary works.

Dance Umbrella

380 Green St., Cambridge. ☎ **617/492-7578.**

Contemporary dance aficionados will want to check out the latest offerings sponsored by Dance Umbrella. It commissions and presents international, culturally diverse works—a broad definition that covers everything from acrobats to well-known groups such as the Mark Morris and Bill T. Jones/Arnie Zane companies. Performances take place at venues in Boston and Cambridge, most often at the Emerson Majestic Theatre (☎ **617/824-8000**), 219 Tremont St., Boston.

THEATER

Local and national companies, professional and amateur actors, classic and experimental drama combine to make the theater scene in Boston and Cambridge a lively one. Boston is one of the last cities where pre–Broadway tryouts are held, presenting the opportunity for an early look at a classic (or classic flop) in the making. It's also a popular destination for touring companies of established Broadway hits.

You'll find most of the shows headed to or on hiatus from Broadway in the Theater District, at the **Colonial Theatre** (106 Boylston St.; ☎ 617/426-9366), the **Shubert Theatre** (265 Tremont St.; ☎ 617/426-4520), the **Wang Center for the Performing Arts** (270 Tremont St.; ☎ 617/482-9393), and the **Wilbur Theater** (246 Tremont St.; ☎ 617/423-7440).

The excellent local theater scene boasts the **Huntington Theatre Company,** which performs at the Boston University Theatre (264 Huntington Ave.; ☎ 617/266-0800), and the **American Repertory Theatre** (ART), which makes its home at Harvard University's Loeb Drama Center (64 Brattle St., Cambridge; ☎ 617/547-8300). Some ART projects and independent productions are at the **Hasty Pudding Theatre** (12 Holyoke St., Cambridge; ☎ 617/496-8400).

The Loeb and the Hasty Pudding also feature student productions. Other college venues include the **Tufts Arena Theater** (☎ 617/627-3493) in Medford, the **Spingold Theatre** (☎ 617/736-3400) at Brandeis University in Waltham, and various performance spaces at **MIT** (☎ 617/253-4720, Theater Arts Hotline).

The Charles Playhouse and the Larcom Theatre are two local institutions that offer entertaining family theater.

Charles Playhouse, Stage II

74 Warrenton St. ☎ **617/426-5225.** Tickets $23–$28.

The "comic murder mystery" *Shear Madness* has been turning the stage at the Charles Playhouse into a unisex hairdressing salon since 1980, and the show's never the same twice. One of the original audience-participation productions, the play changes at each performance as the spectator-investigators question suspects, reconstruct events, and then name the murderer. *Shear Madness* is the longest-running nonmusical play in theater history. Performances are Tuesday through Friday at 8pm, Saturday at 6:30 and 9:30pm, and Sunday at 3 and 7:30pm.

Larcom Theatre

13 Wallis St., Beverly. ☎ **508/927-3677.** Tickets $10–$15.

Three generations of magicians make up Le Grand David and His Spectacular Magic Company, a nationally acclaimed troupe of illusionists that performs at two theaters (in addition to the Larcom, the troupe does shows at the Cabot Street Cinema Theater at 286 Cabot St.) in Beverly, about 40 minutes from Boston by car. Le Grand David has received national attention for his sleight-of-hand and has performed at Easter parties at the White House.

A MAJOR MUSIC FESTIVAL

Tanglewood

Lenox. ☎ **413/637-5165,** or 617/266-1492 out of season. Music Shed $14–$74, lawn $11.50–$15.50; open rehearsals $12.50. To order tickets, call Symphony Charge (☎ 800/274-8499) or Ticketmaster (☎ 800/347-0808).

The Berkshires are a favorite summer destination for many eastern Massachusetts residents, including the Boston Symphony Orchestra. Tanglewood concerts, from the end of June through the end of August, also feature guest conductors and artists and run the gamut from classical to popular music, from chamber music to jazz. Acoustically, the best seats are in the Koussevitzky Music Shed and Seiji Ozawa Hall, but a picnic on the lawn is delightful, especially for those attending with children. Performances are Friday and Saturday evenings and Sunday afternoons, open rehearsals are on Saturday mornings, and student concerts take place on certain evenings. From Boston, Lenox is about a three-hour drive on the Massachusetts Turnpike.

CONCERT VENUES

FleetCenter

Causeway St. ☎ **617/624-1000** (events line) or 617/931-2000 (Ticketmaster).

The state-of-the-art FleetCenter opened in September 1995, replacing legendary (but woefully outdated) Boston Garden as the home of the Bruins (hockey), the Celtics (basketball), and touring rock and pop artists. Concerts are presented in the round or in the arena stage format.

Great Woods Center for the Performing Arts

Route 140, Mansfield. ☎ **508/339-2333,** or 617/426-NEXT to order tickets. Web site http://www.greatwoods.com.

For major mainstream and alternative rock acts out on summer tours, with a smattering of folk, pop, country, reggae, and light classical, head about an hour south of Boston to a sheltered (it has a roof but no sides) auditorium surrounded by a lawn.

✪ Harborlights Pavilion

Fan Pier, Northern Ave. ☎ **617/374-9000,** or 617/426-NEXT to order tickets. Web site http://www.harborlights.com.

Soft rock, pop, folk, and jazz performers draw crowds to a giant white tent on the waterfront that holds single-level seating for evening events from June through September. The pleasant, airy setting, convenient location, and reasonable size make Harborlights a wonderful place to spend a few musical hours.

CONCERT SERIES

Free Lunchtime Concerts

Federal Reserve Bank of Boston, 600 Atlantic Ave. ☎ **617/973-3453.**

Jazz, classical, and contemporary music are performed by local groups in the bank's auditorium, Thursdays at 12:30pm.

King's Chapel Noon Hour Recitals

58 Tremont St. ☎ **617/227-2155.** Donations requested.

Organ, instrumental, and vocal solos fill this historic building with music and make for a pleasant break along the Freedom Trail. Concerts are at 12:15pm on Tuesdays.

Fridays at Trinity

Trinity Church, Copley Sq. ☎ **617/536-0944.** Donations accepted.

Trinity Church features organ recitals by local and visiting artists on Fridays at 12:15pm. The music can be soothing and inspiring, and it's a good time to look around this architectural showpiece.

MUSIC IN THE MUSEUMS

A treat for the eyes and the ears, live music at a museum could be the offering that helps you plan your visit. If you're off on a sojourn to Lexington and Concord, see if your trip coincides with one of the occasional concerts at the **DeCordova Museum and Sculpture Park** (☎ 617/259-8355), on Sandy Pond Road in nearby Lincoln.

✪ Isabella Stewart Gardner Museum

280 The Fenway. ☎ **617/734-1359.** Concert fees, including museum admission, are $15 for adults, $9 for seniors and students, $7 youths 12–17.

This glorious museum, originally a home modeled after a 15th-century Venetian palazzo, features soloists and chamber music in the Tapestry Room Saturday and Sunday at 1:30pm, from September through April.

Museum of Fine Arts, Boston

465 Huntington Ave. ☎ **617/267-9300** or 617/369-3300. Tickets $13, $11 seniors and students, $4 under 12.

The "Concerts in the Courtyard" series brings folk and jazz artists to the MFA on Wednesday evenings from June through September. Performances begin at 7:30pm, and the courtyard opens to picnickers at 6pm. Bring your own dinner, or buy it there. Chair seating is limited, and you're encouraged to bring a blanket or lawn chair.

2 The Club & Music Scene

The club scene in Boston and Cambridge is multifaceted and constantly changing, but somewhere out there is a good time for everyone, regardless of age, clothing style, musical tastes, and budget. Check the *Phoenix,* the *Improper Bostonian,* the

"Calendar" section of the Thursday *Globe,* the "Scene" section of the Friday *Herald,* or the *Tab* while you're making plans.

Boston offers lively but relatively brief nights on the town; a lot of action is packed into a relatively short time. Most bars close by 1am, clubs close at 2, and the "T" shuts down between 12:30 and 1am. The drinking age is 21, and a valid driver's license or passport is required as proof of age (this, of course, is true all over the U.S., but in Boston it is actually enforced, and with a consistency that has made the city notorious for "carding" all prospective buyers of alcohol—or even cigarettes—who look younger than 35).

At most nightspots, unless otherwise specified, the admission or cover charge varies according to the night of the week and the entertainment offered, from up to $3 for a bar to more than $20 for a well-known jazz headliner.

COMEDY CLUBS

The days when every motel and truck stop had a "laff lounge" are, mercifully, coming to an end. Boston was one of the first cities with a hopping comedy-club scene, and as the fad fades, the quality clubs are hanging in there and skimming off the cream. The goal is to emulate Jay Leno, Steven Wright, Paula Poundstone, Rosie O'Donnell, Denis Leary, Anthony Clark, and others who parlayed success in Boston into careers in film and TV (or at least TV commercials).

✪ Comedy Connection at Faneuil Hall

Quincy Market, Upper Rotunda. ☎ **617/248-9700.** Cover $8–$30.

A large room with a clear view from every seat, the oldest original comedy club in town, established in 1968, draws top-notch talent from near and far. Big-name national acts lure crowds, and the openers are often just as funny but not as famous—yet. You can order munchies or come early for dinner (served only before the show). Shows are nightly at 8:30 with late shows on Friday and Saturday at 10:30pm. The cover charge seldom tops $12 during the week, but soars for a big name appearing on a weekend.

Nick's Comedy Stop

100 Warrenton St. ☎ **617/482-0930.** Cover $8–$15.

This reliable old entertainment venue in the Theater District doesn't have the cachet of the Comedy Connection, but it's still a good time. Shows are nightly at 8:15 or 8:30; late shows are on Saturday and some Sundays at 10:30.

FOLK

Platform shoes are back, punk rock is back, and you might say folk is back. In Cambridge, where folk musicians crowd the sidewalks of Harvard Square (Tracy Chapman is just one famous "graduate" of the Square's street performance scene), you'd say it never left.

Club Passim

47 Palmer St., Cambridge. ☎ **617/492-7679.** Cover $5–$10.

Passim has launched more careers than the mass production of acoustic guitars—Joan Baez, Suzanne Vega, and Michelle Shocked started out here. Located in a basement on the street between buildings of the Harvard Coop, this coffeehouse is still building on a reputation for more than 30 years of nurturing new talent and showcasing established musicians. There's live music four to six nights a week and Sunday afternoons, and coffee and light meals are available all the time. Open Sunday to Thursday 11am to 11pm, Friday and Saturday 11am to 4am.

Ⓢ **Nameless Coffee House**

3 Church St., Cambridge. ☎ **617/864-1630.** Cover $3.

The Nameless represents a foot in the door for a wide range of musicians. The young crowd comes for the promising talent, the storytelling, and the free refreshments (coffee, cider, tea, cocoa, and cookies). Don't worry if half the patrons suddenly get up and leave—they're probably friends of the person who just finished performing. Open September to June, Friday and Saturday 7:30pm to midnight.

ROCK

Mama Kin and Mama Kin Music Hall

41 Lansdowne St. ☎ **617/536-2100.**

Members of the Boston-based band Aerosmith co-own Mama Kin and the adjacent music hall, which opened in December 1994 to wide acclaim and instant popularity. You probably won't see Steven Tyler, but you will see up-and-comers early in the week, and more established artists toward the weekend. Open seven nights; doors open at 8 or 9. Some shows are 19-plus (you must be 21 to drink alcohol).

Middle East

472–480 Massachusetts Ave., Central Sq., Cambridge. ☎ **617/864-EAST.** Cover $3–$9.

The name notwithstanding, the Middle East is a restaurant that books progressive and alternative rock in two rooms (upstairs and downstairs) seven nights a week. Serving tasty Middle Eastern fare (try the chicken shish kebab sandwiches and the stuffed grape leaves) and showcasing some of the best local talent as well as bands with international reputations, the Middle East has become a very popular hangout among young people in Boston and Cambridge. The bakery next door, under the same management, showcases acoustic artists most of the time and belly-dancers on Wednesdays. Many shows are 18-plus (you must be 21 to drink alcohol); some are all-ages.

Ⓞ **The Rathskeller (The Rat)**

528 Commonwealth Ave. ☎ **617/536-2750** or 617/536-6508 (concert line). Cover downstairs only, $5–$7.

For 23 years, the Rathskeller (known far and wide as "the Rat") has been in the heart of Kenmore Square dispensing rock and riding out the fickle whims of musical fashion. There's nothing glamorous here—just live music Tuesday through Sunday nights and Sunday afternoons in the street-level room, tables and pool tables upstairs, and pretty good food. The menu features chicken and burgers and also includes vegetarian offerings and sandwiches. The restaurant is open 11am to 10pm, the bar until 2am.

T.T. the Bear's Place

10 Brookline St., Central Sq., Cambridge. ☎ **617/492-0082** or 617/492-BEAR (concert line). Cover $6–$10.

T.T.'s admits people 18 and older (you must be 21 to drink alcohol), and its cutting-edge alternative music attracts a young crowd. Entertainment is offered from 9pm on. Monday night is Stone Soup Poetry night, and on Sunday Ethiopian food is served from 2pm to midnight.

JAZZ AND BLUES

If you're partial to jazz and blues, consider timing your visit to coincide with the ***Boston Globe*** Jazz Festival (☎ 617/929-2000), usually scheduled for the third week of June. Constellations of jazz and blues stars (large and small) appear at after-work, evening, and weekend events, some of them free, many of them out-doors. The festival wraps up with a free Sunday afternoon program at the Hatch Shell.

On summer Fridays at 6pm, the **Waterfront Jazz Series** (☎ **617/635-3911**) brings amateurs and professionals to Christopher Columbus Park, on the water-front, for a refreshing interlude of music and cool breezes.

❖ House of Blues
96 Winthrop St., Cambridge. ☎ **617/491-BLUE.** Cover $6–&15; $3 Saturday matinees.

The original House of Blues packs 'em in for evening and weekend matinee shows, attracting big names and hordes of fans. Reservations are highly recommended. Call the above number for tickets and show times. (See Chapter 6, "Dining," for a full listing.)

Regattabar
In the Charles Hotel, 1 Bennett St., Cambridge. ☎ **617/661-5000** or 617/876-7777 (Concertix). Tickets $5–$25.

The Regattabar features a selection of local and international artists considered the best in the area; Cassandra Wilson, Ellis and Branford Marsalis, Tito Puente, the Count Basie Orchestra, and Karen Akers have appeared within the past two years. The large third-floor room holds about 200 and has a 21-foot picture window over-looking Harvard Square. Buy tickets in advance from Concertix (there's a $2 per ticket service charge) or try your luck at the door one hour before the performance is scheduled to start. Open Tuesday through Saturday and some Sundays with one or two performances per night.

Ryles Jazz Club
212 Hampshire St., Inman Sq., Cambridge. ☎ **617/876-9330.** Cover $5–$10.

During an evening at Ryles you can shuttle back and forth between the two levels or settle on one floor for the evening. True music buffs turn out here, for dining in the downstairs room with tunes in the background, and a wide variety of first-rate jazz, world beat, and Latin performances upstairs. Both levels offer good music and a friendly atmosphere. Open Tuesday through Sunday and some Mondays.

Scullers Jazz Club
In the Doubletree Guest Suites Hotel, 400 Soldiers Field Rd. ☎ **617/783-0811.** Cover $6–$23.

Overlooking the Charles River, Scullers books top jazz singers and instrumentalists in a comfortable, newly expanded room. Shows are usually Monday through Saturday. There's also an excellent monthly dinner/jazz show.

Wally's
427 Massachusetts Ave. ☎ **617/424-1408.** No cover.

Wally's is an intimate jazz and blues cavern on a busy corner in the South End. Every night a notably diverse crowd—gay, straight, black, white, affluent and indi-gent—lines up outside for free jazz performances by students and professors from the Berklee College of Music, local ensembles, or, infrequently, internationally renowned jazz musicians. Though there is no cover, patrons are expected to buy at least one drink (alcoholic or non).

Willow Jazz Club
699 Broadway, Somerville. ☎ **617/623-9874.** Cover $5–15$.

Alternative jazz is featured here nightly. Unless you're a student from nearby Tufts University, the Willow isn't particularly easy to get to, but the top-notch acts lure jazz aficionados from miles around.

ECLECTIC

○ Johnny D's

17 Holland St., Davis Sq., Somerville. ☎ **617/776-2004** or 617/776-9667 (concert line).

This family-owned and -operated restaurant and music club is one of the best in the area. You might catch acts on national and international tours, or acts that haven't been out of the 617 area code. The music ranges from zydeco to rock, rockabilly to jazz, blues to ska. The food's even good. Johnny D's is worth a long trip, but it's no more than 20 minutes from Harvard Square on the Red Line.

Kendall Cafe

233 Cardinal Medeiros Way, Cambridge. ☎ **617/661-0093.** Cover $5–$10.

This friendly neighborhood bar near the Kendall Square office-retail complex showcases three up-and-coming artists each night. Folk predominates, but you might also hear rock, country, or blues in the tiny back room, where waitresses weave through the crowds to serve bar food. Or just stay at the bar—you won't be able to see, but it's such a small place that you'll have no trouble hearing. Shows are Monday through Saturday at 8pm, Sunday at 4pm.

The Western Front

343 Western Ave., Cambridge. ☎ **617/492-7772.** Cover $3—$10.

This casual spot on a nondescript street south of Central Square attracts a multi-cultural (p.c. Cambridge parlance for "integrated") crowd for world-beat music, blues, and especially reggae. Sunday is dance-hall reggae night, but the infectious music makes every night dancing night. Open Tuesday through Sunday from 5pm to 1:30am; live entertainment begins at 9.

DANCE CLUBS

Boston has its share of dance clubs, and caters to a wide range of musical tastes. Many dance clubs are located in the area surrounding Kenmore Square (there's a particularly impressive strip along Lansdowne St.), which makes club-hopping easy, but also means that on Friday and Saturday nights the neighborhood is completely overrun by college students. If you don't feel like dealing with huge crowds of loud teenagers and 20-somethings clogging the streets, stick to slightly more upscale and isolated nightspots.

○ Avalon

15 Lansdowne St. ☎ **617/262-2424.** Cover $5–$10.

A cavernous space divided into several levels, with a full concert stage, private booths and lounges, large dance floors, and a spectacular light show, Avalon is either great fun or a sensory overload. When the stage is not in use, you'll hear international music and, particularly on Saturday (suburbanites' night out), mainstream dance hits. The dress code calls for jackets, shirts with collars, and no jeans or athletic wear; the crowd is slightly older than at Axis. Open Thursday ("Euro night") to Sunday (gay night).

Axis

13 Lansdowne St. ☎ **617/262-2437.** Cover $6–$8.

Progressive rock and "creative dress" attract a young crowd to Axis. There are special nights for hard rock, heavy metal, and alternative rock. Open Tuesday to Sunday 10pm to 2am.

The Roxy

279 Tremont St., in the Tremont House. ☎ **617/338-7699.** Cover $8–$10.

A hotel ballroom-turned-dance club, the Roxy boasts excellent deejays and live music, a huge dance floor, concert stage, and balcony (perfect for checking out the action down below). It's open from 10:30 to 2am on Thursday (African-American professional night), Friday (international night), Saturday (top 40 night), and some Sundays for special events.

Zanzibar
1 Boylston Pl. ☎ **617/351-2560.** Cover $5.

An atrium with a balcony and 25-foot-tall palm trees is the setting in which enthusiastic dancers gyrate to contemporary hits. The upscale clientele take breaks from dancing in the billiard room. The dress code (jackets and shirts with collars for men; no jeans or athletic wear) is strictly enforced. Open Wednesday to Saturday 9pm to 2am.

3 The Bar Scene

Bostonians may have some quibbles with the TV show "Cheers," but no one ever complained that the concept of a neighborhood bar where the regulars practically lived was implausible. From the Littlest Bar (the actual name of a closet-sized downtown watering hole) to the Bull & Finch (on which "Cheers" is based), the neighborhood bar occupies a vital niche in Boston. It tends to be a fairly insular one—as a stranger, you probably won't be confronted, but don't expect to be welcomed with open arms, either. This is one area where you can and probably should judge a book by its cover. If you poke your head in the door and see people who look like you and your friends, give it a whirl. The patrons will tend to reflect the neighborhood. You'll find wrung-out lawyers drinking $7 martinis all over downtown, yuppies quaffing Chardonnay in the Back Bay, beeper-wearing doctors having a quick Guinness on Beacon Hill, middle-aged ex-hippies and artists drinking ale in funky Cambridge taverns, and townies drinking Bud from the bottle in the college areas. And, of course, there are students everywhere. Have your ID ready.

BARS, PUBS & LOUNGES

The Alley Cat Lounge
1 Boylston Pl. ☎ **617/351-2510.** Cover $2.

In an alley off Boylston St. near the Public Garden, the Alley Cat caters to a post-collegiate crowd more interested in dancing and mingling than in seeing and being seen. Open Thursday through Sunday.

Bill's Bar
7 Lansdowne St. ☎ **617/421-9678.** Cover (around $5) for live music only.

Less glitzy than some of its neighbors, Bill's is a real hangout, with a great beer menu and communal television watching (ask about "Melrose Place" night). Bill's takes pride in its jukebox and sometimes features live local bands, and you might take a crack at singing karaoke. Open nightly, 9:30pm to 2am.

Bull & Finch Pub
84 Beacon St. ☎ **617/227-9605.** No cover.

If you're out to impersonate a native, try not to be completely shocked when you walk into the Bull & Finch and realize it looks nothing like the bar on "Cheers" (the outside does, though). It really is a neighborhood bar, but today it's far better known for attracting legions of out-of-towners, who find good pub grub, drinks, and plenty of souvenirs. Food is served from 11am to 1:15am.

Cantab Lounge
738 Massachusetts Ave., Cambridge. ☎ **617/354-2685.** Cover $3–$5.

Follow your ears to this friendly neighborhood bar in Central Square: Whenever the door swings open at night, the deafening music comes spilling out. The source on weekends most likely is Little Joe Cook and the Thrillers, headliners since the early '80s whose catchy tunes you'll dance to all night and hum all the next day (because your ears will still be ringing).

Custom House Lounge
In the Bay Tower, 60 State St., Faneuil Hall Marketplace. ☎ **617/723-1666.** No cover.

The view from the 33rd floor of any building is bound to be amazing; from 60 State St., you'll be mesmerized by the harbor, the airport, and Faneuil Hall Marketplace directly below. There's live music and dancing from 5 to 7:30pm Monday to Thursday and from 9pm to 1am Friday and Saturday.

Hard Rock Cafe
131 Clarendon St. ☎ **617/353-1400.** No cover.

Still going strong since its establishment in London in 1971, the Hard Rock Cafe chain is perhaps the most successful restaurant network in the world, and this link in the chain is a fun one. The restaurant menu leans toward salads, burgers, and sandwiches (including the house specialty, "pig sandwich"). The bar is shaped like a guitar; the taped music bounces off all the hard surfaces and keeps the volume at a dull roar; stained-glass windows glorify rock stars; and the room is decorated with memorabilia of John Lennon, Jimi Hendrix, Elvis Presley, the local heroes from Aerosmith, and others. T-shirts and other goods are for sale at the Hard Rock store. Open daily 11am to 1am for food and until 2am at the bar.

The Harvest
44 Brattle St., Cambridge. ☎ **617/492-1115.** No cover.

Just off Harvard Square, the Harvest caters to Harvard faculty members, visiting celebrities, and young professionals. The outdoor terrace, with its umbrellas and trees strung with tiny lights, is delightful on a warm summer evening. (See chapter 6, "Dining," for restaurant listing.)

Top of the Hub
Prudential Center. ☎ **617/536-1775.** No cover.

Boasting a panoramic view of greater Boston, Top of the Hub is 52 stories above the city. There is music and dancing nightly. Dress is casual but neat. (See chapter 6, "Dining," for restaurant listing.)

HOTEL BARS

Many popular nightspots are associated with hotels and restaurants (see chapters 5 and 6); the following are worth a separate listing.

The Bar at the Ritz
15 Arlington St. (in the Ritz-Carlton). ☎ **617/536-5700.**

Famous for its superb martinis, the Bar at the Ritz is an elegant room with walnut paneling, an intimate fireplace, and a magnificent view of the Public Garden. The spectacular setting and service make it an excellent place for a celebration. Open Monday to Saturday from 11:30am to 1am, Sunday from noon to midnight. Lunch is served Monday to Saturday from noon to 2:30pm.

✪ Bristol Lounge
200 Boylston St. (in the Four Seasons Hotel). ☎ **617/351-2000.**

This is a perfect choice after the theater, after work, or any time at all. An elegant room with soft lounge chairs, a fireplace, and fresh floral arrangements, it features a fabulous weekend dessert buffet. There's live piano music every day. An eclectic menu is available from 11am to 11:30pm.

Plaza Bar
In the Copley Plaza Hotel, Copley Sq. ☎ **617/267-5300.**

The sophisticated Plaza Bar is a splendid setting for romance. The lighting is muted, the chairs and couches are of soft leather, and the drinks and food are excellent. The entertainment is a cabaret-style singer-pianist. Proper dress is required. Open Monday to Saturday, 5pm to midnight.

IRISH BARS

The Black Rose
160 State St. ☎ **617/742-2286.**

Sing along with the authentic entertainment—you might be able to make out the tune on a fiddle over the din—at this jam-packed tavern at the edge of Faneuil Hall Marketplace. Open daily 11:30am to 2am.

The Harp
85 Causeway St. ☎ **617/742-1010.**

Live music on Thursday, Friday, and Saturday draws a young crowd that mills about in lines along Causeway Street, across from Boston Garden and the FleetCenter. Open Monday through Saturday 11am to 2am, Sunday noon to midnight.

Mr. Dooley's Boston Tavern
77 Broad St. ☎ **617/338-5656.**

The selection of imported beers on tap may be more of a draw than the live music at this Financial District spot, but sometimes a brogue and an expertly poured Guinness are all you need. Open daily 11am to 2am.

GAY/LESBIAN CLUBS & BARS
In addition to the clubs listed below, one night a week is gay night at some mainstream clubs. At Avalon, Sunday is gay night, and it's the largest gathering of gay men in town; the Sunday night "tea dance" at Ryles Jazz Club caters to women. Check *Bay Windows* or the monthly *Phoenix* supplement "One in Ten" for listings.

Club Cafe
209 Columbus Ave. ☎ **617/536-0966.**

This trendy South End spot draws men and women for conversation (the noise level is reasonable), dining, live music in the front room, and video entertainment in the back room, called Moonshine. Open daily from 2pm to 2am; dinner is served from 5:30 to 10 Sunday through Wednesday, and until 11 Thursday through Saturday. Sunday brunch starts at 11:30am.

Coco's Lazy Lounge & Dance Club
965 Massachusetts Ave. ☎ **617/427-7807.**

Boston's only women-only club boasts three dance spaces filled with patrons of all descriptions and often features lesbian performers. In a desolate part of town, Coco's offers valet parking and is well-known to local cabbies. Open Friday and Saturday 9pm to 2am.

Luxor
69 Church St., Park Sq. ☎ **617/423-6969.**

This 10-year-old video bar draws a diverse crowd to see the latest music clips and compilations of snippets from movies and old TV shows concocted by the veejays. Downstairs is Jox, a small sports bar. Open daily, 4pm to 1am.

4   More Entertainment

BREW PUBS

One of first cities to develop microbrewery overload was Boston, where hanging copper tubing on a brick wall and proclaiming yourself a master brewer is practically an industry. If you're secretly harboring such aspirations, check out these places first. None have cover charges, but beers here will set you back at least $3 a mug, more if there's something fancy involved. The pubs are also popular dining destinations—all have kitchens serving full meals, some as good as the brews, and all a step up from burgers and nachos.

Back Bay Brewing Company
755 Boylston St. ☎ **617/424-8300.**

The goofiness factor is a bit high here—the motto is "Where Boston Hops," and microbrew offerings include Freedom Trail Ale and Park Square Porter. The selection of four ales and one lager changes regularly. Nevertheless, this bar and restaurant located across from the Prudential Center and filled with locals and visitors will grow on you, especially if you like your bar food sophisticated. Open daily, 11:30am–midnight.

Boston Beer Works
61 Brookline Ave. ☎ **617/536-2337.**

Across the street from Fenway Park, this cavernous microbrewery with vats right out on the floor is chaotic anyway, and before and after Red Sox games it's a madhouse. Visit during a road trip for excellent bitters and ales, seasonal concoctions such as Bambino Ale, lager with blueberries floating in it (not as dreadful as it sounds), hard cider, and particularly the cask-conditioned offerings, seasoned in wood till they're as smooth as fine wine. Sweet potato fries make a terrific snack, but don't plan on being able to hear anything your friends are saying. Open daily, 11:30–12:45am.

Brew Moon Restaurant & Microbrewery
115 Stuart St. ☎ **617/523-6467.**

Hand-crafted beer meets wonderful food at this popular Theater District bar-bistro, where little plates of bar food mingle with freshly made brews. The dark ales are especially celebrated; if you're looking for something lighter, try the Grasshopper IPA. Open daily, 11:30–2am. In the works at press time was a branch in Harvard Square at 50 Church St.

Commonwealth Brewing Company
138 Portland St. ☎ **617/523-8383.**

Boston's first brew pub is still going strong 10 years after it started the trend. It doesn't hurt that the "Commonwealth Brewery," as you'll often hear it called, is a block from North Station and madly popular with the crowds heading to the FleetCenter (and before that, Boston Garden). The English-style brews are top-notch and served alone and in traditional combinations such as the snakebite (lager and hard cider) and shandy (ale and lemon soda). Here, too, the food is quite good—try the hummos plate. Open from 11:30am till midnight Sunday through Thursday, till 1am

Friday and Saturday. There's live music and dancing downstairs Friday and Saturday nights.

John Harvard's Brew House
33 Dunster St., Cambridge. ☎ **617/868-3585.**

This subterranean Harvard Square hangout pumps out English-style brews in a club-like setting (see if you can make out the sports figures in the stained-glass windows) and prides itself on its food. The selection of beers changes regularly, and aficionados will have fun sampling John Harvard's Pale Ale, Nut Brown Ale, Pilgrim's Porter, and brewmeister Tim Morse's other concoctions. Open daily 11:30am–3:30pm and 5–10pm.

MOVIES

The number of mainstream film outlets downtown shrinks by the year (this is the age of the multiplex), but there are several excellent outlets for art, independent, and classic films.

It doesn't get much more mainstream than **Free Friday Flicks at the Hatch Shell** (☎ **617/727-1300,** ext. 555), family films (*The Wizard of Oz* or *Raiders of the Lost Ark* are favorites) shown on a large screen in the amphitheater on the Esplanade usually used for concerts. The lawn in front of the Hatch Shell turns into a giant, car-less drive-in as hundreds of people picnic and wait for the sky to grow dark. Bring sweaters in case the breeze off the river grows chilly.

Classic films are shown as part of series at the **Boston Public Library** (☎ **617/536-5400**) and the **Museum of Fine Arts** (☎ **617/267-9300**). The BPL's free films are usually organized by actor or a theme (say, all Audrey Hepburn or all sports). There is a charge for films at the MFA, which also features premieres of independent and avant-garde films. Ticket prices (usually less than $10) vary according to the filmmaker's reputation and whether the showing is a premiere. The area theaters closest to true revival houses—they feature lectures and live performances in addition to foreign and classic films—are the **Brattle Theater** (40 Brattle St., Cambridge; ☎ **617/876-6837**) and the **Coolidge Corner Theater** (290 Harvard St., Brookline; ☎ **617/734-2500**).

For inexpensive second- and third-run movies as well as classic and independent films, check the offerings at one of the local colleges. Most are open to the public. For showings at **Boston College, Boston University, Harvard University,** the **MIT Film Society, Northeastern University,** and **Tufts University,** check the local publications.

LECTURES

The Thursday *Globe* "Calendar" section is the best place to check for listings of lectures, readings, and talks on a wide variety of subjects, often at one of the local colleges.

The longest-running public lecture series in the country is presented by **Ford Hall Forum.** Tickets are sold on a subscription basis, but there are usually extra seats in the large lecture halls, and the public is admitted free of charge 15 minutes before the program begins. The range of topics is what you might find in a good civics class—politics, the American justice system, civil rights—all discussed by experts who range from high-ranking government officials to celebrated professors. For advance program information write to Ford Hall Forum, 271 Huntington Ave., Suite No. 240, Boston, MA 02115 (☎ **617/373-5800**).

The **John F. Kennedy Library Public Forums** (☎ **617/929-4571**) offer discussions of political and social issues. They're free, but reservations are suggested.

POOL

Plenty of bars have pool tables, but at the new, relatively upscale pool palaces that have invaded Boston, drinking is what you do while you're playing pool, not the other way around.

Boston Billiard Club

126 Brookline Ave. ☎ **617/536-POOL.** Weekend evenings $11 an hour for two players. Each additional person $2 an hour. Prices lower during the day and on weekday nights.

The Boston Billiard Club, decorated with hunting prints, brass wall sconces, and a mahogany bar, has 42 pool tables and has been rated the number one billiard club in the United States by *Billiard Digest Magazine.* There is full liquor service at the tables. Open Monday to Saturday 11am to 2am, Sunday noon to 2am.

Flat Top Johnny's

1 Kendall Sq., Cambridge. ☎ **617/494-9565.** Weekend evenings $10 an hour for two players, $12 for three or more players. Prices lower during the day and on weekday nights.

A spacious room with a huge bar and 12 red-topped tables, Flat Top Johnny's has a neighborhood feel despite being in a rather sterile office-retail complex. Open daily 3pm to 1am.

The Grill & Cue

256 Commercial St. ☎ **617/227-4454.** Weekends $18 an hour. Prices lower on weekdays.

What a concept: pool as an activity for a special occasion. At the prices it charges, the Grill & Cue had better be pretty special, and it is, with half a dozen purple felt-covered tables arranged around the second floor of an excellent restaurant (see chapter 6, "Dining," for a complete listing).

Jillians Entertainment

145 Ipswich St. (corner of Lansdowne St.). ☎ **617/437-0300.** $9–$11 an hour for pool; $7 for a round of golf.

The owners of Jillians revived an interest in pool in Boston and have continued expanding their horizons as entertainment technology has become more sophisticated. A 50,000-square-foot roller rink was transformed into this 56-table pool parlor, and the complex has branched out to include 18 holes of miniature golf, a 200-game video midway, darts, table tennis, and more. There are three full bars and a cafe. Jillians is open Monday to Saturday from 11am to 2am and Sunday from noon to 2am. Children under 18 can be admitted with an adult before 7 on Saturday and Sunday.

11 Side Trips from Boston

Boston is surrounded by sights and attractions of great beauty and historical significance. All of the destinations described here—Lexington and Concord; the North Shore and Cape Ann; and Plymouth—make fascinating, manageable day trips and also offer enough diversions to fill several days.

1 Lexington & Concord

The actual shooting in the Revolutionary War started here, and parts of Lexington and Concord still look much as they did in April 1775, when the fight for independence began. Start your visit in Lexington, where colonists and British troops first clashed. On the border with Concord, spend some time at Minute Man National Historical Park, investigating the historic traces of the landmark battle that raged there over 200 years ago. Decide for yourself where the "shot heard round the world" was fired, bearing in mind that Ralph Waldo Emerson, who wrote the line, lived in Concord. Emerson's house and Orchard House, the family home of Louisa May Alcott (also in Concord), are open to visitors. Some attractions are closed from November through March or mid-April, opening after Patriots Day, which is celebrated on the Monday closest to April 19.

LEXINGTON

6 miles NW of Cambridge; 9 miles NW of Boston

Lexington, now a Boston suburb, takes great pride in its history. The Battle Green, next to a bustling business district, is an open common where you can see the oldest Revolutionary War monument, the Minuteman statue. Occupying British troops marched from

Lexington

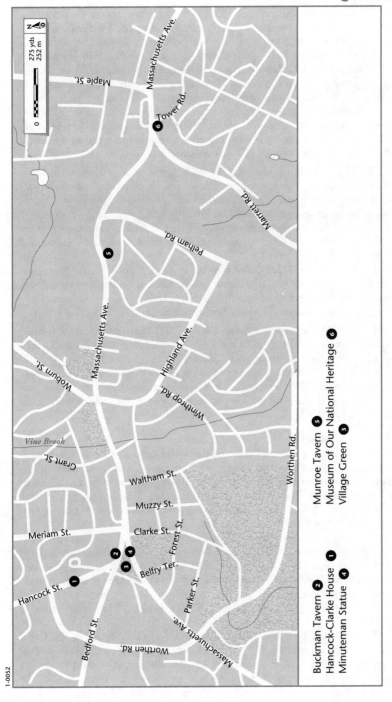

Buckman Tavern ②
Hancock-Clarke House ①
Minuteman Statue ④

Munroe Tavern ⑤
Museum of Our National Heritage ⑥
Village Green ③

1-0052

Boston to Lexington late on April 18, 1775 (no need to memorize the date; you'll hear it everywhere), preceded by patriots Paul Revere and William Dawes, who sounded the warning. Members of the local militia, called "Minutemen" for their ability to prepare for battle quickly, were waiting at the Buckman Tavern. John Hancock and Samuel Adams, leaders of the revolutionary movement, were sleeping (or trying to) at the Hancock-Clarke House nearby. The warning came around midnight, followed about five hours later by some 700 British troops headed to Concord to destroy the rebels' military supplies. Ordered to disperse, the patriots—fewer than 100, and some accounts say 77—stood their ground. Nobody knows who started the shooting, but when it was over, eight militia members were dead, including a drummer boy, and 10 were wounded.

GETTING THERE Modern-day Route 2A approximates Paul Revere's path, but if you attempt to follow it during rush hour, you'll wish you had a horse of your own. Instead, take Route 2 from Cambridge through Belmont, and follow the signs for Route 4/225 into the center of Lexington. Or take Route 128 (I-95) to Exit 31 and proceed to the center of town. Massachusetts Avenue (a continuation of the street you might have seen in Boston and Cambridge) also runs through central Lexington.

The **MBTA** (☎ 617/222-3200) runs bus routes 62, "Bedford," and 76, "Hanscom," from Alewife Station (the last stop on the Red Line) to Lexington every hour during the day and every half hour during rush periods, Monday to Saturday. There is no public transportation between Lexington and Concord.

ESSENTIALS In Lexington the **area code** is 617. Sketch maps and information about Lexington can be obtained at the Chamber of Commerce's **Visitor Center,** at 1875 Massachusetts Avenue (☎ 617/862-1450).

Before you set out, you might want to read "Paul Revere's Ride" by Henry Wadsworth Longfellow, a classic but historically questionable poem that will provide you with a sense of the area's important history by dramatically chronicling the events of April 18–19, 1775.

WHAT TO SEE AND DO

Start your visit at the **Visitor Center,** on the Battle Green. It's open daily, 9am–5pm (9:30am–3:30pm, October through June). A diorama and the accompanying narrative illustrate the Battle of Lexington. The **Minuteman Statue** on the Green is of Capt. John Parker, who commanded the Minutemen. When his troops were confronted by the British, Parker called: "Stand your ground. Don't fire unless fired upon, but if they mean to have a war, let it begin here!"

Three important destinations in Lexington were among the country's first "historic houses" when restoration of them began in the 1920s. All three are operated by the **Lexington Historical Society** (☎ 617/862-1703), which conducts guided tours. Hours are Mon–Sat 10am–5pm and Sun 1–5pm, April through October. Admission is $4 per house, $10 for all three; children 6–16, $1 per house, $2 for all three; family (two adults, two children), $20 for all three. The last tour starts at 4:30; tours take 30–45 minutes.

The **Buckman Tavern,** at 1 Bedford St., is the only building still on the Green that was there on April 19, 1775, and the interior is restored to its appearance that day. Built around 1710, the tavern is where the Minutemen gathered to wait for word of British troop movements, and where they brought their wounded after the conflict. Within easy walking distance, the **Hancock–Clarke House,** at 36 Hancock Street, is where Samuel Adams and John Hancock were sleeping when Paul Revere arrived. They were evacuated to nearby Woburn. The house, furnished in colonial style, was originally built in 1698 and also houses the Historical Society's museum of the Revolution. The **Munroe Tavern,** about one mile from the Green at 1332 Massachusetts Avenue, was the British headquarters and, after the battle, infirmary. The building dates to 1690 and is packed with fascinating artifacts and furniture carefully preserved by the Munroe family, including the table and chair President Washington used when he dined here in 1789.

The **Museum of Our National Heritage** (33 Marrett Rd., Route 2A, at Massachusetts Ave.; ☎ **617/861-6559** or 617/861-9638) is known for exhibits that explore history through popular culture. The installations in the six exhibition spaces change regularly, but you can start with another dose of the Revolution, the exhibit "Lexington Alarm'd." Other topics have ranged from gravestones to jigsaw puzzles, auto racing to George Washington. Lectures, concerts, and family programs are also offered. Admission is free. The museum is open Monday to Saturday from 10am to 5pm and on Sunday from noon to 5pm. Closed Thanksgiving Day, Christmas Eve, Christmas Day, New Year's Eve, and New Year's Day. Sponsored by the Scottish Rite of Freemasonry.

WHERE TO DINE

Bel Canto
1709 Massachusetts Ave., Lexington. ☎ **617/861-6556.** Main courses $5.50–$10.95; pizzas $5.75–$13.95; sandwiches and salads $4.50–$6.75. AE, DISC, MC, V. Mon–Thurs 11am–10pm; Fri–Sat 11am–11pm; Sun noon–10pm. ITALIAN/PIZZA.

One floor above the bustle of downtown Lexington, at peak times this local favorite can seem almost equally busy, but you won't feel rushed. The spacious, whitewashed room fills with the chatter of diners sharing garlic bread and pizza or generous servings of pasta. The antipasto plate of meats, cheeses, tuna and marinated vegetables makes an excellent appetizer to share. Pizzeria Regina pizza is a recent addition to the menu, but you can get thin-crust pizza anywhere—go for the thick whole-wheat crust with your choice of more than two dozen toppings that is a house specialty. Or try the light, filling chicken lasagna. There's also a children's menu ($3.50–$3.95) with kid-size portions of Italian favorites.

CONCORD
18 miles NW of Boston; 15 miles NW of Cambridge; 6 miles W of Lexington

GETTING THERE From Lexington, take Route 2A west from Route 4/225 at the Museum of Our National Heritage; follow signs reading "Battle Road" along the route the British took between the towns. From Boston and Cambridge, take Route 2 into Lincoln. Where the road makes a sharp left, go straight onto Cambridge Turnpike, and follow signs to "Historic Concord."

There is no bus transportation to Concord, but MBTA (☎ **617/222-3200**) commuter trains take about 45 minutes from North Station in Boston and stop at Porter Square in Cambridge. There is no public transportation between Lexington and Concord.

ESSENTIALS The **area code** in Concord is 508. The **Chamber of Commerce** (☎ **508/369-3120**) maintains an information booth on Heywood Street, one block southeast of Monument Square, from April to October. It's open weekends in April and daily May to October, 9:30am–4:30pm. One-hour tours are available starting in May on Saturday, Sunday, and Monday holidays, or on weekdays by appointment. Group tours are available by appointment.

Concord

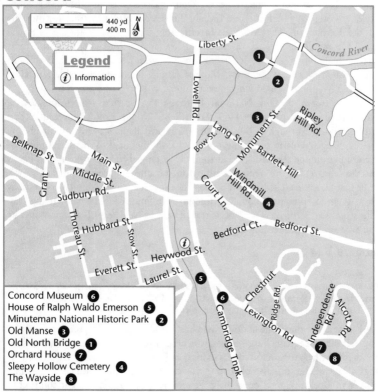

Legend

ⓘ Information

Concord Museum ⑥
House of Ralph Waldo Emerson ⑤
Minuteman National Historic Park ②
Old Manse ③
Old North Bridge ①
Orchard House ⑦
Sleepy Hollow Cemetery ④
The Wayside ⑧

1-0053

Concord also has a web site (http://www.concordma.com), which includes interesting and useful information for visitors.

Concord (pronounced "conquered") revels in its legacy as a center of groundbreaking thought and its role in the country's political and intellectual history. Not only did the first official battle of the Revolutionary War take place here at the North Bridge (now part of Minute Man National Historical Park), Concord has also been an important literary center for over a century. After just a little time in this charming town, you may find yourself adopting the local attitudes toward two of its most famous residents: Ralph Waldo Emerson, who is popularly regarded as a well-respected uncle figure, and Henry David Thoreau, everyone's favorite eccentric cousin. These two contemplative writers wandered the countryside nearby and did much of their writing and reflecting in Concord, forming the nucleus of a group of several important writers who settled in the town. By the middle of the 19th century, Concord was the center of the transcendentalist movement, and the former homes of Emerson, Thoreau, Nathaniel Hawthorne, and Louisa May Alcott are open to visitors. Lovers of literature can also visit Sleepy Hollow Cemetery, where all of the above-mentioned are buried.

MINUTE MAN NATIONAL HISTORICAL PARK Minute Man National Historical Park preserves the scene of the first Revolutionary War battle at Concord on (all together now) April 19, 1775. After the skirmish at Lexington, the British moved on to Concord in search of stockpiled arms, but they had already been moved by the colonial militiamen, who had been warned of the British advance and were preparing to confront them. The Minutemen crossed the North Bridge, evading the British soldiers who were standing guard, and waited for reinforcements on a nearby hilltop. In Concord the British searched homes and burned any guns they found. The Minutemen saw the smoke and, thinking the British were razing their town to the ground, attacked the soldiers standing guard at the bridge. The gunfire that ensued is remembered as "the shot heard round the world," the opening salvo of the revolution.

The park is open daily, year-round. To reach the North Bridge, follow Monument Street out of Concord Center until you see the parking lot on the right; park and walk a short distance to the bridge (a reproduction), stopping along the way to read the narratives and hear the audio presentations. On one side of the bridge is a plaque commemorating the British soldiers who died in the Revolutionary War; on the other is the *Minuteman* statue by Daniel Chester French.

You can also start your visit at the **North Bridge Visitor Center** (174 Liberty St., off Monument St.; ☎ **508/369-6993**), which overlooks the Concord River and the bridge from a hilltop. A diorama illustrates the battle, and exhibits include uniforms, weapons, and tools of colonial and British soldiers. Park rangers are on duty if you have questions. Outside, picnicking is allowed, and the scenery (especially the fall foliage) is lovely. The North Bridge Visitor Center is open daily in summer 9am–5:30pm and in winter 9:30am–4pm. Closed Christmas and New Year's Day.

At the Lexington end of the park, the **Battle Road Visitor Center** (off Route 2A, one-half mile west of I-95; ☎ **617/862-7753**) is open mid-April through October, 9am–5pm daily. The park includes the first four miles of the Battle Road, the route the defeated British troops took as they left Concord on the afternoon of April 19, 1775. At the visitor center, you can see displays about the Revolution and a diorama illustrating the path of the retreat. A pamphlet is available that describes a self-guided tour of a small part of the park near the visitor center; on summer weekends, park rangers lead tours—call ahead for specific times.

WHAT TO SEE AND DO

Concord Museum

Lexington Rd. and Cambridge Tpke. ☎ **508/369-9763**. Admission $6 adults, $5 seniors, $3 students and children 15 and under, $12 families. Apr–Dec, Mon–Sat 9am–5pm, Sun noon–5pm; Jan–Mar, Mon–Sat 11am–4pm, Sun 1–4pm. Follow Lexington Rd. out of Concord Center and bear right at the museum onto Cambridge Tpke.; the entrance is on the left. Parking on the road is allowed.

Just when you start to suspect that the only interesting events to ever happen in this area occurred on April 18 and 19, 1775, a visit to the Concord Museum proves otherwise. On the front lawn, what appears to be a shed is actually a replica of the cabin Henry David Thoreau lived in at Walden Pond from 1845–47 (the furnishings are in the museum). Inside, the self-guided tour traces the history of the town. You'll see Native American archaeological artifacts, silver pieces from colonial churches, a fascinating collection of embroidery samplers, and rooms furnished with period furniture and textiles, all with explanatory text that places the exhibits in historical context. One of the lanterns that signaled Paul Revere from the steeple of the Old

North Church is on display, as are the contents of Ralph Waldo Emerson's study arranged the way it was just before he died in 1882, and a collection of Thoreau's belongings. There are changing exhibits in the New Wing throughout the year. The new History Galleries are scheduled to open with an installation called "Why Concord?" in April 1997.

Ralph Waldo Emerson House

28 Cambridge Tpke. ☎ **508/369-2236.** Guided tours $4.50 adults, $3 seniors and children under 17. Call to arrange group tours (10 people or more). Mid-April–Oct, Thurs–Sat 10am–4:30pm, Sun 2–4:30pm. Follow Cambridge Tpke. out of Concord Center; just before you reach the Concord Museum, the house is on the right.

Emerson, a philosopher, essayist, and poet, moved here in 1835—soon after his second marriage, to Lydia Jackson—and remained until his death in 1882. He called Lydia "Lydian," and she called him "Mr. Emerson," as the house staff still does. You'll see original furnishings and some of Emerson's personal effects (the original contents of his study are in the Concord Museum).

The Old Manse

Monument St. at North Bridge. ☎ **508/369-3909.** Guided tours $5 adults, $4 students and seniors, $2.50 ages 6–12, $12 families (three to five people). Mid-Apr–Oct, Mon–Sat 10am–5pm and Sun and holidays 1–5pm. From Concord Center, follow Monument St. about three-eighths of a mile until you see signs for the North Bridge parking lot; the Old Manse is on the left.

The Reverend William Emerson built the Old Manse in 1770 and watched the Battle of Concord from the yard. He died during the Revolutionary War, and the house was occupied for almost 170 years by his widow, her second husband, their descendants—and two friends. Nathaniel Hawthorne and his bride, Sophia Peabody, moved in after their marriage in 1842 and stayed for three years. This is also where Ralph Waldo Emerson (William's grandson) wrote the essay "Nature." Today you'll see mementos and memorabilia of the Emerson and Ripley families and of the Hawthornes, who scratched notes on two windows with Sophia's diamond ring.

Orchard House

399 Lexington Rd. ☎ **508/369-4118.** Guided tours $5.50 adults, $4.50 seniors and students, $3.50 children ages 6–17, $16 families (up to 2 adults and 4 children). Apr–Oct, Mon–Sat 10am–4:30pm, Sun 1–4:30pm. Nov–Mar, Mon–Fri 11am–3pm, Sat 10am–4:30pm, Sun 1–4:30pm. Closed Jan 1–15, Easter, Thanksgiving, Christmas. Follow Lexington Rd. out of Concord Center past the Concord Museum; the house is on the left.

The 1994 movie *Little Women* dramatically increased interest in Louisa May Alcott's best-known work, and in Concord you can visit Orchard House, the home in which the book was set and written (though the movie was filmed elsewhere). Louisa's father, Amos Bronson Alcott, was a writer, educator, philosopher, and leader of the transcendentalist movement. He created the house by joining and restoring two early 18th-century homes already on the 12 acres of land he purchased in 1857. The family lived here from 1858 to 1877, socializing in the same circles as Emerson, Thoreau, and Hawthorne. Bronson Alcott's passion for educational reform eventually led to his being named superintendent of schools, and he ran the Concord School of Philosophy in Orchard House's backyard.

The rest of the Alcott family is equally well known for artistic and cultural contributions, and for being the models for the characters in *Little Women*. Anna, the eldest, was an amateur actress, and May was a talented artist. Elizabeth died before the family moved to Orchard House. Bronson's wife, Abigail May Alcott, was a social activist and frequently assumed the role of family breadwinner—Bronson, as Louisa wrote in her journal, had "no gift for money making."

The Wayside

455 Lexington Rd. ☎ **508/369-6975.** Guided tours $3 adults, free for ages 16 and younger. Mid-Apr–Oct, Thu–Tue 10:30am–4:30pm. Closed Nov–mid-Apr. Follow Lexington Rd. out of Concord Center past the Concord Museum and Orchard House; the Wayside is on the left.

Part of Minute Man National Historical Park, the Wayside was Nathaniel Hawthorne's home from 1852 until his death in 1864. The Alcott family also once lived here, as did Harriett Lothrop, who wrote the *Five Little Peppers* books under the pen name Margaret Sidney and owns most of the current furnishings. A new exhibit, housed in the barn, consists of audio presentations and figures of Louisa May and Bronson Alcott, Hawthorne, and Sidney.

Sleepy Hollow Cemetery

Entrance is on Route 62 West.

Follow the signs for "Author's Ridge" up the hill to the graves of some of the town's literary lights, including the Alcotts, Emerson, Hawthorne, and Thoreau. Emerson's grave, notably lacking in religious symbolism, is marked by a great uncarved quartz boulder. Thoreau's grave is nearby, where he was laid to rest in 1865 in a ceremony in which he was eulogized by his old friend Emerson: "Wherever there is knowledge, wherever there is virtue," Emerson said in bidding his friend good-bye, "wherever there is beauty, he will find a home."

WHERE TO STAY AND DINE

Colonial Inn

48 Monument Sq., Concord, MA 01742. ☎ **800/370-9200** or 508/369-9200. Fax 508/369-2170. 45 rms (some with shower only), 4 suites. A/C TV TEL. Apr–Oct, $159–$165 main inn; $99–$159 Prescott wing; $200–$240 cottage. Nov–Mar, $135–$139 main inn; $95–$135 Prescott wing; $170–$195 cottage. AE, DC, DISC, MC, V.

The Colonial Inn overlooks Monument Square and has since 1716, when the main building was constructed. Additions since it became a hotel in 1889 have left the inn large enough to offer modern conveniences and small enough to feel friendly. The 12 original colonial-era guest rooms (one of which is supposedly haunted) are in great demand, so reserve early if you have your heart set on staying in the main inn. Rooms in the three-story Prescott wing are a bit larger and have country-style decor. The public areas, including a sitting room and front porch, are decorated in colonial style.

In addition to overnight accommodations, the Colonial Inn has two lounges that serve drinks and bar food, and a lovely restaurant that offers salads, sandwiches, and pasta at lunch and traditional American fare at dinner.

Aïgo Bistro

84 Thoreau St. (Route 126), at Concord Depot. ☎ **508/371-1333.** Reservations recommended at dinner. Main courses $7–$9 at lunch, $14–$25 at dinner. Prix fixe dinner (three courses) $16.95. AE, MC, V. Daily 11:30am–2:30pm and 5–10pm. MEDITERRANEAN.

"Aïgo" is Provençal patois for "garlic," which perfumes the air half a block away from this delightful spot. It's pronounced "I go," and you'll want to, for scrumptious food and top-notch service in a sophisticated setting—one dining room overlooks the train tracks, the other is decorated with murals. Settle in on a tapestry banquette, play with the brightly colored salt and pepper shakers, and prepare to be delighted. The emphasis is on garlic and grilling, so you might start with the house-special soup, aïgo bouïdo, a puree of roasted garlic, onion and almond. Carnivores will relish the beef fillet au poivre, served in a cognac and roasted garlic glaze, or pork chop in sage jus with horseradish mashed potatoes. At least two vegetarian entrees (one a daily special risotto) are available. The lunch menu is heavy on salads and sandwiches, served on focaccia. Desserts are few but delectable—try the lavender mascarpone cheesecake.

2 The North Shore & Cape Ann

Cape Ann is a rocky peninsula so enchantingly beautiful that when you hear the slogan "Massachusetts' *other* Cape," you may forget what the first one was. Cape Ann and Cape Cod do share some attributes—scenery, shopping, seafood, traffic—but the smaller cape's proximity to Boston and manageable scale make it a wonderful day trip as well as a good choice for a longer stay. You can explore the area's rich nautical history and its evolution into a popular destination for artists. Cape Ann can be reached from Boston via I-93 and Route 128 in about an hour. Take a more leisurely drive on Route 1A if you want to explore the North Shore towns of Swampscott, Marblehead, and Salem on your way to Gloucester and Rockport, the artists' colony at the tip of Cape Ann.

The **North of Boston Convention & Visitors Bureau** (P.O. Box 642, Beverly, MA 01915; ☎ 800/742-5306 or 508/921-4990) publishes a visitor's guide to the area. And the **Cape Ann Chamber of Commerce** (33 Commercial St., Gloucester, MA 01930; ☎ **800/321-0133** or 508/283-1601) information center is open year-round (summer, weekdays 8am–6pm, Saturday 10am–6pm, and Sunday 10am–4pm; winter, weekdays 8am–5pm).

THE ROAD NORTH OUT OF BOSTON   You'll probably want to travel by car even if your plans include visiting only one town. Although public transportation in this area is good, it doesn't go everywhere, so scheduling may prove difficult, and in many towns the commuter rail station is some distance from the attractions.

Try to plan to visit on a spring, summer, or fall weekday; many parts of this area are ghost towns from November through March, and traffic is brutal on warm weather weekends. To go straight to Gloucester and Rockport (or to start there and work your way back), take I-93 north; where it turns into I-95 (signs point to New Hampshire and Maine), stay left on 128 and take it to the end. The last exit, number 9, puts you in East Gloucester. To take Route 1A, check a map or ask at the front desk of your hotel for directions to the Callahan Tunnel. It's at the heart of a huge construction site and the signs are usually fairly clear, but the whole arrangement is confusing. East Boston is at the other end of the tunnel; ignore signs for the airport and continue on Route 1A north. If you miss the tunnel and wind up on I-93, follow signs to Route 1 and pick up Route 1A in Revere. You can also stay on Route 1 until it converges with I-95 and 128, but the traffic can be unbearable, especially during rush hour.

MARBLEHEAD
15 miles NE of Boston

One of the area's most popular day trips, for residents and visitors alike, is a visit to Marblehead. It's also a good place to spend a night or more. One of the most picturesque neighborhoods in New England is "Old Town" Marblehead, where the narrow, twisting streets lead down to the magnificent harbor that helps make this the self-proclaimed "Yachting Capital of America." There is sailboat racing in the

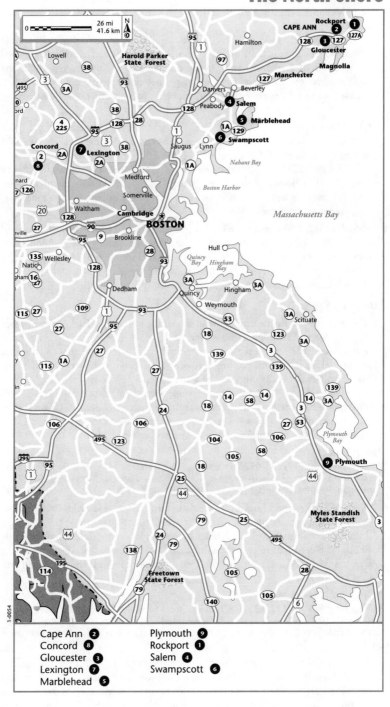

Cape Ann ②   Plymouth ❾
Concord ❽   Rockport ❶
Gloucester ❸   Salem ❹
Lexington ❼   Swampscott ❻
Marblehead ❺

outer harbor all summer, and "Race Week" in July attracts enthusiasts from all over the country.

Marblehead celebrates its history without wallowing in it. As you walk around Old Town, you'll see plaques on the houses bearing the date of construction as well as the names of the builder and original occupant—a history lesson without any studying. Many of the houses have stood since before the Revolutionary War, when Marblehead was a center of merchant shipping. Two historic homes are open for tours.

GETTING THERE   By car, take Route 1A north through Revere and Lynn; pick up Route 129 where you see signs for Swampscott and Marblehead. Or take I-93 or Route 1 to Route 128, then Route 114 through Salem into Marblehead.

MBTA (☎ **617/222-3200**) bus route 441/442 runs from Haymarket (Orange or Green Line) in Boston to downtown Marblehead. The trip takes about an hour. The 441 bus detours to Vinnin Square shopping center in Swampscott; otherwise, both routes are the same.

ESSENTIALS   The **area code** is 617. The **Marblehead Chamber of Commerce** (62 Pleasant St., P.O. Box 76, Marblehead, MA 01945; ☎ **617/631-2868**) publishes a visitor's guide and operates an information booth (daily in season, 10am–5:30pm) on Pleasant Street near Spring Street.

Marblehead also has a web site (http://www.marblehead.com).

WHAT TO SEE & DO

Whatever else you do, be sure to spend some time in **Crocker Park,** on the harbor off Front Street. Especially in the warmer months, when boats jam the water nearly as far as the eye can see, the view is breathtaking. There are benches and a swing, and picnicking is allowed. You may not want to leave, but snap out of it—the view from **Fort Sewall,** at the other end of Front Street, is just as mesmerizing.

Marblehead is a wonderful town for aimless wandering, but try to have enough direction to find the **Lafayette House,** at the corner of Hooper and Union streets. One corner of the house was chopped off to make room for the passage of the Marquis de Lafayette's carriage when he visited the town in 1824.

Abbot Hall

Washington Sq. ☎ **617/631-0528.** Free admission. Year-round, Mon, Tues, Thurs 8am–5pm, Wed 7:30am–7:30pm, Fri 8am–1pm; May–Oct, Fri 8am–5pm, Sat 11am–6pm, Sun 9am–6pm. From the historic district, follow Washington St. up the hill.

The town offices and Historical Commission share Abbot Hall with Archibald M. Willard's famous painting *The Spirit of '76* (you'll probably recognize the drummer, drummer boy, and fife player), which is on display in the Selectmen's Meeting Room. The deed that records the sale of the land by the Native Americans to the Europeans in 1684 is also on view. The building's clock tower is visible from all over Old Town.

✪ Jeremiah Lee Mansion

161 Washington St. ☎ **617/631-1069.** Guided tours $4 adults, $3.50 students, free for children under 10. Mid-May–Oct, Mon–Sat 10am–4pm, Sun 1–4pm. Closed Nov–mid-May. Follow Washington St. until it curves right and heads up the hill to Abbott Hall; the house is on the right.

The prospect of seeing original hand-painted wallpaper in an 18th-century home is reason enough to visit this house, built in 1768 for a wealthy merchant and considered an outstanding example of pre-Revolutionary Georgian architecture. Original rococo carving and other details complement historically accurate room arrangements, and ongoing restoration and interpretation by the Marblehead Historical Society place the 18th- and 19th-century furnishings and artifacts in context. The displays on the third floor draw on the Historical Society's collections of children's furniture, toys, and nautical and military memorabilia. A tip: On the hill between the mansion and Abbott Hall, the private homes at 187, 185, and 181 Washington Street are other good examples of the architecture of this period.

King Hooper Mansion

8 Hooper St., Marblehead. ☎ **617/631-2608.** Tour: Donation requested. Mon–Sat 10am–4pm, Sun 1–5pm. Call ahead; tours are not held during private parties. Where Washington St. curves right at the foot of the hill, bear left; the building is on the left.

Shipping tycoon Robert Hooper got his nickname because he treated his sailors so well, but it's easy to think he was called "King" because he lived like royalty. Located around the corner from the home of Jeremiah Lee (whose sister was the second of Hooper's four wives), the King Hooper Mansion was built in 1728 and gained a Georgian addition in 1747. The period furnishings, though not original, give a sense of the life of an 18th-century merchant prince, from the wine cellar to the third-floor ballroom. The building houses the headquarters of the Marblehead Arts Association, which stages monthly exhibits and runs a gift shop where members' work is sold. The mansion also has a lovely garden; enter through the gate at the right of the house.

WHERE TO STAY

The Chamber of Commerce can provide you with accommodations listings that include many inns and bed-and-breakfasts. If you prefer to use an agency, try **Bed & Breakfast Reservations North Shore/Greater Boston/Cape Cod** (P.O. Box 35, Newtonville, MA 02160; ☎ **800/832-2632** or 617/964-1606; fax 617/332-8572; e-mail bnbinc@ix.netcom.com).

The Nautilus

68 Front St., Marblehead, MA 09145. ☎ **617/631-1703.** 4 rms (none with bath). $55–$60 double. No credit cards. Ask for parking suggestions when you call for reservations.

This guest house is as close to the harbor as you can get without being drenched. Rooms are on the second floor of the home, plain but comfortable, and have semi-private bathroom facilities. Make your reservations well in advance, because the combination of location and cheerful, homey service makes the Nautilus a popular destination.

Pleasant Manor Inn Bed and Breakfast

264 Pleasant St. (Route 114), Marblehead, MA, 01945. ☎ **800/399-5843** or 617/631-5843. 12 rms (some with shower only; one room's bath is across the hall). A/C TV. $68–$80 double. Rates include continental breakfast. No credit cards.

Just outside the historic district, the Pleasant Manor Inn is a three-story Victorian mansion built as a private home in 1872 and operated as an inn since 1923. Innkeepers Richard and Takami Phelan took over in 1975. The spacious rooms open off a magnificent central staircase and are tastefully decorated with Victorian prints and some antiques. Aviation aficionados can request the room where Amelia Earhart stayed. Guests have the use of a tennis court in the backyard. Children are welcome, and smoking is not allowed.

Spray Cliff on the Ocean

25 Spray Ave., Marblehead, MA 01945. ☎ **800/626-1530** or 617/631-6789. Fax 617/639-4563. 7 rms (some with shower only). Memorial Day weekend–late Oct $175–$205 double; lower rates off season. Extra person $25. Rates include continental breakfast, evening

refreshments, and use of bicycles. AE, MC, V. Take Atlantic Ave. (Route 129) to Clifton Ave. and turn east (right if you're driving north, left if you're driving south); parking area is at the end of the street.

Spray Cliff, a three-story Victorian Tudor built in 1910 on a cliff overlooking the ocean, is five minutes from town and a world away. Five of the large, sunny rooms face the water, three have fireplaces, and all are luxuriously decorated in contemporary style with brightly colored accents. Roger and Sally Plauché have run their "romantic, adult inn" on a quiet, residential street one minute from the beach since 1994. Smoking is not permitted.

WHERE TO DINE

The Barnacle

141 Front St. ☎ **617/631-4236.** Reservations not accepted. Main courses $3.95–$12.95 at lunch, $10.95–$15.95 at dinner. No credit cards. Daily 11:30am–4pm and 5–10pm. SEAFOOD.

This unassuming spot doesn't look like much from the street, but at the end of the gangplank-like entrance hall is a front-row seat for the action on the water. Even if you don't land a seat on the deck or along the counter facing the windows, you'll still have a shorebird's-eye view of the mouth of the harbor and the ocean from the jam-packed dining room. The food won't provide much of a distraction, but it's tasty and plentiful. The chowder and fried seafood, especially the clams, are terrific, and there's no better place to quaff a beer and watch the boats sail by.

Driftwood Restaurant

63 Front St., Marblehead. ☎ **617/631-1145.** Main courses $1.60–$9.50. No credit cards. Summer, daily 5:30am–5pm; winter, daily, 5:30am–2pm. DINER/SEAFOOD.

At the foot of State St. next to Clark Landing (the town pier) is an honest-to-goodness local hangout. Whether you're in the mood for pancakes and hash or chowder and a seafood "roll" (a hot dog bun filled with, say, fried clams or lobster salad), join the crowd. The house specialty, served on weekends and holidays, is fried dough, which is exactly as good-tasting and unhealthy as it sounds.

King's Rook

12 State St. ☎ **617/631-9838.** Reservations not accepted. Main courses $4.50–$8. MC, V. Mon–Fri noon–2:30pm; Tues–Fri 5:30–11:30pm; Sat–Sun noon–11:30pm. CAFE/WINE BAR.

There's no better place to complete the sentence "I'm thirsty and I'd like . . ." than this cozy spot, a favorite long before coffeehouses ruled prime-time television. Coffees, teas, hot chocolates, soft drinks, and more than two dozen wines by the glass are available, and the food has a sophisticated flair. The intimate atmosphere and racks of newspapers and magazines make this a great place to linger over a pesto pizza, a salad, or a sinfully rich dessert—and, of course, a beverage.

Kitchen Witch Eatery

78 Front St. ☎ **617/639-1475.** Most items under $6. No credit cards. Summer, Sun–Thurs 11am–10pm, Fri–Sat 11am–11pm. DELI.

This storefront oasis, where you can eat in the tiny dining area or order everything you need for a picnic, is across the street from Clark Landing. Sandwiches, salads, and soups are fresh and delicious, and the muffins and other baked goods are excellent. This is also the perfect place to grab some ice cream or frozen yogurt (in dozens of flavors) and set off to explore the town.

SALEM

17 miles NE of Boston; 4 miles NW of Marblehead

Salem was settled in 1626 (four years before Boston) and later became known around the world as a center of merchant shipping and the China trade, but it's internationally famous today for a seven-month episode in 1692. The witchcraft trial hysteria led to 20 deaths, three centuries of notoriety, countless lessons on the evils of prejudice, and dozens of bad puns ("Stop by for a spell" is a favorite slogan).

Unable to live down its association with witches, Salem has embraced it. The high school sports teams are called the Witches, and the logo of the *Salem Evening News* is a silhouette of a witch. Today you'll see plenty of witch-associated attractions as well as reminders of Salem's rich maritime history.

GETTING THERE By car, take Route 1A north into downtown Salem, being careful in Lynn, where the road turns left and immediately right. Or take I-93 or Route 1 to Route 128, then Route 114 into downtown Salem. Once there, follow the signs, which are color-coordinated—brown for the Visitor Center, blue for parking, and green for museums and historic sites.

From Boston, the MBTA (☎ **617/222-3200**) runs bus route 450 from Haymarket (Orange or Green Line) and commuter trains from North Station. The bus takes about an hour, the train 30 minutes. At the Salem station, a long staircase runs from train level to street level.

ESSENTIALS The **area code** is 508. An excellent place to start your visit is the **National Park Service Visitor Center** (2 New Liberty St., ☎ **508/741-3648**), where exhibits highlight early settlement, maritime history, and the leather and textiles industries. The center (summer, daily 9am–6pm; winter, daily 9am–5pm) also has an auditorium where a free film on Essex County provides a good overview. The **Salem Chamber of Commerce** in Old Town Hall (32 Derby Sq., Salem, MA 01970; ☎ **508/744-0004**) maintains an information booth (summer, weekdays and Saturday 9am–5pm, Sunday noon–5pm; winter, weekdays 9am–5pm), and collaborates with the **Salem Office of Tourism & Cultural Affairs** (93 Washington St., Salem, MA 01970; ☎ **800/777-6848**) to publish a free visitor's guide.

Salem has a web site (http://www.star.net/salem).

What to See & Do

Downtown Salem is spread out but flat, and the historic district extends well inland from the waterfront. Many 18th-century houses still stand, some with original furnishings. Ship captains lived near the water at the east end of downtown, in relatively small houses crowded close together. The captains' employers, the shipping company owners, built their homes away from the water (and the accompanying aromas). Many of them lived on **Chestnut Street,** which is preserved as a registered National Historic Landmark. Residents along the ravishingly beautiful thoroughfare must, by legal agreement, adhere to colonial style in their decorating and furnishings.

At the Essex Street side of the Visitor Center, you can board the **Salem Trolley** (☎ **508/744-5469**; daily April through October, weekends March and November) for a one-hour narrated tour. Tickets ($8 adults, $7 seniors and students, $4 children 5–12) are good all day, and you can reboard as many times as you like at any of the 15 stops—a great deal if you're spending the day and don't want to keep moving the car or carrying leg-weary children.

Should you find yourself in town at the end of October, you won't be able to miss **Haunted Happenings,** the city's two-week Halloween celebration. Parades, parties, and tours lead up to a ceremony on the big day.

The **Heritage Trail** is a 1.7-mile walking route that begins at the Visitor Center, near the two-block pedestrian mall on **Essex Street.** It's marked by a red line painted on the sidewalk and connects many of the major attractions. In the immediate downtown area, walking is the way to go.

Pickering Wharf, at the corner of Derby and Congress streets, is a cluster of shops, boutiques, restaurants, and condos adjacent to a marina. The waterfront setting makes it a good place for strolling, snacking, and shopping. The **Pickering Wharf Antiques Gallery** (☎ **508/741-3113**) collects 40 dealers of all stripes under one capacious roof. You can also take a harbor cruise or go on a whale watch.

Three destinations on the outskirts of the historic district are worth the trip. By car or trolley, **Salem Willows,** a waterfront amusement park, is five minutes away (many signs point the way) and a wonderful place to bring a picnic. Admission and parking are free. To enjoy the great view without the arcades and rides, have lunch one peninsula over at **Winter Island Park.** Up-market gift shops throughout New England sell the chocolate confections of **Harbor Sweets,** and you can visit the source in Salem (Palmer Cove, 85 Leavitt St.; ☎ **508/745-7648**). The retail store overlooks the floor of the factory—call ahead to see if the machinery is running, if you want to see it in action. The shop is open weekdays 8:30am–4:30pm and Saturday 9am–3pm.

Finally, if you can't get witchcraft off your mind, several shops specialize in the necessary accessories. The **Broom Closet** (3–5 Central St.; ☎ **508/741-3669**) and **Crow's Haven Corner** (125 Essex St.; ☎ **508/745-8763**) sell everything from crystals to clothing and cast a modern-day light on age-old customs—just bear in mind that Salem is home to many practicing witches who take their craft very seriously.

Salem Maritime National Historic Site

174 Derby St. ☎ **508/745-1470.** Free admission. Guided tours $3 adults, $2 seniors and ages 6–16, $10 family. Summer, daily 9am–5pm; winter, Mon–Fri 10am–4pm, Sat–Sun 9am–5pm. Closed Thanksgiving Day, Christmas Day, and New Year's Day. Take Derby St. east; just past Pickering Wharf, the orientation center is on the right, at the head of Derby Wharf.

With the decline of the shipping trade in the early 19th century, Salem's wharves fell into disrepair, a state the National Park Service only began to remedy in 1938 when it took over a small piece of the waterfront. Derby Wharf is now a finger of parkland extending into the harbor, part of the nine acres, dotted with explanatory markers, that make up the historic site. The warehouse that houses the orientation center dates from around 1800 and was moved to the head of the wharf in the 1970s. Ranger-led tours, which vary according to seasonal schedules, expand on Salem's maritime history. Yours might include the Custom House (1819), where Nathaniel Hawthorne worked, and the Derby House (1762), a wedding gift to shipping magnate Elias Hasket Derby from his father. If you prefer to explore on your own, you can see the free film at the orientation center and wander around Derby Wharf, the West India Goods Store, the Bonded Warehouse, the Scale House, and Central Wharf.

The House of the Seven Gables

54 Turner St. ☎ **508/744-0991.** Guided tours $7 adults, $4 ages 13–17, $3 ages 6–12. June 1–Labor Day daily 9am–6pm; off-season daily 10am–4:30pm. Closed Thanksgiving Day, Christmas Day, and New Year's Day. From downtown, follow Derby St. east three blocks past Derby Wharf; historic site is on the right.

Built by Capt. John Turner in 1668, this building was later occupied by a cousin of Nathaniel Hawthorne's, and his 1851 novel was inspired by stories and legends of the house and its inhabitants. If you haven't read the book, don't let that keep you away—begin your visit with the audiovisual program, which tells the story. The house holds six rooms of period furniture, including pieces referred to in the book, and a narrow, twisting secret staircase. Costumed guides lead tours of the historic site, which include a visit to Hawthorne's birthplace (built before 1750 and moved to the grounds) and describe what life was like for the house's 18th-century inhabitants. Also on the grounds, overlooking Salem Harbor, are period gardens, the Retire Beckett House (1655), the Hooper-Hathaway House (1682), and a counting house (1830) where financial records were once kept. Combination discounted tickets for the House of the Seven Gables and Salem 1630 (see below) are available at both sites.

✪ Peabody Essex Museum

East India Sq. ☎ **800/745-4054** or 508/745-9500. Admission (good on two consecutive days) $7 adults, $6 seniors and students, $4 ages 6–16, $18 families (two adults, one or more children). Free first Fri of each month 5–8pm. Mon–Sat 10am–5pm, Sun noon–5pm, Fri until 8pm. Closed Thanksgiving Day, Christmas Day, New Year's Day, and Mon Nov–Memorial Day. Take Hawthorne Blvd. to Essex St., following signs for Visitor Center. Plummer Hall (Essex Institute) is on the right; East India Hall (Peabody Museum) is at the corner of Liberty St., at the east end of the pedestrian mall.

The 1992 merger of the Peabody Museum and the Essex Institute combined fascinating collections that illustrate Salem's adventures abroad and its development at home. The Peabody Museum, the nation's oldest in continuous operation, was founded in 1799 by the East India Marine Society, a group of sea captains and merchants whose charter included provisions for a "museum in which to house the natural and artificial curiosities" brought back from their travels. The collection of the Essex Institute (1821), the county's historical society, encompasses American art, crafts, furniture, and architecture (including nine historic houses), as well as dolls, toys, and games.

This all adds up to the impression that you're in Salem's attic, but instead of opening dusty trunks and musty closets, you find all the work done for you and the treasures arranged in well-planned displays that help you understand the significance of each artifact. If you want to learn more, there are two research libraries, but you'll probably be more than happy wandering the galleries until you find something that interests you, as you surely will. Trace the history of the port of Salem and the whaling trade, study figureheads of ships or portraits of area residents (including Charles Osgood's omnipresent rendering of Nathaniel Hawthorne), learn about the witchcraft trials, immerse yourself in East Asian art and artifacts or the practical arts and crafts of the East Asian, Pacific Island, and Native American peoples. The Asian Export Art Wing displays decorative art pieces made in Asia for Western use from the 14th to 19th centuries. Sign up for a tour of one or more houses—the Gardner-Pingree House (1804), a magnificent federal mansion, was the site of a notorious murder in 1830 and has been gorgeously restored. You can also sign up for a gallery tour or select from about a dozen pamphlets for self-guided tours on various topics.

The museum operates a cafe that serves lunch daily and dinner on Fridays.

Salem 1630: Pioneer Village

Forest River Park, off West Ave. ☎ **508/745-0525** or 508/744-0991. Admission $4.50 adults, $3.50 seniors and ages 13–17, $2.50 ages 6–12. Daily Memorial Day–Halloween 10am–5pm. Closed Nov 1–last week in May. Take Lafayette St. (Rtes. 114 and 1A) south to West Ave., turn left and follow the signs.

A re-creation of life in Salem just four years after European settlement, this Puritan village is staffed by costumed interpreters who lead tours, demonstrate crafts, and tend to farm animals. When the 1996 film version of Arthur Miller's play about the witchcraft trials, *The Crucible,* was completed, the village inherited a large collection of authentic and reproduction props that have been put into use. Combination discounted tickets for Salem 1630 and the House of Seven Gables (see above) are available at both sites.

Salem Witch Museum

19 ½ Washington Sq. ☎ **508/744-1692.** Admission $4 adults, $3.50 seniors, $2.50 ages 6–14. Sept–June, daily 10am–5pm; July–Aug, daily 10am–7pm. Closed Thanksgiving, Christmas Day, and New Year's Day. Follow Hawthorne Blvd. to the northwest corner of Salem Common.

Actually a three-dimensional audiovisual presentation with life-size figures, the Witch Museum is a huge room lined with displays that are lighted in sequence. The 30-minute narration tells the story of the witchcraft trials and the accompanying hysteria. (One man was pressed to death by rocks piled on a board on his chest— smaller children may need a reminder that he's not real.) On the traffic island across from the entrance is a statue, easily mistaken for a witch, that actually is of Roger Conant, who founded Salem in 1626.

WHERE TO STAY

Coach House Inn

284 Lafayette St. (Rtes. 1A and 114), Salem, MA 01970. ☎ **800/688-8689** or 508/744-4092. 11 rms, 9 with bath (some with shower only). A/C TV. $65–$72 double with shared bath; $72–$95 with private bath; $125–$155 suite with kitchenette. Extra person $15. Rates include continental breakfast. AE, MC, V.

Built in 1879 for a ship's captain, the Coach House Inn is two blocks from the harbor, a 20-minute walk or five-minute drive from downtown Salem. The high-ceilinged rooms in the three-story mansion have elegant furnishings and fireplaces, many of marble or carved ebony. Breakfast arrives at your door in a basket. Smoking is not allowed.

Hawthorne Hotel

18 Washington Sq. (at Salem Common), Salem, MA 01970. ☎ **800/729-7829** or 508/744-4080. Fax 508/745-9842. 83 rms, 6 suites. A/C TV TEL. $88–$145 double, $185–$225 suite; lower rates off-season. Extra person $12. Children under 16 stay free in parents' room. Senior discount. AE, DC, DISC, MC, V.

This historic hotel, built in 1925 and nicely maintained—the lobby was remodeled in 1995—is as convenient as it is comfortable. The six-story building is centrally located, and some of the attractively furnished rooms overlook Salem Common. Guests have the use of an exercise room, and there are two restaurants on the ground floor.

Salem Inn

7 Summer St. (Rte. 114), Salem, MA 01970. ☎ **800/446-2995** or 508/741-0680. Fax 508/744-8924. 31 rms (some with shower only). A/C TV TEL. Mid-Apr–mid-Oct, double $109–$179; Halloween week $140–$175; Nov–mid-Apr $99–$169. Rates include continental breakfast. AE, DC, DISC, MC, V.

The hubbub of downtown falls away as you enter the two ship's captain's homes that make up the Salem Inn. The 1834 West House and the 1854 Curwen House (around the corner on Essex Street) are one block from historic Chestnut Street and offer guests large, tastefully decorated rooms, some with fireplaces, canopy beds and whirlpool baths. Have breakfast in the Courtyard Cafe or wander out to the rose garden and brick patio at the rear of the main building.

Where to Dine

Whether you're sitting down for three courses or grabbing a muffin and running, Salem offers a good selection. In addition to the restaurants listed below, **Pickering Wharf** has a food court as well as a link in the **Victoria Station** chain (☎ 508/745-3400), where the deck has a great view of the marina. For a quick bite, you might want to try **Brothers Restaurant & Deli** (283 Derby St.; ☎ 508/741-4648), an inexpensive cafeteria-style family deli with home-cooked Greek meals that serves breakfast all day.

✪ Lyceum Bar & Grill

43 Church St. (at Washington St.). ☎ **508/745-7665.** Reservations recommended. Main courses $6–$9 at lunch, $9–$18 at dinner. AE, DISC, MC, V. Mon–Fri 11:30am–3pm, Sun 11am–3pm, daily 5:30–10pm. AMERICAN.

Alexander Graham Bell made the first long-distance telephone call at the Lyceum, and you may want to place one of your own, to tell the folks at home what a good meal you're having. The elegance of the Lyceum's high-ceilinged front rooms and glass-walled back rooms is matched by the quality of the food. Grilling is a favorite cooking technique here—be sure to try the marinated, grilled portabella mushrooms, even if you have to order a plate of them as an appetizer. They're also scattered throughout the menu, for example in delectable pasta with chicken, red peppers, and Swiss chard in wine sauce, or with beef tenderloin, red pepper sauce, and garlic mashed potatoes. Spicy vegetable lasagna is also tasty. Try to save room for one of the traditional yet sophisticated desserts. The brownie sundae is out of this world.

⑤ Red's Sandwich Shop

15 Central St. ☎ **508/745-3527.** Most items under $6. No credit cards. Mon–Sat 5am–3pm, Sun 6am–1pm. DINER.

There's no telling what the Drivases, who run Red's, will do for their next trick—here they manage to run a place where locals and visitors feel equally comfortable. Hunker down at the counter or a table and be ready for your waitress to call you "dear" as she brings you pancakes and eggs at breakfast or soup (opt for chicken over chowder) and a burger at lunch. **Red's Winter Island Grille** (☎ 508/744-0203), which is run by the same management, is open seasonally at Winter Island Park.

Stromberg's

2 Bridge St. (Rte. 1A). ☎ **508/744-1863.** Reservations recommended at dinner. Main courses $3.95–$9.95 at lunch, $9.95–$14.95 at dinner; lobster priced daily. AE, DISC, MC, V. Tues–Thurs 11am–9pm, Fri–Sat until 10pm. Closed Tues on long holiday weekends. SEAFOOD.

For generous portions of well-prepared seafood and view of the water, head to this wildly popular spot near the bridge to Beverly. You won't care that Beverly Harbor isn't the most exciting spot, especially if it's summer and you're out on the deck enjoying the live entertainment (weekends only). The fish and clam chowders are excellent, daily specials are numerous, there are more chicken, beef, and pasta options than you'd think, and crustacean lovers in the mood to splurge will fall for the world-class lobster roll. There's also a children's menu ($2.50–$3.95).

En Route to Gloucester & Rockport

If you approach or leave Cape Ann on Route 128, turn away from Gloucester at the Route 133 exit and head west to **Essex,** known for Essex clams, salt marshes, a long tradition of shipbuilding, an incredible number of antique shops, and one legendary restaurant.

Woodman's of Essex (Main St.; ☎ **800/649-1773** or 508/768-6451) supposedly was the birthplace of the fried clam in 1916. Today it's a great spot for lobster "in the rough," steamers, corn on the cob, onion rings, and (you guessed it) fried clams. Expect the line to be long, but it moves quickly and offers a good view of the regimented commotion in the food preparation area. Eat in a booth, upstairs on the deck, or out back at a picnic table. If this all sounds just plain uncivilized, call ahead for a reservation and head across the street to **Tom Shea's** (122 Main St.; ☎ **508/768-6931**) for table service, a more sophisticated menu, and a calmer atmosphere. You'll want to be well-fed before you set off to explore the numerous antique shops along Main Street.

Approaching Gloucester from the south on Route 127, or detouring from Route 133 onto Route 127, you'll see signs for Magnolia and **Hammond Castle** (80 Hesperus Ave., Gloucester; ☎ **508/283-2080** or 508/283-7673 for recorded directions). Eccentric inventor John Hays Hammond, Jr., designed the medieval castle, which was constructed of Rockport granite and cost more than $6 million when it was built from 1926 to 1929. Guided tours are no longer offered, so you're on your own with a pamphlet to direct you around the castle, which has 85-foot towers, battlements, stained-glass windows, a great hall 60 feet high, and an enclosed "outdoor" pool and courtyard lined with foliage, trees, and medieval artifacts. The pipes in the ceiling "rain" on command. Many 12th-, 13th-, and 14th-century furnishings, tapestries, paintings, and architectural fragments fill the rooms. A pipe organ with more than 8,200 pipes is used for monthly concerts. Write for a copy of the events calendar. Admission is $6 for adults, $5 for seniors, and $4 for children 4–12; children under 4 are free. The museum is open daily Memorial Day through Labor Day from 10am–6pm, Thursday through Sunday from Labor Day through mid-October 10am–4pm, and weekends only 10am–4pm November through May.

GLOUCESTER

33 miles NE of Boston; 16 miles NE of Salem

The ocean has been Gloucester's lifeblood since long before the first European settlement in 1623. The French explorer Samuel de Champlain called the harbor "Le Beauport" when he came across it in 1604, some 600 years after the Vikings, and its configuration and proximity to good fishing gave it the reputation it enjoys to this day.

The fleet sets out early in the morning from the downtown part of the harbor, where processing plants—Clarence Birdseye invented the process for blast-freezing foods here—await the catch, which is unloaded on **State Fish Pier,** Parker Street.

On Stacy Boulevard west of downtown is a reminder of the sea's danger. Leonard Craske's bronze statue of the **Gloucester Fisherman,** known as "The Man at the Wheel," bears the inscription "They That Go Down to the Sea in Ships 1623–1923." More than 10,000 fishermen lost their lives during the city's first 300 years, and a statue honoring the women and children who waited for them is currently in the works.

GETTING THERE   From Salem, follow Route 1A across the bridge to Beverly, pick up Route 127, and take it through Manchester (near, not on, the water) to Gloucester. From Boston, the quickest path is I-93 (or Route 1, if it's not rush hour) to Route 128, which runs directly to Gloucester. Route 128 is almost entirely inland; the exits for Manchester allow access to Route 127 if you want to combine speed and scenery.

The MBTA (☎ **617/222-3200**) commuter rail line runs from North Station in Boston to Gloucester. The trip takes about an hour. The Cape Ann Transportation Authority, or CATA (☎ **508/283-7916**) runs buses from town to town on Cape Ann.

ESSENTIALS   The **area code** is 508. The **Gloucester Tourism Commission** (22 Poplar St., Gloucester, MA, 01930; ☎ **800/649-6839** or 508/281-8865) operates a Visitors Welcoming Center that's open daily from 9am to 5pm during the summer at Stage Fort Park, off Route 127 near the intersection with Route 133. The **Cape Ann Chamber of Commerce** (33 Commercial St., Gloucester, MA 01930; ☎ **800/321-0133** or 508/283-1601) information center is open year-round (summer, Mon–Fri 8am–6pm, Sat 10am–6pm, Sun 10am–4pm; winter, Mon–Fri 8am–5pm).

Gloucester has a page on the Cape Ann web site (http://wizard.pn.com/capeann).

What to See & Do

Business isn't what it once was, but fishing is still Gloucester's leading industry (as your nose will tell you), and the fishermen need all the help they can get. Every year the fleet enjoys some divine intervention during **St. Peter's Fiesta,** a colorful four-day event at the end of June. The Italian-American fishing colony's festival features parades, music, food, sporting events, and, on Sunday, the blessing of the fleet.

Moby Duck Tours (☎ **508/281-3825**) are 50-minute sightseeing expeditions that travel on land before plunging into the water. The "amphibious" vehicles leave from **Harbor Loop** downtown, where tickets ($12 adults, $10 seniors, $8 children under 12) are available. Also at Harbor Loop, you can tour the two-masted schooner *Adventure* (☎ **508/281-8079**), a 121-foot fishing vessel built in Essex in 1926. The "living museum," a National Historic Landmark, is open to visitors from Memorial Day to Labor Day, Thurs–Sun 10am–4pm. (Suggested donation $5 adults, $4 children.)

To reach East Gloucester, follow signs as you leave downtown or go directly from Route 128, Exit 9. On East Main Street, you'll see signs for the world-famous **Rocky Neck Art Colony,** the oldest continuously operating art colony in the country. Park in the lot on the tiny causeway and walk two blocks west along Rocky Neck Avenue, which is jammed with studios, galleries, restaurants, and people. The real draw is the presence of working artists, not just shops that happen to sell art. Some of the locally produced art winds up at the **North Shore Arts Association** (197 E. Main St., rear; ☎ **508/283-1857**), founded in 1923 to showcase local artists' work. It's open June through September, Monday to Saturday 10am–5pm, Sunday 1–5pm, and admission is free.

Stage Fort Park (off Route 127 near the intersection with Route 133) offers an excellent view of the harbor and is a good spot for a picnic, swimming, or just playing on the cannons in the Revolutionary War fort.

Whale Watching

The depletion of New England's fishing grounds has led to the rise of another important seagoing industry: whale watching. The waters off the coast of Massachusetts are prime whale-watching territory, and Gloucester is a center of whale-watching cruises. Stellwagen Bank, which runs from Gloucester to Provincetown about 27 miles east of Boston, is a rich feeding ground for the huge mammals, mainly fin- and humpback whales, who feed on sand eels and other fish that gather along the ridge. The whales often perform for their audience, too, by jumping out of the water, and occasionally dolphins join the show.

Dress warmly, because it's much cooler at sea than in town, and take sunglasses, sunscreen, a hat, rubber-soled shoes, and a camera with plenty of film. If you're prone to motion sickness, take appropriate precautions, as you'll be out on the open sea.

Check the local marinas for sailing times, prices ($20–$25 for adults, less for children and seniors), and reservations. Most companies offer a morning and an afternoon cruise as well as deep-sea fishing excursions. In downtown Gloucester, try **Seven Seas Whale Watching** (☎ 800/238-1776 or 508/283-1776), **Captain Bill's Whale Watching** (☎ 800/33-WHALE or 508/283-6995), or **Cape Ann Whale Watch** (☎ 800/877-5110 or 508/283-5110). At the Cape Ann Marina, off Route 133, you'll find **Yankee Whale Watch** (☎ 800/WHALING or 508/283-0313).

Beauport (Sleeper-McCann House)

75 Eastern Point Blvd. ☎ **508/283-0800.** Guided tours $6 adults, $5.50 seniors, $2.50 ages 6–12. Tours on the hour Mid-May–mid-Oct, Mon–Fri 10am–4pm; mid-Sept–mid-Oct Mon–Fri 10am–4pm, Sat–Sun 1–4pm. Closed mid-Oct–mid-May. Take East Main Street south to Eastern Point Boulevard (a private road), drive one-half mile to the house and park on the left.

The Society for the Preservation of New England Antiquities, which operates it, describes Beauport as a "fantasy house," and that's putting it mildly. Interior designer Henry Davis Sleeper used his summer residence as a retreat and a repository for his vast collections of American and European decorative arts and antiques. From 1907 to 1934 he decorated the 40 rooms, 26 of which are open to the public, to illustrate literary and historical themes. You'll see architectural details rescued from other buildings, magnificent arrangements of colored glassware, an early American kitchen, the "Red Indian Room" (with a majestic view of the harbor), and "Strawberry Hill," the master bedroom. Note that the house is closed on summer weekends.

Cape Ann Historical Association

27 Pleasant St. ☎ **508/283-0455.** Admission $3.50 adults, $3 seniors, $2 students, children 6 and under free. Tues–Sat 10am–5pm. Closed Feb. Follow Main St. west through downtown and turn right onto Pleasant St. (at the Salvation Army store); the museum is one block up on the right. Metered parking is available on the street or in the lot across the street.

This meticulously curated little museum makes an excellent introduction to Cape Ann's history and artists. An entire gallery is devoted to the wonderful work of Fitz Hugh Lane, the American Luminist painter whose light-flooded paintings show off the best of his native Gloucester. The nation's single largest collection of his paintings and drawings is here, along with new galleries featuring 20th-century artists such as Maurice Prendergast, Milton Avery, and Paul Manship. The maritime and fisheries galleries feature entire vessels (including one about the size of a station wagon that actually crossed the Atlantic), exhibits on the fishing industry, ship models, and historic photographs and models of the Gloucester waterfront. The Capt. Elias Davis House (1804), decorated and furnished in the Federal style with furniture, silver, and porcelain, is part of the museum.

WHERE TO STAY

Atlantis Oceanfront Motor Inn

125 Atlantic Rd., Gloucester, MA 01930. ☎ **508/283-0014.** 40 rms (some with shower only). TV TEL. Late June–Labor Day $100–$115 double; spring and fall $65–$95 double. Extra person $8. AE, MC, V. Closed Nov–mid-Apr. Follow Route 128 to the end (Exit 9, East Gloucester), turn left onto Bass Ave. (Route 127A) and follow a half-mile. Turn right and follow Atlantic Rd.

The stunning views from every window of this motor inn would almost be enough to recommend it, but it also has a friendly staff and a heated outdoor pool. The redecoration of the guest rooms in comfortable, contemporary style was completed in 1995. Every room has a terrace or balcony and a small table and chairs, and there's a coffee shop on the premises.

Best Western Bass Rocks Ocean Inn

107 Atlantic Rd., Gloucester, MA 01930. ☎ **508/283-7600.** Fax 508/281-6489. 48 rms. A/C TV TEL. Mid-April–Memorial Day $90–$105 double; Memorial Day–Labor Day $115–$135 double; Labor Day–Oct $110–$125 double. Extra person $8. Rollaway bed $12. Children under 12 stay free in parents' room. Rates include continental breakfast. AE, CB, DC, DISC, MC, V. Closed Nov–mid-April. Follow Route 128 to the end (Exit 9, East Gloucester), turn left onto Bass Ave. (Route 127A) and follow a half-mile. Turn right and follow Atlantic Rd.

A family operation since 1946, the Bass Rocks Ocean Inn offers modern accommodations in a traditional setting. The guest rooms overlook the ocean from a sprawling, comfortable motel, with the office and public areas in a Colonial revival–style mansion built in 1899 and known as the "wedding-cake house." The rooftop sundeck, balconies, and swimming pool all offer excellent views of the surf. The large rooms have balconies or patios; each has a king-size bed or two double beds. Each morning a cold buffet breakfast is served, and each afternoon coffee and chocolate chip cookies are offered. A billiard room and library are available, and bicycles are at the disposal of the guests. Rooms for nonsmokers are available.

WHERE TO DINE

The Gull

75 Essex Ave. (Route 133), at Cape Ann Marina. ☎ **508/283-6565.** Reservations recommended for parties of eight or more. Main courses $5.95–$11.95 at lunch, $6.95–$20.95 at dinner. MC, V. Daily 5am–9:30pm. Take Route 133 less than 2 miles west of the intersection with Route 127, or approach along Route 133 eastbound from Route 128. SEAFOOD.

The Annisquam River is visible through the floor-to-ceiling windows from almost every seat at the Gull. This big, friendly restaurant specializes in seafood but is also known for its prime rib, and it draws locals, visitors, boaters, and families for large portions at reasonable prices. Ask about the daily specials. The seafood chowder is famous (with good reason), appetizers tend toward bar food, and fish is available in just about any variety and style. At lunch, there's an extensive sandwich menu. The Gull has a full bar.

The Rudder Restaurant

73 Rocky Neck Ave., East Gloucester. ☎ **508/283-7967.** Reservations required for weekends. Main courses $12.95–$19.95. DISC, MC, V. Memorial Day–Labor Day, daily noon–10:30pm; call for open hours and days spring and fall. Closed Dec–mid-Apr. SEAFOOD/ INTERNATIONAL.

A meal at the Rudder is not just a meal—it's a party. Overlooking Smith Cove, in the heart of the Rocky Neck Art Colony, the Rudder is jam packed, floor to ceiling, with gadgets, colored lights, antiques, photos, menus from around the world, and other collectibles. Ask for a seat on the deck (if it's not low tide) and be prepared for anything, because the Rudder is known for its "spontaneous entertainment." You might hear live piano music or see Susan's invisible flaming baton twirling act. The chefs are creative (try the shrimp farcis for an appetizer), and main course offerings run the gamut from shrimp scampi over fresh linguini to chicken picatta. There's also a children's menu ($7.95).

ROCKPORT

40 miles NE of Boston; 7 miles N of Gloucester

This lovely little town at the tip of Cape Ann was settled in 1690 and over the years has been an active fishing port, a center of granite excavation and cutting, and a thriving summer community whose specialty seems to be selling fudge and refrigerator magnets to out-of-towners. There's more to Rockport than gift shops—you just have to look. It's also popular with working painters (Winslow Homer is only one of the famous artists who have captured the local color), and for every year-round resident who seems genuinely startled when legions of people with cameras around their necks descend on Rockport each June, there are dozens who are proud to show off their town.

The **Rockport Art Association** is an active organization, and there are many art galleries in town. You'll also find interesting places to stay and some good restaurants.

GETTING THERE By car from Boston or anywhere else described here, Rockport is north of Gloucester along Route 127 or 127A. At the end of Route 128, turn left at the signs for Rockport to take 127, or continue until you see the sign for East Gloucester and turn left onto 127A, which runs along the east coast of Cape Ann. Route 127 is a loop that cuts across the peninsula inland and swings around to follow Ipswich Bay.

The MBTA (☎ **617/222-3200**) commuter rail line runs from North Station in Boston to Rockport. The trip takes about an hour. The Cape Ann Transportation Authority, or CATA (☎ **508/283-7916**) runs buses from town to town on Cape Ann.

ESSENTIALS The **area code** is 508. The **Rockport Chamber of Commerce** (3 Main St.; ☎ **508/546-6575**) is open in summer from 9am–5pm daily, and on winter weekdays from 10am–4pm. The chamber also operates a seasonal (mid-May to mid-October) information booth on Upper Main Street (Route 127), about a mile from downtown. At either location, ask for the pamphlet "Rockport: A Walking Guide," which has a good map and descriptions of three short walking tours. Out of season, Rockport closes up tighter than an Essex clam—from January through mid-April, it's pretty but somewhat desolate.

If you can schedule only one weekday trip, make it this one. For traffic and congestion, downtown Boston has nothing on Rockport on a summer Saturday afternoon. Whenever you go, circle the square once to look for parking (mind the limits on many meters), and if there's no place to park, try the back streets, even if they're some distance from the center of town. Or use the parking lot on Upper Main Street (Route 127) on weekends. Parking from 11am–6pm will cost about $6, and a free shuttle will take you downtown and back.

WHAT TO SEE & DO

The most famous example of what to see in Rockport is surrounded by something of an "Emperor's New Clothes" aura—it's a wooden fish warehouse on the town wharf, or "T-Wharf," as it's called, in the harbor. The barn-red shack (often erroneously rendered in bright red), known as Motif No. 1, is far and away the most frequently painted object in a town filled with lovely buildings and surrounded by rocky coastline. The color certainly catches the eye in the neutrals of the surrounding seascape, but you may find yourself initiating or overhearing conversations about what the big deal is. Originally constructed in 1884 and destroyed during the blizzard of 1978, Motif No. 1 was rebuilt through donations from the local community and tourists. It stands again on the same pier, duplicated in every detail, and reinforced to withstand storms.

Nearby is a phenomenon whose popularity is easier to explain—**Bearskin Neck,** named after an unfortunate bear who drowned and was washed ashore here in 1800, has perhaps the highest concentration of gift shops anywhere. It's a narrow peninsula with one main street (South Road) and several alleys lined—make that crammed—with galleries, snack bars, antique shops, and ancient houses. You'll find literally dozens of little shops carrying clothes, gifts, toys, inexpensive novelties, and expensive handmade crafts and paintings.

More than two dozen art galleries display the works of both local and nationally known artists. The **Rockport Art Association** (12 Main St.; ☎ 508/546-6604), open daily year-round, sponsors major exhibitions and special shows throughout the year. Chamber music fans will want to contact the Chamber of Commerce for information about the **Rockport Chamber Music Festival,** an early-summer highlight.

If the mansions of Gloucester are too plush to interest you, or if you want some tips on what to do with old newspapers, visit the **Paper House** (52 Pigeon Hill St., Pigeon Cove; ☎ 508/546-2629). It was built in 1922 entirely out of 100,000 newspapers—walls, furniture, even a piano. Every item of furniture is made from papers of a different period. It's open daily from May through October from 10am–5pm. Admission is $1.50 for adults and $1 for children.

To get a sense of the power of the sea in this part of the world, take Route 127 north of town to the very tip of Cape Ann. **Halibut Point State Park** (☎ 508/546-2997) has a staffed visitor center, walking trails, tidal pools, water-filled quarries (swimming is absolutely forbidden), and a rocky beach where you can climb around on giant boulders. Guided tours are available on Saturday mornings in the summer, but this is a great place just to wander around, admire the scenery (on a clear day, you can see Maine), and perhaps do some bird-watching.

And if you'd like to indulge the inexplicable craving for fudge that seizes mild-mannered travelers when they get their first whiff of salt water, you can buy some fudge to consume or just watch it being made at **Tuck's Candy Factory** (7 Dock Sq.; ☎ 508/546-6352), in the window of a retail store.

WHERE TO STAY

Moderate

Captain's Bounty Motor Inn
1 Beach St., P.O. Box 43, Rockport, MA 01966. ☎ **508/546-9557.** 24 rms. TV TEL. Apr 1–mid-May $65 oceanfront room, $68 oceanfront efficiency, $70 oceanfront efficiency suite; mid-May–mid-June 15 and early Sept–Oct $78 oceanfront room, $82 oceanfront efficiency (room with mini-kitchenette), $88 oceanfront efficiency suite; mid-June–early Sept $98 oceanfront room, $105 oceanfront efficiency, $115 oceanfront efficiency suite. Extra person $10, rollaway bed $5. All rates based on double occupancy. DISC, MC, V.

To get closer to the beach than this modern, well-maintained motor inn, you'd have to sleep on a houseboat. Ocean breezes provide natural air-conditioning—each room overlooks the water and has its own balcony and sliding glass door. Rooms are spacious and soundproofed, and kitchenette units are available.

Old Farm Inn
291 Granite St. (Route 127) at Pigeon Cove, Rockport, MA 01966. ☎ **800/233-6828** or 508/546-3237. 10 rms. TEL. July–Oct $88–$125 double, Apr–June and Nov $78–$115 double. Room with kitchenette $115, two-room suite $125. Two-bedroom housekeeping cottage

$995 per week July–Aug. Extra person $10. Rollaway bed $15. Rates include buffet breakfast. AE, MC, V. Closed Dec–mid-Apr.

This gorgeous bed-and-breakfast is a 1799 saltwater farm with antique-furnished rooms in the Inn, the Barn Guesthouse, and the Fieldside Cottage. Each room is uniquely decorated with country-style furnishings (many have beautiful quilts on the beds), and innkeepers Susan and Bill Balzarini are devoted to making your stay enjoyable and comfortable. The buffet breakfast, which includes fresh fruit, home-baked breads, a selection of hot and cold cereals, yogurt, and juices, is excellent. Nine of the rooms have air-conditioning, and most have a refrigerator. About 2½ miles from the center of town, the inn is a stone's throw from Halibut Point State Park.

Motel Peg Leg

10 Beach St., Rockport, MA 01966. ☎ **508/546-6945.** 15 rms. $95–$110 double. AE, DISC, MC, V. Closed Nov–Apr.

Operated by Jim and Polly Erwin, this attractive motel is housed in two buildings on a quiet knoll overlooking Rockport Harbor, next to the Old First Parish Burying Ground, and across the street from the public beach. The rooms are decorated with Ethan Allen furniture, some with rocking chairs or "overstuffed" chairs. All rooms are outfitted with double, queen-, or king-size beds.

Ralph Waldo Emerson Inn

1 Cathedral Ave., P.O. Box 2369, Rockport, MA 01966. ☎ **508/546-6321.** Fax 508/546-7043. E-mail emerson@cove.com. 36 rms. A/C TEL. July–Labor Day $96–$137 double; spring and fall $85–$125 double. Extra person $7. Crib or cot $7. Weekly rates available. DISC, MC, V. Closed Dec–mid-April; open weekends only in Apr and Nov. Follow Route 127 north from the center of town for two miles and watch for large sign; turn right at Phillips St.

Somewhere in the old guest register of the Ralph Waldo Emerson Inn you might find the name of Emerson himself, for the distinguished philosopher was a guest in the original (1840) inn in the 1850s. The oceanfront building was expanded in 1912 and still has an old-fashioned feel, with furnishings such as spool beds and four-posters in the nicely appointed, though not terribly large, rooms. There's no elevator, but rooms that require a climb and face the street or have indirect views of the water are cheaper than the more accessible rooms. A few flights of stairs seems a small inconvenience for the view from the top-floor rooms, however. Guests have the use of a heated outdoor saltwater pool or (for a fee) the indoor whirlpool and sauna. Recreation rooms include areas for playing cards, table tennis, or watching the wide-screen TV.

The dining room is open to the public on an availability basis. Breakfast is served from 8 to 10am, and dinner from 6 to 9:30pm.

Yankee Clipper Inn (Romantik Hotel)

96 Granite St. (Route 127), Rockport, MA 01966. ☎ **800/545-3699** or 508/546-3407. Fax 508/546-9730. 27 rms. A/C TEL. Memorial Day–mid-Oct, $124–$219 double; weekends spring and fall $105–$139 double; weeknights spring and fall $75–$99 double. Extra person $26. Rates include full breakfast in summer, continental breakfast spring and fall. AE, DISC, MC, V. Closed Dec–mid-Mar.

Just north of town on the road to Pigeon Cove, this luxurious lodging is set on extensive lawns overlooking the sea. There are three buildings, of which the three-story main inn—with its Georgian architecture, heated saltwater pool, and rooms with private balconies—is the most attractive. Rooms are large and well-appointed, and many have views of the water, as do many of the common rooms within the inn, especially the large and attractive dining room, which is open to the public. Reservations are required of guests as well as the public.

Inexpensive

$ Inn on Cove Hill

37 Mt. Pleasant St., Rockport, MA 01966. ☎ **508/546-2701.** 11 rms (9 with bath, some with shower only). A/C. $66–$102 double with private bath, $50 with shared bath. Extra person $25. Rates include continental breakfast. MC, V. Closed Nov–mid-Apr.

This three-story inn was built in 1791 from the proceeds of pirates' gold found a short distance away. The money was put to good use: The inn is housed in an attractive Federal-style home two blocks from the head of the town wharf. Although it's close to downtown, the inn is set back from the road and has a hideaway feel. Innkeepers Marjorie and John Pratt have decorated the guest rooms in period style, with at least one antique piece in each room. Most rooms have colonial furnishings and handmade quilts, and some have canopy beds. In warm weather, a continental breakfast with home-baked breads and muffins is served on china at the garden tables; in inclement weather, breakfast in bed is served on individual trays. No smoking is allowed at the Inn on Cove Hill.

If you're coming by train from Boston, the hosts will meet you at the station; if you drive, parking is provided.

Peg Leg Inn

2 King St., Rockport, MA 01966. ☎ **800/346-2352** or 508/546-2352. 33 rms. TV. $80–$130 double, $150 two-bedroom unit mid-June to mid-Oct. Off-season rates are lower. Extra person $10. Rates include continental breakfast. MC, V.

The Peg Leg Inn is made up of five early American houses with front porches, attractive living rooms, and well-kept flower-bordered lawns that run down to a gazebo at the ocean's edge. Rooms are good-sized and neatly furnished in colonial style, and some have excellent ocean views. Guests at the inn may use the sandy beach across the road. The Peg Leg restaurant is next door.

WHERE TO DINE

Rockport is a "dry" community where restaurants are prevented by law from serving alcoholic beverages, but you can brown-bag it with your own bottle. Top prices for main dishes may be as much as $5 more if lobster is involved.

Blacksmith Shop

23 Mt. Pleasant St. ☎ **508/546-6301.** Reservations recommended. Main courses $7.95–$9.95 at lunch, $8.95–$16.95 at dinner. AE, DC, MC, V. Mid-Apr–Memorial Day, Thu–Sun, 11:30am–8pm; Memorial Day–Oct 31, Sun–Fri 11:30am–8pm, Sat 11:30am–9pm. Closed Nov 1–mid-Apr. SEAFOOD.

For tasty food in a refined setting, walk one block from the town wharf to this cavernous restaurant set on stilts jutting into the harbor. The menu runs from basic seafood to more ambitious fare—lobster cakes or cheese tortellini with sun-dried tomatoes, for example—but everything is fresh and good. The room is as pleasing as the food, with picture windows, wooden furnishings, paintings in the gallery, and an old forge, anvil, and bellows preserved from the shop where Rockport's village smithy stood. The main dining room has been enlarged many times since its establishment in 1927; it now accommodates 200—and it still fills up. There is a children's menu ($3.95–$4.95) with kiddie-sized seafood portions as well.

✪ The Greenery

15 Dock Sq. ☎ **508/546-9593.** Reservations recommended at dinner. Main dishes $6.26–$11.95 at lunch, $9.25–$15.95 at dinner; breakfast items $1.25–$6.95. DISC, MC, V. Mid-Apr–Nov Mon–Fri 9am–10pm, Sat–Sun 8am–10pm. Closed Dec–mid-Apr. SEAFOOD/ AMERICAN.

The cafelike front room of this restaurant at the head of Bearskin Neck gives no hint that at the back of the building is a dining room with a great view of the harbor. Both rooms have large windows and are well-lit and decorated with plants. The terrific food ranges from crab salad quiche at lunch to grilled swordfish at dinner to steamers anytime, and there's a huge salad bar available on its own or with many entrees. Breakfast is served on weekends. All baking is done in-house, which explains the lines at the front counter for muffins and pastries. This is a good place to launch a picnic lunch on the beach, and an equally good spot for lingering over coffee and a delectable dessert and watching the action in the harbor.

My Place By-the-Sea

68 Bearskin Neck. ☎ **508/546-9667.** Reservations recommended at dinner. Main courses $4.50–$12 at lunch, $12–$18 at dinner. AE, CB, DC, DISC, JCB, MC, V. Apr–Nov daily 11:30–9:30pm. Closed Dec–Mar. SEAFOOD.

People travel to the very end of Bearskin Neck to dine at My Place By-the-Sea on Rockport's only outdoor oceanfront deck. There are excellent views of Sandy Bay from the two decks and shaded patio. Most menu choices depend on the daily catch, so everything is fresh. The baked fish and seafood pasta entrees are good choices, and you can also have chicken or beef. The dessert menu includes excellent homemade fruit pies.

Peg Leg

18 Beach St. ☎ **508/546-3038.** Reservations recommended. Main courses $6.95–$19. AE, MC, V. In season, lunch daily 11:30am–2:30pm, dinner nightly 5:30–9pm. AMERICAN/ SEAFOOD.

For lunch or dinner in a greenhouse, complete with plants hanging baskets, 5-foot geranium trees, and flowers all around, walk through town to the end of Main Street and around the corner to the Peg Leg. The greenhouse, very romantic in the evening with its recessed spotlights and candles, is behind the cozy and attractive main restaurant. Dinner entrées include the house special chicken pie, seafood "pies" (casseroles), fresh fish, steaks, and lobster. All baking is done on the premises, and bread baskets always include sweet rolls and bread. There is also a children's menu ($6.95).

3 Plymouth

40 miles SE of Boston

Everyone educated in the United States knows at least a little about Plymouth— about how the Pilgrims, fleeing religious persecution, left Europe on the *Mayflower* and landed at Plymouth Rock in December 1620. Many also know that the Pilgrims endured disease and privation, and that just 51 people from the original group of 102 celebrated the first Thanksgiving in 1621 with Squanto, a Pawtuxet Indian associated with the Wampanoags, and his cohorts. What you won't know until you visit Plymouth is how small everything was—the *Mayflower* seems perilously tiny, and when you contemplate how dangerous life was at the time, it's hard not to be impressed by the accomplishments of the settlers.

Cape Cod was named in 1602 by Capt. Bartholomew Gosnold, and 12 years later Capt. John Smith sailed along the coast of what he named "New England," calling the mainland opposite Cape Cod "Plymouth." The passengers on the *Mayflower* had secured the title for a tract of land near the mouth of the Hudson River in "Northern Virginia" from the London Virginia Company; in exchange for their passage to the New World, they promised to work the land for the company for seven years. However, on November 11, 1620, rough weather and high seas forced them to make for Cape Cod Bay and anchor there, at Provincetown. Subsequently, their captain announced that they had found a safe harbor, and he refused to continue the voyage farther south to their original destination. They had no option but to settle in New England, and with no one to command them, their contract with the London Virginia Company became void and they were left on their own to begin a new world.

Today, Plymouth is a manageable day-trip destination particularly suited to families traveling with children. It also makes a good rest-stop between Boston and Cape Cod.

GETTING THERE   By car, follow the Southeast Expressway (I-93) from Boston to Route 3. Take Exit 6 to Plymouth, take Route 44 east, and follow signs to the historic attractions. The whole trip takes about 45 minutes. Or continue on Route 3 to the **Regional Information Complex** at Exit 5 for maps, brochures, and information. To go directly to Plimoth Plantation, take Exit 4.

Plymouth & Brockton (☎ 671/773-9401) buses leave from the terminal at South Station. You can also make connections at Logan Airport, where buses take on passengers at all airline terminals.

ESSENTIALS   The **area code** is 508. If you haven't visited the Regional Information Complex, you'll want to stop in and at least pick up a map at the **Visitor Center** (☎ 508/747-7525), at 130 Water Street, across from the town pier. To plan ahead, contact **Plymouth Visitor Information** (P.O. Box ROCK, Plymouth, MA 02361; ☎ 800/USA-1620 or 508/747-7525).

WHAT TO SEE & DO

The logical place to begin (good luck talking children out of it) is where the Pilgrims first set foot—at **Plymouth Rock.** The rock, accepted as the landing place of the *Mayflower* passengers, was originally 15 feet long and 3 feet wide. It was moved on the eve of the Revolution and several times thereafter, before assuming its present permanent position at tide level, where the winter storms still break over it as they did in Pilgrim days. The McKim, Mead & White–designed portico around the rock was presented in 1920 by the Colonial Dames of America. It's not much to look at, but the accompanying descriptions are interesting and the sense of history is curiously impressive.

To get around town, the open-air trolley is a good choice, especially if you have younger children along. **Plymouth Rock Trolley** (22 Main St.; ☎ 508/747-3419) offers a narrated tour and unlimited reboarding privileges daily from Memorial Day through October and weekends through Thanksgiving. Tickets are $7 for adults and $3 for children 3–12. Trolley markers indicate the stops, which are served every 20 minutes.

To get away from the bustle of the waterfront, you might want to relax at **Town Brook Park** at Jenney Pond, across Summer Street from the John Carver Inn. The centerpiece of the park is a beautiful tree-lined pond with ducks and swans. Across from the pond is the **Jenney Grist Mill** (6 Spring Lane; ☎ 508/747-3715; admission $2.50 adults, $2 children 5–12), a working museum where you can see a reconstructed early American water-powered mill that operates in the summer, daily from 10am–5pm. The specialty shops in the same complex, including the excellent Jenney Grist Mill Ice Cream Shoppe, are open year-round, daily 10am–6pm. There is plenty of parking.

You can shop at the **Village Landing Market,** overlooking the Plymouth waterfront off Water Street near Route 44. The specialty shops and boutiques are clustered along cobblestoned walkways bordered with benches, trees, and flowers. Summer band concerts are held in the gazebo, and it's a nice spot for shopping or browsing.

You can't stay at the historic houses of Plymouth, but they're worth a visit to see the changing styles of architecture and furnishings since the 1600s. Costumed guides explain the homemaking details and the crafts of earlier generations. Most of the houses are open from Memorial Day through Columbus Day and during Thanksgiving celebrations; call for schedules. If you're sightseeing with children, pretend the next sentence is written in capital letters: Unless you have a sky-high tolerance for house tours, pick just one or two from eras that you find particularly interesting. Each tour has something to recommend it; the Sparrow and Howland houses are most interesting for those curious about the original settlers.

Six homes are open to visitors: the 1640 **Sparrow House** (42 Summer St.; ☎ 508/747-1240; admission $1); the 1666 **Howland House** (33 Sandwich St.; ☎ 508/746-9590; admission $3 adults, 75¢ children 6–12); the 1677 **Harlow Old Fort House** (119 Sandwich St.; ☎ 508/746-0012; admission $3 adults, 75¢ children 6–12); the 1749 **Spooner House** (27 North St.; ☎ 508/746-0012; admission $3 adults, 75¢ children 6–12); the 1809 **Hedge House** (126 Water St.; ☎ 508/746-0012; admission $3 adults, 75¢ children 6–12); and the 1754 **Mayflower Society Museum** (4 Winslow St.; ☎ 508/746-2590; admission $2.50, 75¢ children 6–12).

A combination ticket for Plimoth Plantation, the Indian campsite, and *Mayflower II* is $18.50 for adults and $11 for children 6–17. Wear comfortable shoes for the tours. There's a lot of walking involved, and the plantation isn't paved.

Mayflower II

State Pier. ☎ **508/746-1622.** Admisson $5.75 adults, $3.75 children age 6–17, children under 6 free. Apr–Nov 30 daily 9am–5pm.

Berthed only a few steps from Plymouth Rock, *Mayflower II* is a full-scale reproduction of the type of ship that brought the Pilgrims from England to America. Even at full scale, you'll probably be struck by how small she is. Although little technical information is known about the original *Mayflower,* William A. Baker, designer of *Mayflower II,* incorporated the few references in Governor Bradford's account of the voyage with other research to re-create as closely as possible the actual ship. Exhibits on board show what life was like during a 66-day voyage in 1620 on a vessel crowded with 102 passengers, 25 crewmen, and all the supplies needed to sustain the colony until the first crops were harvested.

Men and women in period costumes on board the ship talk about the ocean crossing, answer questions, and dispatch little-known but interesting pieces of information. You will probably want to tour the ship. The vessel is owned and maintained by Plimoth Plantation, which is 3 miles south of the ship. A combination ticket for *Mayflower II* and Plimoth Plantation is $18.50 for adults and $11 for children age 6–17.

Alongside *Mayflower II* are museum shops that replicate early Pilgrim dwellings from 1620–21.

○ **Plymouth National Wax Museum**

16 Carver St. ☎ **508/746-6468.** Admission $5.50 adults, $4.50 seniors, $2.50 children 5–12, children under 5 free. Mar–June and Sept–Nov, daily 9am–5pm; July–Aug, daily 9am–9pm. From Plymouth Rock, turn around and walk up the hill or the steps.

Across New England (and probably across the United States), adults who visited the Plymouth National Wax Museum as children can still tell you all about the history of the Pilgrims. There are more than 180 life-size figures and dramatic sound tracks that tell the story of the move to Holland to escape persecution in England, the harrowing trip across the ocean to the New World, the first Thanksgiving, and even the story of Myles Standish, Priscilla Mullins, and John Smith. This museum is a must if children are in your party, and adults will enjoy it, too.

Pilgrim Hall Museum

75 Court St. ☎ **508/746-1620.** Admission $5 adults, $4 seniors, $2.50 children. Daily 9:30am–4:30pm. Closed January. From Plymouth Rock, walk north on Water St. and up the hill on Chilton St.

The Pilgrim Hall Museum, the oldest public museum in the United States, is listed on the National Register of Historic Places. It contains many original possessions of the early Pilgrims and their descendants, including a chair that belonged to William Brewster (alongside an uncomfortable modern-day model that you can actually sit in), one of Myles Standish's swords, and Governor Bradford's Bible. The building itself dates from 1824. Among the exhibits is the skeleton of the *Sparrow-Hawk*, a ship wrecked on Cape Cod in 1626, which lay buried, undiscovered in the sand until 1863. It's even smaller than the *Mayflower II*.

Plimoth Plantation

Route 3. ☎ **508/746-1622.** Plimoth Plantation and *Mayflower II* $18.50 adults, $11 children age 6–17, children under 6 free. Apr–Nov daily 9am–5pm. From Route 3, take Exit 4, "Plimoth Plantation Highway."

Plimoth Plantation is a re-creation of a 1627 Pilgrim village. You enter by the hilltop fort that protects the villagers and then walk down the hill to the farm area, visiting the homes and gardens along the way, which have been constructed with careful attention to historic detail. Once you get over the feeling that the whole operation is a bit strange (we heard someone mention Pompeii), it's great fun to talk to the "Pilgrims," actors who, in speech, dress, and manner, assume the personalities of members of the original community. You can watch them framing a house, splitting wood, shearing sheep, preserving foodstuffs, or cooking a pot of fish stew over an open hearth, all as it was done in the 1600s. And they use only the tools and cookware available at that time. Sometimes you can join in the activities—perhaps planting, harvesting, a court trial, or a wedding party.

The community is as accurate as research can make it: Accounts of the original Pilgrim colony were combined with archaeological research, old records, and the 17th-century history written by the Pilgrims' leader, William Bradford, who often used the spelling "Plimoth" for the settlement. There are daily militia drills with matchlock muskets that are fired to demonstrate the community's defense system. In fact, little defense was needed, because the local Native Americans were friendly. Local tribes included the Wampanoags, who are represented at a homesite near the village, where members of the museum staff show off native foodstuffs, agricultural practices, and crafts. A visit to the homesite is included in admission to the plantation.

At the main entrance to the plantation you'll find two modern buildings with an interesting orientation show, exhibits, a gift shop, a crafts center, a bookstore, and a cafeteria. There's a picnic area nearby.

Cranberry World

225 Water St. ☎ **508/747-2350.** Free admission. May 1–Nov 30 daily 9:30am–5pm. Guided tours available; call for reservations. From Plymouth Rock, walk north for 10 minutes right along the waterfront.

Cranberries aren't just for Thanksgiving dinner, as Ocean Spray's interesting visitor center will remind you. Exhibits include outdoor demonstration bogs, antique harvesting tools, a scale model of a cranberry farm, and film and slide shows. September and October are harvest time. There are daily cooking demonstrations and free cranberry refreshments.

WHERE TO STAY

On busy summer weekends, every room in town is often taken. It is advisable to make reservations well in advance.

MODERATE

Governor Bradford Motor Inn

98 Water St., Plymouth, MA 02360. ☎ **800/332-1620** or 508/746-6200. Fax 508/747-3032. 94 rms. A/C TV TEL. $89–$124 double in season. Extra person $10. Rates lower in off season. Children under 14 stay free in parents' room. AE, DC, DISC, MC, V.

The Governor Bradford is across the street from the waterfront and only one block from Plymouth Rock, the *Mayflower II*, and the center of town. The rooms, each with two double beds, are attractively furnished in a modern style, with wall-to-wall carpeting, refrigerator, and coffeemaker. More expensive rooms are higher up in the three-story building and have clearer views of the water. There's a small heated outdoor pool.

John Carver Inn

25 Summer St. at Town Brook, Plymouth, MA 02360. ☎ **800/274-1620** or 508/746-7100. Fax 508/746-8299. 79 rms. A/C TV TEL. Apr 11–June 19 $69–$89 double; June 19–Oct 18 $85–$105 double; Oct 19–Nov 25 $75–$95 double; Nov 30–Apr 7 $65–$85 double. Children under 19 stay free in parents' room. Passport to History package rates change seasonally. Senior discount. AE, CB, DC, DISC, MC, V.

This impressive colonial-style building offers comfortable, modern accommodations, a large pool, free cribs, and all the amenities. Many rooms are newly renovated and decorated in colonial style. The inn is within walking distance of the main attractions. A **Hearth 'n' Kettle** restaurant is on the premises. The hotel offers a good deal (the John Carver Inn Passport to History Packages) that includes a two-night, three-day stay for two, four breakfast tickets to the restaurant, two $10 discount dinner tickets at the restaurant, two Plimoth Plantation or whale watch tickets, and two tickets to the trolley or Wax Museum.

Pilgrim Sands Motel

150 Warren Ave. (Route 3A), Plymouth, MA 02360. ☎ **800/729-SANDS** or 508/747-0900. Fax 508/746-8066. 64 rms. A/C TV TEL. $90–$120 double, summer; $70–$95 double, spring and Indian summer; $60–$80 double, fall; $50–$70 double, winter. Higher rates for ocean view. Extra person $8. AE, CB, DC, DISC, MC, V.

This attractive motel is outside town, within walking distance of Plimoth Plantation. The ultramodern units, located right on the ocean, have individually controlled heating and air-conditioning, wall-to-wall carpeting, and tasteful furnishings. In the summer guests have access to the private beach, terraces, whirlpool spa, and outdoor and indoor pools. Most rooms have two double or two queen-size beds. Many rooms have refrigerators. One wing is reserved for smokers, the other for nonsmokers. Open year-round.

Sheraton Inn Plymouth

180 Water St., Plymouth, MA 02360. ☎ **800/325-3535** or 508/747-4900. Fax 508/746-2609. 175 rms. A/C TV TEL. Apr–Oct $100–$160 double; Nov–Mar $85–$125 double. Children under 18 stay free in parents' room. Extra person $15. AE, CB, DC, DISC, JCB, MC, V.

Located at the Village Landing, this attractive hotel faces the harbor from a hill across the street from the waterfront. It's the place to stay in Plymouth for access to both the historic sights and the amenities of a chain. Guest rooms are tastefully furnished in contemporary style and have climate control and in-room movies. Some have balconies that overlook the indoor swimming pool and whirlpool, in a colorful garden setting. The hotel also has an exercise room and a restaurant, the **Harbor Grille,** which serves a delicious Sunday brunch, and the **Pub,** which serves lighter fare and has live entertainment on weekends.

BUDGET

Cold Spring Motel

188 Court St. (Route 3A), Plymouth, MA 02360. ☎ **508/746-2222.** 31 rms. A/C TV TEL. $58–$78 double, $68–$88 cottage in season. Lower rates spring and fall. Extra person $5. AE, DISC, MC, V. Closed mid-Oct–Apr.

Convenient to all historic sites, this pleasant, quiet motel has rooms with wall-to-wall carpeting and private bath. The two-story building is set back from the street two blocks inland, not far from Cranberry World. There's parking at your door.

WHERE TO DINE

Seafood is the specialty at almost all Plymouth restaurants, where much of the daily catch goes right from the fishing boat to the kitchen.

Lobster Hut

Town Wharf. ☎ **508/746-2270.** Fax 746-5655. Reservations not accepted. Luncheon specials $4.50–$7.95, main courses $4.95–$12.95 (lobster meat), sandwiches $1.75–$5.95. MC, V. Daily 11am–9pm in summer; daily 11am–7pm in winter. SEAFOOD.

The Lobster Hut is a clean, shiny, self-service restaurant. Take your order to an indoor table or out on the large deck that overlooks the bay. For starters, have some clam chowder or lobster bisque. The seafood "rolls" (hamburger buns with your choice of filling) are excellent. Or choose from a long list of fried seafood—including clams, scallops, shrimp, and haddock. Or you might prefer boiled and steamed items, burgers, or chicken tenders. Beer and wine are served, but only with a meal.

McGrath's Harbour Restaurant

Town Wharf. ☎ **508/746-9751.** Reservations recommended. Main dishes $9.95–$14.95. AE, MC, V. In season daily 11:30am–10pm. Closed Mon in winter. SEAFOOD.

McGrath's is big, busy, and the choice of many families, local business people, and tour groups. In addition to fish and seafood dinners, the menu features chicken, prime rib, sandwiches, and a children's menu. Ask for a table overlooking the water—the room facing inland is on the gloomy side—and be sure you're in good company, because service can be slow.

AT JENNY GRIST MILL VILLAGE

Run of the Mill Tavern

Jenny Grist Mill Village. ☎ **508/830-1262.** Reservations recommended at dinner. Main courses $6–$11. AE, MC, V. Mon–Sat 11am–10pm, Sun noon–10pm. AMERICAN.

You'll find the Run of the Mill Tavern near the water wheel at Jenny Grist Mill Village at Town Brook Path. It's an attractive setting, surrounded by trees, and the tavern offers good, inexpensive meals. In a welcome surprise, the clam chowder here is fantastic. Other appetizers include nachos, potato skins, buffalo wings, and mushrooms. Entrees are standard meat, chicken, and fish, and there are also seafood specials. The children's menu is a great bargain, with burgers and fish and chips at $2.50 to $3.50.

Index